Cinema & Culture

The History & Art of Cinema

Frank Beaver, *General Editor*

Vol. 2

PETER LANG
New York • Washington, D.C./Baltimore • Bern
Frankfurt am Main • Berlin • Brussels • Vienna • Oxford

E. Deidre Pribram

Cinema & Culture

Independent Film
in the United States, 1980–2001

PETER LANG
New York • Washington, D.C./Baltimore • Bern
Frankfurt am Main • Berlin • Brussels • Vienna • Oxford

Library of Congress Cataloging-in-Publication Data

Pribram, E. Deidre.
Cinema and culture: independent film
in the United States, 1980–2001 / E. Deidre Pribram.
p. cm.—(Framing film; vol. 2)
Includes bibliographical references and index.
1. Motion pictures—United States—History. 2. Independent
filmmakers—United States. I. Title. II. Series.
PN2993.5.U6 P75 **791.43'0973'09048 21** 2001029270
ISBN 0-8204-5217-3
ISSN 1524-7821

Die Deutsche Bibliothek-CIP-Einheitsaufnahme

Pribram, E. Deidre:
Cinema and culture: independent film in the United States,
1980–2001 / E. Deidre Pribram. –New York; Washington, D.C./Baltimore; Bern;
Frankfurt am Main; Berlin; Brussels; Vienna; Oxford: Lang.
(Framing film; Vol. 2)
ISBN 0-8204-5217-3

Cover design by Joni Holst

The paper in this book meets the guidelines for permanence and durability
of the Committee on Production Guidelines for Book Longevity
of the Council of Library Resources.

© 2002 Peter Lang Publishing, Inc., New York

All rights reserved.
Reprint or reproduction, even partially, in all forms such as microfilm,
xerography, microfiche, microcard, and offset strictly prohibited.

Printed in the United States of America

For RHP

Table of Contents

Acknowledgments ix
Introduction xi

Part I:
History and Industry

Chapter One: Codependence: The Independent Industry 3
Chapter Two: Film as Artifact:
    Alternative Influences on Independent Cinema 41

Part II:
Textual Analysis and Discursive Fields

Chapter Three: "Fixing" Difference:
    Identity Cinema and Independent Distribution 81
Chapter Four: Telling Tales: Narrativity and Independent Film 113
Chapter Five: Psychic Cleavage: Reading the
    Art Against the Politics in Independent Film 141
Chapter Six: Independent Auteurism: From Modern
    Existentialism to Postmodernism as Nostalgia 167

Conclusion 199
Illustrations 207
Notes 221
Filmography 235
Works Cited 275
Title Index 291
Index 299

ACKNOWLEDGMENTS

I would like to thank Sylvia Harvey for her sustained support and continued wise advice, Christine Gledhill and Steve Neale for their incisive comments, Andrew Weeks for numerous helpful conversations, and Tim Corrigan for his valuable observations. My appreciation also to Sophy Craze, Frank Beaver, and Lisa Dillon at Peter Lang and to Toby Miller who got me there. I was the beneficiary of hours of insightful talk and immeasurable moral support from Jenny Harding and Lisa Henderson. I owe a special, heartfelt thanks to the "film guys"—Tom Keiter, Mike Podolski, Ned Faust, David Goodman, and Dorn Hetzel—for many years of always pleasurable, always meaningful discussions about film and life. Finally, my deepest gratitude to Cliff Jernigan—for pretty much everything.

INTRODUCTION

Contemporary independent film is a distinct system of cinematic representation, although a complex and heterogeneous one. Independent American and non-American films distributed in the United States from 1980 to the present have evolved into a discrete cultural site formulated in the interactions between principles of mainstream popular film and legacies of the avant-garde. Bearing traits characteristic of both Hollywood and alternative cinema, independent film, as it has manifested itself in the 1980s and 1990s, is a shifting, malleable discursive field, positioned somewhere in the substantial expanse between, and as a hybrid of, dominant and avant-garde practices.

Social recognition of independent film as an operative category is both familiar and widespread. The success since 1980 of such films as *Blood Simple* (1983), *Stranger than Paradise* (1985), *She's Gotta Have It* (1986), *My Beautiful Laundrette* (1986), *The Thin Blue Line* (1988), *Drugstore Cowboy* (1989), *Straight out of Brooklyn* (1991), *Paris Is Burning* (1991), *The Crying Game* (1992), *Reservoir Dogs* (1992), *Like Water for Chocolate* (1993), *The Piano* (1993), *Orlando* (1993), *Clerks* (1994), *Hoop Dreams* (1994), *Il Postino* (1995), *Trainspotting* (1996), *Secrets & Lies* (1996), *The Full Monty* (1997), *Happiness* (1998), *The Blair Witch Project* (1999), *Boys Don't Cry* (1999), and *Crouching Tiger, Hidden Dragon* (2000) has made independent film an often-cited (in reviews), easily recognized (by audiences), and heavily marketed (by the industry) classification of film. But as Christine Gledhill says of genre studies, "While the existence of genres is in some ways a self-evident fact, the business of definition and demarcation is less clear-cut" (59).

In quoting Gledhill, I do not intend to link independent film to a genre but rather to say something about the business of definition and demarcation. Indeed, independent film, like its cinematic counterparts commonly identified as Hollywood and the avant-garde, encompasses multiple genres. Once one has established that the object of study—in this case, independent film—exists as a cultural site, the more significant task is to determine what it is and what are its cultural implications. However, the difficulty of using classifications like *Hollywood*, *avant-garde* or *independent* cinemas is that what they point to is as vast, diversified, and contingent as it is "self-evident." In order to disentangle some of the social structures and cultural functions of independent film, discourse analysis is the theoretical framework I use in this book. That is to say, independent film is treated here as a discursive formation.

A discursive formation is a set of cultural practices and institutions that cohere into an identifiable body or domain of knowledge that has been historically constituted within specific discursive and institutional power relations. Undertaking cultural criticism based on discourse analysis in the Foucauldian sense necessitates equal consideration of textual aspects and contextual conditions. This, in turn, involves two phases. In the first phase, it requires an analysis of how texts and contexts (including, for instance, "content" issues and the particular historical and geographical moments of a text's appearance) operate as separate arenas of influence in the processes of cultural production and the construction of cultural meanings. And in the second phase, it demands an exploration of the complex, multiple ways texts and contexts interact. This is to follow a cultural product, a text, from the social world within which it originates through to the social world(s) to which it ultimately returns, while examining how all the intervening discursive layers, textual and social, affect the accompanying production of meanings.

I consider four main discursive fields to be operative in the discursive formation of independent film (and, potentially, in other forms of representation as well).

1. *Representational discourses.* These involve the formal and narrative languages enacted; the historical aesthetic traditions within which cultural producers work; the role of cultural producers as artists or authors; and the actual production of an artifact or text.
2. *Material and institutional discourses.* These include the many structural, organizational, and economic complexes involved in the production and dissemination of cultural artifacts or commodities.
3. *Interpretive, audience, or reception discourses.* This set entails how specific social beings, groups linked by identity, and other communities forge meanings and utilize texts.
4. *Cultural and historical discourses.* This category includes ideological and political claims and refers to the cultural context in which a text is embedded and the historical moment at which readings occur. Involved here are categories of identity, such as gender and race, and the complex ideological frameworks that surround and create them, as well as normative cultural constructs, such as concepts of justice and jurisprudence or discourses of heterosexual romance.

Introduction

In any discursive formation, sites or fields of meaning production are multiple, complex, and interactional. All the above are fields of meaning production that interact together as a larger system of meaning construction, in this instance, the discursive formation of independent film. The specific meanings constructed at any site or at any moment are sometimes complementary to each other, sometimes conflicting, but they are ultimately coherent because they are held together by the discursive rules and behaviors that, in turn, create the discursive object, independent film.

Each field—representational, institutional, interpretive, and cultural/historical—embodies multiple layers of signification occurring at multiple sites. The aim here is to disentangle some of these, to trace their trajectories, and to weigh their effects. And equally, the goal is to identify points of intersection among the various fields and to analyze their interactions. It is necessary to pursue both courses because within each discursive field some meanings are produced or operate separately, while other meanings are tied together and gain coherency only in the movement between differing processes of signification—representational and cultural; institutional and interpretive; institutional, representational, cultural; and other combinations.

In describing a body of work as *independent*, the subtextual assumption is that it is independent of something other than itself. The implicit referent in this case is the ubiquitous presence of the Hollywood industry. At any given historical moment, independent film shapes itself in relation to contemporary attributes of mainstream production, staying at least one step in contradistinction to dominant cinematic practices. Such differentiation can take one or a combination of forms: narrative formation, that is, the kinds of stories told and the ways they are recounted; formal and structural characteristics, entailing the aesthetic means used to relate stories; and cultural referents, for instance, which individuals and groups are represented and how their social and political lives are depicted.

There are no fixed criteria for what constitutes an independent film, its outlines shifting as dominant standards evolve, as long as it remains in some accountable (usually marketable) measure alternative to Hollywood practice. Once a specific innovation has been absorbed by mainstream film, independent practice responds by reinventing itself otherwise.

However, the ways in which independent film differentiates itself in order to stake out its distinctive cinematic domain are significant. Contemporary independent film of the last two decades has repeatedly formulated itself as the heir to avant-garde traditions and experimental practices. "New," "cutting-edge," "radical," and "alternative" are all self-styled properties of independent cinema. Claiming its position at the perimeter rather than at the center of cultural production, independent films are exhibited largely through art-house theaters in urban settings instead of at the studio-dominated cineplexes dotting the overall demographic landscape (although there are increasingly significant exceptions). In general, the independent industry has aimed for reasonably sized, specifically targeted audiences rather than for the mass appeal mandated by Hollywood's blockbuster budgets. Independent film's identity as a commodity stresses its differences from Hollywood's output; the independent industry is not supposed to be ruled by the same economic, political, aesthetic, and historical imperatives as Hollywood cinema. This creates an arguably autonomous filmic enterprise able to represent alternative political views and aesthetic perspectives.

Yet the independent industry remains driven by marketplace demands and competition for consumers similar to Hollywood's, particularly as it grows in popularity, profile, and market share. While often encompassing elements of an alternative cinematic language, independent cinema must also be concerned with a greater degree of narrative and formal accessibility than much experimental work in order to achieve a sufficiently wide viewership and therefore economic viability.

Independent film's avant-garde heritage is evident in the two overarching realms the contemporary movement has carved out for itself: the aesthetic and the political. If a film is aesthetically original, if it can be deemed "cutting-edge," or if in form it is sufficiently distinctive, it falls within the purview of independent practice. Also within the parameters of its aesthetic mandate is the tradition of the "art" film. While no longer necessarily an experimental departure in either form or content, such films are usually identified by the greater intellectual demand they make of viewers or by their dramatic seriousness. The legacy of the art film, traditionally dominated by European filmmakers like Ingmar Bergman, François Truffaut, and Bernardo Bertolucci, continues in such contemporary examples as *Babette's Feast* (1987), *Women on the Verge of a Nervous Breakdown* (1988), *Cinema Paradiso* (1990), *Howard's End* (1992), *Shine* (1996), *Life Is Beautiful* (1998), and *The Red Violin* (1999).

Formed in the wake of the activism of the 1960s and 1970s, independent film's political mandate is largely liberal to left wing. One of the industry's focuses has been identity politics, in films such as *Desert Hearts* (1986), *Working Girls* (1987), *Poison* (1991), *Daughters of the Dust* (1992), *The Living End* (1992), *Mi Vida Loca* (1994), and *Three Seasons* (1999). Traditionally underrepresented groups are frequently both the subject matter and the target audiences of independent film.

An individual work may conform to either the aesthetic or the political purview, or to both at the same time. A film like *Slacker* (1991) can be viewed as

Introduction

structurally innovative in its method of following a single character for a period of time and then, with seeming narrative arbitrariness, switching to another. Simultaneously, the film was viewed as having a cultural impact because it helped define a generation or, from an industry perspective, a demographic group, now named after the film.

While a film's popularity and therefore its profitability are overriding considerations, an independent film cannot be sold solely on the basis that it will be exciting, funny, or action-packed. An individual work must fall within the aesthetic or political mandate, at least to the extent that it can be promoted that way, regardless of whether there is general agreement on its fit within those parameters. Films perceived as purely entertainment are left to Hollywood's purview.[1] An alternative form of pleasure, whether formal, demographic, or in terms of subject matter (like breaking sex and violence taboos) must be established or at least argued for an independent entry.

In addition, all genres are not equally represented in independent practice. On the one hand, melodrama and romantic comedy, for example, are infrequent unless also used in depicting a subcultural group, as in the cases of *The Wedding Banquet* (1993) and *Go Fish* (1994). On the other hand, certain genres, such as the gangster or criminal film, are overrepresented, for instance with *Blood Simple, Henry: Portrait of a Serial Killer* (1990), *The Krays* (1990), *Reservoir Dogs, Bad Lieutenant* (1992), *One False Move* (1992), *Killing Zoe* (1994), *The Last Seduction* (1994), *Pulp Fiction* (1994), *The Funeral* (1996), *Lost Highway* (1997), *The General* (1998), *Suicide Kings* (1998), *Run Lola Run* (1999), *The Limey* (1999), and *The Way of the Gun* (2000).

The term *independent* has been used throughout movie history in varying ways. When United Artists was founded in 1919 it was considered independent, set apart from the dominant studios by providing "a mechanism for the distribution and release of independently-produced features" made by its founders—Mary Pickford, Charlie Chaplin, Douglas Fairbanks, D.W. Griffith—and others who sought more control over their own films and profits (Gomery 173–74). In the aftermath of the 1948 consent decrees, when exhibition divestiture was mandated, the studios, no longer enjoying the income from their theaters or having automatically guaranteed exhibition outlets for their films, moved toward what was recognized as independent production. "The studios gradually fired their contract personnel and phased out active production, and began leasing their facilities for independent projects, generally providing co-financing and distribution as well" (Schatz 11). For instance, a contemporary company like Castle Rock (until its 1993 buyout by Turner, then Time Warner) is an independent producer under this definition, with such films as *When Harry Met Sally* (1989), *City Slickers* (1991), *A Few Good Men* (1992), and *In the Line of*

Fire (1993). Following the demise of the B studios in the late 1940s and 1950s, *independent* also came to signify low-budget genre or exploitation pictures. As actor Tom Hanks notes, at the time he began in the business, the concept of *independent* was synonymous with exploitation fare like slasher movies (*Two Hollywoods* 124). It was in the 1980s and 1990s that independent film took on its current sense of respected specialty fare, often self- or privately financed and released by a handful of specialty distributors.

Given the many, changing meanings of the term *independent*, it is quite likely that an alternate designation would have helped identify the attributes of the 1980s and 1990s movement in distinction from other senses of the term. Instead, on occasion, the use of *independent film* tends to blur its differences from precursor movements. Indeed, efforts have been made to name the contemporary movement in other ways, a gesture that is evident in the 1987 study commissioned by the Sundance Institute and the Independent Feature Project, *Off-Hollywood: The Making and Marketing of American Specialty Films* (Rosen and Hamilton) or in the title of Richard Ferncase's 1996 book, *Outsider Features*. Despite such efforts, the appellation *independent film* appears to have stuck in popular, professional, and critical usage. The term is used in this book to refer specifically to the system of cinematic representation that solidified in the 1980s and continues into the new century.

Generally, a film released in the United States is considered independent if it has received no studio financing, is distributed by a non-major, and has no prominent stars. How then does one classify a film like Robert Altman's *The Player* (1992), a satire of the movie industry? It was distributed by independent Fine Line Features, yet had well-known actors in fictional roles (Tim Robbins, Whoopi Goldberg) as well as stars making cameo appearances (Bruce Willis, Julia Roberts, Cher). In addition, Altman is a director with a track record—although he had been out of the Hollywood loop for the previous decade; indeed, *The Player* was perceived in those quarters as his comeback film.

Or take the case of *Il Postino*, which was financed in Europe, produced in Italy on an original budget of $4 million, and distributed in the United States by Miramax Films. As a foreign film, distributed by a non-major, its independent standing is clear. But is its independent status altered by the fact that Miramax spent $7 million in promotional and print costs in the months preceding the Academy Awards in order to garner the film's five Academy Award nominations, including Hollywood's prestigious Best Picture?[2]

Even more ambiguous is Michael Moore's low-budget documentary *Roger & Me* (1989), a specific indictment of General Motors and a general indictment of corporate capitalism's treatment of workers. Moore was a former journalist who struggled to accumulate the production costs including, according to the promotional materials, mortgaging his own home. By the time the completed film played the festival circuit it had created such attention that it was sold to and distributed by a major, Warner Brothers.[3]

Measured in terms of institutional criteria, one of the ways independent film can be defined is by an existing mechanism of distribution—the kinds of films picked up by independent or specialty distributors determine an independent typology. However, this still begs many questions. Which films are independent distributors picking up and on the basis of what selection criteria? Who are their audiences? That is, who are the distributors selling their products to, and how, in turn, does that influence their selection patterns? How are they selling or promoting these films?

Further, while the constitutive elements of a project's financing and distribution are an attempt to identify independent film by material and institutional criteria, this identification omits considerations of narrative formulation and aesthetic practice—in other words, representational discourses. It also omits the effects of interpretive practices on independent films as well as extratextual cultural/historical resonances. This book examines independent film in its material and other discursive dimensions as both a specific industry and as a larger cultural site of meaning production.

However, because the object under investigation—independent film as a system of representation—is large and complex, this study will focus on the *consumption* side of independent cinema, that is, on its distribution and reception. First, material and institutional dimensions will be considered by analyzing the corporate structures, operating mechanisms, and current status of independent distribution. Unfortunately, choosing such an approach necessitates slighting other significant industry infrastructures that contribute to the production and dissemination of independent cinema. Included in these infrastructures are financing entities, an array of producers and producing mechanisms, production personnel (directors, actors, crew), exhibitors, festivals, and so on.[4] Because the focus of this study is on consumption, the appendix provides two filmographies, one listing films by title, the other by distributor.

Second, the nonmaterial discursive dimensions of independent film can be approached through considerations of the reception aspects of filmic consumption. Which films receive viewership (distribution, positive or negative audience response), and why? What are the specificities of textual forms available to independent film within its current accepted parameters? What are the various interpretations given such films by cultural commentators, by movie reviewers, and, where data exist, by audience members? Discursive analysis of independent film, in terms of its reception, is undertaken through close textual analysis of a number of specific films coupled with careful consideration of the multiple readings such films have prompted.

Although the largest independent distributors may also produce some of their films, it is standard industry practice to select and purchase the material they distribute, their product, from a constantly renewed, existing field of already-made films. In this sense, mechanisms of distribution and exhibition form a first tier of consumption for independent films—a process in which independent productions are viewed by distributors and exhibitors who then select only a very small minority for purchase or exhibition. In this study I analyze independent distribution as a mode of consumption, a part of the "taste-setting" business of defining and demarcating that also functions as the dissemination process for independent productions. End-users are thus consumers as well as part of the overall production process. Movie reviewers and other cultural commentators whose influence can be fairly considerable, as will be seen, are considered to compose a second tier in the processes of consumption. Audience members, viewers who transmit their interpretations by word of mouth, formulate the third and most traditionally analyzed tier of consumption. One of the principal concerns of this book is the way that, in the process of consumption, each of these tiers also constructs the object it consumes.

In order to analyze more clearly the impact of reception, the close investigation of specific texts is limited to feature-length films that have received some measure of general play through theatrical release and that continue to have a videocassette shelf life. Being on the more popular or monetarily successful end of the independent spectrum often means that a film has generated more industry attention, critical interest, and popular discussion, and this data provides a base for an analysis of the effects of varying interpretations. I also wish to discuss in detail films that are easily available to this book's readers. Additionally, although nonfiction films like *The Atomic Cafe* (1982), *The Times of Harvey Milk* (1984), *The Thin Blue Line*, *Roger & Me*, *Paris Is Burning*, *Thank You and Good Night* (1991), *American Dream* (1992), *Brother's Keeper* (1992), *The War Room* (1993), *Hoop Dreams*, *The Celluloid Closet* (1995), *Fast, Cheap & Out of Control* (1997), *Buena Vista Social Club* (1999), and *On the Ropes* (1999) form a significant part of independent cinema's profile, I will limit the films I analyze to fiction, which continues to dominate the independent spectrum despite a number of documentary successes.

It should also be noted that although this study examines a national market—the United States—independent film in the American context is not a national cinema. It incorporates both indigenous and foreign work. Although the few studies of independent film that exist tend to view it as an American phenomenon, international cinema is a strong element in the constitution of independent fare.⁵ Hollywood, by contrast, is very much a national cinema but the inclusion of foreign film in the American independent landscape has offered both film viewers and filmmakers a more global perspective. That said, an international presence is dominated by work from Europe and other developed nations like Australia, while English-language films, with a few exceptions such as *Life Is Beautiful* and *Crouching Tiger, Hidden Dragon*, do better at the box office than subtitled ones.

The book is divided into two parts. Part I, comprising chapters 1 and 2, presents an overview of significant historical and institutional aspects of independent film. Because there are so few studies of independent film to refer to, in contrast for instance to the rich analytical tradition covering Hollywood, part I follows a fairly meticulous descriptive approach in an attempt to provide a much-needed foundation. Part II, chapters 3 through 6, uses close textual analysis to focus more carefully on specific films and the issues they generate.

Chapter 1, "Codependence: The Independent Industry," concentrates on material and institutional aspects of independent practice. The characteristics that act toward defining a work as independent are itemized and described. Factors contributing to the rise of contemporary independent film are explored, including Hollywood and cult film precursors. This chapter also provides a profile of independent distributors, their history, and current economic and cultural parameters.

Chapter 2, "Film as Artifact: Alternative Influences on Independent Cinema," offers an overview of the theoretical reasoning or aesthetic justification behind a number of experimental filmic practices. Six categories of alternative artistic practice are outlined, with the respective terrain and concerns of each delineated. The six are the aesthetic avant-garde, the political avant-garde, art cinema, personal cinema, identity cinema, and postmodernism. Numerous examples of contemporary independent films are given, indicating each film's most significant alternative influence.

Chapter 3, "'Fixing' Difference: Identity Cinema and Independent Distribution," provides an analysis of identity politics, one of the foundations on which independent film as a discursive formation is based. More specifically, this chapter explores how the attributes and limitations of independent distribution interact with the discourses of identity politics. The chapter examines the distribution history of three films: *To Sleep with Anger* (1990), whose distributor, the Samuel Goldwyn Company, received much criticism for its handling of the film; *Daughters of the Dust*, a film of alternative aesthetic, political, and narrative sensibility that nearly failed to receive theatrical distribution; and *Just Another Girl on the I.R.T.* (1993), which was championed by the independent industry in *Daughters of the Dust*'s stead.

Chapter 4, "Telling Tales: Narrativity and Independent Film," deals with the complex subject of narrative theory. While independent film has claimed certain aesthetic approaches and subject matter (cultural referents) to be within its purview, it has been markedly less clear on its relation to issues and aspects of narrativity. This is due in part to the current state of film narratology, which is much more willing to grapple with narrativity as a formal and structural system than it is equipped to take on the challenge of the ideological aspects of narrative as representation. Chapter 4 examines Mike Leigh's *Naked* (1993) as an independent film that is influenced by the political avant-garde in its aesthetic presentation and subject matter but is limited in the extent to which it departs from traditional models in its process of narrative signification around heterosexual relationships and the male as redemptive hero. To highlight the contrasts and resemblances, *Naked* is compared with Hollywood's *Shoot the Moon* (1982) as well as to *Trainspotting*.

Chapter 5, "Psychic Cleavage: Reading the Art Against the Politics in Independent Film," evaluates reception as a political imperative. The chapter takes three films connected by gendered political issues—spousal abuse, rape, social and legal sexual discrimination, or a combination of these—but differentiated in the aesthetic and narrative approaches brought to bear on their respective subject matter. *The Piano* bridges mainstream attributes with feminist avant-garde practices; *Orlando* is more "purely" avant-garde; and *The Accused* (1988) is a product of Hollywood (normative realist) narrative. Questions addressed include: What effects do these varying modes of representation have on meaning production? What are the implications of multiple, often conflicting, available readings within a single text? How does a fragmented, multicultural society begin to negotiate fragmented, multiply inflected story interpretations?

Chapter 6, "Independent Auteurism: From Modern Existentialism to Postmodernism as Nostalgia," assesses whether the much-discussed films of Quentin Tarantino represent a stylistically revamped version of modernist auteurism or, rather, a shift to a postmodern practice. This brings into play contemporary discussions around postmodernity and looks at the degree to which and in what ways ongoing extratextual cultural discourses might be reflected in, formulated by, or struggled over in independent film. The chapter's assessment is conducted through an exploration of the reception of the films *Pulp Fiction, Reservoir Dogs,* and *Natural Born Killers* (1994) in two national contexts, the United States and Great Britain. The analysis considers responses to the films' depictions of violence and morality (or lack of) in comparison to the work of modernist auteurs, exemplified by Martin Scorsese and Paul Schrader.

Introduction

Each of the chapters in part II analyzes aspects of one or more of the principal discursive fields—institutional, representational, interpretive, cultural/historical—that together, in varying ways and to varying degrees, generate the larger discursive formation of independent film. The look at specific films in chapters 3 through 6 is an attempt to examine each of these discourses in operation, as well as an effort to locate and explain how two or more of these discourses might interact together, whether in complementary or conflicting ways, in the process of textual signification. Chapter 3 is concerned with material and institutional discourses (distribution); representational discourses are highlighted in chapter 4 (narrativity); interpretation and reception are dealt with in chapter 5 (reviewers and marketing, an art versus politics dichotomy); and chapter 6 incorporates important contemporary cultural/historical discourses (postmodernism, modernism). Although each chapter foregrounds a specific discursive field, any particular field cannot be considered in isolation but also must be understood in terms of its interactions with other discursive fields. So chapter 3, for instance, which traces specific implications of distribution, an institutional perspective, is also concerned with identity politics, a key contemporary cultural discourse that has a formative influence on independent film.

The discursive and material elements that together construct a system of cinematic representation are manifold; the specific aspects discussed here—mechanisms of distribution, artistic practices, identity politics, narrativity, reception, postmodernism—are representative but certainly not all-inclusive. This book is intended not as an exhaustive account but rather as an introduction to thinking about the qualities and cultural influence of that multifaceted, increasingly conspicuous practice identified as independent film.

My reasons for undertaking this inquiry are varied. First, when I think of the films of recent years available in a popular format (in a cinema or at the video store) that have grabbed my attention, I rarely recall work that originated in Hollywood. Consistently, it has been independent film that has intrigued me and pointed the way to imagining new possibilities in the processes of aesthetic and narrative signification. Second, independent film seems a potential way out of the deadlock associated with the political avant-garde, which, although dedicated to activism and change, has not found a way to appeal to larger audiences. The potential I see in independent film is connected with a refusal to believe, as did the feminist avant-garde of the 1970s and 1980s that *popular* of necessity equals *oppressive*. Third, interest in identity politics, and especially the representation of women, urges investigation of an institutional practice that has claimed that politics as its own, while only inadequately representing it. One of the most pressing tasks facing our multicultural, postmodern world is to theorize and put into practice means by which multiple, complex identities—all with distinct voices, experiences, and interests—might come to coexist across the spectrum of an entire social formation and at the many points of intersection within its domain. Independent cinema is important in that it is a cultural site where some competing voices, issues, and identities are being played out. Although often unsuccessful in specific achievement(s), independent film does operate as an arena, material and discursive, wherein various conditions and identities of multiculturalism are tested and contested. As a consequence, this study devotes considerable attention to the identity politics aspects of independent film.

Fourth, I am motivated by an awareness that independent film is a category of cinematic practice already "out there," a discursive formation frequently experienced by film viewers and filmmakers but not, to date, sufficiently theorized. I spent much of the 1990s identifying myself as an independent filmmaker and as such I encountered people in every facet of the filmmaking enterprise, from financing to production through exhibition and distribution, who also identified themselves as working within the independent industry or within an independent paradigm. Over the same time period, I taught film students in a university setting, a significant number of whom wanted to be independent filmmakers. When they described their ambitions as such, their conception of *independent* seemed to refer to a mode of filmmaking, as well as to a certain lifestyle. On the one hand, it signified not wanting to be a hired director, director of photography, gaffer, or other crew member on a Hollywood project controlled by numerous other, more influential functionaries. But on the other hand, they did not want to exist from grant to grant, scraping money together for the next project to be shown to tiny audiences in highly specialized venues for the sake of the purity of their work, as has been so often the case with the avant-garde. They seemed quite willing to sacrifice some of that purity as long as they could retain a measure of control over or a degree of personal stamp on their product, and as long as the exchange also included a dimension of commercial success and public identity, that is, calculable audience response. In other words, they were willing to trade off the extreme benefits of both ways of working—purity and absolute control or potentially extraordinary fortune and celebrity—in order to have *some* of both worlds.

My concern in analyzing independent cinema is twofold, pertaining to both practice and theory but engaged in an effort to link them. First, the goal for filmmakers is to take what has been formulated in theoretical spaces and to come to some understanding of how those structures of representation are made operational. The achievement for filmmakers who contest dominant practices (whether radically or marginally) is to imagine or produce otherwise. My analysis focuses on how alternative independent discursive possibilities might function textually while paying attention to institutional, industrial, and other discursive factors that mitigate in favor of or against their enactment. Second, one of the purposes of theory is to analyze the configuration(s) of cultural practices in terms of the parts they play in a larger arena of cultural politics. The larger arena in the instance of this study is a rapidly intensifying, multiply identified society. Independent film as an enterprise that attempts to be representative of certain of these social changes urges an exploration of the ways and the degree to which various identities are tested and contested within this particular cultural practice. This analysis also raises issues of how this practice's examples, beneficial or detrimental, might be applied to more general concerns of identity politics. My aim, then, is to pursue an integrated approach to cultural theory, cultural politics, and cultural production as they are applied to some of the parameters, limitations, and possibilities of that system of cinematic representation known as independent film.

 Part I

History and Industry

CHAPTER ONE

Codependence: The Independent Industry

Defining Independent Film

Following the 1997 Academy Awards, in which the only studio film nominated for Best Picture was Columbia TriStar's *Jerry Maguire*, the balance consisting of *The English Patient* (Miramax), *Shine* (Fine Line), *Secrets & Lies* (October), and *Fargo* (Gramercy), the *New York Times Magazine* devoted an entire issue to what they termed "the two Hollywoods": studio and independent. "One is a global blockbuster business, the other a scrappy independent cinema" (cover). In calling the special issue *The Two Hollywoods*, the *New York Times* signals mainstream recognition of independent film as a consequential commodity, industry, and body of signifying practices. *Independent film* is confirmed as an already-existing cultural formation, that is, the term is commonly used to identify and categorize certain films. Existing conceptualizations of what exactly is meant by independent film might be vague but people apparently recognize it when they see it.

No longer located in the peripheral cultural space of "alternative," independent film is identified as moving solidly toward the center—indeed, how much more central could it get than in being designated a "Hollywood"? Yet while the edges of its work might increasingly be blurring with studio product, independent cinema's cultural currency is based on its ability to remain recognizably or arguably distinct: "Audiences now choose among the products of two entirely distinct movie businesses, each with its own sensibility, economic model, cast of characters and lifestyle" (Introduction 75). Studio Hollywood is suddenly competing with independent film as the *New York Times Magazine* portrays it, with a cover photo of actors Tom Hanks and Ben Affleck standing head to head and growling at each other. Or at least Hollywood is beginning to take notice of this other industry. Indeed, 1997 could be considered a moment of significance in the relations between the two industries. Having realized there was money to be made in independent film, studio personnel had been invading independent turf—principally the Sundance Film Festival—since 1989. But the 1997 Oscar season appeared to many to suggest that the reverse was also true, that independent film was now staking claims in studio territory. However, as the issue's coverage of "two entirely distinct movie businesses" makes clear, the independent arena as a discursive field must maintain some degree of difference from Hollywood in order to avoid being encompassed, and thus dissolved, by the more dominant industry. Dawn Hudson, executive director of the Independent Feature Project/West describes independent cinema's necessary identity as "filmmaking that challenges the prevailing aesthetic, political and narrative conventions of American cinema" (8). As it gains cultural prominence and success, independent cinema can continue to exist only as long as it sustains its distinction as the second, the other of, Hollywood.

Nineteen ninety-six, culminating in the 1997 Academy Awards and widely touted as the year of the independents (Corliss, "Independents" 62–66; Clark, "Smaller Films" D5), saw Miramax receive twenty nominations, more than any studio, including twelve for *The English Patient* and two for *Sling Blade*; in addition, Fine Line collected seven for *Shine*, while October earned six for *Secrets & Lies* and *Breaking the Waves*. But the emergence of a competing industry (however economically nonthreatening) is evident over the course of a number of Oscar seasons throughout the 1990s.

In 1993 *The Crying Game* (Miramax) was nominated alongside *Unforgiven* (Warner Brothers). In 1994 *The Piano* (Miramax) competed against *Schindler's List* (Universal). Although a *Schindler's List* sweep, *The Piano* won for original screenplay, as well as lead and supporting actresses. Nineteen ninety-five saw what Tom Hanks refers to as "the *Pulp Fiction-Forrest Gump* superbowl of 1995." He goes on to add, "Which we won by the way!" (*Two Hollywoods* 28). *Pulp Fiction* (Miramax) received only the award for original screenplay, as had *The Piano* and *The Crying Game* in their years, marking the writing Oscar as something of a "consolation prize" for independents in place of Best Picture or Best Director. Nineteen ninety-six had *Il Postino* (Miramax) up against *Braveheart* (Paramount) and *Babe* (Universal), and 1997 featured the independent sweep led by *The English Patient*. In 1998 Hollywood seemed to recover with its own sweep, led by *Titanic* (Paramount). And 1999 saw *Shakespeare in Love* (Miramax) and *Life Is Beautiful* (Miramax) up against *Saving Private Ryan* (Dreamworks). Although *Saving Private Ryan* won five awards, including Best Director, *Life Is Beautiful* won three and *Shakespeare In Love* won seven, including Best Screenplay and the prestigious Best Picture award.

At the same time, there has been considerable debate over whether some of the independent films that have made it to the Academy Awards could even be considered independent. Cited in the journal *Filmmaker*, San Francisco experimental filmmaker Jay Rosenblatt (*Smell of Burning Ants*, 1994; *Human Remains*, 1997) finds it "ludicrous" that a film like *The English Patient* could be labeled independent given its multimillion-dollar budget (which ensures, among other things, prominent actors) and its Hollywood-like storytelling mode, both narratively and aesthetically (Moran and Willis 22).[1] Janet Maslin goes further, calling the 1997 Academy Awards "Parallel Universe Night" because "in their gravity, scale and unlikely beauty" *The English Patient* and *Schindler's List* have much in common and because neither *Shine* nor *Sling Blade* are more avant-garde than *Forrest Gump* (103). And the prominent independent producer's representative John Pierson contends that "you have to bend over backward and jump through hoops to define *Pulp Fiction* as independent" because of its stars, its $8 million budget, and its twelve hundred print release by Miramax. He asks, "if *Pulp [Fiction]* is independent, why isn't a Miramax Woody Allen release or a New Line Jim Carrey romp?" (Pierson 332–33).

I would suggest that the difference rests with the fundamental necessity outlined above: independent cinema's cultural existence is based on its ability to remain recognizably or *arguably* distinct from Hollywood's product. *Pulp Fiction* has an arguably distinctive or original storytelling structure and style, while Woody Allen and Jim Carrey have made effectively identical films, on every count, within Hollywood parameters.

The case for *The English Patient*'s status as independent, however, is a much more difficult one to make. In addition to its budget, stars, experienced director, wide release, and promotional strategy, all comparable to *Pulp Fiction*, it has a familiar, even formulaic, narrative and aesthetic approach. But the argument for *The English Patient*'s independent standing was made—certainly by the film's promoters—on the basis of its distributor, Miramax, and because it falls within the parameters of a certain conception of "art film": both as a foreign film to U.S. audiences and as a historical epic.[2] So while the film's qualifications as independent were not immediately recognizable and are doubtful at best, they were perceived, in some quarters, as arguable.

The most commonly used criteria for determining what is or is not an independent film include the following factors.

Budget Size

Independent films are generally considered to have low or "no" budgets. While the ceiling amount continually changes due to the usually rising costs of making a film as well as to fluctuating expectations of what constitutes "low," a film of

$1 million or under would qualify as low-budget while a film made for $100,000 or less would be a no-budget. Independent films generally have budgets of under $5 million although mini-majors like Miramax are pushing that ceiling up to $10 million or higher.

Source of Funding

Traditionally, in order to be considered independent a film must have nonstudio financing. This is, however, an increasingly murky criterion to apply because there are so many independent production companies who produce films that would not, by any other criteria, be considered independent (see introduction). Further, the major independent distributors are now owned by studios, therefore any films they produce or otherwise help finance have, de facto, studio financing although they might legitimately be considered independent based on a number of other criteria. This criterion applies easily, however, when a film is financed by nonindustry sources, such as grants, personal resources, private investors, although this almost invariably goes hand-in-hand with a low- or no-budget, as outlined above, making the funding sources themselves something of a moot point (e.g., *Clerks,* 1994; *She's Gotta Have It,* 1986).

Distributor

A nonstudio or independent distributor, more often based in New York rather than Los Angeles, is a widely used means of classifying a film as independent. Throughout the 1980s and into the mid-1990s there were four large independent distributors who, because of their size and industry dominance, were also referred to as the "mini-majors": Miramax Films, Fine Line Features, Sony Pictures Classics (formerly Orion Classics) and the Samuel Goldwyn Company. In 1995 Goldwyn was put up for sale because of financial difficulties and in 1997 it went out of business. Around the same time, the industry presence of October Films was on the rise until it too was sold and dissolved into USA Films in 1999. In the latter part of the 1990s several other larger ventures, such as Artisan and Lions Gate (formerly CFP), entered the field. In addition, there are numerous smaller independent distributors, some currently in operation: First Run Features, Roxie Releasing, First Look Pictures, Strand Releasing, New Yorker Films, Northern Arts Entertainment, Arrow Entertainment, Zeitgeist, and Lot 47; others that have appeared and failed over the last two decades include Cinecom, Island/Alive, Aries, Avenue Pictures, Circle Releasing, IRS Releasing, Triton Pictures, Spectrafilm, and Savoy Pictures.

The appellation *mini-major* for the larger distributors has become increasingly fitting. Independent film's rise to cultural prominence in the 1990s has prompted studio involvement. Some of the larger companies are now, indeed, mini-majors and are entirely or partially studio owned: Miramax by the Walt Disney Company; Fine Line Features, a division of New Line Cinema, was bought by Turner Broadcasting and then became part of Time Warner, owner of Warner Brothers Studios, in the subsequent Turner–Time Warner merger (now AOL Time Warner); Sony Pictures Classics has always been studio affiliated and is currently owned by Sony (TriStar and Columbia); and in 1997, October completed a deal with Universal Pictures that gave the studio 51% ownership. Two years later, Universal, in turn, sold October to USA Networks. While all the mini-majors have some arrangement with the studios ensuring that their specialty companies remain "independent," that is, that they retain (varying degrees of) separate control over their operations and output, each has gained the advantage of access to significant studio resources, especially increased capitalization. These and other issues related to distribution are examined in further detail later in this chapter.

Actors

For the purposes of this discussion, actors can be classified into three loose categories: stars (Bruce Willis, Harvey Keitel), known (Steve Buscemi, Lili Taylor), and unknown. Known actors include those who usually or often perform in independent films as well as non–A-list actors who make the occasional foray into independent film in an attempt to rekindle their careers or to set it off in other directions (TV actors trying to move into film, for instance). Normally, having a cast of unknown or known actors (but not stars) is part of what defines a film as independent. However, this distinction too is blurring. As independent films have become more prominent—and fashionable—more A-list actors are willing to undertake independent roles as a career-enhancing step.

Director's Experience

The usual independent director falls into one of two categories: someone who is directing his or her first or second feature as a reputation-building training ground prior to moving to Hollywood financing and distribution (e.g., Spike

Lee, Steven Soderbergh); or certain directors who have made career-long commitments to working independently (e.g., John Sayles, Jim Jarmusch).

Specialized Audiences

Instead of appealing to a mass market, independent film is viewed as addressing a spectrum of specialized audiences (hence the reason they are also referred to as specialty films). This perception of likely audiences results in niche marketing or aiming a film at a specific demographic(s), much like television's strategy since the advent of cable but in contrast to Hollywood's blockbuster approach of reaching the widest possible viewership. The specialized audience for independent film might overlap with a political identity (see Subject Matter, below) as in the case of gay and lesbian cinema, or it might address a more traditionally statistical demographic, for instance, older or urban viewers.

Release Pattern

Different conceptualizations of audience translate into dramatically different release and advertising strategies (and budgets). Hollywood films, aimed at a mass audience, usually follow a wide pattern of release: thousands of prints opening simultaneously across the nation, buttressed by saturation newspaper and television advertising. A specialty film, in contrast, aims to locate and build its audience more slowly by releasing far fewer prints (from a mere handful to the low hundreds, and consequently, far less costly), with staggered openings that move from city to city and rely on the inexpensive but effective advertising of good reviews and positive word-of-mouth.[3]

International Cinema

In the United States the vast majority of international films, and certainly foreign-language films, are distributed by the independents. As such, international films are almost invariably inscribed as independent or "art" films. This categorization, in turn, makes it more likely that distributors will select work from foreign territories that conforms to notions of art film. Additionally, no other nation has a film industry as comparably monolithic as Hollywood's. That is, all national cinemas, like independent film in the United States, also must compete with Hollywood, making them more closely affiliated, in this sense, to independent than to studio sensibility.

Subject Matter

Certain subjects are considered the dominant (or de facto) prerogative of independent film, principally those that take up an overtly or oppositional political stance. A tremendously important strain of independent film throughout the past two decades is that associated with identity politics: gay and lesbian cinema, African American cinema, Asian and Asian American cinema, Latino/Latina cinema, women's cinema, and so on. I discuss this critical aspect of independent film in greater detail in chapters 2 and 3.

Aesthetics

Whether reflected in structure, style, or specific formal attributes, aesthetic experimentation is considered the province and one of the hallmarks of independent film. Avant-garde and alternative practices provide one of the most recurring and fundamental bases for independent cinema. Various alternative filmic legacies which have influenced independent film are detailed in chapter 2.

Narrative

While complexly interwoven with aesthetic considerations, and as such difficult to separate from the previous category, narrativity focuses on a film's modes or means of storytelling, its narrative processes of signification, and its relation to or reflections of ideology. Every film has a process of signification, the system by which it accumulates and conveys its meanings which, in turn, add up to its "story." Aspects of narrative and independent film are examined in chapter 4 and again in chapter 6. Further, while aesthetic or formal variation is the more dominant means of classifying a film as independent, and while many independent films are both aesthetically and narratively experimental, there are some films encompassed within the framework of independent cinema that take an arguably alternative narrative approach but not an alternative aesthetic one. This is touched on in chapter 2.

An independent film consists of some combination, even if a minimal number, of the attributes I have outlined. For a film to be even remotely considered independent, it must exhibit at least one or two of these characteristics. It should also be noted that these are diverse attributes, sometimes overlapping (a low budget generally ensures no name actors), sometimes competing (a foreign film could well have a Hollywood-sized budget or aesthetic approach). Further, these are not equally weighted criteria; some count more or less, in varying configurations, depending on the case and context in any given filmic instance (*Pulp Fiction*'s aesthetic impact arguably outweighs its budget and stars).

The independent films that reach mainstream venues such as the Academy Awards or the front page of the entertainment section of the *New York Times* or *USA Today* exist at the most prominent, visible, and financially successful edge of independent film—they are the most "centered." In storytelling modes they are often the most similar to Hollywood's products and are almost always released by one of the mini-majors. Obviously, though, there is much independent work beyond these culturally profiled notables.

A film like *Poison* (1991), for example, fits the criteria of a low-budget, nonstudio financed, independently distributed—by Zeitgeist—film. It has no known actors, was Todd Haynes's first feature film (he had previously made shorts, including *Superstar: The Karen Carpenter Story*), was viewed as being of particular interest to gay and lesbian audiences, and took time to build its audiences through slow release, good reviews, and positive word-of-mouth. Its subject matter, which involves themes of homosexuality, corresponds with independent cinema's identity politics mandate. Its aesthetic and narrative attributes—three separate stories told in three genres—depart from the formulaic, marking it as stylistically and structurally alternative. It encompasses almost all the defining traits of independent film outlined above, and it is unlikely that many people would challenge *Poison*'s independent status.

By the time of Haynes's 1998 film, *Velvet Goldmine*, the categories become less clear-cut. While its independent standing holds, it is not as easily or unambiguously a fit as *Poison*. No longer low-budget ($8 to $10 million compared to under $300,000 for *Poison*), it features a star (Ewan McGregor) and known actors. Its distributor, Miramax, although an independent is the most prominent of the mini-majors. The company is known for not pursuing a slow-release pattern based on positive word-of-mouth and good reviews but, rather, for following a model similar to Hollywood's of a wide opening bolstered by newspaper and television advertising. Still, *Velvet Goldmine*'s subject matter, glam rock, and its themes around bisexuality and homosexuality are hardly usual Hollywood fare. And while the film does have a narrative through-line, it is not constructed in either a narratively or an aesthetically linear fashion. So, although *Velvet Goldmine*'s representational attributes fit within independent parameters, its material or production factors correspond less comfortably. And of course the problems of attribution grow even murkier the closer one moves to the most widely attended but materially and representationally debatable independent status of films such as *The English Patient* or *Shakespeare in Love* (both, in fact, Miramax films).

As I discussed in my introduction, the business of definition and demarcation is a difficult one, made particularly so by independent film's shifting discursive parameters or floating boundaries. The borders are malleable and shifting for two principal reasons. First, independent film defines itself against other cinematic systems (Hollywood and alternative) and redefines itself as those other systems, particularly Hollywood's, change. Reinvention becomes even more necessary as studio practice appropriates independent qualities. Second, independent film is constructed as a malleable, shifting entity quite purposefully. It is not programmatic and with rare exceptions, such as Dogme 95, it is not a film movement. While the eleven attributes outlined above constitute independent film, there are no fixed criteria for the configurations in which they might occur. It is precisely the open-endedness of potential configurations that gives independent film its malleable signature, as long as the films take shape somewhere in the expanse between, and as a hybrid of, mainstream and alternative practices. So, for instance, low-budget genre pictures made in the Hollywood mold or exploitation films do not fit, nor do entirely nonnarrative avant-garde films.

On the one hand, from the perspective of analysis, independent film's malleability poses real challenges because there is no overarching theory that grounds and connects the films, no specific set of guidelines that fixes their boundaries, unlike the precision of the ten Dogme 95 rules and the reasoning behind them.[4] On the other hand, such open-endedness manages to avoid the delimitation of boundaries that proved so problematic for the political and aesthetic avant-gardes. Attempts to pinpoint the exact perimeters of independent film often have led to the imposition of largely arbitrary points of demarcation and to unhelpful arguments about which specific films "count" and which do not.

However, the example of *Velvet Goldmine* indicates that the eleven characteristics of independent film fall into two broad groupings: the "means of production and 'the vision thing'" as Manohla Dargis notes ("Vision Thing" 32), that is, the institutional and material factors in contrast to textual or representational attributes. In other words, filmic production is understood as both commodity and cultural artifact, the latter in the sense of a means of human expression. Institutional and material factors often are considered the more reliable determinants for purposes of definition precisely because they are more tangible. One can argue whether a film is or is not independent based on its budget (does $8 million count?), but at least one can determine what that budget is. Representational factors are far more elusive to quantification.

James Schamus, the copresident of Good Machine and producer of such films as *Poison, The Wedding Banquet* (1993), *The Brothers McMullen* (1995), *Walking and Talking* (1996), *Happiness* (1998), and *Crouching Tiger, Hidden Dragon* (2000), suggests that American independent filmmakers define themselves in terms of a common enemy, Hollywood, and that this is "a peculiarly romantic (and free-market capitalist) notion of artistic identity, one that posits the heroic individual artist fighting for his [sic] vision" ("American Independents" 36). At the same time, however, American independent film does not eschew Hollywood but rather engages "the dominant film industry in surprising ways, parodying Hollywood's representational and narrative strategies while at the same time paying homage to the ethics of the avant-garde past" (36). A major indicator of engagement with the dominant industry is independent film's reliance on plot-based, relatively linear narrative, which is like Hollywood's but in contrast to much of the avant-garde.

As a result, Schamus defines independent film as a "blending of American and European sensibilities," a blending that does not take the form of a singular school or style and instead maintains an ambiguous stance to both (37). Independent film draws on both popular mainstream culture and avant-garde culture without upholding one over the other in its entirety or in a simplistic manner. Schamus adds, "Unlike earlier avant-garde strategies, it doesn't ask its audience to take a totally (and illusory) oppositional stance to mass culture, but neither does it buy into that stance uncritically" (37).

I would agree with this analysis of independent film as a hybrid moving between popular culture and avant-garde culture. In one guise, Hollywood is the projected common enemy for independents, the ubiquitous presence against which independent film constantly strives to define itself. Simultaneously, however, independent film's textual strategies are not simply oppositional to Hollywood practices, as was at times the case for avant-garde movements. Quite the contrary, independent film, in taking an ambiguous stance toward Hollywood, borrows heavily from, pays homage to, plays to, and plays on the discourses of the dominant, mass culture industry, just as it does with avant-garde and art film traditions.

Or in the less positive spin of Steven Bickel, at the time the head of international sales at Goldwyn, "There's no such thing as independent films. They're really co-dependent films" (qtd. in Amedeo 11*)*. They are codependent, rather than wholly independent, in the sense of always requiring, by definition, a dominant industry to define themselves against. And as the following chapter argues, independent film's discursive existence is also codependent on the language and strategies of the avant-garde, although not, as in the instance of Hollywood, as a formation largely to be defined in opposition to, but rather as a respected tradition to be honored, borrowed from, and cited. In this sense of codependence, independent film is a relational industry and aesthetic. While it forms its own distinct system of cinematic representation, it is one that exists only in relation to other cinematic systems.

Other attempts at definition include one by Jim Stark, the producer of a number of independent films including Jim Jarmusch's *Down by Law* (1986), *Mystery Train* (1989), and *Night on Earth* (1991). Stark's definition links the two broad groupings of factors—material and representational—by focusing on independent film as an economy of means that results in aesthetic invention: "in general these filmmakers looked not to star actors, crowd scenes, fancy optical effects or plot twists, but to character pieces where the story was told visually, often with striking and inexpensive devices such as unrealistic or 'moody' lighting, long takes or jump cuts" (13). Scott Macauley, editor of *Filmmaker*, makes a similar point when he describes *Reservoir Dogs* (1992), *Clerks*, and *What Happened Was...*(1994) as a "new generation of talkies." These are films "in which witty conversation and few locations provide a model of indie-film economy" ("Take" 34). Although Stark stresses visual techniques and Macauley the centrality of dialogue, both link economy of means to a creatively inventive aesthetics of necessity. Or as Derek Jarman puts it, speaking of financial constraints imposed on his film, *Wittgenstein* (1993), "the budget again becomes the aesthetic" (13).[5]

Another view, and one that is contrary to most independents' recognition of the distinctions between Hollywood and independent fare, is that of Sundance Festival's founder Robert Redford. He describes his goal as wanting to break down the distinction between independent and studio films, so that "there won't be a distinction between types of movies, just a broader menu. I think the reason independent film got categorized in the first place was because by and large, it wasn't very good" (qtd. in Kim 85).[6] This is both a questionable goal, given that independent film's currency is based on its distinction from studio product and its ability to do things otherwise limited by Hollywood's vast and particular infrastructures, and a questionable analysis of independent film ("it wasn't very good").

Ted Hope, the producer of Hal Hartley's films *Simple Men* (1992), *Amateur* (1994), and *Flirt* (1995), and James Schamus's partner in the production company Good Machine, takes either a cynical or pragmatic view—depending on one's perspective—arguing that independent film has become solely a marketing concept:

> Acquisitions are driven by marketability, and marketability alone. Art has no value. Sure a film has to be 'good' to be picked up, but what does a distributor truly look for when it acquires a film? Uniqueness of vision? Independent spirit? Discipline? A controlled or unique aesthetic? Try again. Like their Hollywood counterparts, the first item on their menu is a marketable concept, one they already know how to package. (18)

By a marketable concept that independent distributors "already know how to package," Hope means that the new acquisition must fit the model of a financially successful film that has preceded it, in terms for instance, of its subject matter, narrative style, specialized audience, or some other "hook."

Schamus responds by acknowledging that acquisitions are driven almost solely by marketability but counters that the function of current manifestations of independent film is precisely to identify and define such markets:

> Many people who used to be shut out of the public sphere—women, gays and lesbians, African-Americans—have found a place in our problematic cultural landscape precisely through the process of getting organized as a "market."...a market *can* be a kind of community and the consumption of cultural commodities *can* help people form and articulate identities and solidarities of real importance. ("Don't Worry" 22)

Schamus's point here is a critical one and an argument that has been put forth by others.[7] In this view, the current function of independent film is to help define multiple and alternative markets or identities. While acknowledging that independent film is a business driven by economics and that selection of films is overwhelmingly based on marketability, Schamus suggests that within these market constraints there is still room for political activity. The question is whether this is a viable position or itself a romantic notion of independent film. This important issue of how well and in what ways independent film helps shape "emerging" identities and provides them with a means of expression and communication is one I explore in greater depth in chapter 3.

Without doubt the market context of late capitalism is a critical determining factor for independent film. Some analysts believe contemporary national and global developments signify a later phase of modernity while others mark them as a shift to postmodernity. This is a significant distinction profoundly shaping one's understanding not just of economic effects but of other social and cultural occurrences as well.

I would argue that while most—indeed, the great majority—of independent cinema's specific texts are not themselves postmodern, independent film as an industry and as a cultural practice operates in an increasingly postmodern landscape. Among the effects produced by this landscape are fragmentation, diversity, and an anticanonical approach. For example, Larry Grossberg points out: "If one makes an effort to construct such a postmodern aesthetics, the generic diversity is overwhelming. One would have to include, or at least justify excluding, a wide range of texts" (273). His statement pinpoints both an accuracy about and the difficulties involved in analyzing representational practices under postmodernity/postmodernism. I would suggest that instead of attempting to justify the inclusion or exclusion of specific texts, a more fruitful approach is to identify significant signposts or landmarks in the landscape of independent film. This is perhaps akin to receiving directions in a small town in relation to markers such as a church, a convenience store, the local post office, or the Wal-Mart. These do not demarcate the town's boundaries, but they do reveal the significant features of the town from the perspective of its occupants—those who use it.

An approach that attempts to define by signposts and landmarks avoids the limitations of modernism's master narratives and canons—fixed texts and located perimeters. But I am also aware that an approach insisting on postmodernism's migratory boundaries is open to charges of critical evasiveness. Nonetheless, this is the approach taken in part II. It is an effort to define, not by securing the perimeters of independent film or determining inclusivity and exclusivity but by locating significant markers and by mapping from the interior out.

History

As with a definition, there is no clear consensus on a moment of emergence for the contemporary wave of cinema known as independent film. However, often cited seminal films include *The Return of the Secaucus Seven* (1980), *Chan Is Missing* (1982), *Smithereens* (1982), *Stranger than Paradise* (1984), and *She's Gotta Have It* (1986).

A number of infrastructural and technological conditions enabled the emergence and development in the early to mid-1980s of independent film in its current configurations. The most frequently cited factor is the rapid growth of the home video market in the mid-1980s, the result of home video cassette players becoming available in the late 1970s. "For a brief period from 1984 to 1987 (when the home video business was new), independent video companies sprang up, seemingly overnight, each one hungry for product" (Stark 12).[8] "Overnight" video production and distribution companies such as Vestron, Cannon, and Lorimar spurred the development of the independent industry with an influx of money for low-budget movies ($1 to $3 million), which they could sell to the burgeoning home-use market. Although short-lived, this boom in financing triggered a lot of independent production, helped develop institutional infrastructures, and succeeded in drawing a number of people into the orbit of independent production and distribution. The money dried up rather rapidly, however, as video distributors found themselves going out of business despite overstocked shelves and catalogs. The idea that successful video releases needed theatrical showcasing or some other kind of marketing hook became entrenched. From then on, the home video market looked increasingly to "name actors, experienced directors and…conventional scripts" (Stark 12).

A second factor that contributed to the rise of independent cinema in the 1980s and 1990s was the concurrent events taking place in Hollywood. Beginning with *Jaws* in 1975 and *Star Wars* in 1977, Hollywood saw the rise of the blockbuster, large-scale action and special-effects driven films aimed at the widest possible audience but appealing especially to young men, the largest and most committed movie-going demographic group.[9] As Thomas Schatz argues, "the composition and industry conceptualization of the youth market…was shifting from the politically hip, cineliterate viewers of a few years earlier to even younger viewers with more conservative tastes and sensibilities" (19). The era of the blockbuster (in the strictest sense, films that earn $100 million or more in domestic theatrical box office) is often referred to as *the new Hollywood* (distinguishing it from "classic" Hollywood).[10] In addition to the blockbuster text of action and effects, new Hollywood practices include high-cost films, large promotional budgets, generation of media hype, tie-in and spin-off merchandising around films poised as events, and a film's simultaneous opening in thousands of theaters (Tasker 217, 219). Schatz suggests that for the most part "the New Hollywood's calculated blockbusters are themselves massive advertisements for their product lines" of books, CDs, television programming, video games, videocassettes, comic books, theme park rides, and assorted merchandise (19).

In 1996, the year that "belonged" to independent film at the Academy Awards, the highest grossing Hollywood successes were among the most expensive to make: *Independence Day, Twister,* and *Mission: Impossible*. The average cost to produce and market a film in 1996 was between $57 and $61 million.[11] In 1997, the year of *Titanic* and *Men in Black*, Jack Valenti, the President of the Motion Picture Association of America, cited the average cost of producing and marketing a film as $75.6 million (Rea, "On Movies," March 22, 1998: F9).

Simultaneously, over the same two decades, Hollywood's box-office intake has come increasingly from foreign markets, which can now yield as much as 50% of a studio's grosses. In 1998, for example, of the $13.8 billion generated worldwide, international theaters accounted for $6.84 billion. Similarly in 1999, foreign markets were responsible for $7.1 billion of the year's $14.6 billion in gross earnings (Martin, "Tiger" D1). And blockbuster action and genre films, in particular, fare well with international audiences.[12] In Hollywood's current estimation, pursuing the blockbuster is a better financial strategy and less risky than turning out medium- or low-budget (by Hollywood standards) productions. "Though the size of a picture's budget obviously doesn't guarantee a large audience, virtually every film that has had a megagross has also had a megabudget" (Gabler 77). Domestic audiences "like big-budget extravaganzas, such as *Independence Day*, more than character dramas like *Fargo*" (Lieberman B2). Indeed, *Independence Day* "earned more at the domestic box office than Miramax's entire 1996 slate" ("1997's Most Influential People" 52), although that was considered the year of the independents. Or as Ron Weiskind put it in 1996:

> *The Postman [Il Postino]*, which ranks as the highest-grossing foreign-language film released in the United States, has racked up $22 million in this country after more than a year in release. In contrast, *Star Trek: First Contact* reported a $30 million box-office take on its first weekend alone. (G11)

As for the international market, "Foreign audiences don't want small, sensitive, serious pictures from America. They can get those from their own national film industries" (Gabler 78). This is a view seconded by Isisara Bey, an African American studio executive who writes of his experiences at the 1993 Pan African Film and Television Festival in Burkina Faso, "Make no mistake about it, Africans go to see African films—in droves. Folks get all dressed up and stand in long lines, especially when it's a film by one of their favourites." But, he explains, the African films at the festival dealt with "issues of political and social significance. There were films of substance holding an unflinching mirror to the contradictions of African life." What Africans look for from the American film industry are the bigger budget, high-gloss productions of action-adventure, romantic comedy, and other genre pictures. This desire is welcomed by a Hollywood that continues to consider Africa as "the repository for the latest shoot 'em-up, cut 'em-up, action and karate flicks" (Bey 42).

Hollywood's pursuit of the blockbuster strategy, which relies increasingly on action, effects, genre films, and stars with domestic or international appeal (what Peter Bart, the editor-in-chief of *Variety*, describes as "marketing plans pretending to be movies" [qtd in Ryan F5]),[13] has left an opening in the marketplace precisely for those "small, sensitive, serious" pictures that incorporate greater cultural specificity. A successful independent film grosses between $1 and $3 million: *Clerks*, $3 million; *Happiness*, $2.9 million; *Reservoir Dogs*, $2.8 million; *Straight out of Brooklyn*, $2.7 million; *Go Fish*, 2.4 million; *The Incredi-*

bly *True Adventure of Two Girls in Love*, $1.97 million; *High Art*, $1.93 million; *I Shot Andy Warhol*, $1.8 million; *Daughters of the Dust*, $1.7 million; *To Sleep with Anger*, $1.16 million; *Living in Oblivion*, $1.08 million; *Velvet Goldmine*, $1.05 million; *Slacker*, $1 million; *Box of Moonlight*, $782,000; *Safe*, $460,000; *Swoon*, $340,000.[14] *She's Gotta Have It* at $7.1 million is a stand-out. As the *Wall Street Journal* notes, for "independent motion pictures that attract an 'arthouse' crowd and are popular with critics a box-office gross of $10 million is a home-run and [distribution] costs must be tightly scrutinized" (King and Turner B13).

At the other end of the spectrum are the rare breakthroughs, the exceptions such as *The Crying Game* ($65 million), *The English Patient* ($78.7 million), *Pulp Fiction* ($100 million), *Life Is Beautiful* ($57.5 million), *Shakespeare in Love* ($100 million), and *The Blair Witch Project* ($140 million). With the exception of *The Blair Witch Project*, an Artisan release, all of these, along with *Il Postino*, are Miramax releases, which explains that company's industry dominance, often credited to its outstanding marketing savvy. It should also be noted that only about 10% of the independent films made manage to recoup their costs and only about 1% achieve some measure of profitability (Dawes 10). As Christopher Cherot, director of *Hav Plenty* (1997) put it: "My film is what you call a modest success. It got distributed—that's the successful part about it" (Lechner 49).

Other factors that have contributed to the establishment of independent film include the rise of film schools, which provide a training ground and a source for collaborators; the financial accessibility and physical portability, beginning in the 1940s and 1950s, of 16 mm and other low-budget technologies; a growing tendency to consider specific demographic groups or target markets when looking at the consumer population;[15] and the existence of a repertory theater tradition in the 1960s and 1970s, which established an audience base of certain viewers (e.g. college, urban) who were later to become the foundation for specialized audiences. The expertise of repertory theaters rested in screening classics, foreign art films, and cult films. The home video market of the 1980s effectively ended repertory exhibition because the films that were their stock-in-trade could now be seen at home on a VCR. However, the repertory tradition, in its viewer base and viewing practices, helped pave the way for "the modern era of first-run, off-Hollywood features" (Pierson 20), that is, theatrical premieres of original, lower-budget films rather than rescreenings of classics.

Repertory exhibition as one of the precursors of contemporary independent film is evident in the influence that works of the repertory era have had on current independent cinema. In 1996, the independent film journal *Filmmaker* asked forty-seven critics, curators, distributors, and producers from the independent community to pick what they considered "the most important American independent films of all time." Because the selection criterion was "most important," respondents chose films "that were pioneering in some historical, cultural or business context," in addition to those of aesthetic significance (Fall 1996: 40–60).[16] It should be noted that because discussion was limited to American films, the enormous influence of foreign, especially European, cinema is not factored in.

Many films of the recent wave of independent film were cited, for instance, *Stranger than Paradise* (1985), second on the list; *She's Gotta Have It* (1986), third; *Return of the Secaucus Seven* (1980), fifth; *Blood Simple* (1984), ninth; *Reservoir Dogs* (1982), thirteenth; *Daughters of the Dust* (1992), fourteenth; *Chan Is Missing* (1982), thirty-seventh; *Trust* (1990), forty-fifth; and *The Living End* (1992), forty-eighth.

Along with the many notable examples from contemporary independent film, the list also included a significant number of earlier works that would fall into the classic, avant-garde, or cult film categories. Indeed, the film that placed first is John Cassavetes's classic, *A Woman under the Influence* (1974). Cassavetes is described as "the quintessential American indie," his films receiving more votes than any other director's, and his methods of private financing and self-distribution much admired (40). Also on the list, as the thirty-second, is Sam Fuller's *The Naked Kiss* (1965), a B film classic.

Films considered experimental or influenced by the avant-garde included *Scorpio Rising* (1964), eighth; *A Movie* (1958), twelfth; *Meshes of the Afternoon* (1943), twentieth; *Eraserhead* (1977), twenty-first; and *Film About a Woman Who…* (1974), twenty-ninth. I discuss films that fall within the avant-garde or art paradigms in the next chapter.

Cult or exploitation films that made the list were: George Romero's low-budget horror film, *Night of the Living Dead* (1968), fifteenth; *Sweet Sweetback's Baadasssss Song* (1971), an inspiration for blaxploitation films and the concept of target or niche markets, twenty-sixth; *Easy Rider* (1969), the counter-culture road movie, twenty-seventh; *Pink Flamingos* (1972), John Waters's camp outing, thirty-fifth; action and sexploitation picture, *Faster, Pussycat! Kill! Kill!* (1966), forty-sixth; and the very financially successful, hardcore *Deep Throat* (1972), fiftieth. Exploitation films are low-budget genre pictures aimed at target markets of the genre's specific fans. Labeled as such because they "'exploit' sensational' material" (Bordwell and Thompson 23), they are often categorized together with cult films. Indeed, *Night of the Living Dead; Faster, Pussycat! Kill! Kill!;* and *Deep Throat* are all exploitation films that developed cult followings. In contrast, Melvin Van Peebles's *Sweet Sweetback's Baadasssss Song* is less blaxploitation and more political (as is, arguably, *Easy Rider*, although based on low-budget generic biker flicks), while *Pink Flamingos* can be seen as having art film intentions.[17]

Exploitation and cult films have their roots in the B movies of classical Hollywood. From the mid-1930s through the 1940s it was standard practice to present the movie-going public with a program consisting of two features (plus a newsreel, cartoons, and previews of coming attractions) (McCarthy and Flynn 15). Hollywood studios provided the A picture or top of the bill and collected the majority of the box-office take in a percentage split with (then studio-owned) theaters. There was not, however, sufficient financial incentive for the studios to produce the B or second half of the double bill. Rather than program two A features together, it was more profitable to hold the second A picture for a subsequent week and present it to a new ticket-buying public.

The B half of the program was paid a fixed rental fee for exhibition rights instead of a percentage of box-office take, so while there were not the opportunities for runaway hits and large amounts of money, the prospect of regular, reasonable profits existed for those who could make sixty to seventy-five minute features cheaply and rapidly. Further, the risks were low because the films were guaranteed exhibition by being block-booked with the major studios' product. The result was the rise of substudios or B studios, like Republic and Monogram, that made Westerns, gangster films, and other genre pictures, often at the pace of one a week (McCarthy and Flynn 17; Ferncase 4). In time, the term *B film* came to stand apart from its B studio origins. That is, it came to stand for a style of film—low-budget, gritty, based on generic formulas—whether produced by B studios or the majors.

The demise of the B studio system began in the late 1940s. The first blow came in 1948 with the ruling in the antitrust case of *United States v. Paramount Pictures* that determined that the studio's control of production, distribution, and exhibition constituted a monopoly and ordered studios to sell off their theater chains. Over the next few years, as the Paramount consent decrees forced studios to divest themselves of their exhibition outlets, the practice of block booking B or second features disappeared (Ferncase 3; McCarthy and Flynn 15).[18] The second set back, the rise of television in the 1950s and the accompanying drop in movie attendance, caused the B studios' final decline (Gomery 188). By the 1950s only a few survived and those that did existed in transformed configurations, evolving into producing "exploitation" movies.

Prominent among these was American-International Pictures (AIP), which was one of the first companies to identify and capitalize on the burgeoning youth market of the mid to late 1950s and 1960s (Hoberman and Rosenbaum 115–16; Ferncase 7). And prominent at AIP during this era was Roger Corman who worked with a number of genre formulas—sci-fi, horror, sexploitation, action—and who helped pioneer contemporary low-budget filmmaking techniques at AIP and subsequently at his own production company, New World Pictures, founded in 1970 (Ferncase 7; McCarthy and Flynn 63).

The development of the exploitation film and the opening up of exhibition practices led to the repertory tradition, well established by the 1970s, and to the rise of the cult film. Cult fare included B film revivals such as *Freaks* (1932, re-released 1972) and *Reefer Madness* (1940, re-released 1972), as well as more recent exploitation ventures such as *Night of the Living Dead*, camp art films like *Pink Flamingos* and *The Rocky Horror Picture Show* (1975), and more politicized filmmaking, such as *The Harder They Come* (1972) and *Girlfriends* (1978).

Cult films are dependent on repeat viewers, often at late-night showings, for their success. In *Midnight Movies*, J. Hoberman and Jonathan Rosenbaum argue that "films tend to inspire a cult only after they have become devalued or otherwise estranged from mainstream acceptance" (30–31). They attribute the success of a film like *The Rocky Horror Picture Show* to the fact that it "translated many intellectual and avant-garde ideas about sexuality and culture into terms that teen-agers could relate to" (211).

As the spread of videocassettes in the 1980s undermined much of the reason for repertory cinemas, all these antecedents—B movies and low-budget features, exploitation, avant-garde, and cult films—contributed to the makeup of theatrically released, first-run independent film in the 1980s and 1990s.

Distributors

A number of independent distributors also grew out of the repertory tradition. New Line Cinema, founded by Robert Shaye, began with cult and art films aimed at the college-aged audience. Initially, it distributed Jean-Luc Godard's *Sympathy for the Devil* (1970), the re-release of *Reefer Madness* (1972), and John Waters's *Pink Flamingos* (1972), and continued with such films as *Smithereens* in 1982. Simultaneously throughout the 1980s, New Line was branching out into specialized genre pictures like the *Nightmare on Elm Street* series. Successes like these and the *Teenage Mutant Ninja Turtles* series allowed New Line to begin financing and releasing higher-budget, glossier commercial productions, such as *The Mask* (1994), *Se7en* (1995), *Last Man Standing* (1996) and *Wag the Dog* (1997), and so to function as a virtual studio. In 1990, however, New Line established Fine Line Features, its specialty film division, which subsequently oversaw the release of its smaller, independent films ("In-House Boutiques" 9). Headed by Ira Deutchman, Fine Line's early films included *Trust* (1990), *My Own Private Idaho* (1991), *Night on Earth* (1991), *The Player* (1992), *Swoon*

(1992), *Naked* (1993), *Dear Diary* (1994), and *The Incredibly True Adventure of Two Girls in Love* (1995). Under the leadership of Ruth Vitale (1995 to 1998) and Mark Ordesky (from 1998), subsequent Fine Line releases include *Shine* (1996), *The Sweet Hereafter* (1997), *Gummo* (1997), *Pecker* (1998), *Tumbleweeds* (1999), *The Cup* (1999), *An Affair of Love* (2000), *Saving Grace* (2000), and *Before Night Falls* (2001). Using the definitions I've established for independent films in this book, almost all films from New Line are excluded whereas films distributed by Fine Line are included.

Other "virtual studios" have existed. There are, for instance, British-based Polygram Filmed Entertainment and its U.S. distribution company Gramercy Pictures, cofounded with Universal Studios. Polygram Filmed Entertainment, a division of the international music and entertainment group, Polygram, was sold in May 1998 by the Dutch electronics company Philips to Canadian-owned Seagram, which also owned MCA/Universal, comprising its music, film, and television interests (Glaister 4; "Seagram" 24). But even before that sale, Gramercy was established as a fifty-fifty joint venture between Polygram and MCA/Universal, its function being "to distribute and market films from both MCA and Polygram that are judged to be commercially viable but not 'blockbuster' material" (Magiera 42). Polygram/Gramercy films have included *Four Weddings and a Funeral* (1994), *Dead Man Walking* (1995), *Shallow Grave* (1995), *The Usual Suspects* (1995), *Fargo* (1996), *The Big Lebowski* (1998), *Your Friends and Neighbors* (1998), *Elizabeth* (1998), and *Lock, Stock and Two Smoking Barrels* (1999). Although something like *Shallow Grave* could certainly be considered independent in many respects and *The Usual Suspects* has been influential for independent film, Gramercy releases largely have been excluded from this study (for instance, Gramercy also distributed *Barb Wire* [1996] with Pamela Anderson Lee). In April 1999, Barry Diller of USA Networks bought Gramercy and reshaped it into USA Films.

The concept of a classics or specialty division, as in the case of New Line and Fine Line, originated with United Artists Classics, which existed from 1980 to 1983 as a division of United Artists, releasing such films as *The Last Metro* (1980), *Diva* (1981) and *Entre Nous* (1983). Ira Deutchman, Tom Bernard, and Michael Barker all established themselves at UA Classics, which Bernard and Barker's promotional material describes as "the first modern-day specialized distribution company" (bio. sheet, Sony Classics PR material). In 1983, Tom Bernard and Michael Barker, along with Donna Gigliotti, formed Orion Classics under Orion's auspices,[19] releasing such films as *My Beautiful Laundrette* (1986), *Babette's Feast* (1987), *Wings of Desire* (1988), *Women on the Verge of a Nervous Breakdown* (1988), *Mystery Train* (1989), and *Europa, Europa* (1991). In 1992, when Orion was facing Chapter 11 bankruptcy, Bernard and Barker, along with Marcie Bloom, who had replaced Gigliotti in 1990, established Sony Pictures Classics under the ownership of the Sony Corporation, which also controlled the Columbia and TriStar studios. Sony Pictures Classics began in business in 1992 with *Howard's End* and continued with such films as *Orlando* (1993), *Mi Vida Loca* (1994), *Safe* (1995), *Living in Oblivion* (1995), *Welcome to the Dollhouse* (1996), *Lone Star* (1996), *In the Company of Men* (1997), *Ma Vie en Rose* (1997), *The Governess* (1998), *Central Station* (1998), *Run Lola Run* (1999), *The Emperor and the Assassin* (1999), *Kikujiro* (1999), *The Tao of Steve* (2000), *Crouching Tiger, Hidden Dragon* (2000), and *Beijing Bicycle* (2001).

Independent producer's representative John Pierson describes Orion Classics as having had "a consistent game plan throughout the eighties and into the nineties based on intelligent conservatism and savvy taste in world cinema" (120). In other words, it has been conservative in its spending for a film's rights and its promotional budget, and relies more than other American independent distributors on foreign films, particularly European auteurs, for its product. Pierson believes that Sony Pictures Classics continues to be run in the same manner, as if by "old dogs who don't believe in any of the new tricks," keeping promotional budgets low by relying on word of mouth, and holding print numbers down by opting for a slow release pattern. In contrast, those who head Sony Classics "bash Miramax's profligacy at every opportunity" (334) for the latter's high expenditures in purchasing distribution rights and for exorbitant promotional costs.

Miramax, founded and run by brothers Harvey and Bob Weinstein (and named after their parents, Miriam and Max), also began as an art/cult film distributor. The turning point for the Weinsteins came in 1989, the year in which Miramax released *sex, lies & videotape* and *My Left Foot*. *Sex, lies & videotape*, in particular, altered Miramax's direction. Grossing $24.7 million in domestic box-office receipts, it also altered expectations about independent film. From there, Miramax climbed steadily in box-office intake with *The Crying Game* in 1992 at $65 million, *The Piano* in 1993 at $40 million, crossing the $100 million studio blockbuster magic number with *Pulp Fiction* in 1994, grossing $78 million domestically with *The English Patient* in 1996, $57.5 million with *Life Is Beautiful* in 1998, and $100 million for *Shakespeare in Love* in the same year.

Miramax's successes and industry dominance are usually attributed to two factors. The first is its astute marketing skills and assertive business practices. *Forbes* describes Miramax as bringing to the scene "a brand of street-smart marketing that the art-world had rarely seen before" (Gubernick 110; King and Turner B13). The second factor is that since 1993 the Walt Disney Company has owned Miramax. Ironically, in an early interview, Bob Weinstein, describing studios as standing armies and themselves as "guerrillas," says, "We don't want to grow up to be another Walt Disney" (Gubernick 110).

The Disney buyout provided substantial financial resources to the smaller company, allowing Miramax to change, or at least broaden, its marketing strategy, often promoting and releasing a film widely, in a manner based more on a studio model than an independent one. "Miramax spends so much marketing a film that, even though a film may gross a nice amount, the exorbitant price that Miramax spends in P&A (prints and advertising) for its releases eats up all the profits" (Johnson and Harris S23). The argument is that Disney can afford to subsidize Miramax, whether it makes a profit or not; stand-alone independent distributors cannot afford to do so but are dependent on profits to survive.

While Miramax's industry dominance has been unquestionable—it has a film list consisting of hundreds of titles—its business practices sometimes provoke "anger and vitriol" (Johnson and Harris S21) from competitors. It has been accused of using its Disney backing to buy up films for fees other independents cannot afford. Speaking of the 1998 Sundance Film Festival in which Miramax bought three films for a total of $14.75 million—*Next Stop, Wonderland* and *The Castle* for $6 million apiece, and *Jerry and Tom* for $2.75 million—Bingham Ray, then of October Films, stated, "It was a headline-buying move: We're the players, nobody else. That's what those buys signal to me" (qtd. in Horn F11). Miramax has also been accused of buying up more films than it is able to release and subsequently shelving them, while managing to keep them out of competitors' hands (Hope 18). At the 1999 Independent Feature Project Spirit Awards, Miramax was presented with a fake award called "The Shelf," "for the most films acquired for distribution but never actually released" (Garrett, "Beach Blanket Bingo" 18).

Charges against Miramax also include inflating box-office figures, for instance, boosting the opening weekend take for *Pulp Fiction* by $400,000 (Grove). The reason for the figure inflation, according to CNN, was to ensure that the film could claim to be number one at the box office. In a practice followed by studios, the *New York Times* reports, initial box-office earnings are inflated because of studio belief that audiences measure the appeal of a movie based on its opening, that is, public perception of a film will be more favorable if it opens at number one (Lewis 68).[20]

Still, regardless of the charges aimed at it, Miramax is the distributor who has set the standard of expectations for independents. The desire to compete with Miramax and to replicate some of its successes has caused a number of other studios besides Disney to set up their own specialty divisions (Fox Searchlight, Paramount Classics, Universal Focus, Screen Gems). Miramax has also prompted the entry of larger, better financed new distributors into the marketplace (Artisan, Lions Gate). And it has altered the kinds of films independents acquire in their quest for the "crossover" or exceptional box-office successes.

The Miramax effect has been felt industry-wide, prompting, for instance, the leadership shake-up beginning in the mid-1990s at Fine Line. Ira Deutchman was replaced as president by Ruth Vitale, who was given "the mandate to compete more aggressively with Miramax as well as to move into the production of higher-budget films" (Glucksman, "Pushing Films" 21; Cox 22). Bingham Ray, after his departure from October, described Universal's buyout:

> One of the fatal flaws at October [was that] Universal wanted to turn us into Miramax. They wanted us to compete, go toe to toe with Harvey [Weinstein]. And there were those of us who said, "Look, that's not going to fly. October is October, let us grow, give us the financing to grow, but at the same time, let us maintain our niche." And that was a constant war that I lost. (qtd. in Hernandez and Rabinowitz, "Part 1A"; brackets in original)

Even at Sony Classics, the "old dog" who has carved out its own market niche and largely stuck to it, higher-profile, higher-budget films have crept onto their list since the latter part of the 1990s. For instance, it has picked up several films that have a wider appeal or can be marketed more easily because of the presence of stars, such as *Dancing at Lughnasa* (1998) with Meryl Streep, *The Opposite of Sex* (1998) with Christina Ricci and Lisa Kudrow, and *Pollock* (2000) with Ed Harris. In its promotion of *Crouching Tiger, Hidden Dragon* (2000), the company has also pursued a strategy of wide-release coupled with expensive television and newspaper advertising in place of its more traditional reliance on a slow-release pattern and word-of-mouth marketing.

Fox Searchlight Pictures, owned and operated by Twentieth Century Fox, began releasing films in 1995–96. It is run by Lindsay Law, longtime head of PBS-affiliated American Playhouse. Fox Searchlight has had a number of notable successes, including *The Brothers McMullen* (1995), *The Full Monty* (1997), *Waking Ned Devine* (1998), and *Boys Don't Cry* (1999). These films, however, have had the financial and institutional backing to pursue a more studio-like promotional and release operation. Other Fox Searchlight films include *Girl 6* (1996), *The Van* (1996), *Star Maps* (1997), *Slums of Beverly Hills* (1998), *Woman on Top* (2000), and *The Deep End* (2001). In 1998, Paramount formed Paramount Classics, headed by Ruth Vitale and David Dinerstein. Their most prominent films to date are *The Virgin Suicides* (1999) and *You Can Count on Me* (2000). Although their list is still small, other films include *Girl on the Bridge* (1999), *Passion of Mind* (2000), *Sidewalks of New York* (2000), *Sunshine*

(2000), *Our Lady of the Assassins* (2001), and *My First Mister* (2001). Universal's specialty division, Universal Focus, released its first film, *Billy Elliot*, in 2000, following with *The Man Who Cried* (2000), *The Caveman's Valentine* (2001), *Better Housekeeping* (2001), and *Julie Johnson* (2001). Universal Focus's mandate, like other studio specialty branches, is to pursue films in the "midrange" budget of $3 million to $20 million but which also hold the potential for widespread appeal or breakout success (Harris, "Outside Investors" A1; McNary 3).

The push toward higher production budgets for independent films—in the $5 to $20 million range—has altered significantly the kinds of independent films which have dominated in the latter half of the 1990s and into the new century. Geoffrey Gilmore, longtime programmer at Sundance, defends the festival's choices in 2001 and in the years immediately preceding by explaining that "the middle level of production—the $5–$15 million budget range—has proved to be a profitable arena, so companies are comfortable funding those types of films. Consequently, they have become a big part of the independent spectrum" (Geffner, "Sundance" 56). Such market shifts result in, for example, Sony Pictures Entertainment's launching of a second specialty division called Screen Gems, aimed at medium-budget films that fall into the space between the low-budget of Sony Classics and the wide releases of Columbia Pictures. Describing Sony Classics as "highly valued," Sony Pictures gave assurances that Screen Gems would not intrude upon Sony Classics's established terrain (Rabinowitz). Forming Screen Gems as a separate midrange division closer to the level of Miramax meant that Sony Classics's "branding" would not be undermined by forcing it to acquire and distribute higher-profile, more competitive films, the situation that had occurred with Fine Line and October. Yet the new company allows Sony to participate in the more highly visible, generally higher-return range of the independent arena. Ironically, though, it is the Sony Classics released *Crouching Tiger, Hidden Dragon* which earned the most prestige, attention, and box-office returns of any independent film in 2001. Screen Gems releases include *Limbo* (1999), *Arlington Road* (1999), *Black and White* (1999), *Timecode* (2000), and *Girlfight* (2000). Some of these films are not properly independent at all, others are only marginally so (similar to *The English Patient* and *Shakespeare in Love*). In the former category is *Arlington Road* with Jeff Bridges, Tim Robbins, and a $35 million budget; in the latter is *Black and White* with Brooke Shields, Robert Downey Jr., and a $10 million budget.

The term *branding* is being bandied about increasingly among independents. See, for example, David Geffner's article in *Filmmaker,* which depicts Miramax and Artisan as the two most successful distributors to have established a brand identity ("Cars" 22, 68). Many in the independent community see the development (or incorporation from other cultural areas) of concepts such as branding to be proof of the commodification of independent film in the 1990s, supplanting its previous existence as an "art" or a "passion." Contrary to this position, I would argue that independent film has always been a commodity (as well as an art and passion). However, during the 1990s it became a more popular and profitable one, raising the level of attention it received and intensifying its commodification. As Bingham Ray notes, "the Hollywood-ization of the independent marketplace.... is targeting essentially the same audience that we were targeting in the early 90's and late 80's, but the stakes are much, much higher" (qtd. in Hernandez and Rabinowitz, "Part 1"). And in fact it is precisely principles such as branding that have kept independent companies from being absorbed into the operations of their larger studio owners. Their separate existence is assured (only) to the degree that independent film's cultural currency remains rooted in its being recognizably or arguably different from Hollywood's product and that it is bought and sold in the marketplace on the basis of those arguments and brand identity.

Another notable development has been the entrance of larger, more substantially nonstudio-financed distributors into the field, better able to compete at Miramax's level. The most visible of these new entrants is Artisan Entertainment, presided over by Amir Malin, formerly of October and Cinecom. Its financial foundation is built on a video library of thousands of titles from former companies Live and Carolco which bring in a sizable and steady income. Artisan's astonishing success with *The Blair Witch Project* is attributed to its ingenious marketing based on the Internet, and the company's clarity about its target audience—"young, hip" (Malin qtd. in Germain 12).

Artisan's marketing skills were evident in their difficult, earlier release, *Pi* (1998). The film was purchased at the 1998 Sundance Film Festival for $500,000 according to Malin, although John Horn put the figure between $500,000 and $1 million: "With minimal marketing costs, the black-and-white movie about a psychotic mathematician needs to generate some $2 million in receipts to be on pace to break even" (Horn F11). Malin acknowledged that "everyone told me we'd be lucky to do $300,000 [at the domestic box-office]" and that they thought his purchase price of $500,000 was excessive (qtd. in H. Jacobson E2; brackets in original). But contrary to expectations, with successful marketing including the Internet, *Pi* earned $3.2 million (IMDb). Artisan is also the distributor of *Permanent Vacation* (1998), *The 24 Hour Woman* (1999), *My Name Is Joe* (1999), *Chuck & Buck* (2000), *Ghost Dog: The Way of the Samurai* (2000), *Requiem for a Dream* (2000), and *The Center of the World* (2001), as well as the second and third sequels of *The Blair Witch Project* (2000 and 2001).

Another significant new and larger distributor is Lions Gate Releasing. Formed from the smaller company CFP—*The Monster* (1994), *Flirt* (1995), *Heavy* (1996), *The Young Poisoner's Handbook* (1996), *Sunday* (1997), *The Daytrippers* (1997)—in January 1998 it received access to increased financing through its new parent company, Lions Gate Entertainment. Among Lions Gate's films are: *Eve's Bayou* (1997), *Gods and Monsters* (1998), *Buffalo 66* (1998), *The Dinner Game* (1998), *Dogma* (1999), *American Psycho* (2000), *8 ½ Women* (2000), *Love & Sex* (2000), *Steal This Movie!* (2000), *Shadow of the Vampire* (2000), and *Urbania* (2000).

Of the four original mini-majors (Miramax, Fine Line, Sony Classics, and Samuel Goldwyn), Goldwyn is the only one that has gone out of business. Its chair and CEO was Samuel Goldwyn Jr., son of the legendary Hollywood figure, and the company owned a number of concerns, including an exhibition chain of fifty "mostly art-house theaters" and a film library of 850 Hollywood classics (Grover 42).

Goldwyn's distribution division was headed by, most notably, Jeff Lipsky from 1983 to 1986 and by Tom Rothman until the summer of 1994. Debt-ridden and up for sale in 1996, the Goldwyn Company was bought by Metromedia International Group and then, in turn, sold to MGM (Elsen n.p.). MGM disbanded Goldwyn in 1997, but over the years it had released an impressive array of independent films, including *Gregory's Girl* (1982), *Stranger than Paradise* (1985), *Sid and Nancy* (1986), *Desert Hearts* (1986), *Prick up Your Ears* (1987), *To Sleep with Anger* (1990), *Straight out of Brooklyn* (1991), *Mississippi Masala* (1992), *Much Ado about Nothing* (1993), *32 Short Films about Glenn Gould* (1993), *Ladybird, Ladybird* (1994), *To Live* (1994), *Go Fish* (1994), and *I Shot Andy Warhol* (1996).

October Films, also no longer in business, was founded in 1991 by Bingham Ray and Jeff Lipsky, who began with Mike Leigh's film of the same year, *Life Is Sweet*. Lipsky left in 1995 and was replaced by Amir Malin and John Schmidt. October's releases included: *Tout les Matins du Monde* (1992), *The Living End* (1992), *Un Coeur en Hiver* (1993), *Ruby in Paradise* (1993), *The War Room* (1993), *The Last Seduction* (1994), *Breaking the Waves* (1996), *Secrets and Lies* (1996), *Girls Town* (1996), *The Celebration* (1998), *High Art* (1998), *Cookie's Fortune* (1999), and *Three Seasons* (1999). October's catalog also had offered a number of independent "classics" originally released by Cinecom (which has been out of business since the early 1990s), such as *El Norte* (1983), *The Times of Harvey Milk* (1984), *The Brother from Another Planet* (1984), *A Room with a View* (1986), *Sammy & Rosie Get Laid* (1987), and *Salaam Bombay!* (1988).

In 1997, Universal Pictures, then a division of Seagram (subsequently bought by Vivendi), purchased a 51% share in October Films. Universal obtained a prestige specialty unit, and October, a rapidly growing company since its 1991 inception, received increased capitalization to support its expansion. However, in April 1999, Universal sold a majority share of October and Gramercy (which it had acquired through Seagram/Universal's buyout of Polygram) to USA Networks, headed by Barry Diller. The two companies—October and Gramercy—were combined to form a new distribution entity, USA Films (of which Universal continues to own 45%). Intended to be a hybrid between studio and independent sensibilities, USA Films has released high-profile films with star casts like *Being John Malkovich* (1999) and *Nurse Betty* (2000). But USA Films has also released *Series 7* (2001), as well as lower-budget, foreign language films like *The Idiots* (1999) and *Rosetta* (1999).

WinStar Cinema is a new subsidiary of USA Films, formed out of a merger of Fox Lorber, primarily a video distributor, and two smaller companies. It appears to be USA Films's smaller independent outlet, to date handling primarily documentaries and foreign films like *On the Ropes* (1999), *Humanité* (2000), *Winter Sleepers* (2000), and *Yi Yi* (2001).

Smaller distributors like Arrow, Cowboy, First Look, First Run, Frameline, Kino, Lot 47, New Yorker, Northern Arts, Phaedra, Roxie, Seventh Art, Strand, and Zeitgeist have done their best to keep up with the mini-majors, but they have difficulty competing with the financial resources of the bigger distributors. In place of paying millions to buy up a film's distribution rights, a small company may pay a maximum of $100,000 or, in some cases, as little as nothing, guaranteeing only that it will spend a certain amount on prints and advertising to promote the film.

First Run Features, a longtime survivor that has been in existence since 1979, has released such films as *Gal Young 'Un* (1979), *Northern Lights* (1979), *The Life and Times of Rosie the Riveter* (1980), *Born in Flames* (1983), *Enormous Changes at the Last Minute* (1985), *Sherman's March* (1986), *Sleepwalk* (1987), *The Big Dis* (1990), *Strangers in Good Company* (1992), *The Watermelon Woman* (1996), and *The Quarry* (1998). Seymour Wishman and Marc Mauceri, who run the company, complain they find "little they like that competitors with deeper pockets don't beat them to" (Glucksman, "Pushing Film" 23).

Steve Fagan, the sales manager for Arrow, whose releases include *Combination Platter* (1993), *My Life's in Turnaround* (1994), *Ponette* (1996), *Restless* (1998), *Jump* (1999), and *30 Days* (2000), speaking of the high prices being paid for purchasing a film's rights at Sundance, comments, "We can't compete against that. We don't have Walt Disney's money" (Horn F11). And Jonathon

Dana, the president of Triton, which went out of business in 1994 after releasing such films as *Hearts of Darkness* (1991), *Mindwalk* (1991), *In the Soup* (1992), *Toto le Héros* (1992), and *A Brief History of Time* (1992), argues that the "whole system's being co-opted by the studios," likening that to "General Foods doing gourmet coffees" (Glucksman, "State of Things" 24). The reason for the undermining of smaller companies, Dana explains, is that independent distribution requires "more intense capitalization than ever," referring to the money involved to purchase and successfully promote independent films, the necessary steps before they can earn a profit at the box office.

As James Schamus of Good Machine points out, the significant cost in the current market is not what it takes to make a film but what it takes to market it to American, European, and other theatrical audiences (Pincus, "Manifest Destiny" 107–8). The advent of digital video and other technologies has opened up the possibility of making films more cheaply, but marketing and promotion is moving in the inverse direction, growing ever more costly.

On the surface, the recent example of *The Blair Witch Project* seems to contradict this axiom. It was hailed as rewriting "the record book on indie success" (H. Jacobson D2) for its extensive and ingenious Internet marketing begun by filmmakers Daniel Myrick and Eduardo Sánchez, and then taken over and elaborated on when Artisan picked up the film. In principle, Internet promotion provides wide access at no cost, "the great equalizer for independent filmmakers," as Sánchez describes it (qtd. in Geffner 22). But *The Blair Witch Project's* release was accompanied by saturation television and newspaper advertising, and its strong "buzz" was capitalized on through costly wide release. Two weeks after its opening it was playing on 1,100 screens and at its widest went to 2,538 screens (IMDb; Box Office Guru). While the Internet does provide a new outlet for promotion, one with the potential for inexpensive, huge success, it does not appear (yet) to replace other costly aspects in the business of getting films to audiences. However, Internet marketing does appear to significantly augment the amount a film can earn at the box office.

That the specific distributor and the company's distribution strategy, in turn, are pivotal to a film's ultimate success or failure can be seen in the response of filmmakers to the exhibition histories of their films. Writing in *Box of Moonlight & Notes from Overboard,* Tom DiCillo described his experience with his crowd-pleasing film *Living in Oblivion* (1995). He had concerns about the length of time the film was in release at all, and noted that when it made some of the "Year's Ten Best" lists in December 1995 (for instance, Janet Maslin's in the *New York Times*), it wasn't possible for new viewers to go see it because it was no longer playing anywhere. DiCillo reported that he queried the heads of his distribution company—Sony Pictures Classics, although he does not name it in the book—on their plans for garnering Academy Award nominations. "He said he was living up to his commitment to seek a nomination for Best Original Screenplay by sending video cassettes to members of the Academy. I asked if he was taking out ads in the trade papers, offering the film for the Academy's consideration. He said they planned to do that sometime in January, not wanting to 'overdo it' right away because the Academy members were too smart for that stuff and it tended to backfire" (DiCillo 36).

On the same day of that conversation, DiCillo picked up an issue of *Variety* and found "a full-color advertisement for *The Brothers McMullen*, offering the film 'for your consideration' as Best Picture, Best Screenplay, Best Director, Best Actor and Best Actress." He continued:

> My distributor took *Living in Oblivion*, admittedly a small film and made it smaller....The distributor of *The Brothers McMullen*, took a very small film, and made it enormous. The amount they spent is irrelevant. No matter what it cost it worked. People saw the film. People are still seeing the film. (36)

Living in Oblivion was considered a success because it earned $1.14 million and received positive critical response. DiCillo's point, however, is that in comparison *The Brothers McMullen* earned over $10 million and was seen by a much wider audience.

The countervailing argument, of course, is that the amount spent *is* relevant. Trimark Pictures paid $3 million for rights to DiCillo's next film, *Box of Moonlight* (1997). Because Trimark is primarily a generic film distributor (*Warlock, Leprechaun*, both 1991) it has the resources to pay higher prices for a film's rights. *Box of Moonlight* went on to earn only $782,000 in domestic box office, despite John Turturro's presence in the cast and positive reviews (Horn F11).

DiCillo expressed disappointment over *Living in Oblivion*'s exhibition history although Sony Classics is a mini-major. Even if a fiscally conservative company, he was not dealing with one of the smaller distributors who lack even Sony Classics's resources. In contrast, Fox Searchlight, distributor of *The Brothers McMullen* and mandated to seek prestige and notice, is bankrolled by $150 million in capitalization from Twentieth Century Fox (Glucksman, "State of Things" 24).[21]

Another instance of a disgruntled filmmaker, this one dealing with one of the smaller, micro distributors, is longtime independent Jon Jost, whose film *All the Vermeers in New York* won the Los Angeles Film Critics Award for best experimental film in 1992. In the summer 1993 issue of *Filmmaker*, Marcus Hu, one of the founders and copartners of Strand Releasing (*Claire of the Moon;*

Crush; Totally Fu**ed Up; Clean, Shaven; Nenette and Boni; Latin Boys Go to Hell; Love Is the Devil; Signs and Wonders as well as *All the Vermeers in New York*), wrote an article titled "Guerrilla Releasing: A Guide to No-Budget Film Distribution." In it, Hu contends:

> An independent filmmaker with rejection letters from Miramax, Goldwyn and Fine Line needn't begin sharpening a straight-edged razor. Despite the dominance of the larger specialty distributors, many of the new, smaller 'cottage industry' distributors are achieving success by carefully placing and niche-marketing their films....Such recent films as *All the Vermeers in New York, Henry [Portrait of a Serial Killer], Vincent, Man Bites Dog, The Vanishing, Together Alone,* and *Mala Noche* are prime examples of independent films which might never have had a theatrical life if it weren't for the newer micro distributors. (34)

Although Strand is considered one of the survivors among the micro distributors, receiving a retrospective showing of twenty-five of its films at the Museum of Modern Art in the summer of 1999 on the occasion of its tenth anniversary, filmmaker Jost did not share Hu's optimism. In a detailed and angry letter in the spring 1992 issue of *Off Hollywood Report*, Jost outlined his efforts and frustrations in seeking a distributor for *All the Vermeers in New York*. "Finally, throwing in the towel on securing any of the legit so-called art film distributors in the States, we signed up with tiny Strand Releasing out of Venice, California" (9). The "legit" art film distributors that Jost specifically itemizes as either ignoring the film or turning him down are Orion Classics, Goldwyn, Fine Line, Island, Avenue, and Aries. The outcome of having had to go with Strand is, according to Jost, that the film opened "in barebones fashion," only at specific theaters in select cities. Hu cited the expenses spent for prints and advertising on *All the Vermeers in New York* as totaling only $23,350 and the film's national theatrical gross as $157,046 (39).

There is little question that for a film to earn $10 million, as *The Brothers McMullen* did, or even $1 million, requires detailed attention to marketing, often in the form of costly advertising, or in some other, time-demanding, hands-on approach. And as Jost attempted to point out, which films win such money, time, and attention, and for what reasons, are serious issues in what constitutes contemporary independent film. Further, while smaller companies cannot afford to stake the same amount in prints and advertising commitments as the mini-majors do, neither can they hold out hope for a breakout success grossing $45.9 million (*The Full Monty*), or $57.5 million (*Life Is Beautiful*), or even $11.5 million (*Boys Don't* Cry) without such expenditures.

Still, some micro distributors manage to survive and new companies continue to enter the field. A recent example is Shooting Gallery, which began as production facilities, then moved into producing. In a unique deal with exhibitor Loews Cineplex, Shooting Gallery Films released six films in early 2000 for a limited run of twelve weeks, two weeks per film, in nineteen major cities. It then booked each of the films in other venues as interest arose, generated by the initial release. The initial slate of films was *Judy Berlin, Orphans, Such a Long Journey, Croupier, Southpaw,* and *Adrenalin Drive*. The standout success from this group was *Croupier,* which went on to earn $4.7 million, while *Judy Berlin* earned a respectable $467,000. In the fall of 2000, Shooting Gallery, again in partnership with Loews, released another series of six films on the same basis of a limited run in select cities, and continued the practice in 2001. The company described its mandate as small, complex films that have found critical success, and its program consists of a high proportion of international films.[22] Unfortunately Shooting Gallery went out of business in June, 2001 due to a failed Internet venture. But this does not undermine the example it set for independent film distribution. For instance, Miramax has begun a film series with Landmark Theaters patterned after Shooting Gallery's arrangement with Loews.

Shooting Gallery's example illustrates that, despite the industry's received wisdom that says only a certain few films can find success while the majority of independent films are considered to be "unmarketable" (Geffner, "Cars" 18), the few that do receive distribution are not somehow destined or inevitable. They are not the only films that could find an audience and earn a profit and, indeed, their success could be attributed as much to distributors' beliefs in their marketability as to any "inherent" quality in the films. For example, Mark Urman, copresident of Lions Gate, describes many of the films he has viewed at Sundance as "just too fragile for this world," admitting that they might "unjustly fall by the wayside" (qtd. in Anderson 29). This returns to the critical issue of what attributes or hooks are considered marketable, which in turn determines what films are being picked up for distribution, to be sold to which audiences, and on the basis of what criteria, a subject I examine in more detail in chapter 3.

Independent Distribution's "Permanent Government"

A fundamental truism about independent film distribution is that companies are continually going out of business, appearing and disappearing overnight.[23] In a 1996 interview, John Sayles commented, "We've made ten movies, and I'd say seven of the companies that distributed our movies are no longer in business"

(Ratner 35). Sayles's estimate is close—six of the distributors of those ten films are now out of business.[24]

While it is accurate that independent distribution is a risky business and companies have gone out of business with startling regularity, this truism masks an equally significant factor: the individuals who form and run these companies resurface time and again. There may be rapid turnover in the corporate make-up of independent distribution, but the individual players have remained strikingly consistent.

One of the expectations of an industry with high corporate turnover is that it provokes a constant flow of new blood and fresh ideas (or at least power bases) into the institutional arena. In fact, while companies have formed, folded, and formed anew, the founders, owners, presidents, and partners have moved from one corporate entity to the next, encountering and reencountering one another en route. Producer's rep John Pierson refers to this handful of people (himself included) as independent film's "permanent government" (40).

As was pointed out earlier, Tom Bernard and Michael Barker began their distribution careers at United Artists Classics, moved jointly to form Orion Classics, and subsequently established Sony Pictures Classics, which they still run. Tom Rothman, originally an entertainment attorney, was longtime head of distribution and production at Goldwyn before leaving to become the first president of Fox Searchlight and, following that, moving to Twentieth Century Fox proper.

Amir Malin was a cofounder (in 1982) and CEO of Cinecom, which released such films as *Come Back to the 5 & Dime Jimmy Dean, Jimmy Dean* (1982), *Eating Raoul* (1982), *El Norte* (1983), *A Room with a View* (1986), *Matewan* (1987), and *The Handmaid's Tale* (1990), before going out of business in the early 1990s. Subsequently, Malin became one of the partners in October Films before, most recently, serving as cofounder and president of Artisan Entertainment (*Pi; The 24 Hour Woman, The Blair Witch Project*).

Ira Deutchman was head of marketing at United Artists Classics in the early 1980s till he left to oversee distribution at Amir Malin's newly formed Cinecom. After Cinecom's demise, Deutchman served as producer's representative for *Metropolitan* (1990) which was sold to and released by New Line. In the wake of that deal, Deutchman became head of Fine Line Features, New Line's newly established art-house division. He is now CEO of Studio Next, a digital video production company.

Another notable figure is Ben Barenholtz, who owned the Elgin Theater in New York and originated the concept of the midnight movie there in 1970 with *El Topo*, following that up with *Pink Flamingos* in 1973. When the theater went out of business in 1978, Barenholtz, moving from exhibition to distribution, founded Libra Films, which released *Eraserhead* in 1977 and *The Return of the Secaucus Seven* in 1980. In 1985, a new company Barenholtz was partnered in, Circle Releasing, distributed *Blood Simple* and went on to produce several later Coen Brothers films, including *Raising Arizona* (1987), *Miller's Crossing* (1990), and *Barton Fink* (1991).

Jeff Lipsky began working in distribution in 1974 as a sales rep for John Cassavetes's self-distributed *A Woman under the Influence*—he describes Cassavetes as having "invented the wheel" of independent distribution (43). Later in the 1970s he served as head of distribution at New Yorker Films and then as head of distribution at Goldwyn from 1983 to 1986, years that saw the release of films such as *Stranger than Paradise* and *Desert Hearts*. From there he went to Skouras Pictures (*Belizaire the Cajun*, 1986; *Waiting for the Moon*, 1987; *Living on Tokyo Time*, 1987; *The Wizard of Loneliness*, 1988; *Apartment Zero*, 1989), and subsequently, in 1991, cofounded and ran October Films with Bingham Ray, before leaving in 1995. More recently, Lipsky resurfaced as head of distribution and marketing at Samuel Goldwyn Films, a newly formed entity established by Samuel Goldwyn Jr. in the wake of the Samuel Goldwyn Company's sale and demise. To date, Samuel Goldwyn Films has released only a handful of films (*The Hanging Garden*, 1997; *Desert Blue*, 1998; *Better than Sex*, 2000; *Faithless*, 2001) and Lipsky has since departed to Lot 47 (*Venus Beauty Institute*, 1999; *The War Zone*, 1999; *The Price of Milk*, 2000; *L.I.E.*, 2001; *Chunhyang*, 2001).

Bingham Ray first managed the Carnegie Hall and Bleeker Street cinemas, then worked at New Yorker Films at the same time as Lipsky. Ray moved to Goldwyn during Lipsky's era as head of distribution (1983–86) and took over Lipsky's position when the latter left in 1986. He did subsequent stints at Alive Pictures (*The Moderns*) in 1988 and Avenue Pictures (*Drugstore Cowboy*) in 1989 before co-founding October Films in 1991, which he left when it was bought out and transformed into USA Films.

While not an exhaustive list, the above examples provide some indication of how independent film's intimate "permanent government" has recurringly resurfaced. These individuals provide a consistency, indeed an institutional dominance, in what is otherwise perceived as an industry of flux and upheaval. Their prevalence may well prevent the flow of new ideas and alternate strategies; insider experiences and viewpoints do not change dramatically, although the corporate entities within which they function do. This creates a certain sedimentation embedded within the field and makes upheaval and change a much more limited reality than industry mythology suggests.

Studio Ownership

Another of the most significant aspects of the current composition of independent distribution is ownership of the mini-majors by Hollywood studios. The primary reason independent distributors agree to studio buyouts is to increase their capitalization. In the current marketplace, purchasing, marketing, and sometimes producing films requires tremendous financial resources.[25] For instance, through the deal with Universal, October got "a huge injection of cash to bid more aggressively on films, and to start producing them as well" (Rea, "On Movies" May 11, 1997: F7). Sufficient capitalization has always been an issue in the film industry. One of the reasons for the disappearance of the B studios in the 1950s, for example, was thin capitalization: "their physical assets, cash on hand, and borrowing power were never very great" (McCarthy and Flynn 24, 36), leaving them no financial cushion to fall back on during stretches of poor business.

From a studio perspective, the prestige in owning a specialty film division is the dominant incentive:

> Disney executives sat helplessly as rival Sony Corp., with its Columbia and TriStar studios, bought ads in the trade newspapers trumpeting its "30 Academy Award nominations." More than a third of these came from art-house pictures such as *Howard's End* and *Indochine*, that were released by its tiny 'Sony Classics' unit....Disney seeks this prestige. (King and Turner B13)

But while obtaining award-winning stature may be a greater motivator than commerce in studio acquisition of independent companies (or more accurately, the motivator of prestige as it affects commerce), Hollywood began to take notice of independent film only after several striking box-office successes. The moment of change is widely regarded as the 1989 release of *sex, lies & videotape* which earned $24.7 million at the box office, grabbed Hollywood's attention, and brought large numbers of studio representatives to subsequent years of the Sundance Film Festival, where the film had premiered, in search of other independent "discoveries." And Disney's purchase of Miramax occurred in the wake of Miramax's 1992 success *The Crying Game* ($65 million) and Sony Classics's *Howard's End* ($25 million).

Harvey Weinstein insists Disney's only influence on Miramax is financial, "Disney is our big daddy or rich uncle. You can say Disney or you can say Chase Manhattan." Disney publicly concurs. CEO Michael Eisner states, "They're completely autonomous. And they should be. They keep their costs down and their ideas up" (Weinstein and Eisner qtd. in Corliss, "Independents'

Day" 64). And Joe Roth, the studio's chair after Jeffrey Katzenberg's 1994 departure, seconded the sentiment calling it, "'euphemistic and silly' to say the Weinsteins report to him" (J. Williams D2). But early predictions of tension between "strong-willed Disney executives and the Weinstein brothers, who have a reputation as sometimes abrasive entrepreneurs" (King and Turner B13) seem to be borne out.

Disney-imposed restrictions at the time of the buyout stipulated that Miramax stay within its budget guidelines and not release films rated NC-17 (Corliss, "Independents' Day" 64; J. Williams D2). In the past Miramax had distributed such X-rated films (since replaced by the NC-17 rating) as *Tie Me Up, Tie Me Down* (1990) and *The Cook, the Thief, His Wife and Her Lover* (1990). Miramax released them into theaters without their ratings, as they were permitted to do, after using the ratings controversy surrounding the films to generate publicity. However Disney, as a member of the Motion Picture Association of America (MPAA), which oversees the ratings process, is not permitted to distribute unrated films. Further, Disney, as a self-styled family-oriented company maintains a corporate policy against NC-17 films. Such films also make marketing harder as many newspapers will not run NC-17 ads, a number of theaters do not show them, and certain video stores (for example, Blockbuster) will not carry them.

To date, Miramax and Disney have fought over the release of such NC-17 films as *You So Crazy* with Martin Lawrence (1994), which was sold by Miramax, at Disney's insistence, to Goldwyn; *Priest* (1995), a story woven around the character of a homosexual priest; *Kids* (1995), for which Disney demanded the repayment of its $3.5 million purchasing price and which was subsequently distributed by Shining Excalibur, a subsidiary established by Miramax to distribute the film in disassociation from Disney; and *Dogma* which Disney officials found "inappropriate" (Hernandez), particularly in light of protests by Catholic groups. As a result, Miramax resold the film to Lions Gate, which distributed it instead.

Miramax is not the only independent to be affected by such restrictions. The distribution of Fine Line's *Crash* (David Cronenberg, 1997) was delayed for six months by Ted Turner who considered the film "really weird" (Rea, "Driving" F4). Steven Schiff, screenwriter of *Lolita* (1998), states that studio ownership kept independents like Miramax and October from distributing the film which, as a result, premiered in the United States on the cable movie channel, Showtime, rather than in theaters (Schiff xxv–xxvi). In contrast, non–studio-affiliated Artisan was free to release Wayne Wang's *The Center of the World* (2001) without restriction, despite its having been given an NC-17 rating. Artisan distributed the film uncut and unrated.

But perhaps the most highly publicized case to date of studio intervention is that of Todd Solondz's *Happiness*, a black comedy-drama with a subplot involving pedophilia. Having financed the film and being set to release it, October was forced to back out of the deal by Universal. Opposition to *Happiness* is reported to have reached the highest echelons of Universal and perhaps even its parent company, Seagram.[26] Except for October's initial announcement on July 1, 1998, that it was going to back out of releasing the film because *Happiness* did not "fit Seagram/Universal's image"(Pener 41), October and Universal officials refused to comment on the situation. It is worth noting, however, that the film was not renounced as unfit for October. On the contrary, the controversy-generating, Cannes Critics' Prize-winning *Happiness* is precisely the kind of film October would desire for its slate. The hope of October executives that retention of 49% financial ownership in the company would ensure October its desired autonomy apparently did not materialize. *Happiness* was distributed, instead, by its producers, Good Machine (Holden 41; Schamus, "Pursuit of Happiness" 34+).[27] Such studio interference threatens independent film's foundational distinction from Hollywood, risking the independent arena's dissolution through the enforced absorption of Hollywood standards. In other words, such studio mandates force independent film to imitate the more powerful industry, instead of allowing it to emphasize its distinction by stressing differences between the two. This tends to eliminate or mitigate a cutting edge quality, one of the characteristic attributes of independent film.

For example, in the instance of *Happiness*, objections from Universal seemed to focus not on the fact that a pedophiliac character, Bill Maplewood (Dylan Baker), is portrayed, but rather on *how* he is characterized. "It's not that the character's crimes are shown (they aren't) but that Solondz refuses to demonize him. He finds it far more interesting to try to understand what makes him tick. This is what is truly shocking to some" (Ansen, "Comedy" 87).[28] In other words, if Bill Maplewood's character had been demonized, clearly and simplistically, his presence in the film would not be a problem. Yet the film does not validate him in any sense for what he has done—he, we, the represented community, and his entire family know that what he has done is wrong. However, he is presented as an average, familiar social type. As *USA Today* explains, the problem is "the character is presented as a normal, upstanding member of the community" (Puig, "Happiness" D1). This is only to suggest that pedophiliacs do not take shape in some immediately recognizable monstrous guise but are, indeed, concealed within the community at large.

Further, the character of the pedophiliac is hardly significantly worse than the rapist, the stalker, or the wife batterer in the film. In fact, *Happiness* can be read as an initiation into the sordidness of male sexuality. After futile masturbatory efforts, when Billy (Rufus Read), the film's eleven-year-old protagonist, announces to his mother, aunts, and grandparents gathered around the dining table, "I came," his exuberant innocence seems shallow, illusive, and transitory as he steps into the world of adult male sexuality, governed by the disturbing cultural and psychological factors the film depicts. The criticism of the pedophiliac character in *Happiness* is that he is presented in a positive light; yet, he is actually a cornerstone in the film's distressing, cumulative portrait of male sexuality. Bill Maplewood is, however, a complex character, just as the angry, verbally violent stalker, Allen (Philip Seymour Hoffman), is depicted as an insecure, social outcast. Such complexity of character may well be equated in corporate studio minds, among others, as a positive portrayal—as if being represented in detail, being made visible, or being shown to exist as a human being is in itself dangerous.

Although issues of censorship may be one of the most overt indications of the consequence of studio ownership on independent companies, a bigger influence could well prove to be the effect of Hollywood expectations on the independent industry. Most notably, there is an increasing pressure toward "mini-blockbusters"—an effort to duplicate such hits as *Pulp Fiction, Shine, Shakespeare in Love,* and *The Blair Witch Project*. The model here is Miramax, an exception in the independent industry in many ways, but now the standard-bearer in terms of studio expectations. As a result, Fox Searchlight manages to replicate a Miramax-type success with *The Full Monty*, and the minimum performance expectation for a successful film rises from $1 or $2 million to $10 million (*The Brothers McMullen*). As Mark Urman, the president of Lions Gate, put it, "Hollywood and the indies are now cohabiting, and they've given one another their virus. Indies are dreaming about money, and studios are dreaming about prestige" (Puig, "Sundance's Shifting Beat" D1). While independent film has always been codependent on Hollywood in the sense of requiring a dominant industry to create and measure itself against, the independent industry is increasingly institutionally and financially dependent as well.

The studios may value their specialty divisions primarily for their prestige rather than for their financial earnings, but the more widespread the audience for a film, the more widespread the accompanying prestige factor. Only with breakout films such as *Life Is Beautiful, The Full Monty,* or *Crouching Tiger, Hidden Dragon* does one achieve both the box-office benefits of a hit and the widespread attention that wins high-profile, mainstream accolades like Academy Award nominations, the kind of prestige the studios seek (instead of, say, the recognition a film receives at the Telluride, Berlin, or New York film festivals which is of far less interest to the studios).[29] The desire for prestige and profit causes studio executives to pressure their independent subsidiaries for highly visible, widely aesthetically appealing, and financially successful results, pushing independent films toward a more mainstream, more audience-populated "center." Simultaneously, it usually takes the expensive promotional efforts of newspaper and TV advertising and the wide release strategy that ensures a film's accessibility before breakout success can occur. These requirements cause independent distributors to be that much more dependent on studio capitalization in order to achieve their mandate. Tom Bernard of Sony Classics describes the current climate as, "an insatiable appetite to become bigger businesses, to carve out a bigger slice of the market" (qtd. in Rea, "Madness" F12), a situation fueled by studio pressure. The effect of these developments is to further intensify the distances and the differences in product between the mini-majors and the micro distributors.

In this chapter I have outlined some of the institutional and historical dimensions of the independent film industry. In the next chapter I examine certain of the representational discourses that have most affected independent cinema: avant-garde and alternative filmmaking practices. Then in chapter 3 I explore how institutional and representational discourses coexist, that is, the interaction of "the means of production and the vision thing."

CHAPTER TWO

Film as Artifact: Alternative Influences on Independent Cinema

In the winter 1998 issue of *Filmmaker: The Magazine of Independent Film*, Jim Moran and Holly Willis respond to criticisms that the magazine, like the surrounding independent industry, promotes only a narrow and commercialized strand of independent film (Moran 22). Indeed, the cover of the issue promises updates on recent work by Vincent Gallo, Robert Duvall, Alan Rudolph, Paul Schrader, and Penelope Spheeris. Except for first-time feature director Gallo (*Buffalo 66*), all the others have long-standing name recognition and substantial ties to Hollywood.

Acknowledging the criticism that, overall, the independent industry is creating and promoting increasingly generic films, "dominated by the success stories of college-age men," Moran and Willis leave open the question, "Given the relative failure of much radical film practice to achieve the political goals it strove for as well as the fundamental shifts in how we question naive notions of 'vision' and the role of the artist in contemporary society…what would we choose to celebrate in the independent cinema of the '90s?" (22).

Although heavily influenced by mainstream filmmaking practices—the dominance of features, plot-driven modes of storytelling, a central focus on character development, casting of stars, Hollywood-type promotional and marketing techniques, and so on—independent cinema also embodies the legacies and effects of a number of alternative filmmaking practices.

Often used interchangeably, terms such as *avant-garde, experimental*, and *alternative* are modes of cultural production meant to signify in opposition to *dominant* forms of cultural activity. While the histories and traditions of avant-garde, experimental, and alternative work are complex, and the meanings of each term far from fixed, for the purposes of this study, *avant-garde* refers to two specifically historical modernist movements, as delineated below. *Experimental* denotes current work, in contrast to avant-garde's association with a historical moment. And *alternative* is the encompassing term, applied here to include avant-garde, experimental, and all forms of oppositional artistic practice in their various manifestations.

Concepts of dominant cultural production, from which alternative work seeks to signify differently, are far too complex and intricate to be given justice in this study. But, in general, in film theory dominant practices often have been encompassed by the notion of "classic realist cinema," also known as "classical Hollywood cinema" for its intimate association with that industry. However, classic realist cinema has come most commonly to designate a specific era in Hollywood film practice stretching from the late 1920s to the 1960s, comprising a specific narrative and aesthetic style based on principles of temporal and spatial continuity and cause-and-effect coherency, which in turn, forge a particular ideological configuration of "the world" or "reality."

Equally problematic are ideas of what constitutes *realism*. In much current theory, all textual schools or artistic styles are material, social, and ideological representations of some portion of the world. Particular forms of realism are presented in such a way that they conceal their representative qualities so that they can more convincingly stand in for "the truth" or reality. Graeme Turner, citing Colin McCabe, describes dominant realism as "a set of representational codes that offers the viewer a comfortable position from which to see even bitter political struggles as natural and inevitable." Hollywood realism "precodes the reality it represents within commonsense understandings of the world" (Turner 100). In this analysis, then, realism is a function of hegemony.

To function effectively as natural, invisible, or commonsensical views of reality, styles of realism must constantly revise and update their representational codes and signifying landscapes in order to keep up with changing historical circumstances. In "On Realism in Art," for instance, Roman Jakobson describes realism as a highly relational notion based on prevailing social and cultural formations (38–46).[1]

To avoid the historical, geographical, and stylistic specificities associated with classic realist cinema and, equally, to capture the resonances of various forms of realism as shifting and evolving discursive formations, this study refers to the range of dominant cinematic practices, most commonly but not solely emanating from Hollywood, as *normative realism*. Normativity designates the changing natural, invisible, and commonsensical qualities that attach to prevailing modes of representing the world at any specific time. The term *normative realism*, which is itself relational, permits an evolving sense of what independent film and alternative cinema are working in opposition to at any historical or contemporary moment.

Although influenced by various forms of alternative cinema, independent film stands in distinction to its avant-garde precursors and experimental contemporaries. This is indicated, for instance, by the manner in which the journal *Filmmaker* speaks of *Orlando*'s (1993) place in the cinematic landscape compared to Sally Potter's former filmic output. "With her new feature, *Orlando*, Sally Potter has risen from the respectable obscurity of avant-garde fame into the upper echelons of the independent film world" (Zeig 24). Alternative practices have the tendency to involve sharp breaks with dominant cinema, while independent film is inclined to formulate itself as a hybrid with allegiances to both alternative and normative realist cinematic practices.

Although it is not always apparent where independent film departs from alternative practices—for example, *Orlando*, *Daughters of the Dust* (1992) and *Poison* (1991) all exhibit strong avant-garde or experimental traits—certain distinctions are evident. Avant-garde and experimental film- and videomaking are much more likely to encompass short works, while independent film is dominated by features. Respective institutional and economic structures account for this. The outlet for alternative work is largely film and video festivals, so the lack of income-generating exhibition, as well as the characteristics of experimental aesthetic forms, tends to make shorts a more viable option. In contrast, independent films are intended for theatrical release, videocassette, and television, with festival play viewed largely as an intermediary step in acquiring any of the former. In turn, the greater potential market for independent film over alternative work, as well as the greater costs associated with making features over shorts, affects the nature of the artifact produced.

Although alternative modes of working are distinguished from independent ones as in the case of Sally Potter, in Moran and Willis's open question about which aspects of independent film should be celebrated and preserved as independent film evolves, the subtextual suggestion points to alternative representational practices. In a view expressed repeatedly in various independent forums, the concern put forth is that independent film continues to be a hybrid, incorporating alternative strategies without veering too closely to mainstream or dominant models. Indeed, it is through its borrowing or absorption of alternative traditions that independent film receives much of its respectability and credibility.

This chapter unravels some of the representational discourses from which independent film is composed. Just as the last chapter looked at how economic and institutional factors affect the specific composition of independent cinema, this chapter details how certain representational discourses are made operational and what they "stand for" or come to mean. Representational discourses involve the historical aesthetic traditions within which cultural producers perform, as well as the formal and narrative languages their specific works put into play. The representational discourses analyzed here, then, are certain alternative filmmaking practices; the issue is how these discourses work toward shaping the specificity of the artifacts produced.

Representational discourses do not exist apart from their material form, variously called a work of art, an aesthetic object, a cultural product, a text, or an artifact. Each of these terms for the tangible formation in which representational discourses take shape bears its own resonances. A *cultural product*, for instance, carries the spin of the economic and social forces which shape it—an object intended to be produced, distributed, and consumed.

An *artifact*, like a text, conveys meanings beyond its tangible form, just as a more traditional archaeological artifact, such as an ancient shard of pottery, imparts a sense of or is open to interpretations about the past. An artifact is trace evidence of other qualities: concepts, beliefs, meanings, times, and places. More than a material entity, an artifact is a means of expression and communication that absorbs aesthetic, social, and ideological concepts and practices. In other words, it absorbs histories.

Another contemporary term for the material form resulting from representational discourses and practices, *text*, has a certain dichotomization attached to its usage, for instance, signified and signifier often lapsing into a form/content parallelism, or debates about whether meaning is located in the text or brought to it by audiences. In order to avoid these dichotomizations, this chapter uses the concept of artifact to signify the material object created through representational, institutional, interpretive, and cultural/historical discourses. *Artifact* seems to allow for a sense of greater openness to the conception of multiple, layered, interactionally crisscrossing discourses, which together, in complicated relations, formulate the entity that is the end product of aesthetic activity.

In the following sections I offer an examination of six alternative practices: the aesthetic avant-garde, the political avant-garde, art cinema, personal film, identity cinema, and postmodern film. Each section briefly outlines how and why that practice functions as a representational discourse—that is, "the institutional processes, ideological preferences, vested interests and aesthetic judgements" (Wolff, *Aesthetics* 107) behind each approach—and indicates how all these alternative practices have influenced, and continue to affect, current configurations of independent film.

It should be noted that this chapter deals with the history of alternative cinema, not as it affects alternative or experimental film and video in the 1980s and 1990s but in terms of how it has affected independent film, as defined in this study, during these decades. Independent film and various forms of contemporary experimental film and video share alternative precursors and traditions. However, experimental film and video have used these differently than independent film, and their lines of development have followed different trajectories.

The Aesthetic Avant-Garde

The avant-garde has been described as having two principal tendencies: one aesthetic, the other political. The first concerns itself with "an exploration of the means of representation, and with a revolutionising of the language of cinema" (Harvey, *Independent Cinema* 11), while the second is "radically opposed to the dominant or mainstream cinema at the level of its content or subject matter" (10).

Terry Eagleton, clearly signaling his own position, calls these two avenues of the avant-garde "negative" and "positive." The first, the aesthetic, is

> shock, outrage, mustaches on the Mona Lisa. It is difficult to base a politics on it, and difficult to do it twice. This current of the avant garde takes up the negative aesthetic of modernism and destroys meaning. What is it, in the end, that the bourgeoisie cannot take? Meaninglessness.

The second, the political, is the

> positive moment of the avant garde, that of Brecht rather than Dada. This proclaims: there is indeed a way of resisting incorporation by the ruling order, whatever the fashionable jeremiads about how they will simply hang Picassos on the walls of their banks....The positive avant garde understands that the question of integration stands or falls with the destiny of a mass political movement. (Eagleton 371–72)

The avant-garde is generally considered to originate with the modernist art movements of the twentieth century, in particular with cubism. In some analyses, cubism marks a juncture in which the aesthetic and political avant-gardes are unified, but this unity soon dissolves in the work of subsequent modernist schools. Peter Wollen, for instance, describes cubism as "a critical semiotic shift, a changed concept and practice of sign and signification, which we can now see to have been the opening-up of a space, a disjunction between signifier and signified and a change of emphasis from the problem of signified and reference, the classic problem of realism, to that of signifier and signified within the sign itself." The "classic problem of realism" is to show something "transparent" about an accessible social reality (the signified) through verisimilitude (the signifier). Cubism, in fracturing its subjects into numerous planes, addresses the problematic of being able to access social reality at all by means of representation or language (the signifier). Wollen continues, "When we look at the development of painting after the Cubist breakthrough, however, we see a constant trend towards an apparently even more radical development: the suppression of the signified altogether, an art of pure signifiers detached from meaning as much as from reference" (Wollen, "Two Avant-Gardes" 95). In Wollen's analysis, the problem of realism is the accurate depiction of social reality through representation; the problem of Cubism is our limited capacity to use representation in order to get at or perceive social reality at all. But the problem of abstract and other modernisms is solely that of a now free-floating, nonanchored image or sound without representative power of anything beyond itself.

Sylvia Harvey takes up a similar point: "Modernist aesthetics induces a reflection upon, a consideration of, the means of representation, and for lovers of art it generates aesthetic pleasure out of a series of 'frame-shifts' (the procedures whereby the art work playfully refers to itself and its own processes of production)" (*May '68* 82). And it is this last that becomes identified as film's aesthetic avant-garde, beginning with surrealist filmmakers in the 1920s such as Salvador Dali and Luis Buñuel (*Un Chien andalou*, 1928), Fernand Léger and Dudley Murphy (*Ballet mécanique*, 1923–24), and the work of Man Ray. It revives and achieves perhaps its "purest" form with the structuralist/materialist filmmakers in Britain in the 1950s and 1960s (the co-op movement), and with the structuralist/minimalist filmmakers of North America in the 1950s, 1960s, and 1970s (Michael Snow, Hollis Frampton, Andy Warhol).

Wollen's, Harvey's, and Eagleton's descriptions of the aesthetic avant-garde are fairly condemnatory (to varying degrees) because the absence of representation linked to referent undermines the ability to establish a clear-cut political perspective or position from which to operate. A free-floating signifier makes it almost impossible to comment on the world, or on conceptions of the world, in any shape or form. "The danger of this position is that in concentrating on the 'reality of reflection,' on the means of representation alone, the sense of a productive tension between means of representation and that social reality which the means of representation strive to analyse and account for is lost" (Harvey, *May '68* 66). The issue, then, is to what degree such a modernist project is able to refer to a larger social and ideological environment or the extent to which it can refer only to its own processes of production. The perceived value of aesthetically driven film hinges on the outcome of this assessment. For some, like Harvey, the "struggle within representation" can be considered political if it is understood to refer only to a limited "politics of form" (*Independent Cinema* 12). For others, however, as Harvey notes, summarizing the 1969 argument of the film journal *Cinéthique*, the cinema produces its own specific ideology, the "impression of reality," an ideological construct that creates film's power of illusion, the sense that it is replicating "reality." The function of materialist cinema, which refuses the codes of realism, is to disrupt the "illusion-generating mechanisms" and so the "illusory reflections of reality" of dominant cinema (*May '68* 38).

Lisa Cartwright and Nina Fonoroff argue this position in an essay from 1983, with an updated 1992 introduction, "Narrative Is *Narrative*: So What Is New?" Approaching the issue from a feminist perspective, they defend the political value of a nonnarrative, experimental film practice.

> Much feminist study has been devoted to the development of a discourse that addresses the ways in which narrative functions to reproduce the patriarchal order. Processes of identification (with camera point of view, with characters depicted within the film), temporal continuity, the "kind" of viewing required for narrative films—these are just a few aspects of narrative cinema that are called into question. (128)

Cartwright and Fonoroff strive to sever the belief, propagated, they argue, by the dominance of narrative film, that there is a necessary or natural link between image and referent, between pleasure and narrative, and between narrative and film (128). Calling for an experimental, nonnarrative aesthetic instead, they believe that "structuralist, visionary and personal film" (124) is capable of breaking down the ideological association of (narrative) film with (the illusion of) reality.[2] An embedded narrative tradition, based on a diegesis, psychologically developed characters, spatial and temporal continuity, and so on, will not serve to disconnect the elision between film as a time-based, photographic medium and its ability to replicate reality. Greater attention to the language of cinema and its means of (re)production, however, is more appropriate to rendering its representative and ideological qualities apparent.

As a result, certain currents of underground cinema completely abandoned working narratively. But in the 1970s, another tendency developed—the deconstructive film or new narrative. These films signaled a return to narrativity but only to deconstruct it by constructing nontraditional experimental narratives that specifically undermined or called into question aspects of classical or normative narrative. Deconstructive films achieved their results by adopting and adapting many of the stylistic techniques of the more abstract North American avant-garde (visionary, lyrical, and structuralist film). Influential deconstructive films include Yvonne Rainer's *Lives of Performers* (1972) and *Film about a Woman Who...*(1974), Joyce Weiland's *The Far Shore* (1976), Chantal Akerman's *Jeanne Dielman, 23 Quai du Commerce, 1080 Bruxelles* (1976), Raoul Ruiz's *The Hypothesis of the Stolen Painting* (1978), and Sally Potter's *Thriller*

(1979). The result was a blending of the sensibilities and concerns of the aesthetic and political avant-gardes.

The Political Avant-Garde

Sylvia Harvey outlines four points in her critique of the aesthetic avant-garde. First, it dwells on a concept of art about art, using that notion "to replace an interest in the *relationship* between specific means of aesthetic representation and a social reality." Second, it pursues an essentialist position in which form becomes content, wherein for example, "a particular style is essentially progressive or essentially reactionary." Third, its meaning is embedded solely in the text and not in the political, economic, social, or cultural institutions and discourses surrounding it, that is, "within a system of consumption, distribution or exchange specific to a particular society and a particular historical moment." And fourth, it emphasizes "high" art and disregards issues of audience accessibility by offering "a puritanical defence of the 'work'...and an accompanying underestimation of the importance of pleasure and entertainment" (*May '68* 69–70).

Concern about the inability to reference an explicit social reality is taken up by Marxist theorists such as literary scholar Peter Bürger, who argues that the term *avant-garde* should be applied solely to artists (for instance, dadaists and futurists) who undermine the institution of art, while *modernist* should be reserved for all those who pursue only formal aesthetic issues (*Theory* 47–54). Jochen Schulte-Sasse, in his introduction to Bürger's *Theory of the Avant-Garde* explains that Bürger is concerned mainly with the differences between formalist modernism and the political avant-garde. "Modernism may be understandable as an attack on traditional writing techniques, but the avant-garde can only be understood as an attack meant to alter the institutionalized commerce with art" (xv). Although modernist artists may alter aesthetic technique, they continue to work within established paradigms of art; it is avant-garde artists who demolish the paradigms themselves by attacking the institutions and discourses of art, as in the case of Marcel Duchamp, who with his readymades questioned what constitutes art or what defines the artist as individual creator.

According to Bürger, "When the avant-gardists demand that art become practical once again, they do not mean that the contents of works of art should be socially significant. The demand is not raised at the level of the contents of individual works. Rather, it directs itself to the way art functions in society, a process that does as much to determine the effect that works have as does the particular content" ("Negation" 239). The way art functions in society has to do with issues such as what constitutes the art object, with notions of originality and authenticity, as well as with exhibition practices and structures of economic transactions. As such, the avant-garde artist maintains concern with the social environment while formal modernism, in this argument, ceases to be connected with social practice.

Within film theory, similar arguments have been taken up by, most notably, Peter Wollen. Wollen understands the problem as originating in false divisions within the conception of *cinematic codes*. In the modernist attempt to define a "pure" cinema, all noncinematic codes are refused. Noncinematic codes are attributes that do not appear exclusively in film, such as music, verbal language (theater), and narrative (literature and theater) ("Ontology" 197). Next, the material itself is focused on rather than the semiotic or representational aspects of the solely cinematic codes: film emulsion, light, projection, and so on. "The modernist current, in complete contrast, has sought to expel the noncinematic codes, leaving the residue called 'film'....Film is now directed not towards the 'nature' of the pro-filmic event, but towards the 'nature' of its own material substrate" (206). In other words, elements of mise-en-scène, what occurs in front of the camera, are no longer of comparable concern to what occurs in the camera, on the film base, and in the process of projection.

From Wollen's perspective, the crisis of modernism that occurs across all the arts in the 1960s, which he associates with the social changes of May 1968, presents, rather than a decline, an opportunity for the political avant-garde, "creating a host of new areas of commitment and inquiry: women's art, political art, popular imagery, environment, performance" ("Mexico" 114). Although the social changes are widely seen as threatening the demise of the avant-garde, "in fact it represents a revival," from a sociopolitical perspective. Like Bürger, Wollen terms the aesthetic avenue *modernism*, believing only the political strand fully *avant-garde*, sometimes also referring to it as the "historical avant-garde" (113–14).

Wollen's avant-garde lineage descends from Sergei Eisenstein and Bertolt Brecht to the counter-cinema of Jean-Luc Godard.

> In Godard's post-1968 films we glimpse something of an alternative route between contentism and formalism, a recognition that it is possible to work within the space opened up by the disjunction and dislocation of signifier and signified....Godard takes the idea of formal conflict and struggle and translates it into a concept of conflict, not between the content of images [like Eisenstein], but between different codes and between signifier and signifier....He wants not simply to represent an alternative "world" or alternative "world-view," but to investigate the whole process of signification out of which a world-view or an ideology is constructed. ("Two Avant-Gardes" 99–100)

From the perspective of the political avant-garde and its attempts to repoliticize modernism, the solution became the establishment of two avant-gardes, one aesthetic and the other political, creating a division into two distinct, even oppositional, projects. But having once defined two dichotomous avant-garde practices, politically concerned theorists had then to work to reunify them. From *Cahiers du Cinéma*, for instance: "We would stress that only action on both fronts, 'signified' and 'signifier,' has any hope of operating against the prevailing ideology. Economic/political and formal action have to be indissolubly wedded" (qtd. in Harvey, *May '68* 67). While exploration of the means of representation alone is insufficient, a work is fully avant-garde in this argument only if it employs both aesthetic and political innovation—at the levels of signifier *and* signified.

To indicate how deep the bifurcation is that needs to be overcome, we have the commentary of Terry Eagleton, the symmetrically inverted form of *Cahiers du Cinéma's* position. Speaking of Theodor Adorno, Eagleton writes: "It is possible to read his work as a retreat from the nightmare of history into the aesthetic....these two facets of thought [the aesthetic and the political] are closely intertwined, as a defeatist politics generates a compensatorily rich aesthetics" (359–60). Here the two are seen as mutually exclusive operations, the aesthetic rising to fullness only as the political diminishes.

In its urging of an either/or oppositional conception of alternative artistic practice, the bifurcation of the two avant-gardes raises other issues. First, members of the aesthetic avant-garde rightly could argue that much of the work is not as apolitical as the political avant-garde claims. After all, alternative artistic practices are not a series of permanently fixed behaviors and activities (drip painting, scratch films) nor are they constituted by only certain, recurring aesthetic works or styles (such as abstraction). Alternative film is defined, and continually redefined, in contradistinction to changing forms of normative cinematic practices and changing conceptions of the hegemonic. As such, aesthetic experimentation gains cultural currency and political value from the contexts in which it is located, that is, it has an effect whether shock or critique. Second, is such a clean or extreme distinction between the political and aesthetic avant-gardes possible when many specific films do not fall neatly into one or the other category but are more likely to encompass elements of both avant-gardes? Instead of an inclusive-exclusive opposition, a looser, more floating notion of alternative artistic activity would be better in keeping with the multiple, vast potential of the permutations that artifacts can and do take. Further, the paradigm establishes a "canon" of two avant-gardes. Why not more or others instead? For instance, the possibility of a narrative avant-garde is conceivable, perhaps descending through the work of filmmakers such as R. W. Fassbinder.

The concept of an alternative narrative practice might open up a space for a filmmaker such as John Sayles, who is determinedly independent in his method of working but who is difficult to classify as such because his work is not formally experimental. Yet, he has made a career-long commitment to exploring narratives of multiple, and shifting, perspectives (e.g., *The Return of the Secaucus Seven*, 1980; *Matewan*, 1987; *City of Hope*, 1991; *Lone Star*, 1996; *Men with Guns*, 1998).

The issue of narrative raises another troubling concern for the conception of a political avant-garde. While the aesthetic avant-garde is largely antinarrative, the position Cartwright and Fonoroff argue, the political avant-garde requires a referent in order to comment on the sociocultural landscape. Wollen's strategy for dealing with the problem of referent is to argue in favor of a narrative cinema, but one that is simultaneously antirealist, or at any rate, anticlassic; in other words, it must still remain experimental at the level of signifiers. He points out that the Soviet directors of the 1920s, although aesthetically alternative, were also preoccupied "with the problem of realism" and remained "within the bounds" of narrative cinema ("Two Avant-Gardes" 98). Similarly, Brecht did not "abandon the whole realm of reference outside the play," nor did he equate "anti-illusionism with suppression of any signified" ("Ontology" 201). Instead, his definition of anti-illusionism is meant to put forth a different "version of realism" ("Semiotic Counter-Strategies" 212), while always retaining a representation of something, a referentiality to dynamics beyond the bounds of the play or stage.

However, although he argues for the inclusion of narrative codes in avant-garde work, Wollen is also adamant in maintaining that "new content" requires new means of expression, that experimentation at the level of signifiers is also necessary. Alternative approaches at the level of content or politics are not sufficient in and of themselves ("Two Avant-Gardes" 98–99). The difficulty here, as Wollen acknowledges, is that the disruption of "norms of diegesis, subversion and deconstruction of codes" unless "thought through carefully or stopped arbitrarily at some safe point, leads inevitably straight into the positions of the other avant-garde" (101). That is, because there is no clearcut boundary between on the one hand the deconstruction of narrative and aesthetic codes necessary to the political avant-garde and on the other hand the unlimited exploration of the means of representation by the aesthetic avant-garde, the former can easily, perhaps inevitably, overlap with and merge into the activities of the latter.

Similarly and conversely, Wollen, equating words and stories with signifieds, recognizes that the appropriation of narrative by the political avant-garde has no "naturally visible" or logical demarcation from the more conventional narrative approaches of Hollywood or art cinema (102–3). With the reintroduction of narrative practices to avant-garde work, where then is the turning point between representation as illusion and politically productive, alternative "versions of realism"?

The Avant-Gardes and Independent Film

The issues Wollen raises concerning the dissolution of boundaries between work that critiques prevailing perspectives or offers alternative realisms or does both and work that replicates existing beliefs, values, and practices are critical questions for independent film. Many would argue that independent cinema is a watered-down version—some would say, compromised version—of the avant-gardes.

Concerns around marketability translate into limited aesthetic experimentation. Narratives based on psychologically developed characters are largely adhered to. But at the same time, a high status and a considerable degree of respect are given to formal experimentation in independent film. Aesthetic experimentation remains one of the principal, weightiest determinants of whether a film is considered independent.

A political perspective, if present at all in independent film, primarily takes the shape of identity politics. No longer is there the general coherence that was provided by left-wing politics for many of those in alternative film movements who worked in clear opposition to Hollywood's humanist tendencies. Indeed, independent film can be said to have lost both the aesthetic and the political clarity of previous avant-garde film movements.

Political positions or aspirations are hard to sort out; that is, it is difficult to extract a suggested political agenda from individual independent films or from independent film overall. Aesthetic departures, when they exist, are not necessarily coherent. It may not be clear to what ends they are being used within individual films, nor is there the coherency of repeated use over a group of films (with rare exceptions such as Dogme '95). In contrast, many earlier alternative film movements displayed a general coherency or interconnectedness attributable to communication among films and filmmakers who were developing theories in common and exploring similar concerns.

The absence of coherent aesthetic or political lines cutting across independent film reflects the demise of the same certainties in the larger social, postmodern landscape. The loss of formulated political and aesthetic agendas is a result of the shattering and splintering of the social body into a multiplicity of perspectives with diverse political concerns and, consequently, diverse, fragmented ways of working. A local view—or many local views—is identifiable. Individual films become "specific bits" that are recognizable. But there is a lack of certainty at the level of a global view, of an overall, coherent entity.

Although losing the avant-gardes' strength of coherency, independent film's aesthetic and political splintering is not necessarily a limitation to the degree that it reflects a changed set of social circumstances. In principle, independent film's fragmentation into a diversity of styles and concerns is better able to represent, to make sense of and explore, a fragmented social landscape of competing values, meanings, and lives. In practice, as we shall see, this is not always the case. Nonetheless, the many localized views of independent film hold the potential of more appropriately representing contemporary culture.

That the social landscape of the 1980s and 1990s marks a changed set of circumstances for filmmakers is clear. Filmmakers such as Michelle Citron (*Daughter Rite*, 1978), whose work originates within the discourses and aesthetics of the feminist avant-garde, have argued that such a differing context requires an accompanying shift in modes of production.

> The context has changed since the 1970s, so those of us working within it must also change. On the simplest level, we have lost our audiences as previously defined (for example, the large network of broad-based women's centres has greatly diminished)....Only two distributors of women's films remain in the United States: New Day Films (which has expanded to include labour movement and health films) and Women Make Movies. Other films are occasionally picked up by broader-based independent distributors, this in itself is a kind of mainstreaming....In some cases, this can have the advantage of broadening a film's audience; in others, it can bury them out of sight.(54–55)

It is the development of these broader-based independent distributors in the 1980s and 1990s, and the cultural climate that made them possible, that has helped create independent film. Citron argues that audiences are no longer "out there" in the same way they were in the 1970s, an era and political climate that fostered the production of experimental film. The move to more popular, narrative forms is a question of filmmakers following their audiences (55), a corollary argument to the charge that the political avant-garde failed to reach the very audiences to and for which it claimed to speak.

Lisa Cartwright and Nina Fonoroff elaborate a position contrary to Citron's that is quite prescient, if disapproving, about the forthcoming development of independent film.

> The issue of economic survival is of paramount importance, and the move to narrative reflects this concern. As funds for filmmaking become scarce, it becomes increasingly difficult and risky to depend on granting systems for support. Much current work is

done with a view toward marketing potential: larger budgets, "better" production values, and more topical themes all signal the move toward making films that are commercially viable products—lifted from obscurity to greater "public acceptance," from small film-screening spaces to art-movie houses—and, by design or default, a shift from a concern for the possibilities of new uses of film to a concern for marketability and accessibility. (130)

For Cartwright and Fonoroff, as for others associated with the political avant-garde, it is impossible to have a cinema of politics without an accompanying practice of nonconventional signifiers. This is so because dominant forms only replicate dominant ideologies, reexerting existing power relations and defeating whatever else might be achieved at the level of content. To claim a political cinema without the necessary aesthetic subversions is to advocate a (or the same old) cinema of illusory reality.

But Citron is not unaware of the losses and compromises her position entails, nor of the criticisms it engenders.

We wanted to make films that challenged the status quo. Whether documentary or avant-garde, these were films for a purpose, for political organizing and consciousness-raising in the broadest sense. This film practice challenged ideas about film language, the relationship between viewer and film, and the function of cinema in our society....What we sacrificed in a particular compromise was not in that context as important as what we gained. A film-maker might make a seventeen-minute film that would be seen by no more than 10,000 women. But the film had a clarity of political and aesthetic vision completely in the film-maker's control....But the shifting historical moment creates both a willingness and a need to make different compromises. Today, a woman can make a low-budget feature which gets theatrically distributed and seen by hundreds of thousands of women. But in this case, the demands of the market as "safeguarded" by the producer circumscribe risks at the level of either form or content. (58–59)

Despite the attendant sacrifices, filmmakers like Citron, and unlike Cartwright and Fonoroff, see adaptation to the cultural moment as the most effective strategy.

Yet we now can return to Moran and Willis's question, What would we choose to celebrate in the independent cinema of the 1990s? Although the shift to independent film may be the most effective strategy in light of the changed social circumstances, for many the most valuable aspects of contemporary independent cinema are precisely those associated with the avant-gardes: the explicitly experimental qualities of *Surname Viet Given Name Nam*, *Privilege*, *The Bloody Child*; the breaks in temporal and spatial continuity of *Orlando* or Derek Jarman's *The Last of England* and *Wittgenstein*; the quirkiness of *The Hours and the Times*, *Stranger than Paradise*, *Women on the Verge of a Nervous*

Breakdown, Sweetie; the non-linear, poetic quality of *Daughters of the Dust, Young Soul Rebels, Man Facing Southeast*; the low-budget, grainy, home-movie texture of *The Living End, Clerks, Straight out of Brooklyn, Go Fish*; the in-your-face political factor of *Born in Flames, Ladybird, Ladybird,* and *My Name Is Joe*; the level of discomfort elicited by the treatment of subjects in *Poison, Happiness, The Nasty Girl,* and *The Celebration.* Independent film simultaneously departs from avant-garde practice *and* maintains a complex, indebted relationship towards it.

Art Cinema

Contemporary art cinema developed in the late 1950s and solidified in the 1960s with the work of a number of European directors. Seminal directors and films include Ingmar Bergman with *The Seventh Seal* (1956) and *Wild Strawberries* (1957), Federico Fellini and *La Dolce Vita* (1959), Alain Resnais with *Hiroshima Mon Amour* (1959), and Michelangelo Antonioni's *L'Avventura* (1960). Andrew Tudor argues that these films are united and distinguished from mainstream classic realist cinema because they are "deliberately and obviously intellectual" and because each bears "extremely visible individual stylistic characteristics" (9). By "obviously intellectual" Tudor seems to mean that art cinema appeals to "reason," to films that require careful decoding in order to make sense of events, characters, symbolic objects, and so on, and additionally, that demand a weighing through of the dramatic problems depicted to reach such interpretive determinations as "right" or "wrong." This is in contrast to the more immediately visceral audience positioning associated with being swept along by Hollywood-generated filmic events, in which what characters and objects stand for is usually transparent, as is the location of moral authority, for instance, where "good" and "bad" reside (this, of course, is not to simplify the ideological impact of Hollywood films).

Similarly, Annette Kuhn, citing David Bordwell, speaks of "being challenged or 'made to think' by art cinema" (Kuhn 216). She explains that in Bordwell's argument this objective is achieved by an approach that is different from mainstream film's treatment of narrative structure, an approach in which concepts of causality are less strictly adhered to. So, for instance, the connection between character motivation and plot events may not be clearly defined. Indeed, the narrative may be driven more by a character's subjective states than by plot at all (216–17). This conforms to the conventional understanding that European films are character-oriented in contrast to Hollywood's material, which is considered plot-driven. Even so, character motivation may not be linear or causally explained and can, in turn, be further disrupted by the voice and concerns of the filmmaker, for instance by various means of filmic self-reflexivity or by a series of events or objects of focus that can only be united, that is, made sense of, as the vision or preoccupation of the artist/filmmaker.

Further, art cinema has traditionally had its own distinct distribution and exhibition system in which, for instance, films tend to be shown in art houses, at film societies, and so on, many of which forums became the exhibition base for recent independent cinema. Separate venues, too, lead to "different expectations" on the part of the audience (Kuhn 216), primed to take in more intellectually or aesthetically challenging fare.

Such a concept of a different level of movie-going experience has its origins in more general cultural distinctions between "high" and "low" art. Len Masterman suggests that the turning point for film, enabling such a distinction to be made, came with the 1964 book by Stuart Hall and Paddy Whannel, *The Popular Arts*, in which the argument was put forth that "discrimination ought to be exercised, not *against* mass-media products, but *between* them" (Masterman 299). Instead of finding all media texts artistically suspect and deficient, as had been the widespread critical practice until that point, some texts could be elevated to the level of "art" or high culture, such as the work of directors Bergman, Buñuel, Vittorio de Sica, Antonioni, Jean Renoir, and Akira Kurosawa.

In addition, in *The Popular Arts* Hall and Whannel forge a third category of film existing between the banality of Hollywood-inspired mass art and the exemplary creations of high art. Their intermediate grouping is *popular art*, a hybrid of popular culture and high art:

> [A] number of popular cinema-forms—such as the western, the thriller and the musical—have developed; and although most examples of these genres are banal, routine treatments of well-worn formulae (as is common in mass art), a number of gifted popular artists have been able to fulfill themselves while working within this popular tradition and using the familiar conventions. (77)

Among such popular filmmakers, Hall and Whannel include, for example, Howard Hawks. While not quite reaching the upper echelons of high art, his "creative intention" (80) enables him to exceed the superficiality of mass art.

Subsequently, under the influence of the French New Wave, a group of filmmakers and critics who came to the fore in the 1960s, the work of such Hollywood genre directors as Hawks and Alfred Hitchcock was upheld as high art, along with the output of the French New Wave itself. In addition, the increased textual presence of filmmakers (through self-referentiality, highly individualized stylistic characteristics, and so on) led members of the French

New Wave to take up and further develop the concept of *auteurism*, an idea closely linked to the whole notion of art cinema. *Auteur* signifies the director as identifiable, individual author, the creative genius or visionary artist recognizably responsible for the work of art. They "stamp the marks of their personal genius on films bearing their names" (Kuhn 216). Auteurism is based on the notion that a body of films expresses a director's personal vision of life, and that this vision can be traced from film to film through repeating or progressive stylistic and thematic patterns. Art cinema largely has been built around the concept of auteurism.

However, the auteur theory has been much criticized. One argument is that because cinema is a collaborative and highly institutionalized endeavor, a single individual cannot be considered responsible for a film's total effects. Auteurism has also been included in a more widespread criticism, as have the avant-gardes, of the very notion of an elitist "high" art. Still, concepts of auteurism continue to influence both mainstream and independent film, Martin Scorsese and Quentin Tarantino serving as current prominent examples. The influence of auteurism is indicated as well by the common journalistic and academic practice of identifying films by director and year.

No clear boundaries exist between art cinema and avant-garde work nor between art cinema and mainstream narrative film. For instance, the French New Wave encompasses both of the former, with members like Godard and Resnais more likely to be considered avant-garde, while Claude Chabrol and François Truffaut would tend to be thought of as makers of art films. While the exact boundary between art and avant-garde films is unclear, art cinema has been criticized by proponents of the avant-gardes for being insufficiently alternative and adhering too closely to Hollywood narrative norms.

In the 1980s and 1990s, independent film absorbed art cinema as part of its terrain or discursive formation. Indeed, independent film has been much influenced by art cinema and the concept of the auteur. In independent film, more adamantly than in Hollywood, it is very often the writer/director who envisions and oversees the project, functioning very much as auteur. Despite its theoretical limitations, auteurism also continues to be influential as a method of critical classification for independent film. For instance, in *Cinema of Outsiders*, Emanuel Levy describes "individual filmmakers and directorial careers as the central organizing principles" (x) for his material.

It is useful to outline some of the independent films that fall within various categories of art cinema. All the following categories conform to some tendency of art cinema, and all are considered to fall under independent film in the United States. It should be stressed that the lists are exemplary, not exhaustive, and many, if not most, of the examples cited could fit into more than one of the five categories.

1. Films that are formally, narratively, or formally and narratively experimental but that have some recognizable classic realist attribute(s), separating them from avant-garde work

Films which apply here are: Derek Jarman's *The Last of England* (1988), *Edward II* (1992), and *Wittgenstein* (1993); Patricia Rozema's *I've Heard the Mermaids Singing* (1987); the works of Peter Greenaway (*Drowning by Numbers*, 1987; *The Cook, the Thief, His Wife & Her Lover*, 1990; *Prospero's Books*, 1991; *The Pillow Book*, 1996; and *8 ½ Women*, 2000); *Wings of Desire* (1987); Jim Jarmusch's films, for example, *Stranger than Paradise* (1985), *Down by Law* (1986), and *Mystery Train* (1989); Raoul Ruiz's *On Top of the Whale* (1987), *Three Lives and Only One Death* (1996), and *Genealogies of a Crime* (1997); *The Icicle Thief* (1989); *Poison* (1991); *Zentropa* (1991); *River of Grass* (1995); *Female Perversions* (1996); *Schizopolis* (1996); *Run Lola Run* (1999); Harmony Korine's *Gummo* (1997) and *julien donkey-boy* (1999); and *Memento* (2001).

2. Films that are dense or intellectual

The distinctions between this category and the first are very murky and many of the films listed could be placed in either category. However, the categories are maintained separately because it is arguably possible for a film to be formally or narratively experimental without being intellectually provocative or for a densely challenging film to contain no formal or narrative experimental gestures. For example, *Run Lola Run* with its one story told three times in which in each version slight shifts in timing significantly alter events and outcomes, can be considered formally experimental. However, it is not intellectually dense or complex. In contrast, *Happiness,* if not intellectually dense is certainly intellectually provocative, but it is not formally experimental.

Films in this category might include the following: Eric Rohmer's ongoing work, for instance *Boyfriends and Girlfriends* (1987), *A Tale of Summer* (1997), and *Autumn Tale* (1999); Akira Kurosawa's *Rhapsody in August* (1991) and *Ran* (1994); Krzysztof Kieslowski's *The Colors Trilogy: Blue, White,* and *Red* (1993, 1994, and 1994, respectively); Hal Hartley's output, including *The Unbelievable Truth* (1990), *Trust* (1991), *Simple Men* (1992), *Amateur* (1995), and *Henry Fool* (1998); *Metropolitan* (1990) and *Barcelona* (1994) by Whit Stillman; *Waiting for the Moon* (1987); *My Dinner with Andre* (1981); *Distant Voices, Still Lives* (1989); and Atom Egoyan's work, including *The Adjuster* (1992), *Exotica* (1994), *The Sweet Hereafter* (1997), and *Felicia's Journey* (1999).

3. Historical or epic dramas

During a talk at the Toronto Film Festival in the early 1990s, Hanif Kureishi, the screenwriter of *My Beautiful Laundrette* (1986), *Sammy and Rosie Get Laid* (1987), and *My Son the Fanatic* (1998), referred to these kinds of films as "museum pieces," in a statement that makes their link to high art overt. Films here would include Merchant/Ivory productions such as *A Room with a View* (1985), *Howard's End* (1992), and *The Golden Bowl* (2001); *Camille Claudel* (1988); *Henry V* (1989); *Enchanted April* (1992); *The Madness of King George* (1994); *Queen Margot* (1994); *The English Patient* (1996); *Mrs. Brown* (1997); *Oscar and Lucinda* (1997); *The Red Violin* (1998); *Topsy-Turvy* (1999); and *Up at the Villa* (2000).

4. Films that are based on a work of art in a different medium or whose subject matter is art

For instance, adaptations of novels and other literary works: *Madame Bovary* (1991); *Much Ado about Nothing* (1993); *Smooth Talk* (1986) from the short story by Joyce Carol Oates; *Persuasion* (1995) from Jane Austen's novel; *Angels and Insects* (1996) based on the work by A. S. Byatt; Henry James's *The Wings of the Dove* (1997); and Virginia Woolf's *Mrs. Dalloway* (1998).

There are also stories based on the lives of an artist or group of artists: *Prick up Your Ears* (1987) about playwright Joe Orton; *My Left Foot* (1989) centered on the painter Christy Brown; *Tom and Viv* (1994) depicting poet T. S. Eliot's marriage and its relation to his work; *The Moderns* (1988) detailing artistic Paris in the 1920s; *Mrs. Parker and the Vicious Circle* (1994) focusing on writer Dorothy Parker and the members of the Algonquin Round Table; *Basquiat* (1996), about the painter Jean-Michel Basquiat, and *Before Night Falls* (2001), a look at Cuban poet, novelist, and activist Reinaldo Arenas, both directed by prominent painter Julian Schnabel; *I Shot Andy Warhol* (1996); *Wilde* (1997) about the life of playwright Oscar Wilde; *Shakespeare in Love* (1998), a fictional interpretation of Shakespeare's working process and times; *Love Is the Devil* (1998) on British painter Francis Bacon; *Pollock* (2000), which portrays abstract expressionist Jackson Pollock and his marriage to fellow painter Lee Krasner.

While the majority of films in this category focus on classical art, as in the instance of classical pianist David Helfgott and his mental illness in *Shine* (1996), there is some range in this area as, for example, in the arguably thematically comparable film, *Sid and Nancy* (1986) about punk rocker Sid Vicious, or in *Gods & Monsters* (1998) focusing on the later years of James Whale, the director of *Frankenstein* (1931) and *Bride of Frankenstein* (1935).

5. International cinema

International cinema very easily could comprise its own category—or multiple categories—given the breadth, variety, and complexity of world cinema. However, it appears here as a subcategory of art cinema because of the place it traditionally has been accorded in U.S. culture. Further, this category deals only with foreign-language rather than English-language films although, obviously, films shown in the United States from Australia, New Zealand, Canada, Great Britain, and Ireland are international cinema also, and they form a significant part of independent film. (English-language foreign films have been enveloped within other categories in this study). It should also be noted that although there is some representation from various regions of the world, for instance Asia and Central and South America, international cinema has been dominated by and continues to be overshadowed by European cinema.

Foreign films served as the foundation for art cinema in the 1950s, 1960s, and 1970s. Indeed, international cinema, with a few American exceptions such as John Cassavetes, was equivalent to art cinema during those decades. Heavily influencing subsequent independent film, art cinema was represented by filmmakers/auteurs such as Bergman, Buñuel, Fellini, Antonioni, and Kurosawa. Historical film movements of particular importance for later independent film included Italian neorealism (Roberto Rossellini, Vittorio de Sica, Luchino Visconti) with its location shooting, focus on the details of everyday life, and noncausally connected scenes. Also very significant was the French New Wave (Godard, Truffaut, Chabrol, Resnais, and Agnès Varda), which combined elements such as lost heroes and existential anxiety, narratives based on chance events and digressions, references to other films and aspects of popular culture, and stylized or "artificial" dialogue. The single most influential filmmaker for independents is Godard, who is considered to have reinvented narrative structure by fragmenting it and revised aesthetic style by making it raw and apparent through such techniques as hand-held camera and jump cuts. Godard's inclusion of pop culture elements is also frequently cited as having had a significant impact.

In the context of the United States, international cinema has been pivotal in defining what an art cinema, and subsequently, what an independent cinema might be. This can be seen in filmmakers such as Jim Jarmusch, who explicitly includes international characters in his narratives—a Hungarian cousin (Eszter Balint) in *Stranger than Paradise*, a jailed Italian tourist (Roberto Benigni) in *Down by Law*, and Japanese visitors (Masotoshi Nagase, Youki Kudoh) in *Mystery Train*—to Hal Hartley whose films comprise causal disconnects, a slowed rhythm, and only partially explained motivations for characters. International influence is evident in quite different ways in the work of Quentin

Tarantino whose production company, A Band Apart, is named after the Godard film, *Bande à part* (1964). Or it can be seen in Steven Soderbergh's *sex, lies & videotape* (1989), in which introspective characters are driven to explore their sexuality and relationships, a frequent theme in certain strands of European cinema. And it can be found in Gus Van Sant's *My Own Private Idaho* (1991) where, in startling, disjointed juxtaposition, the story of two gay male hustlers is mixed with Shakespearean dialogue and further fragmented by intertitles.

Most international films distributed in the United States tend to be character-oriented, thought-provoking dramas that continue in the tradition of the art film, although there are generic exceptions, such as action-adventure or gangster and crime films from Asia (*Fallen Angels*, 1995, Hong Kong; *Shanghai Triad*, 1995, China; *Adrenaline Drive*, 2000, Japan; *Non-Stop*, 2000, Japan). And while international cinema carries high cultural status, subtitled foreign-language films have never achieved widespread popularity or box-office clout, although again with occasional exceptions (*Life Is Beautiful; Crouching Tiger, Hidden Dragon*). Due to limited revenues, which also limit larger competitors' interest, as well as to their considerable cultural capital value, international cinema became a significant component of independent film in the 1980s and 1990s. In fact, foreign cinema was formative in the foundation of independent film with such cases as *The Last Metro* (1980), *Erendira* (1981), *Diva* (1981), *Entre Nous* (1983), *The Funeral* (1984), and *Ran* (1984). What we call independent film would be sadly depleted without the contribution of both foreign-language and English-language international cinema.

Table 1 presents examples of notable foreign-language independent films by country of origin.

Table 1

Title	Director	Year	Distributor
Argentina			
Man Facing Southeast	Eliseo Subiela	1987	Film Dallas
Belgium			
An Affair of Love	Frédéric Fonteyne	2000	Fine Line
Golden Eighties	Chantal Akerman	1986	World Artists
Ma Vie en Rose	Alain Berliner	1997	Sony Classics
Man Bites Dog	Remy Belvaux, André Bonzel and Benoit Peolvoorde	1992	Roxie
Night and Day	Chantal Akerman	1992	International Film Circuit

Table continued on next page

Table continued from previous page

Rosetta	Jean-Pierre Dardenne and Luc Dardenne	1999	USA Films
Spetters	Paul Verhoeven	1980	Goldwyn
Toute une Nuit	Chantal Akerman	1982	World Artists

Brazil

Bye Bye Brazil	Carlos Diegues	1980	Unifilms
Central Station	Walter Salles	1998	Sony Classics
Me You Them	Andrucha Waddington	2001	Sony Classics

China

Beijing Bicycle	Wang Xiaoshuai	2001	Sony Classics
East Palace, West Palace	Zhang Yuan	1997	Strand
The Emperor and the Assassin	Chen Kaige	1999	Sony Classics
Farewell My Concubine	Chen Kaige	1993	Miramax
Not One Less	Zhang Yimou	1999	Sony Classics
Raise the Red Lantern	Zhang Yimou	1991	Orion Classics
The Road Home	Zhang Yimou	1999	Sony Classics
Shanghai Triad	Zhang Yimou	1995	Sony Classics
The Story of Qui Ju	Zhang Yimou	1992	Sony Classics
Suzhou River	Lou Ye	2000	Strand
To Live	Zhang Yimou	1994	Goldwyn
Xiu Xiu: The Sent-Down Girl	Joan Chen	1998	Stratosphere
Yi Yi	Edward Yang	2001	WinStar

Cuba

Guantanamera	Tomás Gutiérrez Alea and Juan Carlos Tabio	1997	CFP
Strawberry and Chocolate	Tomás Gutiérrez Alea and Juan Carlos Tabio	1994	Miramax

Czech Republic

Kolya	Jan Sverák	1996	Miramax

Denmark

Breaking the Waves	Lars von Trier	1996	October
The Celebration	Thomas Vinterberg	1998	October
Dancer in the Dark	Lars von Trier	2000	Fine Line
The Idiots	Lars von Trier	1999	USA Films
Mifune	Soren Kragh-Jacobsen	1999	Sony Classics

Finland

Leningrad Cowboys	Aki Kaurismäki	1989	Orion Classics

Table continued on next page

Table continued from previous page

France

Amélie	Jean Pierre Jeunet	2001	Miramax
Beau Travail	Claire Denis	2000	New Yorker
Betty Blue	Jean-Jacques Beineix	1986	Alive
Chocolat	Claire Denis	1989	Orion Classics
Un Coeur en Hiver	Claude Sautet	1993	October
Criminal Lovers	François Ozon	2000	Strand
Delicatessen	Marc Caro and Jean-Pierre Jeunet	1991	Miramax
Diva	Jean-Jacques Beineix	1981	United Artists Classics
The Dreamlife of Angels	Erick Zonca	1998	Sony Classics
Edith and Marcel	Claude Lelouch	1983	Miramax
Entre Nous	Diane Kurys	1983	United Artists Classics
I Stand Alone	Gasper Noé	1998	Strand
Irma Vep	Olivier Assayas	1996	Zeitgeist
Jean de Florette	Claude Berri	1986	Orion Classics
Late August, Early September	Olivier Assayas	1999	Zeitgeist
The Last Metro	François Truffaut	1980	United Artists Classics
Manon of the Spring	Claude Berri	1986	Orion Classics
Nenette and Boni	Claire Denis	1997	Strand
Sans Soleil	Chris Marker	1982	New Yorker
Subway	Luc Besson	1985	Island
Water Drops on Burning Rocks	François Ozon	2000	Zeitgeist
When the Cat's Away	Cèdric Klapisch	1997	Sony Classics
Wild Reeds	André Téchiné	1994	Strand

Germany

Aimée and Jaguar	Max Färberböck	2000	Zeitgeist
Beyond Silence	Caroline Link	1996	Miramax
Brother of Sleep	Joseph Vilsmaier	1995	Sony Classics
Faraway, So Close!	Wim Wenders	1993	Sony Classics
Marianne and Juliane	Margarethe von Trotta	1981	New Yorker
The Nasty Girl	Michael Verhoeven	1990	Miramax
The Princess and the Warrior	Tom Tykwer	2001	Sony Classics
The Promise	Margarethe von Trotta	1994	Fine Line
Rosa Luxembourg	Margarethe von Trotta	1986	New Yorker
Winter Sleepers	Tom Tykwer	2000	WinStar

Hong Kong

Chungking Express	Wong Kar-wai	1995	Miramax/Rolling Thunder
Fallen Angels	Wong Kar-wai	1995	Kino

Table continued on next page

Table continued from previous page

In the Mood for Love	Wong Kar-wai	2000	USA Films
A Touch of Evil	Tony Au	1995	October

Hungary

My Twentieth Century	Ildiko Enyedi	1990	Aries
Sunshine	István Szabó	1999	Paramount Classics

India

Aparajito	Satyajit Ray	(1958)*	Sony Classics
The Big City	Satyajit Ray	(1963)*	Sony Classics
Charulata	Satyajit Ray	(1964)*	Sony Classics
Devi	Satyajit Ray	(1960)*	Sony Classics
Jalsaghar	Satyajit Ray	(1958)*	Sony Classics
Kama Sutra: A Tale of Love	Mira Nair	1997	Trimark
The Middleman	Satyajit Ray	(1975)*	Sony Classics
Roja	Mani Rathnam	1992	Phaedra
Pather Panchali	Satyajit Ray	(1955)*	Sony Classics
Salaam Bombay!	Mira Nair	1988	Cinecom
Two Daughters	Satyajit Ray	(1961)*	Sony Classics
The World of Apu	Satyajit Ray	(1959)*	Sony Classics

*re-released 1995

Iran

Children of Heaven	Majid Majidi	1999	Miramax
The Color of Paradise	Majid Majidi	2000	Sony Classics
The Day I Became a Woman	Marziyeh Meshkini	2001	Shooting Gallery
Under the Olive Trees	Abbas Kiarostami	1994	Miramax
The Wind Will Carry Us	Abbas Kiarostami	2000	New Yorker

Italy

Cinema Paradiso	Giuseppe Tornatore	1990	Miramax
Dear Diary	Nanni Moretti	1994	Fine Line
Life Is Beautiful	Roberto Benigni	1998	Miramax
Malèna	Giuseppe Tornatore	2000	Miramax
Mediterraneo	Gabriele Salvatores	1991	Miramax
Il Postino	Michael Radford	1995	Miramax

Japan

Adrenaline Drive	Shinabu Yaguchi	2000	Shooting Gallery
Eureka	Shinji Aoyama	2001	Shooting Gallery
The Funeral	Juzo Itami	1984	Republic

Table continued on next page

Film as Artifact

Table continued from previous page

Gohatto	Nagisa Oshima	1999	New Yorker
Kikujiro	Takeshi Kitano	1999	Sony Classics
Maborosi	Hirokazu Kore-eda	1996	Milestone
Non-Stop	Sabu	2000	Shooting Gallery
Ran	Akira Kurosawa	1984	Orion Classics
Remembering the Cosmos	Junichi Suzuki	1999	Phaedra
Rhapsody in August	Akira Kurosawa	1991	Orion Classics
Shall We Dance?	Masayuki Suo	1997	Miramax
Tampopo	Juzo Itami	1987	Republic
A Taxing Woman	Juzo Itami	1988	New Yorker

Mexico

Amores Perros	Alejandro González Iñárrito	2000	Lions Gate
Cronos	Guillermo Del Torro	1993	October
Danzón	Maria Novaro	1991	Sony Classics
Erendira	Ruy Guerra	1983	Miramax
Like Water for Chocolate	Alfonso Arau	1993	Miramax

Netherlands

Antonia's Line	Marleen Gorris	1996	First Look
Broken Mirrors	Marleen Gorris	1984	no distributor
A Question of Silence	Marleen Gorris	1981	Quartet/Sigma

Portugal

On the Run	Bruno de Almeida	1998	Phaedra
Voyage to the Beginning of the World	Manoel de Oliveira	1997	Strand
Women	Luis Galvão Teles	1997	WinStar

Russia

Burnt by the Sun	Nikita Mikhalkov	1994	Sony Classics
Freeze Die Come to Life	Vitali Kanevski	1990	International Film Exchange
Little Vera	Vasili Pichul	1988	Miramax
The Thief	Pavel Chukhraj	1998	Stratosphere

South Korea

Chunhyang	Im Kwon Taek	2001	Lot 47

Spain

All About My Mother	Pedro Almodóvar	1999	Sony Classics
The Flower of My Secret	Pedro Almodóvar	1996	Sony Classics

Table continued on next page

Table continued from previous page

Goya in Bordeaux	Carlos Saura	2000	Sony Classics
High Heels	Pedro Almodóvar	1991	Miramax
How to Be a Woman and Not Die in the Attempt	Ana Belén	1999	First Look
Lovers	Vicente Aranda	1991	Aries
Open Your Eyes	Alejandro Amenábar	1997	Artisan
Tango	Carlos Saura	1998	Sony Classics
Tie Me Up! Tie Me Down!	Pedro Almodóvar	1990	Miramax
Women on the Verge of a Nervous Breakdown	Pedro Almodóvar	1988	Orion Classics

Taiwan

Eat Drink Man Woman	Ang Lee	1994	Goldwyn
Pushing Hands	Ang Lee	1992	Good Machine
A Time to Live	Hou Hsiao-hsien	1985	International Film Circuit
Vive l'Amour	Tsai Ming-liang	1994	Strand

Ukraine

A Friend of the Deceased	Vyacheslav Krishtofovich	1998	Sony Classics

Vietnam

The Scent of Green Papaya	Tran Anh Hung	1993	First Look

COPRODUCTIONS

Title	Director	Year	Distributor	Countries
Babette's Feast	Gabriel Axel	1987	Orion Classics	France/Denmark
Brother	Takeshi Kitano	2001	Sony Classics	Japan/United States
Character	Mike van Diem	1997	Sony Classics	Belgium/Netherlands
Close to Eden	Nikita Mikhalkov	1992	Miramax	Russia/Mongolia
Crouching Tiger, Hidden Dragon	Ang Lee	2000	Sony Classics	Taiwan/China/United States
The Cup	Khyentse Norbu	1999	Fine Line	Bhutan/Nepal
The Double Life of Veronique	Krzysztof Kieslowski	1991	Miramax	France/Poland
East-West	Régis Warnier	1999	Sony Classics	France/Russia
Eternity and a Day	Theo Angelopoulos	1998	Phaedra	France/Greece/Italy
Europa, Europa	Agnieszka Holland	1991	Orion Classics	France/Germany
Journey of Hope	Xavier Koller	1990	Miramax	Switzerland/Turkey

Table continued on next page

Table continued from previous page

Pelle the Conqueror	Bille August	1989	Miramax	Denmark/Sweden
Red Firecracker, Green Firecracker	Ping He	1994	October	Hong Kong/China
Shadow Magic	Ann Hu	2000	Sony Classics	China/United States
Shower	Zhang Yuan	1999	Sony Classics	China/Germany
Toto le Héros	Jaco Van Dormael	1992	Triton	Belgium/France
The Vanishing	George Sluizer	1988	Tara	Netherlands/France
Vertical Ray of the Sun	Anh Hung Tran	2000	Sony Classics	Vietnam/France
West Beirut	Ziad Doueiri	1999	Cowboy	France/Lebanon

Personal Cinema

The heritage of personal film in the United States is often merged with structuralist, minimalist, and other movements as one linear tradition known as the American avant-garde or underground cinema. Lisa Cartwright and Nina Fonoroff unite these movements when they speak of "North American structural, visionary, and personal film" (124–25). Although there is certainly thematic and stylistic overlap among the various strands of underground cinema, personal film has had an important, and distinct, influence on independent film and so will be considered separately here.

Influenced by the avant-garde movements of the 1920s, personal film was made possible by the development and accessibility of 16mm equipment following World War II (Cook, "Point" 54). Sixteen millimeter technology changed the potential for individual filmmaking in several ways. Because it was cheaper than 35mm, it made equipment and film stock available to more people. Because it was lighter in weight, portable, and required fewer necessary accessories, it meant a crew could consist of one or two people who could film in a variety of locations, resulting in a means of production with enhanced autonomy and mobility. The result was "an emphasis on 'self-expression' which is seen as standing in opposition to the representation of the world-view of a dominant class in commercial cinema" (53–54).

Although both structuralist/anti-illusionist and personal/visionary filmmakers claim their legacies from avant-garde movements of the 1920s, personal film, like surrealism, is more heavily influenced by the medium of poetry and the dream world. A North American cinema of personal vision can trace its lineage from the psychological, dream, or "trance" films of Maya Deren (*Meshes of the Afternoon*, 1943), through the mythic psychodramas of Kenneth Anger (*Fireworks*, 1947; *Scorpio Rising*, 1963), and the lyric films of Stan Brakhage (*Anticipation of the Night*, 1958; *Window Water Baby Moving*, 1959) and Marie

Menken (*Notebook*, 1962). In contrast, the structuralists are affected, arguably, by the increasingly materialist-formalist concerns of painting. Both share, however, an antinarrative drive, working in opposition to classic forms of cinematic storytelling.

Personal film also shares strong affinities with an auteurist position in their common emphases on the creative capacity and visionary genius of the individual artist.

> For Brakhage, for instance, the film material represents a passive mass or body which is reorganized by the active agency of the artist into a meaningful system, a notion of the "natural" as passive and the artist as central figure in the world which goes back to the Renaissance....For Brakhage, the camera is an extension of the human eye, and in a hierarchy of discourses the discourse of the artist predominates, providing the overall coherence of the work. (Cook, "Point" 54–55)

Under the growing influence of formalist concerns in the arts, one tributary of avant-garde film of the 1940s and 1950s became, in the 1960s, the structuralist or anti-illusionist movements, while the impetus of personal and visionary production continued as a parallel presence. Personal film was considered by many to be a part of the aesthetic avant-garde, its use of "a private language to convey the personal fantasies and obsessions of a single individual" (53) making it unamenable, in principle, to political applications. Private symbols or personal moods often made a clear interpretation of content or referent difficult.

However, the 1960s and 1970s also saw another development, the rise of various political movements based on arguments of equity and civil rights. In the wake of these political movements, personal filmmaking provided a new logic. Within the women's movement, for instance, in the light of concepts of consciousness-raising and notions of the personal as political, one thread of women's filmmaking resulted in autobiographical pieces and in personal explorations of self and others. A few of the many examples that could be cited include, *Janie's Jane* (Geri Ashur, 1971), *Joyce at 34* (Joyce Chopra, 1972), *Daughter Rite* (Michelle Citron, 1978), and *Rape Stories* (Margie Strosser, 1989). In these "personal" films, "spontaneous self-expression...is replaced by a suggestion that a sense of self is constructed through social processes" (Thompson and Bordwell 687).

Such a fusion of personal experience and social process is evident in independent film in the detailed exploration of one's immediate neighborhood and the "bits" of daily life discovered there in *Chan Is Missing* (1982) or *Slacker* (1991). It can be found in the intimate circle of friends in *Go Fish* (1994), or the intimate relations of family and friends in *Bhaji on the Beach* (1994); neither friends nor family lose sight that theirs are intimacies also forged from commonalities of social circumstances. The fusion of personal and social can also take shape as part of the production process, as in *Mi Vida Loca* (1994), the story of teenage Latina gang members. It is cast with a mix of unknown actors as well as residents from the Echo Park area of Los Angeles where the film is set and which has a large Latino population. Similarly, the personal and the social are combined in the collaborative, improvisational techniques that created the script for *Girls Town* (1996), about four high-school teenagers who, as a group of close friends, deal with single motherhood, date rape, suicide, and everyday life. The four young women who play the leads (Lili Taylor, Brucklin Harris, Anna Grace, and Denise Hernandez) formulated their own characters and dialogue through a lengthy rehearsal process that allowed them to bring their own experiences to the larger story they were telling (Harris 33).³ In a similar manner, *Slam* (1998), centering on an imprisoned slam poet (Saul Williams), cast genuine poets (Williams, Sonja Sohn). The actors not only wrote their own poetry for the film, they also created their own characters and dialogue through a combination of extensive rehearsals and a spontaneous shooting style (Winters 28). It is in all these senses of personal—singular, artistic expression; intimate experience; and political voice—that the legacy of personal filmmaking has an ongoing impact and relevance for the independent enterprise.

Identity Cinema

To many of those who work and believe in alternative cinematic practices, identity cinema represents the most contentious grouping of films to be included under the heading of "alternative cinema." This is because there is no specific aesthetic discourse or formal set of practices that can be associated with identity cinema, which means it is frequently discounted as a genuinely alternative mode of production. While many political or identity films may well be aesthetically experimental, they need not be so. Maria Maggenti's *The Incredibly True Adventure of Two Girls in Love* (1995) is an example of a film which is not. A lesbian romantic comedy—just as *The Crying Game* (1992), for instance, is a play on the traditional heterosexual romance genre—*Incredibly True Adventure* was criticized, in some quarters, for its lack of formal experimentation.

In an interview with Maggenti for *Filmmaker*, Scott Macaulay broached the subject almost apologetically. "What's amazing is that *Incredibly True Adventure* is totally a crowd pleasing film and I don't mean that in a condescending way" ("True Romance" 32). He rushed to assure her his intent was not condescension because "crowd pleasing" is customarily understood as the antithesis of "art," synonymous with *mainstream, apolitical* (or politically suspect), and *sell-out*.

Macaulay's amazement about Maggenti's film stems from his perception that the work manages to be simultaneously crowd pleasing and good, that is, successful in its political agenda.

He continues later in the interview, "In terms of the New Queer Cinema films, there's been a distrust of some of the conventional narrative strategies that you kind of embrace in your film" (33). In something of a tyranny of the formal, Maggenti was placed in the position of responding from a defensive, or at any rate, self-explanatory posture, "I did go through many trials when I began to develop the script and I felt as if I were almost anti-intellectual, as if I were almost letting down the legacy of queer cinema" (32).

Peter Wollen is clear that political militancy alone is no guarantee of being avant-garde; equally necessary is "a break with bourgeois norms of diegesis, [and] subversion and deconstruction of codes" ("Two Avant-Gardes" 101), that is, a departure from normative realist modes of filmmaking. Indeed, theorists like Wollen criticize art cinema for similar reasons, feeling it fails to sufficiently subvert normative codes or effectively break down dominant narrative.

However, the same move away from the principally formal concerns of the aesthetic avant-garde, and that enabled the reemergence of the political avant-garde in Wollen's analysis, made it difficult to mandate or police the boundaries of any future state of production, in order to ensure it was unified in its uses of content *and* form, signified and signifier. It is the 1960s and post-1960s emergence of a diversified body of identities and concerns that results in an accompanying diversification of production practices.

Although the powerful influence of the avant-garde remains, and with it a hierarchy in which the aesthetic takes pride of place, "it soon became clear that the old doctrines of purity, of self-definition, of art about art, had collapsed and been replaced by a new and extremely heterogeneous expansion of art into a whole range of semiotic practices, with new types of audience relationship and with new and unanticipated forms of signification" (Wollen, "Semiotic Counter-Strategies" 213). Along with this diversification—a sudden heterogeneity of politicized concerns—the "purity" of any single style or mode of production, such as the subversion of traditional aesthetic codes and conventions or the development of an antinarrative or a fragmented, dismembered narrative, could not be upheld, opening up the possibility of working in as many aesthetic forms as in politicized perspectives.

Further, the return to narrative, to the issues of "marketing and accessibility" which Cartwright and Fonoroff deplore, offers solutions to two other problems encountered by the tenets of the avant-gardes and art cinema. The first is precisely the issue of audience and the notion of producing an art "for the people" which the people neither appreciate nor find entertaining. As Sylvia

Harvey notes, "While it is not difficult to see how a 'popular,' mass cinema might not objectively serve the interests of the workers, it is much more difficult to see how or for how long the value of a cinema which objectively serves their interests but is *not recognized by them* can be defended" (*May '68* 80; see also 64 and *Independent Cinema?* 20).

The second but linked problem is the connection between the avant-garde and concepts of "high art." The aesthetic and political avant-gardes and art cinema are all profound parts of the legacy and practices of high art. For those concerned with issues of audience accessibility, or the value of the popular, or both, a politicized production that adopts narrative forms and genres, and works within traditional codes holds the potential, in this view, of surmounting the overintellectualization, overaestheticization, and elitism associated with high art. However, the influence of the avant-gardes cannot be easily dismissed and, as formally nonexperimental filmmakers such as Maria Maggenti have found, their "place" within independent practice does not exist without question or some suspicion.

Diane Crane points out that the redefinition of formal and stylistic features "appears to be the most important factor" in an art work's acceptance as avant-garde (and by extension, as independent). "Art movements that confine their iconoclastic activities to the redefinition of social content or the production and distribution of art works are less likely to be labeled avant-garde by members of art worlds. For this reason, the Social Realists in the 1930s and the mural artists in the 1970s who redefined the social content of art and the settings for the production and the distribution of art are not considered to be avant-gardes" (Crane 15). For independent film, in the hierarchy in which the formal predominates, a film is most likely to be considered independent if it is both aesthetically and politically alternative. If a film is aesthetically experimental it is likely to be considered independent even if it is not in any way alternative in content or social agenda. If a film is alternative in social agenda but formally conventional, it is the least likely to find acceptance within the boundaries of independent film.

Identity cinema, whether aesthetically experimental or not (and the range is great), is included here as a constituent of alternative cinema because it is, first, such an important component of independent film as it differentiates itself from normative realist practice. Although sometimes disowned by its precursor, identity cinema is very much heir to the principles of the political avant-garde. Second, while identity is a political category, and therefore more fittingly a cultural/historical discourse, the situation of identity cinema illustrates how representational discourses are inseparable from cultural/historical ones, as the case of the political avant-garde, itself, makes clear. The indissolubility of representational from cultural/historical discourses is the core agenda of the political avant-garde. Third, identity cinema's inclusion as alternative practice points out the problem of the dominance of formal considerations in configurations of alternative representational discourse, excluding other discursive possibilities, for instance, narrativity. I return to the question of narrative in chapter 4.

The following are films that have contributed to the concept of identity cinema.

Other examples of gay and lesbian films besides *The Incredibly True Adventure of Two Girls in Love*, include *Desert Hearts* (1986), *Parting Glances* (1986), *Mala Noche* (1986), *My Own Private Idaho* (1991), *Longtime Companion* (1990), *The Hours and the Times* (1991), *Poison* (1991), *Swoon* (1992), *The Living End* (1992), *Claire of the Moon* (1992), *Go Fish* (1994), *Stonewall* (1995), *Late Bloomers* (1996), *Beautiful Thing* (1997), *Billy's Hollywood Screen Kiss* (1998), *Ma Vie en Rose* (1997), *High Art* (1998), *Boys Don't Cry* (1999), *Trick* (1999), and *But I'm a Cheerleader* (2000).

The range of films exploring race and ethnicity comprise, among others: *Chan Is Missing* (1982), *Dim Sum: A Little Bit of Heart* (1985), *Double Happiness* (1994), *Picture Bride* (1995), *Strawberry Fields* (1999), *Three Seasons* (1999), *She's Gotta Have It* (1986), *Sidewalk Stories* (1989), *Straight out of Brooklyn* (1991), *Daughters of the Dust* (1992), *Sankofa* (1994), *The Glass Shield* (1994), *Eve's Bayou* (1997), *Slam* (1998), *Sammy and Rosie Get Laid* (1987), *Mississippi Masala* (1992), *Bhaji on the Beach* (1994), *My Son the Fanatic* (1998), *Such a Long Journey* (1998), *East Is East* (2000), *American Desi* (2001), *Crossover Dreams* (1985), *Mi Vida Loca* (1994), *Latin Boys Go to Hell* (1997), *La Ciudad* (1999), and *Smoke Signals* (1996).

Films that focus on women and gender are disproportionately fewer (compared to population or audience percentage),[4] although some of the films that appeared in the previous groupings of race and ethnicity and sexual identity are equally appropriate here. Films within this grouping include, for example: *My Brilliant Career* (1980), *A Question of Silence* (1981), *Antonia's Line* (1996), *Born in Flames* (1983), *Working Girls* (1987), *Privilege* (1991), *MURDER and Murder* (1996), *Antonia and Jane* (1991), *Gas Food Lodging* (1992), *My New Gun* (1992), *Orlando* (1993), *The Piano* (1993), *The Ballad of Little Jo* (1994), *Girls Town* (1996), *The 24 Hour Woman* (1999), *Tumbleweeds* (1999), and *Girlfight* (2000).

British filmmakers have been particularly strong on films that focus on class, such as Mike Leigh's *High Hopes* (1989), *Life Is Sweet* (1991), *Naked* (1993), *Secrets & Lies* (1996), and *Career Girls* (1997), and Ken Loach's films, *Ladybird, Ladybird* (1994), *Raining Stones* (1994), *Carla's Song* (1996), *My Name Is Joe* (1999), and *Bread and Roses* (2000). Also falling into this category are *The*

Snapper (1994), *The Van* (1996), *The Full Monty* (1996), *Trainspotting* (1996), *Human Traffic* (2000), and *Ratcatcher* (2000).

In addition, there are films that combine working within two or more political identity categories, for instance, *My Beautiful Laundrette* (1986), *Macho Dancer* (1988), *Young Soul Rebels* (1991), *The Wedding Banquet* (1993), *The Watermelon Woman* (1996), and *Chutney Popcorn* (1999).

Although this study does not cover them, a number of influential documentaries could most readily be described as generically belonging to identity politics, some of which are: *The Thin Blue Line* (1988), *Incident at Oglala* (1991), *Paris Is Burning* (1991), *American Dream* (1992), *Forbidden Love: The Unashamed Stories of Lesbian Lives* (1992), *Silverlake Life: The View from Here* (1993), *Hoop Dreams* (1994), *The Celluloid Closet* (1996), *The Big One* (1998), *Genghis Blues* (1999), *On the Ropes* (1999), and *Southern Comfort* (2001).

Postmodern Film

An understanding of what postmodern film practices or, more generally, postmodern artistic practices might be is still very much in the process of cultural formation. However, certain attributes are fairly widely agreed on, for instance, the admissibility of all forms, elements, affects and variations of popular culture in place of the exclusivity of high art. "Popular culture could no longer be seen simply in terms of the old 'Hollywood' mass-media model" or "summarily dismissed by monolithic reference to 'dominant codes' or 'classic texts'" (Wollen, "Semiotic Counter-Strategies" 213). The change reflected an acknowledgment that the modernist dismissal of popular culture as empty, trivial, and invalid had been a gross oversimplification. "The implications of the developments appeared to be that, in a society dominated by the mass media, popular culture is better able than avant-garde art to provide visual metaphors that reflect the problems and dilemmas of everyday life" (Crane 76).

Additionally, a number of stylistic features have become identified with the postmodern.

1. Compilation. Works that are gathered from various dissimilar sources of origin. Concepts such as pastiche, bricolage, photomontage and collage are associated with the practices of compilation.[5]

2. Repetition. Umberto Eco calls postmodernism an "aesthetics of seriality" in which the concept of manifold reproduction (as in industry and mass media) is no longer seen as alien to the enterprise of art as it was for modernism (qtd. in Frow 22).

3. Lack of an original or novelty. Within modernism, every work of art, "figures out a new law, imposes a *new paradigm*, a new way of looking at the world" (Frow 22). This is displaced in postmodernism; artworks or cultural texts are based in a widely known and mutually experienced cultural imaginary rather than in an individual artistic imaginary.

4. Fragmentation. Concepts of compilation, as well as the constant flow and simultaneous break-up of media information (such as TV commercials and channel surfing), result in far more fragmented texts rather than in the unified and coherent works of modernist art.

5. Referentiality and appropriation. References or appropriations can be taken from other works of art, either in the same medium or across media, from the contemporary moment or from the past. In film this might take the form of incorporation from other films, either by reference to or wholesale appropriation of them, and can occur in any one (or more) of a number of forms—parody, sampling, homage, straight rip-off, and so on.

The above stylistic features of postmodernism overlap with each other; none is distinctly separable. Pastiche, for instance, implies compilation, appropriation, and fragmentation. Repetition and loss of novelty may well encompass, in addition, the referential.

There has also been considerable debate about the originating "moment" of postmodernism and the demise of modernism. The need for determining a specific moment may rest with our desire for clean divisions. Instead of attempting to locate precisely when one movement breaks with the other, perhaps it is more helpful to understand the transformation as the moments when one movement merges with, or emerges from, the other. In this dynamic, figures such as Godard, Robert Rauschenberg, Jasper Johns, Warhol, and other pop artists can be seen as, on the one hand, exemplary of a high point of modernism—in their enshrinement as individual creative forces, artistic geniuses, and auteurs; in their emphasis on work that is novel, original, or "strange"; in the density of their work as well as in its presentation and marketing, all of which render it high art. On the other hand, these same figures can be viewed simultaneously as exemplary of an emergent phase of postmodernism—in Godard's use of appropriation, cultural reference, and fragmentation, for instance; in pop art's seriality, constant citation of popular culture, and so on.

Another tendency has been a kind of "cultural panic" in which postmodernism is assumed to signify the end of artistic practice. Arthur Danto writes, "Recently people have begun to feel that the last twenty-five years, a period of tremendous experimental productiveness in the visual arts with no single narrative direction on the basis of which others could be excluded, have stabilized as the norm....There is no a priori constraint on how art works must look—they can look like anything at all. This alone finished the modernist agenda" (16). Here, diversity of styles and modes of production are identified as another attribute of postmodernism. However, rather than cause for panic, in an era marked by the urgency of social pluralism, the accommodation of differences could prove to be one of postmodernism's richest and most beneficial aspects.

Yet Danto refers to the completion of the modernist project as the end of art: "one mark of art having ended is that there should no longer be an objective structure with a defining style, or if you prefer, that there should be an objective historical structure in which *everything is possible*. If everything is possible, nothing is historically mandated: one thing is, so to say, as good as another. And that in my view is the object condition for post-historical art" (44). By no "objective structure with a defining style," Danto speaks of the loss of the art object, the artifact, in its expression within particular coded modes of representation that have gained certain recognized, exclusive, and valued significances. Although Danto does not decry the onset of such a "post-historical" diversity of styles and practices, it seems somewhat dire (or premature) to refer to this as the end of art. It is the end of modernism, perhaps even the end of art as we have become accustomed to it. But the postmodern, by identifying work in terms of its diversity—calling attention to its specific time, place and voice(s) of origin—can be argued to historicize or provide specificity to art, precisely by removing it from the abstract realms of the universal and the eternal.

The diversity of practices associated with postmodernism, coupled with its inclusiveness toward popular culture, has meant the increased admissibility of more familiarly mainstream modes of storytelling and their accompanying formal approaches. As Craig Owens notes, if modernism "proclaimed the autonomy of the signifier, its liberation from the 'tyranny of the signified'[,] postmodernists instead expose the tyranny of the *signifier*" (59), the tyranny of the formal. For independent film this has meant the reintroduction of concepts such as narrative, entertainment, and pleasure. These have surfaced in ways such as the renewed popularity of genre films, for instance, gangster and crime, or horror like *The Blair Witch Project* (1999). The revived credibility of entertainment and pleasure is found in the humor based on pop culture referencing in *Pulp Fiction* (1992) and *Reservoir Dogs* (1994) or in the comedic moments that play on generic and stylistic visual features, particularly around violence, following in the mold of Tarantino or the Coen brothers.

A postmodern sensibility is also evident in the kind of *listless irony* found in such films as Mary Harron's *I Shot Andy Warhol*. We're not entirely sure why we are following Valerie Solanas (Lili Taylor), what is significant about her story, and what—if anything—we're meant to learn from it. Somehow because of this (rather than despite it), the film is both moving and disturbing. Additionally, it is underwritten with an off-hand, low-key, and running irony in that it is the story of Solanas who is famous for shooting Andy Warhol who is famous for telling us that in the future we'd all be famous for fifteen minutes—which is what Solanas's shooting Warhol and this film about her achieve for Solanas. But achieves rather unjustly, as it transpires, pointing to the inadequacies of the way she, and others, come to be (briefly) known, remembered or understood.

A listless, meandering quality exists in the films of Richard Linklater, Kevin Smith, and Gregg Araki, with their nonheroic, largely noneventful storylines. Similar to these are the nonevents or nonheroes—in contrast to antiheroes—of *Welcome to the Dollhouse* (1996), *Heavy* (1996), and much of *Trainspotting* (1996). In chapter 6 I take up the subject of postmodern film in a more detailed manner, examining some of its possibilities and its possible limitations.

All the previously described traditions and currents of alternative artistic practice enabled and continue to influence the potentialities and parameters of independent film. Independent cinema embraces numerous modernist notions: in, for instance, its construction of the director as primary creative force or auteur; in its emphasis on personal expression; in the value it places on the original, the novel, the shocking, the strange; in the weight it gives to formal experimentation of the material and lingual elements of the medium. And although independent film, in comparison with other alternative practices, reverts more often to the narrative modes of storytelling and the psychological development of characters associated with mainstream cinema, as well as to its concerns of wider marketability, it also frequently retains the more specialized, dense language and the codes connected with high-art cinema. And in some cases, as in certain instances of modernist practice, independent film takes on overtly politicized perspectives and concerns.

The influences of the postmodern can also be seen on independent film, notably in its acceptance of popular culture, resulting in the greater permissibility of narrative (and specifically Hollywood-associated) genres and codes; in its broader (some would say weaker) sense of what constitutes the political; in its increased concern with issues of marketability and accessibility—the latter in the two senses of readily available as well as easily read.

A serious limitation in operative conceptions of representative practice lies in the dual division of form and content, and the similarly binary signifier and signified, in which signifier tends to parallel form and signified to equate with content. Instead, a more suitably complex way would be to understand representation as the process of various discourses—representational, institutional, interpretive, and cultural/historical—operating simultaneously. An artifact, then, is the confluence of meanings from multiple discourses, in varying configurations and states of interaction. The meanings, shapes, psychological and emotional textures, and so on, of an artifact resonate with its precursor movements, its history, as it puts various representational and other discourses into action and interaction. With the artifact paradigm, aesthetic discourses (abstraction, naturalism) converge with narrative discourses (art film or classic realism; fiction, nonfiction or experimental) that interact with cultural discourses (concepts of justice in courtroom dramas and detective stories; heterosexual coupling in romance), and so on. All these are put into play in every artifact in various formulations of relationship to one another, and not necessarily in concert with each other, that is, not working inevitably toward the same meaning constructions. This accounts, in part, for the existence of conflicting textual elements and the possibility of multiple readings. It also helps account for the difficulty in labeling a piece as purely avant-garde in either aesthetic or political terms, precisely because artifacts are multiply layered constructions.

Each discourse (aesthetic, narrative, cultural, institutional) has its own series of codes formulated by signifiers and signifieds. For alternative and independent practices, in their struggle over what is "legitimately" avant-garde in form versus what is genuinely "progressive" in content, a disproportionate emphasis may be placed on the aesthetic as the most immediately visible, and so most easily recognized, aspect of representational discourses in operation. Conversely, films that put alternative narrative and cultural discourses into play may be less readily available to immediate recognition, and so, less amenable to critical consensus that they display characteristics of alternative significance.

It can also be argued that independent film exists as a hybrid not only because it borrows from both Hollywood and alternative filmmaking traditions but also because it borrows from among elements within each of these large configurations, crafting itself by referencing or appropriating within and across a number of, for example, alternative filmmaking practices. Further, it is possible that because of its hybrid qualities, its composition from among various representational discourses, independent film creates an object which may contain gaps and fissures, a cultural product held together to whatever degree of coherency by leaky joints or weak seams. This may help explain why independent film seemingly has been able to take up the representation of multiple, varying identity formations, a subject I cover in the next chapter.

Having outlined here some of the historical and contemporary alternative representational discourses that influence independent film, in chapter 3 I will pursue a more detailed look at how institutional discourses (distributors) interact with alternative representational discourses when those representational discourses are called on to express the cultural/historical experiences of specific identities or communities—in this case, African Americans. The chapter introduces the further layer of cultural/historical discourses, in the particular form of identity politics.

 Part II

Textual Analysis and Discursive Fields

Chapter Three

"Fixing" Difference: Identity Cinema and Independent Distribution

> When a work is so densely seeded within black culture, a lot of people who are not from the culture will say that they find the film inaccessible or they find it is not engaging. What they are saying is that they do not feel privileged by the film.
> —Julie Dash

> I have wanted always to develop a way of writing that was irrevocably black. I don't have the resources of a musician but I thought if it was truly black literature it would not be black because I was, it would not even be black because of its subject matter. It would be something intrinsic, indigenous, something in the way it was put together—the sentences, the structure, texture and tone—so that anyone who read it would realise.
> —Toni Morrison

One of the principal means independent cinema uses to distinguish its cultural mandate from that of Hollywood's is by its choice of the voices of those for whom it ostensibly speaks and of the lives it seeks to represent. Identity politics is one of the constituting threads with which independent film weaves its discourse. Rosalind Brunt suggests that the starting point for a politics of identity is "the issue of representation: both how our identities are represented in and through the culture and assigned particular categories; and also who or what politically represents us, speaks and acts on our behalf. These two senses of 'representation'…. help us think how we both 'make sense' of the world and get a sense of our 'place' in it—a place of many, and increasing, identities" (152). Making sense of the world and of our place in it is a multitiered process in which our identities are shaped by how we come to perceive ourselves as well as by how we are perceived by others: the development of psychic and social being.

The dual inscription of the term *representation* is echoed by Paul Gilroy: "the idea that artists are representative, public figures has become an extra burden for them to carry. Its weight can be felt in the tension between the two quite different senses of a word which refers not just to depiction but to the idea of delegation or substitution" (qtd. in Mercer 239). Representation as substitution, as speaking and acting on behalf of an entire multifaceted social identity, presents its own complexities. While Gilroy indicates the difficulty for members of subcultural groups to both depict and be delegates for the place from which they emerge, Brunt pinpoints the all-too-frequent occurrence in which a cultural outsider with greater access to the means of representation becomes the substitute delegate.

One of the cornerstones of the recent wave of independent cinema that began to consolidate in the 1980s is films associated with an emerging identity politics, following in the wake of the various 1960s and 1970s civil rights movements. Included in this early grouping are films such as *Chan Is Missing* (1982), *Parting Glances* (1986), *Desert Hearts* (1986), *She's Gotta Have It* (1986), and *Working Girls* (1987). As Peter Wollen has noted, the 1960s and post-1960s era saw the emergence of a diversified array of identities and concerns that resulted in an accompanying diversification of production practices (Wollen, "Mexico" 95). A consequence of the political movements of the 1960s and 1970s was a growing awareness of coexisting but distinct social formations—women, gays and lesbians, racial and ethnic minorities, and so on—each with differing needs, desires, and agendas. A universal or homogenous approach no longer was perceived to fit all.

With the 1980s and 1990s this evolved into the urgency of multiculturalism: the opportunities and issues surrounding a multiply identified, multiply experienced society. A recognition of the swiftly diversifying nature of society and the concomitant creation of multiple, "specialized markets," underscored the need for concepts and frameworks which promoted the modes and means of pluralistic existence. These social and political conditions enabled the establishment of independent film in the 1980s and 1990s as a cultural field whose mandate and marketshare involve, precisely, the representation of underrepresented, marginalized, or otherwise ignored subcultural communities and consumers. Independent film has become one of the cultural arenas where, through representational discourses, a number of concepts and strategies for multicultural existence are experimented with and experienced.

In the complexity of its creation and dissemination, independent film embodies both sets of dynamics cited by Gilroy and Brunt: Gilroy's in the work of specific filmmakers trying to make sense of the world and their place in it; Brunt's in the surrounding institutional framework that selects specific work and then markets it back to its originating community and to communities beyond. The intent here is to show how the institutional infrastructures of the independent industry, despite claims of a cultural mandate to the contrary, narrow the permissible range of subcultural representations through the persistent framing of films by, about, and for marginalized social subjects as instances of "otherness." The consequence is that space is created for some versions of particular identities but not for others.

Such an analysis necessitates an examination of the cultural spaces occupied by independent distributors, in terms of their avowed political role as well as their economic relations. This chapter explores how the specifics of the independent industry, at the levels of both individual practices and institutional processes, shape and thus help define the identities of identity politics. I consider how identities are organized by certain external forces, in this instance, distribution and marketing mechanisms, and how this shaping occurs within specific, limited, and set parameters that, in significant ways, are not to the advantage of the particular community being "identified."

As in most cases of hegemonic power structures, the organizing of identities is not the effect of purposeful or straightforward behavior on the part of individuals but rather is mediated through complex, intricate cultural discourses. Such discourses include concepts of history and the complicated processes of reading texts. At issue are such considerations as what is historically valid knowledge and what are "legitimate" representational discourses for transmitting such knowledge. I will utilize the distribution histories of three African American independent films, *Daughters of the Dust* (Julie Dash, 1992, Kino), *To Sleep with Anger* (Charles Burnett, 1990, Goldwyn), and *Just Another Girl on the I.R.T.* (Leslie Harris, 1993, Miramax), giving the closest reading to *Daughters of the Dust*, in order to compare the varying interpretations of each film on the part of independent distributors, the decisions then made about how that picture was handled, and the effects of that treatment on the critical and public reception of the film. Such pragmatic institutional decisions, mediated by preferred readings and discourses of historical knowledge, will be shown to form a significant means by which particular identities achieve or fail to achieve representation.

No doubt independent film provides opportunities and a cultural presence for filmmakers otherwise denied the ability to create and disseminate their work. In turn, their films help further extend the independent arena. For instance, *She's Gotta Have It* enabled Spike Lee's transition to Hollywood, where he largely has worked since as one of the few African American writer-directors to successfully sustain a career with the major studios. At the same time, *She's Gotta Have It* arguably helped pave the way for other films by, about, and for African Americans, both independent (*Hollywood Shuffle*, 1987; *Sidewalk Stories*, 1989; *To Sleep with Anger*; *Straight out of Brooklyn*, 1991; *One False Move*, 1992; *Fresh*, 1994; *The Glass Shield*, 1994; *Hav Plenty*, 1997; *Eve's Bayou*,

1997; *Down in the Delta,* 1998; *Slam,* 1998; *The Caveman's Valentine,* 2001), and emanating from Hollywood (*I'm Gonna Git You Sucka,* 1988; *Boyz N the Hood,* 1991; *New Jack City,* 1991; *The Five Heartbeats,* 1991; *Juice,* 1992; *Devil in a Blue Dress,* 1995; *Set It off,* 1996; *Soul Food,* 1997; *Rosewood,* 1997; *Love and Basketball,* 2000; and Spike Lee's subsequent films).[1]

Simultaneously, however, an independent discursive formation, as currently configured, has restricted depictions of members of marginalized communities in, most notably, three ways. First, the tendency to adopt an "it's-been-done" mentality, referring to having championed one's women's film, gay film, lesbian film, African American film, Latino/Latina film, or any other categorization of social identity that reduces a complex of experiences into a single rendition—once, and for all time.[2] The it's-been-done plea may be applied within an individual distribution company or across the industry. That is, a film may be turned down because a company has already done "its" women's, gay, or black film or because the market for that "type" of film has already been saturated by other companies or because it fails to add anything "new" to our understanding of that particular social category from what's already available. All are arguments that would be unimaginable if applied to films by, about, or for the dominant market group ("Sorry, we've already done our straight white male film for the year").

Second, the independent arena has limited the range of representations through the industry's failure to cultivate a sufficiently wide array of specialized audiences. Instead of recognizing and carefully appealing to new audiences, particularly the communities of origin for subcultural filmmakers, the industry relies on a known and established concept of art film viewers—traditionally white, urban, middle-class ticket buyers. Further, there is a strong tendency within the independent industry to mirror Hollywood's ideal demographic target—young males. This leads to Jim Moran and Holly Willis's description of the independent arena as increasingly "dominated by the success stories of college age men" (Moran 22). Although Moran and Willis refer to the writers/directors making contemporary film, their comment applies equally to the subject matter and target audiences that dominate independent practice. James Schamus, for one, concurs with this widely held analysis of the ascendant trend in independent film.

> Oddly, as the independent infrastructure grays...the subculture that infrastructure promotes grows, depressingly, more and more stupidly ageist and infantilized—a trait shared to great extent by Hollywood, too. The "independent" scene, unlike the earlier Euro-inflected "art-house" culture, has a hard time dealing with mature and experienced voices—we're too busy rushing around looking for the next barely post-pubescent auteur to market. ("Don't Worry" 60)

The desire to reach a young male audience is rationalized by the percentage of the movie-going public that young men represent compared with their percentage in the overall population. Younger viewers do go to the movies in disproportionate numbers to their total population; however, they do not represent a disproportionate percentage of the overall movie tickets sold. That is, while sixteen- to twenty-year olds make up 8% of the total population, they account for 17% of movie tickets sold. However, thirty- to thirty-nine year olds, representing 20% of the overall population, also account for 19% of ticket buyers. Thus the older demographic, although not as sought after an audience, actually exceeds the younger group in the total number of tickets purchased or dollars spent ("USA Snapshot" D1). The emphasis on a youthful male audience is further bolstered by conventional wisdom that suggests that boys and young men will not go to films by, about, and for girls and young women, but that girls and young women will attend movies aimed at male viewers (McKay; Puig, "Little Girl Power" D1). The result is surprise every time a "new" audience is rediscovered, as in the case of young women viewers, following the success of films such as *Clueless* in 1995 (Orenstein 1), and again, in the wake of the box-office achievements of *Titanic* in 1997, and the *Scream* series in 1996, 1997, and 2000 (S. Jacobson 47; Weeks A1).[3]

Third, and as a result of the two previous factors of singular filmic instances deemed sufficient portrayal of entire cultural formations and the invisibility of many particularized audiences, is the narrowing of the diversity of the films promoted. This can be seen in the heralded wave of African American cinema in the 1990s, which solidified largely into the stories of young urban men, depictions dominated by gangs, drugs, and violence, in both the Hollywood and independent spheres. Such confined representation has been much criticized for providing a distorted image of the multifacetedness of African American lives and experiences, as well as playing to negative stereotypes of African Americans in communities beyond. This is not to suggest that the films that do receive distribution are not good in and of themselves but only to emphasize that they are too narrow and repetitive a rendition to be considered anything near a significant depiction of the full range of African American culture. As filmmaker Robert Townsend notes, when complaining that most black films must contain violence in order to be considered marketable, "We've got to do all kinds of stories. If the films all have the same kinds of tones, then it will be another black exploitation period" (qtd. in Lowery and Sabir 108).

While the independent industry can argue that they are merely attempting to compete with what's "out there," or replicating what has previously proved commercially successful, the narrow depictions do in fact coincide with the dominant audience's stereotypical perception of African American existence—

largely inner city, poor, and crime-ridden. In other words, the films are being assessed from, in this instance, a white middle-class viewing position. Independent industry personnel stand in for, and indeed themselves largely conform to, the assumed white, male, middle-class, heterosexual ticket buyer. These industry representatives, for commercial and market reasons as well as ideological identification, ensure that the dominant audience they resemble will be served rather than the subcultural audience that may be portrayed. The narrow spectrum of films available and experiences depicted is not simply a transparent rendering of how various social identities have come to perceive themselves—despite industry marketing and philosophical claims to the contrary. Instead, such depictions are filtered through the perceptions and agendas of those who represent, in the sense of speak on behalf of, marginalized communities. Such delegates, because of their greater access to the means of representation, in this specific instance, distribution, "manage" available subcultural representations.

The issue is not solely the inequity of exclusion for those audiences left unaddressed. At stake is the "fixing" of a given identity in terms of how it is understood by an outsider audience as otherness. The consequence is gay films dealing primarily with sex (and AIDS), black films about race, and so on. As Kobena Mercer points out, "the idea of speaking as a 'representative of the race' reinforces the myth, on which ideologies of racism crucially depend, that 'the black community' is a homogenous, monolithic or singular entity defined by race and nothing but race" (250). Industry promotion and public conviction that films based on identity politics are works in which representatives of specific communities speak for that community too often conceal that what is actually being spoken are the ideologies of those occupying the dominant producing, distributing, and viewing positions.

The distribution history and audience reception of Julie Dash's *Daughters of the Dust* illustrate some of the complex ways in which the narrowing of subcultural representations is made operational. I would like to use its example to examine some of the intricacies of a filmmaker attempting to speak from her own cultural position and experiences within a broader institutional and discursive context to discuss some of the limitations of an industry that advances itself as speaking on behalf of others. As I am myself a white viewer, I will rely for assistance on readings of *Daughters of the Dust* from Toni Cade Bambara, from focus groups of African American women conducted by Jacqueline Bobo, and on writer-director Dash's own comments. This is not to suggest that what results is somehow a racially "neutral" reading. Quite the contrary, it is an attempt to account for racialized readings of the film and to analyze how and why the film was misread by so many white viewers, in particular, industry personnel.

Through close textual and institutional analysis, this chapter tracks a number of discursive interactions. First, how identity groups can use alternative representational discourses to convey cultural/historical meanings and experiences, in the instance of *Daughters of the Dust*, an African American version of history. Second, how alternative means of storytelling, such as the subject matter, aesthetics, and narrative formation of *Daughters of the Dust* can encounter difficulties within an industry formation, even one supposedly designed to represent just such alternative discourses. Third, the ways in which independent institutional entities approach the business of representing various cultural/historical discourses. Fourth, how identity and industry formations may collide over cultural/historical discourses. This consideration also involves the question of power because not all social formations wield the same levels of influence, economic and otherwise. By having slipped through the distribution barriers, and in the way it managed to get released, *Daughters of the Dust* is an exception which illustrates the point. And fifth, the ways in which the cultural/historical discourses of identity politics, as conveyed through representational discourses, can be read differently by other interpretive agents, in this instance independent distributors, and as a result are in political terms "misread." The examples that illustrate this last point are *To Sleep with Anger* and *Just Another Girl on the I.R.T.* The discussion deals with independent distributors as a first tier or line of consumption/interpretation.

Distribution Strategies

As a representative of one of the mini-majors admitted retrospectively (in light of *Daughters of the Dust*'s success at the box office), the film had been "kicking around for a while," meaning it had been offered to, and passed on by, the full range of independent distribution companies.[4] Dash's description of the film's distribution difficulties matches this acknowledgment.

> I was certain that now that the film was completed, distribution would not be a problem. It had been hard in the early days to convey in words the idea of this film. But now that it was done, I figured there'd be no more blank looks. They wouldn't have to imagine a film about African American women at the turn of the century. There it was, right in front of them. I was wrong. All of the distribution companies turned it down. I was told over and over again that there was no market for the film.... Again, I was hearing mostly white men telling me, an African American woman, what my people wanted to see. In fact, they were deciding what we should be allowed to see. (16, 25)[5]

Indeed, it appeared that the film was not going to get theatrical distribution at all when, finally, it was picked up by Kino International, a company dealing primarily in classic foreign films.[6] *Daughters of the Dust* opened at Film Forum, a specialty theater, in New York on January 15, 1992, the first feature film by an African American woman in theatrical release.

Although she was assured that the film would be distributed, Dash remained concerned that a smaller company such as Kino would mean a limited exposure for the film during its initial run (a concern similar to Jon Jost's with *All the Vermeers in New York*). This transpired, for instance, when the film opened only in New York rather than in numerous U.S. urban markets simultaneously. Received wisdom holds that a film needs the initial buzz of wide release and promotion in order to succeed. Otherwise it takes time to build audience awareness and word of mouth publicity. The danger of a limited release and promotional strategy is that a film will be pulled from the theater(s) due to insufficient business before its likely audiences have had a chance to identify it. The widespread view exists—including in Dash's assessment (26)—that this was the fate of Charles Burnett's *To Sleep with Anger*. Indeed, *To Sleep with Anger* has entered industry annals as "a cautionary tale to independent film companies seeking to market to an African-American art-film audience" ("Faithful" 21).

Starring Danny Glover, *To Sleep with Anger* was released in October 1991 in multiple markets. A month later it had earned only $325,000 at the box office, although there had been a strong critical response to the film from the outset. It was runner-up for the Grand Jury Prize at the Sundance Film Festival in 1990, and *Variety*'s very favorable review, following its Sundance screening, described it as a film that "simmers for a long time before it begins to percolate a pungent, stimulating brew. With special handling, pic could appeal to a sizable audience....Once its theme takes hold, *To Sleep With Anger* is a fascinating piece that proves Burnett a filmmaker of rich imagination and talent" (*Variety*, January 31, 1990: 33).

In contrast, when *Daughters of the Dust* screened at Sundance in 1991 it won only the cinematography award, for Arthur Jafa Fielder's work, and received a scathing postfestival review from *Variety*: "Nobly intended as an investigation into a little known African-American culture, *Daughters of the Dust* plays like a two-hour Laura Ashley commercial....Talent is definitely on view here, and certain viewers will assuredly fall in with the slow rhythm and privileged mood Dash sets up. But on any serious level, two hours of visual lyricism do not substitute for good drama and historical substance" (*Variety*, February 11, 1991: 112).

Despite its positive critical response and the assessment that *To Sleep with Anger* had the potential of addressing a "sizable audience," Goldwyn marketed and released it largely as a specialty (i.e., art) film and was subsequently much criticized for this strategy. Tom Rothman, head of production at Goldwyn at the time, argued that their sincere efforts to market to black audiences had met with failure: "The numbers and the pattern have been the same everywhere, regardless of how we use television, radio, newsprint and public appearances to support this picture.... it has performed well in specialty houses, but in so-called black theaters across the country, the performance has been significantly less" (qtd. in Rohter C15). Responses to this by representatives of the film are twofold. The first is that Goldwyn did not know how to promote the film to African American viewers. Writer-director Charles Burnett attributed the film's poor performance among black audiences to "not an absence of interest but rather a lack of effective marketing. 'It's not that the black community is not responding.... It's that they don't know anything about it. The problem has really been trying to communicate with black audiences'" (qtd. in Rohter C15). This even seems borne out by some mainstream newspaper reviewers' responses to the ad campaign. For instance, "Like, who put together that newspaper ad with a fat quote from Vincent Canby of the *New York Times*? 'A Big Movie, Full of Big Comic Scenes!'" (Mills, "Out of Obscurity" G10), and "All of this would suggest that viewers—and perhaps the distributor of the film—may not know just what to make of *To Sleep with Anger*. Curiously, though it is a compelling drama, ads have stressed the film's humor" (Nicholson G11). Second, representatives of the film complained that the amount of Goldwyn's promotional budget was woefully inadequate. A year after its release, coproducer Caldecott Chubb remarked, "In its defense, Goldwyn was the only company that expressed any interest in distributing it. Everyone else thought it too daunting." He goes on to add, however, that eight weeks previously they had released David Lynch's *Wild at Heart* with ten times the promotional budget of *To Sleep with Anger*, "They didn't really focus on this movie until it was too late, they had no strategy for reaching the African-American community" (qtd. in Steinmetz 17).

Rather than revamping the nature of their campaign and increasing the promotional budget in reaction to the film's early slow showing, Goldwyn narrowed its focus and abandoned potential black audiences.[7] Instead, it sold *To Sleep with Anger* as art-house fare, screened only in those specialized theaters, relying on an audience with which it was familiar and where its previous promotional strategies had worked. "Goldwyn executives argue that they cannot afford to aim such efforts primarily at the black audience that had been assumed to identify most closely with the film. 'The audience for any specialized picture is the white audience,' Mr. Rothman said. 'That audience tends to be more review-driven, and this film has gotten absolutely fabulous reviews'" (Rohter C15). In a convoluted argument, Rothman suggests that Goldwyn cannot afford the expense of marketing to African American audiences but must rely instead on the unpaid promotional value of positive reviews. And because it is a white audience who primarily reads and responds to those reviews, the principal audience for *To Sleep with Anger* is white, not black, and the picture generically an art film.

The prominent producer's representative John Pierson,[8] who describes *To Sleep with Anger* as "beautifully made, slightly obscure," comments:

> Glover's name got the film made, but caused terribly confused expectations when Goldwyn later released it. If his screen partner Mel Gibson had been in it, that probably would have changed the commercial prospects. Goldwyn was roundly thrashed for treating it like an art film, which is exactly what it was. Admittedly, their grass roots outreach to the black audience was almost nil. (205)

In this rather self-conflicting analysis, although Pierson reports the criticisms meted out to Goldwyn, he simultaneously defends the company by blaming the film's poor showing on its "mixed-signal" casting which caused "confused expectations"—as if one cannot have Danny Glover without Mel Gibson—and thus rendered the film less- or un-commercial. However, this contradicts conventional industry wisdom which is to cast known actors in independent films precisely in order to have a marketing hook. Pierson further defends Goldwyn's strategy on the basis that they marketed *To Sleep with Anger* for "exactly what it was," an art film, while only half-heartedly acknowledging that the distribution company ignored a large and significant audience base.[9]

Certainly a drama with white characters centering on intergenerational family relations, in the manner of *On Golden Pond* (1981), *A River Runs Through It* (1992), *Dolores Claiborne* (1995), or *Liberty Heights* (1999) would hardly be considered an art film. The criteria which Goldwyn, Pierson, and others used to designate *To Sleep with Anger* an art film appear to have been based on three determinants: known audiences, subject matter, and their own position vis-à-vis the film's address.

First, considering *To Sleep with Anger* as an art film rather than as a drama with black characters aims it at a known category of viewers for independent distributors instead of at an unfamiliar audience that needs to be cultivated. Second, *To Sleep with Anger* does not conform to the subject matter or genre of youth-oriented films preoccupied with inner-city violence, which dominates the perception of what "black film" is;[10] instead, characters from an older generation lead the story which focuses on family relations and community interactions. Third, and in a theme to which I will return in connection with *Daughters of the Dust*, the tendency exists for industry members to classify any film they do not "get" or, in Dash's terms, are not privileged or addressed by as an art film. It is important that the Goldwyn company is not singled out but that these problems are viewed, rather, as industry-wide. Indeed, Goldwyn had at least as good a track record of picking up films by, about, and for African Americans, while not limiting their selections solely to the inner-city genre, as any other independent distributor.[11]

To Sleep with Anger ultimately earned $1.16 million at the box office; *Daughters of the Dust* earned $1.7 million (*Filmmaker* 3: insert preceding 42).[12] While seemingly not an enormous difference in hard figures, at the profit margins involved with independent film $540,000 is a substantial discrepancy, equaling about half of *To Sleep with Anger*'s gross and a third of *Daughters of the Dust*'s. Further, the concept of box-office success is not calculated solely on the basis of box-office gross. Also considered in the equation are what the distributor paid to the filmmakers for the film's rights and the distributor's promotional and marketing costs. For instance, *The Spitfire Grill* sold at the Sundance Film Festival in 1996 to Castle Rock "for a calamitously overpriced $10 million. That price took what might have been a modest success and turned it into a major commercial failure" (James 26). Released through Columbia, although *The Spitfire Grill* earned $12.66 million at the box-office (*Filmmaker* 6: insert preceding 49), its advance costs were disproportionately high compared with what the film could reasonably be expected to earn. So, within the industry the film is widely viewed as a commercial failure.

The difference between *To Sleep with Anger* and the greater box-office success enjoyed by *Daughters of the Dust* appears to be attributable to KJM3 Entertainment Group, a then recently formed African American public relations firm hired by Kino to promote and market the film. KJM3 advertised *Daughters of the Dust* in newspapers and on radio stations with a largely African American audience; arranged interviews and stories on black radio and TV programs and in black newspapers and magazines; placed posters in community bookstores, schools, and churches; and elicited the support of black social and political organizations. The film's opening date of January 15 was planned to coincide with the celebration of Martin Luther King Jr.'s birthday and to closely precede February, which is Black History month. KJM3 vice president Marlin Adams explained: "We knew the audience for this film. We knew that there is a complete cross section of the black community who are concerned with the questions this film addresses—what about ourselves should we retain? Questions around history and identity, the past vs. the future" (qtd. in Godfrey 17). KJM3 and Kino's strategy was to pursue cheaper, grass-roots promotional techniques and then to rely on what turned out to be very positive, and vocal, word of mouth.

These focused efforts to reach and develop the film's likeliest audience(s) resulted in its sold-out run at the Film Forum, attended by nontraditional independent film-viewers, individuals as well as groups from schools and churches, who went to an art theater specifically to see *Daughters of the Dust*. Ninety percent of this initial audience was composed of African American women,[13] and from there the film went on to find a wider release and appeal. For instance, when it subsequently opened for a regular run at New York's Village East Cinemas it played to sold-out audiences, prompting a theater spokesperson to comment, "It's been a big surprise. It's primarily a middle-class black female audience. We sell out weekend performances, and during the week, we get busloads of church groups, high schools, and senior-citizen groups coming in for matinees" (Hoban 27).[14]

It is worth noting that while KJM3's promotional strategies were unusual, the efforts expended to promote *Daughters of the Dust* were not excessive or out of the ordinary for an independent film. For instance, Pierson, who represented the film, describes the difficulties in getting *Slacker* into the pivotal Sundance Film Festival in 1991, where it had been rejected the previous year. Orion Classics had already signed on to distribute *Slacker*, but despite that company's involvement and a highly influential producer's rep, the film's admission to Sundance or to other important festivals was far from a given. Further, Pierson describes the significant efforts made to overcome negative newspaper reviews, such as in the *New York Times*, before *Slacker* ultimately "found" its audience (190–94).[15]

Although the gamut of independent distribution entities insisted there was no market for *Daughters of the Dust*, filmmaker Dash ultimately succeeded in reaching the audiences she had intended to address: "I wanted black women first, the black community second, white women third" (40). The question is why did the independent industry insist there was no market for the film and, when audiences flocked to it, why were these same distributors taken by surprise? In the cases of both *To Sleep with Anger* and *Daughters of the Dust*, why was the industry unable to recognize the films' audiences—an untested potential in the former; proven in the latter instance? What are the specific appeals of *Daughters of the Dust* for its intended audiences and what makes it so difficult for the independent industry to recognize those pleasures?

An Iconography of Appearance

The year is 1902. We meet a family, the Peazants, at a critical moment: several members have elected to migrate north for better jobs and schooling. Nana, the head of the family has called the Peazants together for a reunion picnic. She performs a ritual of protections against the hazards of "crossing over." She creates an amulet from scraps of the ancestral past: her most potent gris-gris is a clump of her mother's hair, a last minute keepsake the mother yanked from her scalp before she was snatched from Nana, the child, and sold down river.

Toni Cade Bambara, Preface to *Daughters of the Dust*

Julie Dash describes the sea islands off the coast of the Carolinas and Georgia, home to Gullah communities and the setting for her film, as the Ellis Island for African Americans, "the processing center for the forced immigration of millions" (6). *Daughters of the Dust* tells the stories of four generations of women and of an important segment in African American history.

One of the aspects that attracted African American women viewers to the film was the direction and nature of the film's gaze. For instance, "The thing that struck me about *Daughters of the Dust* was that there were different-looking black women—different hairstyles, different shapes; the difference within blackness was just really striking to me and nice because they were all very beautiful in their own way" and "In *Daughters of the Dust*, the configuration of all these women together is extremely seductive" (Bobo 55–56). This perspective is affirmed by Toni Cade Bambara: "What draws black women in particular to the lengthy movie theater lines again and again is the respectful attention Dash gives to our iconography—hair, cloth, jewelry, skintones, body language" ("Preface" xv).

Yet it is this same aspect of mise-en-scène that prompted one of the major criticisms of the film. In the same review in which it called the film a two-hour Laura Ashley commercial, *Variety* described it as "gorgeously shot in the style of a fashion layout....On view for reel after endless reel are countless silent shots of women" (*Variety*, February 11, 1991: 112). And Phoebe Hoban in an article probing the film's popularity with African American women, found, "At times, with its one representative Indian and its endlessly kaleidoscopic pairing of women, men, and children with elaborate hairstyles, *Dust* looks like a parody of a Benetton ad" (27).[16] These readings are in stark contrast to the seductive pleasure black women viewers attribute to these same "endless" images. The criticism of tediousness from both reviewers suggests that the film addressed someone else's imaginary, not their own.

What many of the film's African American viewers seemed to recognize but what was consistently missed by white (re)viewers is, precisely, the historical and cultural dimensions of the film's iconography of appearance. In an interview with Dash, bell hooks asked her about criticisms of the film: "we know that a lot of people have crassly said that this is a film about hair....What do you think about the critics and others who have said that there is too much emphasis on the aesthetic elements of appearance—the hair, clothes?" ("Dialogue" 52). Dash responded:

> The hairstyles we're wearing now are based upon ancient hairstyles, and there is a tradition behind those hairstyles. They mean things. In any West African country, you know, if you are a preteen you have a certain hairstyle. If you are in puberty you have another hairstyle. Menopausal, another hairstyle. (53)

And in another context, Dash elaborated further.

> Everything means something; there's a source for everything. You just don't put a scarf up on someone's head. You just don't put jewelry on someone; you put it on in a certain way. People's motor habits—the way they stand and the way they walk, the way they laugh—I tried to maintain the integrity of West African motor habits. An example would be of turning the head slightly to the left when listening to an elder and putting a hand over your mouth when you laugh. All this is approached from an Afrocentric perspective.... Afrocentrism, as I'm applying to this film, is that your actions are derived from West African culture rather than from the hinterlands of Europe. (Davis 116)

In other words, African American women viewers recognize in the film's iconography of appearance precisely what is absent in a Benetton ad: the specificities of individual, cultural, and historical contextualization. Many white (re)viewers, not primarily addressed by the film, were unprepared—perhaps untrained as much as unwilling—to recognize those resonances, and so, were left linking the film to the artifices and superficialities they associate with a Benetton ad. Such ads are purposefully designed to suppress individual, cultural or historical contextualization, and to focus attention, instead, on surface appearance in order to create a universalizing, "we are the world," iconography.[17]

The film's representation of a range of black women is enacted additionally through its depiction of characters in which there is a group dynamic instead of a single protagonist. The resulting diversity of experiences becomes clear in instances such as Jacqueline Bobo's character summary along a continuum of spirituality.

> Nana Peazant places her faith in her ancestors and the relics from their past lives; Yellow Mary clings to her St. Christopher charm and her strong conviction that she can always make her way in the world; and Eula sets a letter beneath a glass of water under her bed to summon the spirit of her mother to guide her. Haagar believes firmly in herself and doesn't need any of what she terms "that hoodoo mess." Viola, more than anyone else, has entrusted her life to the belief systems of the dominant culture. (155)[18]

The diversity of women characters, across generations and life circumstances, is inseparable from a historical context in *Daughters of the Dust*. As Bobo writes:

> Viola's attempts to restrain her sexual feelings were not unusual, for many black women of that era attempted to present themselves as refined and genteel in response to the pervasive sentiment that black women were loose, untamable sexual creatures.... The presentation of Viola and her starched, restrained, religious countenance provide a stark contrast to Eula's rape and to Yellow Mary [a prostitute]. Their two stories, coupled with Nana Peazant's history, are a dramatic reconstruction of one of the most devastating myths about black womanhood. (157–58)

Instead of the complex, confusing, or impenetrable film so often described by white reviewers, African American reviewers pointed to the simplicity or transparency of the narrative's historicizing. Jacquie Jones in *Cineaste* writes, "The irony is that, on a certain level, the film's narrative is quite simple.... In one scene, children pour over a 'wish book' picking out all the things they will be able to buy once they leave their isolated homeland. In this, *Daughters of the Dust* is a familiar immigrant drama. The young reach for change while the old cling to tradition.... the tension between tradition and modernity... is symbolic of a classic African American discourse: reconciling collective memory and the legacy of slavery with upward mobility and the American dream" (68–69). And Valerie Boyd in *American Visions* finds:

> The premise is simple.... The matriarch of the family, Nana, doesn't want them to move north and leave their culture behind, so she evokes the spirits of the ancestors to communicate with the younger people and to keep the family together, in spirit if not in reality.... And African Americans should not depend solely on marketing executives to get the word out. *Daughters* will likely build its audience through black America's oldest marketing strategy—word of mouth....Historically significant and visually sublime, *Daughters of the Dust* is like a sacred secret whispered in your ear. Pass it on. (46, 48)

However, if that historical significance is invisible because it is unknown to a segment of the population, those viewers will see a parade of interchangeable African American women rather than representatives of the range of women's experiences cited earlier by Bobo's focus groups.

The film also addresses the absence, for African Americans, of "history" as a continuous written record, a cultural genealogy, due to forced immigration through slavery, separation from homeland, and the compulsory dissolution of families, followed, in turn, by the mandatory assumption of owners' names in order to be identified as their property. Writing of diasporic people of color, Stuart Hall observes, "Because they are irrevocably the product of several interlocking histories and cultures...people belonging to such cultures of hybridity have had to renounce the dream or ambition of rediscovering any kind of 'lost' cultural purity or ethnic absolutism. They are irrevocably translated" (qtd. in

Mercer 27–28). Such translated people nonetheless still long for cultural and self knowledge. A woman following a screening of *Daughters of the Dust* explained how the film recognized that need: "It makes you feel connected to all those before you that you never knew, to parents and grandparents and great-grandparents.... Whatever color you are, people want to feel that sense of belonging" (Hoban 27).

"The whole film is about memories, and the scraps of memories, that these women carry around in tin cans and little private boxes....'Scraps of memory' is also taken from a paper that W.E.B. DuBois wrote about the fact that African Americans don't have a solid lineage that they can trace. All they have are scraps of memories remaining from the past" (Dash qtd. in Davis 114). It is fitting that the film is told in such bits and pieces—whatever individual characters hold. The "scraps" become a tradition, a way of historicizing, a translation. And in the process, the film contests European-derived notions of what constitutes "the historical," which formed another category of mainstream criticism about the film: "Dash displays an antihistorical, anti-informational bent that is highly frustrating" (*Variety*, 11 February: 112). The film's ostensible "antihistorical bent," its lack of "historical substance" is another factor cited in complaints about the narrative's incomprehensibility. For instance, "Daringly, Dash's moviemaking embraces the rhythms and textures of another culture and age. But she isn't always successful in making it clear or accessible for modern viewers" (Garner n.p.). *Daughters of the Dust*, then, sets in motion questions surrounding which modes of discourse are empowered or authorized as history, and as such, suitable for historical representation.

Narrating History

> Ibo captives, African captives of the Ibo tribe, when they were brought to the New World, they refused to live in slavery. There are accounts of them having walked into the water, and then on top of the water all the way back to Africa, you know, rather than live in slavery in chains. There are also myths of them having flown from the water, flown all the way back to Africa. And then there is the story—the truth or the myth—of them walking into the water and drowning themselves in front of the captors. I was able, in my research, to read some of the accounts from the sailors who were on the ship when supposedly it happened.... Watching the Ibo men and women and children in shackles, walking into the water and holding themselves under the water until they in fact drowned. And then interestingly enough, in my research, I found that almost every Sea Island has a little inlet, or a little area where the people say, 'This is Ibo Landing. This is where it happened'.... It's because that message is so strong, so powerful, so sustaining to the tradition of resistance, by any means possible, that every Gullah community embraces this myth. (Dash 29–30)[19]

The family gathering in *Daughters of the Dust* begins at this particular island's Ibo Landing. The story of the Ibos' drowning as resistance to the conditions of slavery, whether originating as "the truth or the myth," reverts to mythical accounts through its dispersal from Sea Island to Sea Island. It becomes a shared or communal story, flying across space like the Ibos fly back to Africa, occurring everywhere and, hence, in European American terms, occurring nowhere. The refusal to identify a single, specific location in the African American rendition undermines the story's "historical accuracy" in terms of Western historiography. For descendants of an oral tradition and a people of the diaspora, however, this same attribute of dispersal ensures that the message of resistance is embraceable by all.

Western European and European American traditions in the discipline of history are multifaceted and complex, but some cultural theorists argue that a central trait, perhaps *the* central tendency, is the weight given to written and factual material, placing it at the top of the hierarchy of what constitutes the historical, valuing such material as closest to ascertainable and objective truth. In this paradigm, "myths" and other forms of oral cultural tradition are considered less historical and so are relegated to a lower position of value in the recording of a cultural past. Because they are not factually based or factually verifiable, they are, in this estimation, closer to fiction than to science.

Michelle Wallace, who defines African American oral tradition as including "jokes, stories, toasts, black music from spirituals to funk, and black English" (78), argues that a significant part of contemporary African American literary and historical practice is "the writing down, or the translation, of a predominantly oral or mythic tradition." But, she continues, this tradition is viewed by dominant historiography as an inferior process of historicizing, used of necessity by "people who lack the broader, more 'universal' knowledge of the scholar and the historian" (243–44).

Although certain schools of Western history have been formulated to avoid precisely such limitations, as in the cases of social history and, more recently, cultural history (Wolff and Seed 8–9), Ella Shohat and Robert Stam concur that it is an always-potential danger of Eurocentric thinking "to equate the 'non-literate' with the '*ill*iterate'," valuing literacy over orality, and assigning "the prerogative of interpreting history to the literate European." They continue:

> But one can appreciate literacy as a useful tool and still question the equation of the written with the lofty, the serious, the scientific, and the historical, and of the oral with the backward, the frivolous and the irrational. (298)

Or at any rate, one can avoid equating the written with fact and the oral with fiction; the one with truth and the "other" with myth. Raymond Williams explains that the word *myth* came into use in the English language in the early nineteenth century, from its precursor *mythos*, a fable, story, or tale, used as an antithesis to *logos* and *historia*. In Williams's analysis, one significant sense of myth has been to use it "negatively as a contrast to fact, history and science" (210, 212).

The historical tradition that Dash, Wallace, and others critique descends from Enlightenment-based concepts of rationality in which reason and analysis are used to "prove" evidence beyond doubt or subjective interpretation, indeed, to an objective measure of accuracy or "truth." Such notions of history are indicated in nineteenth-century Cambridge historian J. B. Bury's contention that while history "may supply material for literary or philosophical speculation, she is herself simply a science, no less and no more" (qtd. in Gay 189). Or the view of Thomas Macaulay, author in the mid-nineteenth century of *History of England*, who saw "history as a duel between reason and superstition, the modern and the medieval world" (qtd. in Gay 197). In the twentieth century, this idea still held sway: "One of the foundations of modernity has been the distinction between fact and fiction, a distinction that did not have the same preeminence in premodernity, where it was the distinction between sacred and profane that was paramount" (Godzich xiv). In contrast, in some instances of postcolonial theory, history is considered "the discourse through which the West has asserted its hegemony over the rest of the world," in part by equating *history* with *civilization*, and then allocating civilization as a property of the West (Gandhi 170–71). Much is at stake in the conceptualizing of history—what it is and how it should be represented.

Concerns similar to Dash's regarding the processes of historiography, and of history as contested terrain, are taken up by British filmmaker Maybelle Peters in an animated short entitled *A Lesson in History* (1990). Peters's is a lesson in history in two parts. In the first, a male narrator transports us through a European-derived definition of history, through the facticity of dates, major events such as wars, and a recitation of prominent individuals—kings and queens, explorers and conquerors—the categories of people that made up nineteenth-century historian Thomas Carlyle's Great Man theory of history.[20] In this segment of Peters's piece, we find that many events from black history have not been included or made famous within European historical discourse. "1490: Portuguese ascend River Congo about 200 miles and convert King of Congo to Christianity"; "1562: John Hawkins starts slave trade from West Africa to the Indies."

In the second, longer segment, images of blacks largely excluded from the annals of European and American history float past (Madame C. J. Walker, Charles White, Matthew Henson, and so on), and then recur later in the segment gracefully flying among widely known, "crossover" personages such as Sojourner Truth, Martin Luther King Jr., and Ethel Waters. These images interplay with photographs of blacks in political struggle and resistance around the world and animated, constantly moving, cut-out figures and objects of African origin. Set to African music, a woman narrator (Peters herself) provides an African-derived version of history, tales of unnamed people told in narrative form, for instance, "It was said that the slaves flew. That magic words were known. In the sky flew inventors, explorers and artists."

The piece's transformation in content *and* structure from part one to part two, in both the nature of the stories told and the mode of storytelling, occurs as a way to disprove the European-derived view. As Peters's narration tells us, "in order to teach history you need written facts. Otherwise it ceases to exist." The second portion of *A Lesson in History* provides a kind of history that, for many Western eyes, is non-existent. This is elucidated, for example, in the following excerpt from the film's historical account of slavery, told in a narrative mode of anonymous, representative characters not through the facticity of names, dates, and places:

> The young woman falls, begins to rise up. But too late. The driver sees her and uncoils the whip. He brings it down on her back again and again. She falls and is still.... They remember together the words of the ancestors, criss-crossing paths, wandering rivers, the beating of wings, grandmothers' whispers. She climbs to her feet. She grasps her baby and begins to rise above the cotton. Past the crack of the whip she soars over the plantation not looking back.

A Lesson in History dramatizes the proposition that European historical traditions include and exclude certain people and certain ways of understanding experience. "It is said that we flew. I don't know where that is written. There is no evidence of the event. Historians don't look for feathers or listen for patterns in the wind. They look for nests and eggs." Western history tends not to look for the subtextual traces, the whispers; it seeks the tangibles, as exemplified in the following excerpt from a review of *Daughters of the Dust*. "Despite Dash's famous research, it's hard not to wish for more explicit detail. I came away stuffed with questions: What's the economy of the community? Who catches those shrimp? What do the houses look like?" (Brown, "How" 52)

It is the very terms of the concept of history that is the problem, not the omission of content, of certain individuals, and of verifiable events. One kind of history cannot be made to encompass the other, which is not equivalent to saying that the other history does not exist. Instead, it means that those of us who are heir to an absolutist notion of history are restricted in our ability to record or acknowledge the other.

The point that Peters conveys about the interrelatedness of content and form, between the kind of story told and the mode of storytelling, between cultural/historical discourses and the representational discourses chosen to render them, is applicable to *Daughters of the Dust*. It is within the mandate and parameters of Peters's film to provide comparative versions of historicizing, one Western and the other African-derived. But this was not Dash's intent. Her purpose was not to create a translation from one civilization to another—a crossover film, culturally subtitled for a white audience—but was rather to depict what Peters means by a "history of non-existence." This is another way of understanding what is implicated in the privileging of a specific audience, but in this rare instance, "black women first, the black community second."

Storytelling Strategies

Dash chose a structure for the film that mirrors how an African griot (storyteller) might tell a family history within the practices of an oral literature. Rather than a cause-and-effect linearity, the story moves off in tangents and returns: "The model is Black dialogue—how they recount tales, the grammatical patterns, the cadence, the way it digresses, goes forward and back" (Dash qtd. in Thomson 27). Toni Cade Bambara describes the film's storytelling mode as, "the African-derived communal, purposeful handing down of group lore and group values in a call-and-response circle" ("Reading" 124). Criticizing the dominance of the text as the overwhelming determinant on which artistic judgment is rendered in European aesthetics, Paul Gilroy describes antiphony, or call and response, as the principal formal feature of nontextual modes of signifying practices such as, "mimesis, gesture, kinesis, and costume" (78). In other words, the difference is not solely between an oral and a written literature, in which the former involves not only an eloquent and complex use of verbal arts but also a process of narrativity in which nonverbal communication plays a pivotal role. The interactions and relations created by call and response are as central to meaning production as the specifics of the story told. "The *griot* comments on the past in the light of the present and vice versa, communicating not in the disengaged, third person voice that has been the hallmark of conventional Western history, but in a manner fully engaged with the ongoing drama of the group" (Cheryl Chisholm qtd. in Shohat and Stam 298).

According to Adetokunbo Knowles-Borishade, there are three primary participants in a call-and-response speech formation: the caller, the chorus, and the responders. "In classical African rhetoric, the Caller is the primary creative element because s/he initiates the speech ritual. This person bears the responsibility of presenting solutions to the social and political problems of the people. Thus, the individual desires of the Caller are subsumed as s/he becomes a conduit who speaks on behalf of the group" (490). The caller is joined by the chorus, "whose role is to validate, to bear witness to the truth of the Word (Nommo)." In this format, the caller "is accompanied by the echoes of the Chorus with cries of 'teach,' 'that's right,' 'preach,' 'Amen,' and 'Go ahead on!'....In African culture, the concept symbolizes and perpetuates the ultimacy of the collective, whereby decisions are made and actions are taken by consensus rather than by solitary decree" (494). Finally, there are the responders, "who either sanction or reject the message—the Word—based upon the perceived morality and vision of the Caller and the relevance of the message." The significance of this relationship is that "a vital portion of the prepared message is not available to the Caller and must be provided by the Responders spontaneously during the speech act" (497–98).

The lesson in narrativity, here, is that social formations select and shape cultural activities in keeping with their particular, situated identities. This is apparent if we take as an example two classical forms of music—symphony and jazz—one associated predominantly with European Americans, the other with African American audiences. With the former, the audience experience tends to be quiet, orderly, and controlled, down to the moments when people are meant to applaud or coughing is sanctioned, whereas jazz is a more participatory, interactive, and social event. The social functions of these two cultural practices vary along with the musical forms. Part of appreciating the text in both cases is "getting" the social function of the event, whether that entails being quiet during the performance, or conversely interacting with the performance by showing vocal appreciation.

Similar differentiated behavioral patterns have been attributed to black and white moviegoers. For instance, the reactions of some black viewers have been explicitly linked to a call-and-response heritage in which the audience takes up the position of the responders and "either sanctions or rejects the message," just as characters do within the text of *Daughters of the Dust*. The journalist Kevin Carter describes the black moviegoing experience as louder and often funnier, "because, basically, many black folks don't watch a movie. They talk to it" (F1).[21] His article quotes producer Warrington Hudlin (*House Party 1, House Party 2*): "We don't wait and politely applaud at the end: We respond moment to moment." Hudlin continues, speaking to the invisibility and "naturalness" of cultural practices, "When you're born into a tradition, you just continue the tradition. Only when I began studying film in college did I realize that people of European descent think in a different way" (F1).

Such differentiated audience patterns may result in one group's finding the other's viewing behavior "passive," as Hudlin does, or conversely, "disruptive" or, when employed within the text, "confusing." Further, socially differentiated modes of interaction with cultural products contribute to the nature and constitution of specific cultural works. As an interviewee in Carter's article points out, the give-and-take of vocal audiences may enhance some types of movie viewing experiences, but it is not conducive to others, for instance, subtitled art films.

Much is at stake in the manner in which various social formations choose their cultural activities and shape them. Bambara refers to the difficulties for a national community in selecting an appropriate spoken and written language, but what she says could apply equally to cinematic representational discourses.

> In the anticolonial wars and since, language has been the subject of hot debate in both diplomatic and cultural arenas. It is key to the issue of cultural-political autonomy, as in, for example, the development of national literatures and national cinemas. Which language shall a newly independent country adopt—that of the largest ethnic group within its colonialist-created borders, that in which the oldest literature is written, that in which the most compelling oral literature is transmitted, that which has been taught in the schools, namely the colonialists'? ("Reading" 127)

She goes on to argue that what is needed are instances of "noncapitulation to the strategies of containment by official and monied types who argue that vernacular is neither a dignified vehicle for presenting the culture nor a shrewd way to effect a crossover to cosmopolitan audiences who may enjoy your cuisine and appropriate your music but prefer that you speak in standard Europese" (127–28). For Bambara, *Daughters of the Dust* is an undertaking in noncapitulation. If it had attempted to create itself for a crossover, that is white, audience, it would have become an entirely different film and privileged an audience different from the one Dash aspired to reach.

Indeed, with its iconography of appearance, history told in feathers and patterns in the wind, call-and-response mode of narrativity, multiple perspectives, and an entire community rather than a single individual as protagonist, *Daughters of the Dust* may well be what Toni Morrison had in mind when, in the epigraph that began this chapter, she speaks of a literature that is "irrevocably black," not because its characters or author are black but because of "something in the way it was put together—the sentences, the structure, texture and tone" (qtd. in Gilroy 78). However, there are serious risks in a strategy of noncapitulation, for instance, never reaching one's desired audience (or, perhaps, any audience), as was almost the theatrical case for *Daughters of the Dust*.[22]

And it is Dash, herself, who raises the greatest difficulty. In Morrison's terms, such a literature is "irrevocably black" because "anyone who read it would realise." But as Dash's opening epigraph points out, and as the distribution history of *Daughters of the Dust* makes clear, if an audience, particularly the sociopolitically hegemonic audience and its representative gatekeepers of culture, is not privileged by a film, it may well fail to "get it," and therefore cannot make exactly the kind of realization Morrison posits.

Morrison's and Dash's statements reveal a contradiction in possibility at a historical moment when *multicultural* merely nods to the fact of other existences but does not refer to being versed in or informed by other cultures' discourses. This is in contrast to *multilingual,* which can refer to a degree of familiarity and proficiency with languages other than one's first language. This is not to suggest that an outsider can somehow possess another language (or culture) or lay claim to it from an insider's position. Such possession is impossible unless that language or culture is one's own from birth or early life. But it is to say that people can become sufficiently skilled in a nonoriginary language to the extent that they are able to operate or make a good faith effort within another lingual landscape. Multicultural in this sense, like multilingual, not only would entail acknowledging, in principle, that other cultures and practices exist, but, in addition, would signify the ability (training and willingness) to travel in such landscapes. This represents an intermediary stage of cultural understanding—that of a visitor, somewhere between an insider and a stranger.

Distributing Identity

In his book, *Spike, Mike, Slackers & Dykes,* John Pierson writes, "I read once that she [Dash] believed that 'white male gatekeepers' were blocking her film and ignoring its waiting audience, and wondered if she put me in that category." And then, as if inadvertently answering his own question, "I couldn't stay awake through the film, and I had no feeling for her following" (98). This, of course, is precisely the problem Dash identifies. If he, or others in similar positions at the initial tier of interpretation, cannot personally relate to the film at hand or to its intended viewers, then that film has little chance of distribution or, beyond that, the kind of relevant marketing that would favor its positive reception. The political dimension of this is that the void in the personal experiences of cultural delegates, those who speak on behalf of others, results in the larger cultural absence of those subcultures they supposedly speak for. Industry personnel are best equipped to promote films that are relevant to some aspect of their own experiences, for instance, stories about young men grappling with identity—in

Pierson's case, films such as *Slacker* (1991), *Laws of Gravity* (1992), *Amongst Friends* (1993), *Clerks* (1994), and *Chasing Amy* (1997).[23]

Pierson, as he acknowledges, has no affinity for the audiences receptive to *Daughters of the Dust*, which is evident when he retrospectively finds Dash "absolutely right that the college-educated, black, middle-class, female, Toni Morrison-reading audience would line up for her feature" (98). The description makes that viewership sound so narrowly focused it is as if he were suggesting, who, besides one of its own members, would not have overlooked it? In almost identical phrasing later in his book, Pierson again describes those who view *Daughters of the Dust* as "an audience of black women who read Toni Morrison novels" (208), pondering an audience that evidently mystifies him.

In the aftermath of independent distribution's miscalculations with *Daughters of the Dust*, the film most frequently cited as redressing the industry's omission of the audiences appealed to by Dash's film was Leslie Harris's *Just Another Girl on the I.R.T.* It had the early support of Pierson, went on to win the 1993 Jury Prize at the Sundance Film Festival, and was released by Miramax in the same year.

At the time, Pierson was overseeing a completion fund for first-time directors, financed by Island Pictures. Well before *Just Another Girl on the I.R.T.* had even finished principal photography, he was prepared to put $100,000 into the film's post-production. As he described it, between *Daughters of the Dust*'s 1991 premiere at Sundance and its theatrical release a year later, "I found a more contemporary project written and directed by a black woman" (98). Given Pierson's track record and industry standing, this was an enormously influential stamp of approval for *Just Another Girl on the I.R.T.*, although Pierson never did make the investment in the film. Once Harris had finished production, negotiations between the two broke down, though Pierson says he later helped her close the distribution deal with Miramax (99).

Still to be accounted for are the reasons the industry was willing to champion *Just Another Girl on the I.R.T.* but not *Daughters of the Dust*. Why, in Pierson's terms, could they (or at least believe they could) relate better to the text, have a better feeling for its potential audience(s), and see it as more "contemporary"—beyond the obvious fact of the different settings and historical eras? Discussion here is not focused on the merits of specific films but rather on patterns of independent film distribution. Regardless of the strengths or weaknesses of individual texts, certain subjects, genres, and styles of filmmaking find favor while others do not.

The key to industry support for *Just Another Girl on the I.R.T.*, the story of bright, ambitious, seventeen-year-old Chantel (Ariyan Johnson) whose plans for college followed by medical school are derailed when she becomes pregnant, appears to be its familiarity. In contrast to *Daughters of the Dust, Just Another Girl on the I.R.T.*'s modes of storytelling, the representational discourses employed, allow more easily for a range of readings of the text as a known quantity. First, its modes of storytelling conform to culturally dominant forms of narrativity instead of the filmic structure based on oral literature and call-and-response of *Daughters of the Dust.*

Second, with its inner-city setting, the poverty of Chantel's overcrowded housing project residence, and the depiction of the difficulties of growing up as a teenager on the city's "mean streets," the film is an inversion of the urban, young male tales, one of the dominant trends in recent films made by or representing African Americans, and as such, generically familiar. Some commentators on the film deny the similarity; for instance, Peter Rainer in the *Los Angeles Times*: "Most movies about black innercity life have been so male-oriented that *Just Another Girl on the I.R.T.* seems like a bulletin from the other side of the tracks" (F4). But with its dominant theme of teenage pregnancy taking the place of violence and drugs—"babies making babies," a topic as much in the headlines of black urban woes as guns and crack—the film can be read, just as easily, as a remake from the same side of the tracks, with a female lead.

For distributors, generic familiarity translates into a known category of film and, therefore, belief in a ready-made audience as well as a tried-and-true marketing and promotional process. This is the development Good Machine copresident Ted Hope describes when he argues that independent acquisitions have become dependent primarily on a marketable concept that distributors "already know how to package," and not on any artistic criteria (Hope 18). *Just Another Girl on the I.R.T.*'s apparent generic familiarity was not lost on Miramax, which followed a distribution strategy, unsuccessful in this instance, but similar to that employed with films aimed at African American urban male teenagers, by releasing it in mainstream, "downtown" theaters in the hopes of capturing a wide young audience inclined to repeat viewings of favorite films.[24]

Third, and most significant, the reason that *Just Another Girl on the I.R.T.* was more accessible than *Daughters of the Dust* can be seen if one returns to Kobena Mercer's terms of the ideologies of racism in which "the black community is a homogenous, monolithic or singular entity defined by race and nothing but race," leading to black films about race: "blacks tend to be depicted either as the source and cause of social problems—threatening to disrupt moral equilibrium—or as the passive bearers of social problems—victimized into angst-ridden submission or dependency. In either case, the tendency whereby images of blacks become fixed into such stereotypes functions to encode versions of reality that confirm the ideological precept that 'race' constitutes a 'problem' *per se*" (82–83).

If viewed as an affirmation of a dominant cultural perspective of race as a problem per se, *Just Another Girl on the I.R.T.*'s spunky, outspoken, and intelligent hero, Chantel, becomes, in some readings, the "source and cause" of the social problems depicted. Vincent Canby in the *New York Times* determines that it is Chantel's "mouth that gets her in trouble," not what enables her to succeed to the extent that she does nor what accounts for her ambitiousness and self-confidence. Although an A student, "her attitude is impossible" and she's "more wise-mouthed than wise" ("Brains" C12). The failings are all Chantel's and have nothing to do with the world in which she exists. We have, here, an uppity woman who deserves her comeuppance. From Hal Hinson in the *Washington Post*: "if Chantel is confident, she is also willful; that if she's goal-oriented, she's also grasping and materialistic and cruelly selfish.... *Just Another Girl* is really the story of Chantel's comeuppance" ("I.R.T." D6).

Charmed by Chantel in the film's first half, reviewers write her off once she becomes pregnant, reading the film as a "cautionary and heavy-handed" (Rainer F4) message against teen pregnancy and teenage arrogance, rather than what writer-director Harris planned.[25] "Asked whether she sees Chantel as a role model, Harris says she was not developing a character to voice a particular moral position, but just to explore the stresses facing teens on the streets today" (Wechsler D2). The alternative would have been to applaud Chantel's perseverance in the face of mounting pressures, which means that, by film's end, she has managed not to be locked into the welfare system, to be taking classes at a community college, and to be doing all the other things she does to avoid becoming what she so fears: just another girl. Instead, in these reviewers' readings Chantel is a lost cause because she gets pregnant and then fails to abort the baby: "Chantel might also have a future if she can avoid getting pregnant or, at least, if she follows good advice when she does" (Canby, "Brains" C12).

In other words, a (white) spectatorial position and cultural discourse which permits race to be located as the source and cause of the problem per se, are inserted or incised into the text, exactly what was so difficult to do with *Daughters of the Dust*. A cautionary tale about self-destructive behavior bringing one's social ills on one's self is not the only way to read *Just Another Girl on the I.R.T.*, but because that reading is possible the film is more institutionally appealing. It is more familiar material and so more easily marketable to a crossover audience whom distributors have "a feel for." The film is brought into familiar cultural and economic terrain, rendering it more comprehensible to white industry personnel, and therefore, easier to target as a commodity to known audiences. A film must verify its accessibility first to industry members, the initial interpretive audience encountered, and second to reviewers and other commentators before it has any hope of reaching either home or crossover audiences beyond. Every viewing audience interprets, making sense of a film and then endowing it with those meanings. In the case of independent distributors, their interpretations become part of a film's meanings through its acquisition (or nonacquisition) and its marketing and promotional campaign. Put another way, in Stuart Hall's words, "I acknowledge that the spaces 'won' for difference are few and far between, that they are very carefully policed and regulated.... I know that what replaces invisibility is a kind of carefully regulated, segregated visibility" ("What Is This" 24). Completely omitted by many white readers of such films are considerations of the role of whiteness in representations of blackness, and therefore, in the received meanings of those texts. As Sharon Willis says: "In popular representations, as in the world, identity politics is likely to go both ways, to become either a site for the progressive use of diversity or an opportunity for the conservative management of difference within existing power structures" ("High Contrast" 3).

The challenge for white viewers is to determine whether such a reading—or any reading—is a case of managing difference by placing the other in a position of otherness, and of managing one's own anxiety about difference by attributing the problems depicted to individual willfulness. As willfulness, the problem could be rectified if only the individual were to behave "responsibly" or, from an alternative perspective, in keeping with existing power differentials marked out by social norms and expectations of behavior.

This is not to say that minority filmmakers are somehow responsible for referencing whites in their work, that their texts should be culturally subtitled for a white audience. Quite the contrary: the onus falls on the industry if the independent arena does not want to be taken by surprise at every unexpected success of an "unmarketable" film or at the (re)discovery of each new audience base. For it is the distribution and promotional systems that, in the first instance, decide what work the public will have access to and, in the second instance, market and sell that film in specific ways. How a film is promoted, how it is explained for consumption, influences how it will, in turn, be read.

For these same reasons, Julie Dash opposed *Daughters of the Dust*'s label as an art film in her wish to avoid the narrowing of viewership that resulted when *To Sleep with Anger* was perceived to be aimed (in *Filmmaker*'s description) at "an African-American art-film audience" and not a wider African-American audience. Or her desire to avert the limitation in viewer base that occurred due to Goldwyn executive Tom Rothman's conviction that because it was an art film, *To Sleep with Anger*'s primary audience was white. "Dash, justifiably, refuses to accept the film's designation as an experimental, avant garde, or art house film, labels that attempt to distance the film from its desired audience. Dash conceived the film as one that would be accessible to the primary audience at which she aimed it—black women" (Bobo 195). To the audiences for which it was intended, *Daughters of the Dust* is a historical drama. In the eyes of its nonprivileged viewers, it is an art film, the nearest label those not primarily addressed by the film have for categorizing it. This is accomplished by an inversion in which, if the film feels dense or "slightly obscure" (as Pierson says of *To Sleep with Anger*), the text itself is considered unfathomable. The limitation does not rest with the particular viewer who is failing to "get it." A representational category is imposed upon the text—in this instance, "art film"—to avoid acknowledging that the rift between reader and text may be a reflection of the reader's own situated viewing position. But the point is that alternate viewing positions can open up a text to entirely different sets of meanings. The situation is similar with professional film analysts—reviewers, critics, scholars—who form a second tier or level of reception that add to a film's meanings, putting further interpretive discourses into public circulation. David Sterritt, film critic for the *Christian Science Monitor*, comments that critics in major cities see, and prefer to see, most films in private screenings specially set aside for reviewers, rather than in public showings with audiences consisting of the film's intended market segment. He comes to the not too surprising conclusion that critics can learn as much about a film from the responses of its intended audience as from the text itself (B9).

If reviewers as a second tier of interpretation considered it part of their mandate to offer multiple or alternative readings for films such as *Just Another Girl on the I.R.T.*, and if the distributor's marketing campaign helped audiences understand *To Sleep with Anger* as, for example, a drama dealing with a generational transition from a rural southern culture to an urban one, those films might have had a better chance of reaching the audiences who could most relate to them, as did occur with *Daughters of the Dust*. And from there they might have spread to audiences beyond, as also happened with *Daughters of the Dust* due to positive word of mouth, reaching Dash's intended "black community second, white women third." Sparked by its appeal among its primary audience, black women viewers, other audiences attended and attempted to understand the film from another spectatorial perspective.

One of the limitations of identity cinema as currently configured is that it is a means of verifying and maintaining otherness, used to locate and situate categories of difference. Cultural theorists such as Paul Gilroy have raised objections to the concept of identity politics because it demarcates only certain, usually marginalized, people as bearing identities. More centrally located others remain invisible or neutral, for instance, "whiteness" is often excluded from discussions of race. The solution is not to abandon the notion of various, multiple identities but to expand it to be inclusive of all social locations, making all positions visible and apparent.[26] Within the independent film community identity politics is too often a means of "fixing" the other, of securing a cemented position for otherness, while forgetting that industry members, too, are situated beings, located by race among other categories. Their racial identity, like everyone's, is not invisible nor is their viewing position universal.

Fixing is the photographic process that gives substance to an otherwise momentary visual image. It is the agency by which the image is given permanency, solidifying or authenticating the image with a materiality as if of its own essence. *Fixing* is also the act of correcting or solving a problem; the term is prescriptive as well as stabilizing. This returns us to Mercer's critique of the all-too-frequent perception of race as a problem per se, in which the racialized other is either the cause or the passive bearer of social problems. Such a perception of race is in keeping with the preferred white interpretations of Chantel in *Just Another Girl on the I.R.T.* Yet, if race cannot be "fixed" for hegemonic audiences—in both senses of positioned as well as solved, and thereby making the "problems" it poses seem less complex or threatening—it is difficult for representations by, about, or for minorities to be recognized or rendered visible in dominant culture, as was almost the case with *Daughters of the Dust* and was the case, arguably, with *To Sleep with Anger*.

To the dilemma of the dual inscription of representation, in which artists of color are expected, in Paul Gilroy's terms, to both depict and serve as delegates for the place from which they emerge, Mercer's solution is that artists be understood as speaking *from*, not *for*. "The critical difference in the contemporary situation thus turns on the decision to speak *from* the specificity of one's circumstances and experiences, rather than the attempt, impossible in any case, to speak *for* the entire social category in which one's experience is constituted" (92).

Mercer's reframing applies equally well to Rosalind Brunt's twin demarcations of representation: illustrative of identity formations and indicating political delegation. In the latter instance, the concern is that cultural outsiders, with greater access to the means of representation, substitute for or speak on behalf of others. The alternative is to conceive of those with access to the means of production and dissemination, indeed all viewers, as speaking *from* a racially and otherwise situated position, and not *for* communities of others. It is also to recognize that interpretations of a text can vary greatly for a viewer when informed by the readings of other audience members, as the secondary and tertiary audiences (the black community, white women) for *Daughters of the Dust* found after the film's appreciation by its primary audience of black women. This is to take pleasure in a more comprehensive sense of multiculturalism, a state informed by the interpretations and experiences of others. Like a multilingual person, a multicultural viewer in the expanded sense and at all interpretive levels attempts to understand a film from other spectatorial positions and attempts to find multiple or alternative readings to one's own. Seeking to occupy alternative viewing positions opens up a text to divergent series of meanings. And if such a multicultural viewer cannot see an entirely different film—the film its primary audiences recognize—he or she can at least see the same film differently, that is, visit the landscapes of other viewing positions.

The examples of *Daughters of the Dust, Just Another Girl on the I.R.T.*, and *To Sleep with Anger* indicate how institutional and material factors can drastically affect the representation of cultural/historical discourses—in the case of these films, the depiction of various aspects of African American experience. Institutional processes surrounding distribution limit cultural/historical discourses in two principal ways. First and foremost, through the process of selection, determining which (few) films will be seen and which (many) others will not be. Second, distribution mechanisms affect cultural/historical discourses, here identity politics, in terms of how a given film is promoted, how it is presented for consumption to the viewing public.

Institutional discourses are formulated from infrastructural factors such as economic and market considerations. But such discourses are also a function of individual personnel, the makeup of independent film's "permanent government." The people who run the industry perform interpretive acts on films available for distribution (to varying degrees based on respective power), and these readings as well as market factors determine which films will be selected and how they will be promoted.

Institutional and interpretive discourses have profound effects not only in determining which cultural/historical discourses will be made public and how they will be marketed but also in establishing the representational discourses in which cultural/historical discourses or "content" may take shape—which genres, whether nonlinear storytelling or forms more closely resembling normative realism, and so on. These choices, in turn, tend to limit the representational (as well as cultural/historical) discourses available to filmmakers, at least those who work on the assumption of or desire for distribution.

In addition to indicating the effects of institutional processes in determining which films appear or fail to appear, the distribution histories of *Daughters of the Dust, Just Another Girl on the I.R.T.*, and *To Sleep with Anger* reveal how much is at stake and how drastically the meanings, values, and understandings of a film can alter because of the representational discourses that are chosen or are allowed to depict the cultural discourses of identity politics. The next chapter looks more closely at a representational discourse, narrativity. It attempts to locate differences, similarities, and contested terrain that exist between independent and Hollywood films around the subject of narrative. The chapter also explores in greater detail how representational discourses can dramatically affect the meanings and readings of cultural/historical discourses.

CHAPTER FOUR

Telling Tales: Narrativity and Independent Film

In the beginning was the gene. And the gene was hungry; to live was to multiply.
—Donna Haraway, *Simians, Cyborgs, and Women*

I am well aware that I have never written anything but fictions. I do not mean to say, however, that truth is therefore absent.
—Michel Foucault

Discussing the science of biological determinism and human nature, Donna Haraway writes, "one thing is undeniable about biology since its early formulations in the late eighteenth and early nineteenth centuries: biology tells tales about origins, about genesis, and about nature" (72). She calls such tales—for instance, those surrounding what has become known widely as the aggressive and selfish gene—the "fictive strategy for producing facts" (73).

Carolyn Steedman tells a similar story of history:

> [T]he historian can always, in this manner, present a plot that seemingly *had* to be shaped in a particular way, according to what the documents used for its composition authorized, or what they forbade: can always present herself as the invisible servant of her material, merely uncovering what already lies there, waiting to be told. It is as well that readers are alerted to the fact that the historian is able in this way to appropriate to herself the most massive authority as a narrator. ("Culture" 613)

Similarly, Susan Hekman, writing on moral theory, suggests, "we are told stories about who we are and hence what we ought to do. Our belief in those narratives provides us with both an identity and a moral practice" (137).

As more disciplines come to understand their project, and product, as narratively based, it grows increasingly pressing to conceive of narrative as a process of explanation and normalization that establishes power by determining laws (scientific, historical, moral, and so on), values, and codes of behavior. In discursive relations, "[w]e discover not a configuration or a form, but a set of *rules* that are immanent to a practice and define it in its specificity" (Coste 53). This applies to various forms of "nonfictional" narrative such as science and history, as well as to more familiar, fictive configurations like the novel and film.[1]

At issue for film studies are the ways narratology, the study of storytelling practices, is currently framed. Ideological studies of representation appear to have evolved on a separate, distinct path while the field of narratology has largely sidestepped the question of narrative as ideological practice. At issue for independent film is the lack, currently, of a theory outlining what might constitute an independent narrative as an alternative to normative realist film; this remains a largely overlooked, unaddressed subject. However, the breach between ideological discourses and representational ones in the discussion of narrativity is not a problem originating solely in the independent arena but an omission in film studies across the board, including, most notably, theorizations of classic realist and other forms of dominant cinema. Such a forced breach hampers the ability to conceptualize fully narrative discourses or to analyze how they might interact with other discourses in the formulation of a cultural product.

Avant-garde traditions and alternative practices have emphasized formal aesthetic discourses as a primary means of signifying differently from Hollywood, and thus as a fundamental basis of their identity in contradistinction to mainstream practices. In the process, alternative modes of production largely have bypassed or abandoned narrativity (or to be more accurate, a coherent theorization or approach to alternative narrativity has been bypassed, although many instances of alternative work do take on narrative forms). Independent film largely has returned to narrative forms, staking this area out as one aspect of its territory that makes it distinct from alternative work. What remains less clear conceptually, however, is how independent film's use of narrativity departs or could depart from Hollywood usage. The effect of alternative influences on independent film as well as the lack of an integrated approach to narrativity in film studies has resulted in independent cinema's overdetermination of formal (stylistic and structural) aspects, at the cost of narrative considerations, as the means of identifying a film as either mainstream or independent. The outcome of this can be seen in the difficulty of categorizing a film such as Maria Maggenti's *The Incredibly True Adventure of Two Girls In Love* (1995), discussed in chapter 2. Similarly, the emphasis on a film's formal discourse creates difficulties in accounting for an entire body of work such as John Sayles's, which tends to be stylistically straightforward but narratively explores multiple and shifting perspectives.[2] Other filmmakers who might be affected by the absence of a notion of independent narrativity include Victor Nunez and Ken Loach.

Whether it is possible to have a narratively alternative film that is aesthetically normative realist (as is arguably the case with Sayles and Maggenti), or conversely, whether it is possible to have an aesthetically and politically (in subject matter or "content") alternative film that is narratively normative realist, directly affects large sequences or modes of filmmaking practice within independent film. For instance, independent films by women have tended to be, overall, less aesthetically experimental than much male-originated work. As was noted in chapter 2, films that focus on women and gender are disproportionately fewer in the makeup of the independent field than the population and audience percentages of women would warrant. Could one of the reasons that independent films by women have difficulty in getting picked up and disseminated, which accounts in part for their respective paucity, be attributed to the less aesthetically alternative approach some of these films take, for example, in the (successful) instances of *Gas Food Lodging* (1992) and *Working Girls* (1987)? Do such films arguably take an alternative narrative approach? To begin to address these issues I would like to consider the case of *Naked* (1993) as an alternative independent film aesthetically and in terms of political content or certain cultural/historical discourses it invokes but which, in certain other significant ways, conforms to normative realist narrativity.

With films such as *High Hopes* (1989), *Life Is Sweet* (1991), *Secrets & Lies* (1996), *Career Girls* (1997), and *Topsy-Turvy* (1999), as well as *Naked*, British director Mike Leigh has made a significant contribution to independent film of the past two decades. Leigh's work is considered independent because of its non-Hollywood financing and distribution; its subject matter (dominantly an exploration of working-class culture); its production process in which, instead of using a pre-written script, Leigh and his actors are involved in a lengthy period of improvisation and rehearsals before filming begins; its prolonged, seemingly meandering scenes; and its character and dialogue-driven quality.

Distributed by Fine Line, at the time of its release *Naked* was described as a strikingly original departure from traditional models, singled out for its grittiness, bleakness, and "super-realism" (Macdonald 17). The film was characterized as nasty and uncompromising (Kempley C1; Howe, "*Naked*" 38), remarkable, unnerving, and raw (Turan, "Leigh's Truth" F1), and as though it "lunged at us" with a jagged edge (Brown, "Swept" 64). Leigh was hailed as a stubborn individualist (Macdonald 17), a director who has never done anything conventional (Turan, "Leigh's Truth" F1) and whose films spring, successfully, "from their being made within a strictly independent context.... as far from the Hollywood model as can be imagined" (Gritten F14).

In subject matter, structure and form, and in some of the cultural discourses it invokes, *Naked* is rightly considered an important and aggressively original independent film. However, it can equally be argued that from a narrative perspective, *Naked* conforms to familiar Hollywood models as much as it departs from them. I will compare *Naked* to *Shoot the Moon* (Alan Parker, 1982, MGM/UA), the latter as a paradigmatic three-act story of redemption. *Shoot the Moon* serves as a standard or generic sample of Hollywood narrative structure; it is not an exceptional or ground-breaking film. I intend, first, to show how the formal system of three-act structure and the ideological construct of redemption operate in concert, which necessitates some discussion of current narrative theory. Then I offer close, comparative readings of *Shoot the Moon* and *Naked*. For if certain cultural discourses are fundamental to hegemonic narrative traditions and practices, then presumably those ideologically saturated forms of narrativity are another realm against which independent film defines itself and strives to depart. Yet, this is not so with *Naked*. When analyzed by considering the themes of redemption and forgiveness, within the discursive matrices of masculinity, heterosexual relations, and the family romance with its redemptive power of love, *Naked* follows the structural, representational, and ideological contours of *Shoot the Moon* to a remarkable degree.

Defining Narrative

In *The Television Handbook*, Patricia Holland suggests that the gap between film/television practitioners and film/television theorists is widest over narrative theory. She describes the theorists' version as "tortuous complexities," and the practitioners' model as "pragmatic common sense." Yet, she continues, despite the schism, "many of their concerns are similar" (117). Citing Robert Mackie and Syd Field as proponents of the practitioners' three-act structure, Holland outlines their arguments about narrativity: first, there are rules; second, the rules work; and third, they underlie all dramatic construction. "Despite the multitude of actual stories with which the world is filled, there are, underneath, very few narrative structures" (118).

Three-act structure does not refer solely to a narrative's structural aspects (although that too) but to all aspects of textuality, including subject matter, point of view or perspective, principles of continuity (unity of time and space), psychological realism, cause-and-effect ordering—indeed, many of the traits of normative realist film. The system of three-act structure can be viewed as the practitioners' roughly equivalent term for the normative realism of Hollywood or hegemonic production.

Central to the concept of three-act structure, in addition to formal, rhetorical, or narrational concerns, are certain thematics, for instance, that of heroism or redemption and forgiveness. This is made evident in the numerous books that analyze and instruct in the writing of narrative scripts for Hollywood consumption. Linda Seger's *Making a Good Script Great* states:

> Although the hero myth is the most popular story, many myths involve healing. In these stories, some character is "broken" and must leave home to become whole again. The universal experience behind these healing stories is our psychological need for rejuvenation, for balance.... In all cases, something is out of balance and the mythic journey moves towards wholeness. Being broken can take several forms. It can be physical, emotional, or psychological. Usually, it's all three. In the process of being exiled or hiding out in the forest, the desert, or even the Amish farm in *Witness*, the person becomes whole, balanced and receptive to love. Love in these stories is both a healing force and a reward. (141)

The redemption of the individual in these stories normally occurs through love (interest).

Paul Lucey in *Story Sense* writes from a similar viewpoint: "Audiences prefer stories about characters who struggle through to some sort of victory or self-realization. This aesthetic—the cinema of optimism and a strong narrative line—is a defining trait of American movies" (85). Significantly, Lucey refers to this as an *aesthetic* rather than an ideology. And indeed it is. For the formal system of three-act structure is intimately and inseparably bound up with thematics such as redemption or heroism. The design of three-act structure not only assists in, even urges, the formulation of certain cultural/historical discourses such as these but also makes them difficult to resist or avert.

In his introduction to *Narration in the Fiction Film*, David Bordwell defines three ways of analyzing storytelling: "narrative as a *representation*, considering the story's world, its portrayal of some reality, or its broader meanings"; "narrative as a *structure*, a particular way of combining parts to make a whole. This approach is exemplified by Vladimir Propp's analysis of the magical fairy tale and by Tzvetan Todorov's studies of narrative 'grammar'"; and "narrative as a *process*, the activity of selecting, arranging, and rendering story material in order to achieve specific time-bound effects on a perceiver" (*Narration* xi). Bordwell calls the latter *narration*, and while he points out that "the three approaches often crisscross," his concern is to explore narrative as process.

By *narration*, Bordwell refers to the formal elements or stylistic aspects of a narrative film: "all materials of cinema function narrationally—not only the camera but speech, gesture, written language, music, color, optical processes, lighting, costume, even offscreen space and offscreen sound" (20). His concern in analyzing how these elements function narrationally is to redress an imbalance in film studies in which the camera's role is prioritized, followed by editing. Further, Bordwell wishes to establish that a film's formal systems are equal in importance to the processes of plot, or narrative as structure, in the light of the predominance given to the work of the Russian formalists in recent narrative study.

Yet, while limiting himself in *Narration and the Fiction Film* to a study of narration, or narrative as process, Bordwell complains:

> The value of this approach [Russian formalist] for film studies would be a little clearer if there were a wide range of work on narrative theory in the field. Unfortunately, the literature on the problem remains thin. There are virtually no theoretical studies of the representational dimension of film narrative, although some work in the theory of genre has been useful. (xii)[3]

A similar concern is expressed elsewhere by Teresa de Lauretis:

> While narrative film has always been the primary area of reference for critical and theoretical discourses on cinema, narrative structuration has received on the whole much less attention than have the technical, economic, ideological, or aesthetic aspects of filmmaking and film viewing. (106)[4]

The puzzle is how to account for this shared view from scholars working on opposite sides of the dilemma: de Lauretis as a theorist of narrative as representation (in Bordwell's sense of the word) and Bordwell as a contributor to the study of narrative as formal system. Or perhaps more to the point, what keeps their two approaches, despite the mutual recognition of need, from being more easily integrated?

Although Bordwell and de Lauretis lodged their complaints on the state of narrative theory in the mid-1980s, the deficiencies they identify preceded that moment and continue unresolved. For instance, Krystyna Pomorska, in an anthology of the work of the Russian formalists published in 1971, writes: "The question now posed regarding works of literature was not 'What is it about?' or 'Why and how did it appear?' but *'How is it made?'* Thus, the literary work was now defined, not in terms of its subject matter nor its origins, but in terms of its construction" (274).

And Sarah Kozloff, summarizing the state of narrative theory in 1992, explains:

> First, however, we must understand the limitations of narrative theory as a tool. Because this field is concerned with general mappings of narrative structure, it is inescapably and unapologetically "formalist" (that is, it concentrates on describing or analyzing

the text's intrinsic formal parameters), and it is up to the individual practitioner to use the insights gained about narrative structure to analyze a text's content or ideology. (68)

The dilemma rests, therefore, on what aspects of the theory render it "unapologetically 'formalist'" and make the inclusion of work on narrative as representation difficult to incorporate, so that considerations of content, ideology, or cultural/historical discourses are left up to the devices of the individual practitioner (one assumes readers, not solely critics). In order to address this question, it is helpful to look at examples of specific narratological constructs and how those constructs are framed.

Borrowing from the Russian formalist tradition, Bordwell describes *fabula* as the story, "the pattern which perceivers of narratives create through assumptions and inferences" (49). The *syuzhet* is the plot, "the actual arrangement and presentation of the fabula in the film." But Bordwell's model gives greater emphasis to the system of *style*: "the film's systematic use of cinematic devices." "The syuzhet embodies the film as 'dramaturgical' process; style embodies it as a 'technical' one" (50).

Together, the two systems of syuzhet and style appear to equate with or create the fabula: "I take narration to be the all-inclusive process which uses both *syuzhet* and style to cue spectators to construct a *fabula*, or story" (344). Bordwell insists fabula is not equivalent to *histoire* in the *histoire/discours* (story/discourse) split of narratologists such as Gérard Gennette and Seymour Chatman.[5] He also does not consider it equivalent to the diegesis, because the fabula is "never materially present" but occurs in or is created by the perceptions of spectators. This appears to force a breach, in Bordwell's analysis, between *narration* as the material aspects of a film (syuzhet and style), and *the narrative* as imagined construct (fabula). Narrative as imagined construct is conceptualized as such in other quarters as well. The literary theorist Didier Coste, for instance, describes narrative as having "no substance": "The word 'narrative' is basically an adjective, not a substantive" (4). The difficulty in Bordwell's system, however, arises from the split between the *outcome* of the processes of narrativity and the material processes themselves.

While there are efficacious reasons for segregating narration from narrative (for instance, the handling of a vast web of interacting, complex, often competing elements in a narrative text), doing so also produces all the problems of partition. Edward Branigan attempts to explain why narratologists "identify 'narration' as a special area of inquiry within a spectator's overall comprehension of narrative" (73). He cites as a fundamental concept of narrative theory the idea "that narration is concerned with *how* an event is presented, how it happens, rather than *what* is presented or what happens"; narrative is then "construed narrowly as *what* happens in the story—is then seen as the *object* of some mechanism or process—narration" (65). This effectively divides narration and narrative into distinct procedures, indeed into discrete areas of inquiry. Once this fundamental distinction is enacted, Branigan continues, theorists like Kristin Thompson and Bordwell are able to "forcefully argue that the goal of narrative criticism is not to uncover meanings or connotations, or to produce interpretations, but to analyze the actual patterns of the specific and concrete devices in each art medium that engage our perception of narrative" (121).

Similar difficulties and "deep divisions" can be found, for instance, in the application of Roman Jakobson's work on poetic language. Robert Stam summarizes Jakobson's theory of communication: "sender and receiver have a common code, and can send a message via a channel between them, about the context or world. Together this ensemble of elements produces *meaning*" ("Origins" 16) or poetry and prose as signifying practices. However, although Jakobson's model describes a complex of interactive factors in the production of meaning, when applied within film studies the elements of his paradigm become segregated. "Romantic approaches [such as auteurism] might be said to emphasize the role of the sender and therefore the emotive function of art. Realist approaches, including some Marxist and early feminist approaches, emphasize the context and therefore the referential function of art. Formalism emphasizes the message [text] and therefore the poetic function of art," and so on (17).

The difficulty, of course, is how can these elements be separated and considered in distinction? How can narration and narrative be partitioned? To do so is to understand narrative as an act of signification but, disturbingly, to remove narration from the realm of signifying practice to that of simply means or process toward a signifying end. In other words, such a paradigm excises the meaning of production (narration) from the production of meanings (narrative).

Robert Burgoyne concurs with the assessment that the most significant work on ideological aspects of narrative has developed outside of narrative theory, particularly in psychoanalysis (70). He believes this is so because "[n]arrative analysis traditionally endeavors to disclose the deep structural patterning beneath the surface features of the artifact" (75). All textual specificities then, that is any and all elements that historicize or contextualize, are part of the "surface features" of a film; attention in their direction serves only to distract from the ability to recognize the authentic or universal core of the story. In much of narrative theory, film texts are dehistoricized, their aspects, procedures, and meanings universalized, in order "to provide a comprehensive account of the laws of narrative structure which operate across genres and across different media" (75). In order for narrative theory to achieve these goals, the tendency is to exclude from consideration any elements that do not speak of all narrative texts, across genres and across media. In other words, referential aspects are omitted because they are not given to universal applicability—in the same manner as plot functions or character actants are. Specifics of content and context—cultural and historical discourses—become points of exclusion rather than signposts of significance in the production of meanings. Instead attention is directed toward supposedly purely aesthetic discourses.

The tendency to homogenize does not occur solely in the realm of narrative as representation, in Bordwell's sense of referring to a world beyond the text. For instance, Burgoyne points out that although Bordwell argues extensively for the equivalently important role of style along with structure, Bordwell is also aware that style has been excluded or minimized by many narrative theorists because "the inclusion of stylistic features makes it seemingly impossible to derive general patterns of composition which might be applied to a variety of narrative texts in different media" (74–75). The formal and aesthetic discourses of style are overlooked for "confusing" the problem by complicating the ability to draw universal narrative rules, laws, or conclusions, for making the creation of a science of narratology more difficult.

Sheila Johnston cites a parallel strategical logic on the part of Vladimir Propp:

> One of the main sources of confusion and ambiguity in earlier studies of the tale was, Propp found, the researchers' assumption that their material should be classified according to its *theme*. The trouble was that often one tale incorporated either several of their themes at once or none of them. Propp also argued that this kind of taxonomy was fallacious, masking basic similarities between thematically dissimilar tales and lumping together quite different, but thematically related ones. He even asserted that "the division of fairy tales according to themes is in general impossible".... Rather than looking at the apparent subject-matter of his tales, he set out to discern their latent, "skeleton" formation. (234)

This assessment of Propp's position raises the specter of arbitrariness in what is given precedence. Why classify according to skeletal structure rather than theme? What seems to gain priority is what is most manageable, that which is most amenable to "scientific" rationality and precision.

Semiotic analyses of narratives attempt to avoid the problem of the exclusion of narrative as cultural representation by emphasizing the concepts of signifier and signified in place of a fibula-syuzhet split. In principle, because a signifier always signifies something, this brings the role of the referential nature of narrative to the fore. According to Christian Metz, "the filmic signifier is as indicative as its signified of the latent significations of the film, the entire apparent material is open to a symptomatic reading (here we recognize the banal but true observation usually rather badly expressed as 'the form' of a film tells us as much as its 'content' about its 'true meaning')" (32–33).

Yet here, too, similar divisions surface. Citing Metz's "Notes Towards a Phenomenology of the Narrative," Johnston outlines his argument:

> Denotation, in the cinema, is the literal meaning of the spectacle; connotation encompasses all its elusive, symbolic meanings. The artistic status of the cinema resides in its connotative qualities, but it is, Metz argued, through the procedures of denotation that the cinema is *langage*. He hoped that eventually the semiotic model could be refined sufficiently to analyse both these strata and their interplay in producing meaning. Meanwhile however it should confine itself in the first instance to the denotative. (230)

Denotation and connotation are viewed as separate strata, with the hope that one day the two can be examined in terms of their interplay. But without both strata, and in particular their interplay, in conjoined consideration, much of the meanings produced are unrecoverable. What is lost is precisely the slippage, the forming and reforming of meanings through interaction. A narrative cannot be apprehended fully in terms of "component" parts.

Contrary to Bordwell's contention that the three approaches to narrative as representation, structure, and process (or however many categories a theorist chooses to configure) "often crisscross," they are inseparable in the sense that a loss of meanings occurs when the three are not considered in conjunction with each other—contextually and relationally together. Each category considered in distinction produces meanings, certainly; but such a process of separation fails to do justice to the range of meanings surrounding any given text. To equate "narrative as structure," for example, with a fully sufficient notion of narrativity is to be left with an impoverished reading.

Simplifying all narrative texts to the same structure or the same few structures limits the ability to identify two texts that might be similar in unusual but significant respects but not in all respects. It also eliminates the ability to see differences. In any instance of comparison between two signs, intra- or intertextual, the signifiers may be identical while the signifieds depart in intentions, or conversely the signifieds may be comparable although the signifiers vary, the result of the effects of form, style, structure, context of use, and so on. The particular range of meanings available from specific texts are the cumulative effects of representational and cultural/historical discourses in action and interaction.

Much current film narratology exemplifies theoretical approaches to narrative that remove the specificities of content and context—cultural/historical discourses—and create categories, such as narrative and narration, that serve as false divisions. What is required, more helpfully, is an integrationist approach toward narrativity, one of multiple, layered, and interacting discourses. This would better account for similarities and differences simultaneously within, between, and across a variety of narrative texts. It would also entail a view of the processes, products, and meanings of narrativity as shifting and provisional, a theory of continuous relationality.

In describing *narrative* as an adjective, not a substantive, Coste is motivated by concerns similar to Bordwell's: to emphasize narrativity as an imaginary construct, forged in the mind of the spectator from material (narrational) aspects of a text. And in phrases such as *narrative film,* the term indeed functions as an adjective, indicating that the work in question is fictional and that it tells a story. But this far from exhausts the possible meanings of the term. Nor does it negate for narrative a position as a substantive, as an object of knowledge. For narrativity is both a material and an imaginary construct.

Cultural production has been understood too often as a construct of seemingly insurmountable binary structures: form or content, art or politics, aesthetics or ideology. These are conceptualizations based on the recurring break of representational from cultural/historical discourses. I would suggest that what holds these oppositions together, providing the sense of coherency of a single, unified text, is narrativity. Narrativity then is understood both as a material and an imaginary construct, the formulation of representational and cultural/historical as well as interpretive discourses. Such a unified concept of narrativity, as cultural referent, structure, and process, has been insufficiently explored in cinema studies.

From the perspective of ideological investigations in film studies, of narrative invoking cultural/historical discourses, the issue is not solely of recognizing that texts operate ideologically, or of analyzing which ideological positions a particular text might convey but, in addition, of determining how that ideology is made operational. How does it appear in the written text or on the screen? How does ideological content take form—material and imagined—in conjunction with aesthetics? I believe it is questions such as these that concern de Lauretis when she observes that "narrative structuration has received on the whole much less attention than have the technical, economic, ideological, or aesthetic aspects of filmmaking and film viewing."

Further, questions of how ideology is made operational are of critical concern to practitioners who wish to represent alternative identities and experiences. Their task is not limited to analyzing how existing texts function but includes being able to imagine otherwise, to construct other ways of telling stories and understanding a plurality of experiences. This is what is at stake politically in the interlacing of cultural production and identity politics.

Applied to three-act structure as a dominant narrative paradigm, these concerns result in questions such as why is it so difficult to produce around, outside, or beyond the three-act structure of normative realist cinema if it is simply a narrational (formal, aesthetic) structure? Why are certain representational discourses, if oppressive or "complicit with dominant ideology" so difficult to abandon or work in opposition to? What makes some stories possible, or even likely, while others are almost impossible to tell? The answer I would suggest, and as the following close analysis argues, is that narrativity is never solely aesthetic but is always constructed simultaneously from representational and cultural/historical discourses, mobilized by functions such as structure and (the often theoretically underconsidered processes of) characterization.

Relationships and Redemption

Released by MGM/United Artists in 1982, *Shoot the Moon* was greeted with mixed reviews. Some were decidedly negative, such as Andrew Sarris's in the *Village Voice:* "I cannot figure out what it is about, nor why it was made" (43); and *Variety*'s: "A grim drama of marital collapse which proves disturbing and irritating by turns" ("Falls" 20). Other reviewers were laudatory, for instance, Pauline Kael: "there isn't a scene in...*Shoot the Moon* that I think rings false" (104) and Richard Schickel: "something rather special is at hand" (79).

The screenplay was written by Bo Goldman who, at the time *Shoot the Moon* was released, had already won Academy Awards for cowriting *One Flew over the Cuckoo's Nest* (1976) and writing *Melvin and Howard* (1980). He went on to become one of Hollywood's highest paid writers, doing the scripts for such films as *Swing Shift* (1983), *Scent of a Woman* (1992), and *Meet Joe Black* (1998), in addition to becoming a very successful script doctor (a person hired by studios to rewrite screenplays slated for production but plagued by problems). The director for *Shoot the Moon* was Alan Parker. His previous films included *Midnight Express* (1978) and *Fame* (1979), and he went on to direct such films as *Birdy* (1985), *Mississippi Burning* (1988), *The Commitments* (1991), *Evita* (1996), and *Angela's Ashes* (1999). Both men's standings within the film industry as well as the nature of the story, render *Shoot the Moon* an apt exemplification of three-act structure. There is nothing particularly startling or unusual about it as a Hollywood film.

Starring Albert Finney and Diane Keaton, *Shoot the Moon* is the story of George and Faith Dunlap, and of how they cope with the disintegration of their marriage. The first act introduces us to their domestic situation, which includes four young daughters, depicts the strains and hostilities between the couple, and culminates in their decision to separate. The second act is driven by the question of how each will cope with the separation (although the story is more centrally George's). The possibility that they will reunite is raised in the third act, which deals with whether there is a place for George in the family and what he must do to "earn" it.

Naked, winner of best director for Mike Leigh and best actor for David Thewlis (as Johnny) at Cannes in 1993, and released in the United States by Fine Line in 1994, also fits into the divisions of three-act structure. The first act details Johnny's escape to London, his turning up at the flat of Louise (Lesley Sharp) and Sophie (Katrin Cartlidge), and the establishment of his relationships with both women. Act 2 consists of Johnny's two-day journey through the streets of London, in which the audience learns a great deal about his life circumstances even if Johnny as a character learns very little about himself. The last act returns Johnny to the flat, along with Louise, Sophie, and the mysterious but persistent character Jeremy (Greg Cruttwell).

From a narratological perspective, the significant equivalences are not that both films conform to the structural pattern of three acts, per se, but that the lead characters' stories have similar trajectories and the characters receive parallel treatments. That is, similar cultural discourses are invoked (heterosexual coupling, masculinity) through, most notably, the narrative function of characterization. In both instances, the main characters' stories are played out through their central relationships—George and Faith, Johnny and Louise. The main character's search is formulated through his relationship with a woman and his (misplaced) role in the institutions of heterosexuality and masculinity. In both films, the lead character has an affair with another woman, largely in response to or in an attempt to get a response from his female partner. And both films are punctuated by disturbing acts of violence, directed principally at the women surrounding the two leads, but in both instances culminating in one, most brutal beating they themselves experience.

Although the triggering incident for George and Faith's separation is Faith's discovery of George's affair with another woman, Sandy (Karen Allen), the film indicates that the two have been unhappy before the infidelity. It is not entirely clear if Faith's silent hostility is new, but George's anger and dissatisfaction are evidently ongoing. Just before the couple's confrontation and separation, we witness a presumably average morning between the two. The children have just departed for school; George, an award-winning writer, works at home. As Faith clears the breakfast dishes, George begins what appears to be his usual routine, complaining and slamming drawers because he cannot find his glasses, then dissolving into an outburst because, he claims, his daughters take all his pencils and ruin their points.

The previous evening, on the way to an awards presentation, Faith is wordless in the car on the drive from their rural home into San Francisco. George, in contrast, glibly maintains a one-sided conversation. The ability to talk, to philosophize, to prattle on oblivious to whether anyone is listening marks a connection between George and Johnny. While Johnny is skilled at argumentation, lashing others with his point of view, George is adept at making excuses, at using talk to keep up appearances.

Although his wife has barely spoken a word to him that evening, George convincingly feigns warmth in his acceptance speech when thanking her as his friend and helpmate. Later that night as his eldest daughter, Sherry (Dana Hill), questions him about his sleeping alone in a room separate from Faith, he responds, without missing a beat, by providing the excuse that "Mummy hurt her back in the crowd. And I'm all pumped up, I can't sleep, I don't want to keep Mummy up," although Sherry, on the verge of adolescence and aware of his affair, does not believe him. And later, after the separation, when the woman at the local restaurant where George regularly takes his three younger daughters before school, asks after Sherry, George smoothly explains that she's fine but, "[t]akes the bus; likes to go with her friends," instead of admitting that Sherry refuses to speak to or see him. Both George and Johnny use their verbal skills for purposes of denial: George to deny his actual feelings; Johnny to deny his isolation, to fill the void that surrounds him.

The narrative question that drives act 2 of *Shoot the Moon*, the longest portion of the film, is how each partner will cope with the separation. At the outset, the assumption (the audience's as well as George's and Faith's) is that Faith will fare the worse. George has another relationship, another readied domestic situation to step into; in addition, he was the one who seemed to want out of the marriage to begin with. Initially Faith does indeed have difficulties, slipping into an immobilizing depression. But while she continues to have ups and downs, she also is able to put her life back together, step by step. George, in contrast, contains and denies what he feels and ultimately must face up to an escalating series of frustrations: the continued refusal of his daughter Sherry to see or talk to him; his growing jealousy over Frank (Peter Weller), the man Faith becomes involved with; his realization that his family can and will go on without him, triggered by incidents such as Faith's decision to rearrange the dining room and, most of all, by her decision to build a tennis court, which she hires Frank to build.

It seems like morbid understatement to describe Johnny's dilemma as a problem with intimacy. Yet some kind of connection with others that would minimize his isolation and rage is apparently what he desires, especially from

Louise. Johnny's problem, however, is that his only means of getting through to others is to anger or hurt them.

We learn, sporadically, that Louise and Johnny were involved with each other in Manchester, that Louise although terribly homesick will not go back because of Johnny, and that Johnny ended their yearlong relationship. Louise: "Thought you said you never wanted to see me again." Johnny: "I don't, so will you fuck off and go back upstairs."

When Johnny shows up, Louise seems wary of him, seemingly determined not to let him get to her, despite Johnny's relentless baiting. Johnny, in turn, seems bent on setting her off, on triggering some kind of response toward him. When Johnny replies only with smart-ass comments and verbal abuse to Louise's attempts to talk with him, she rips up and throws away the postcard she had sent him, the means by which Johnny had found her. Louise, her roommate Sophie, and Johnny spend some time talking together in the living room, and then Louise asks Johnny if he wants to see her room, an invitation for him to spend the night with her. Johnny follows her upstairs but does not enter the room, merely making a sarcastic remark from the doorway before returning to the living room and to Sophie, with whom he has sex while Louise sits upstairs in the dark, awake and aware of what is going on.

The next evening at home, Johnny follows Louise around the flat as she ignores him and as a love-sick, clinging Sophie follows him. Although Sophie begs Johnny for his attention, Louise seems impervious to him, steadfastly and silently watching TV while Johnny tries various means to get a response from her, including standing in front of the TV, turning it off, taking her cigarette from her and smoking it, and kissing her. His frustration at his failure to anger her, upset her, or otherwise affect her is what apparently propels him out of the flat and into his journey on the streets of London.

When Johnny returns after two days, a beaten and broken figure, it appears that he and Louise will reconcile—or at least that Louise (and the audience) believes this possible. She has finally let down her guard and given into his presence, expressing her desire that they move back to Manchester together. But Johnny is unable to follow through on his part of the commitment. After various moments when the two hold each other and exchange looks of affection, Louise leaves for work to give notice. Johnny first attempts to seduce Louise's other roommate, Sandra (Claire Skinner), and then steals the money Jeremy left behind in the flat before hobbling away on his own.

There is no question that the central characters in both *Shoot the Moon* and *Naked* err drastically and that both men are seriously flawed. We see this from the outset, in Johnny's rape of a woman and George's extramarital affair. It is precisely these characters' errors that both films deliberately explore. More than that, the core concern for both narratives is to examine how and why these two men err so deeply.

In attempting to deal with their problems, each character resorts to violence aimed at the women nearest him. Frustrated by Faith's growing intimacy with Frank and Sherry's continued refusal to forgive him for his affair and departure, George returns to the family home at night with a birthday gift Sherry has previously refused to accept. When Sherry again refuses to see him, George, in a chilling sequence, breaks into the locked house by smashing a window and drags Faith to the porch, barricading her outside ("How do you like being locked out of your own house?"). He then goes after Sherry, spanking her repeatedly and brutally. When a crying Sherry finally manages to break away, George, now presumably realizing what he has done, pleads with her to talk to him: "Honey. Please, honey. Forgive me." At this point Faith, succeeding in getting back into the house, rushes to comfort Sherry and orders George out. Although George's actions have been shocking in their intrusiveness and violence, the scene also closes with some visual sympathy for him. There is a high wide shot of George leaving the house: his family is huddled together on the stairs while he is alone in the frame, as if we are asked to view him as indeed shut out from his family and home.

George's restoration within the family is as narratively dependent on reconciliation with Sherry as it is on his relationship with Faith. It is Sherry who first recognizes he has betrayed them with his affair and who is the least willing or able to forgive him. The possibility for father-daughter reconciliation occurs in the aftermath of a fight between Sherry and her mother. Sherry, having recently found her parents sleeping together, is angered at Faith's continued intimacy with Frank. She shouts at her mother: "You fucked my father last week. You're fucking Frank this week. Who're you going to fuck next week?" Faith's response is to slap her across the face, recalling George's corporal punishment. When Frank attempts to intervene, Sherry adamantly insists, "You're not my father," her first tacit acknowledgment of who is. Sherry then runs away to her father's (and Sandy's) home.

In this instance, and in this instance alone, Faith is the less understanding of the two parents. During the subsequent conversation between father and daughter, when Sherry speaks to him with a similar defiant rebellion (born of confusion), George's immediate response is to get angry and walk away from her, leaving her to sit alone on the dock. However, he stops himself, overcomes his anger, and instead returns to talk with and comfort Sherry. The lesson that George must learn in order to acquire Sherry's forgiveness, his own redemption, and the possibility of a place in the family is to reign in, to manage, his anger. In doing so, by behaving like a "proper" father, he enables Sherry to let go of her adult persona, allowing her, for the first time since her parents' separation, to act like or to be a child. In exchange, Sherry prompts George to admit he still loves Faith, making him take the initial step in acknowledging his genuine feelings.

Johnny's resort to violence takes the form of appalling verbal cruelty (aimed at virtually everyone), as well as physical assaults against women, from the rape he commits in an alleyway at the opening of the film to two episodes of "rough" sex with Sophie. In addition, sexual violence is conveyed through the character Jeremy (identifying himself later in the film as Sebastian, their landlord) who, in multiple scenes intercut with the primary story action abuses and rapes women, culminating in his rape of Sophie. Until his arrival at Sophie and Louise's flat late in the film, Jeremy's connection to the primary story is unclear in a causal or plot sense. This encourages assigning a metaphorical function to his character, reading his place in the story by analogy. And indeed, Jeremy and Johnny are linked by their cruelty to and abject mistreatment of women. Such a metaphorical connection allows two possible modes of linkage: we either compare or contrast the characters. In fact, a correlation of comparison or contrast is what links Johnny to all the characters he encounters on his two-day journey, and especially to Brian, the security guard (Peter Wight).

Seemingly opposites initially—Johnny is jobless, Brian employed; Johnny is brash, Brian timid; Johnny is cynically despairing, Brian naively optimistic—over the course of their lengthy sequence the two progressively reveal their commonalties. Both are connected by their love of reading, by their philosophical conversations, and especially, by their isolation—Brian's exemplified by his gainful employment guarding empty space and his feelings for a woman he knows only voyeuristically through window panes and across buildings. Indeed, Johnny is connected to all the people he encounters in this urban underclass by the analogy of isolation. Most of them, except Brian, have difficulty communicating. In one form or another they fail to articulate either their thoughts or their feelings, from the Scottish couple, Archie (Ewen Bremner) and Maggie (Susan Vidler), whose accents make them almost incomprehensible (for American viewers at any rate) and who spend their entire screen time shouting in search of each other; to the woman Brian watches (Deborah Maclaren), who is drunk and seems largely unable to speak except for non sequiturs and guttural noises; to the waitress (Gina McKee) who gets upset and insists Johnny leave her apartment when he attempts to converse with her on a personal level. Although Brian expresses himself well, he seldom has the opportunity to do so because he is rarely in the company of another human being, which explains his eagerness to spend time with Johnny. It is through Brian and the isolated, inarticulate characters whom Johnny encounters that we begin to realize Johnny's propensity to talk is his means of keeping his own isolation in abeyance.

In contrast, Johnny and Jeremy, linked initially by their violent misogyny, grow increasingly differentiated as the story progresses. By the time Johnny completes his London odyssey, we have been asked to understand and feel pity for his world view. That is, we know why his perspective is as it is, where it comes from, why he is so brutal, violent, and frustrated. Johnny's behavior comes to make sense—although not to earn vindication—because of the social conditions we witness. The narrative, however, never permits Jeremy's character a similar depth of perspective. There is no "other" or "beyond" to Jeremy; he remains one-dimensionally despicable, divided from Johnny by class, money, and status.

The progressive divergence between the characters of Johnny and Jeremy is evident in their respective encounters with Sophie, culminating in Jeremy's arrival at the flat and his brutal sexual attack on her. Jeremy's rape of Sophie can too easily be read as "much worse" than Johnny's previous acts of rough sex with her. Here the narrative arguably solicits us to draw distinctions between Jeremy's treatment of Sophie and Johnny's earlier encounters with her because Jeremy's act is more brutal, hurtful and, unlike Johnny's, nonconsensual.[6]

Such a reading is further emphasized, perhaps overdetermined, by the cutting between action: at the same time Jeremy is raping Sophie, Johnny is enjoying some of his most tranquil moments at the unnamed waitress's flat. Jeremy arrives at Louise and Sophie's, introduces himself as the landlord, and physically threatens Sophie. *Cut to* Johnny waiting for the waitress at the end of her shift to walk home with her. *Back to* an extended sequence culminating in Jeremy raping Sophie. *Back to* Johnny at the waitress's flat, having a bath and then sitting in the warm, cozy living room with her.

When the waitress unexpectedly throws Johnny out of the apartment, he, unlike Jeremy, leaves. He does not hit her or rape her as we might expect or fear—and as is threatened for a moment when he forcefully backs her up against the wall. Instead, he spews words at her in an effort to induce guilt for what he sees as his unnecessary homelessness for the night and for her mean-spiritedness in throwing him out.

It would be much harder to read a contrast between Johnny and Jeremy if, for instance, Jeremy's rape of Sophie were intercut with images of Johnny having forced or rough sex with the waitress, although this is at least as plausible a narrative development as the action shown. Stated conversely, intercutting similar abusive behavior would be more likely to indicate the commonalty between the two characters. Further, Johnny's unexpected shift in behavior, not physically hurting the woman or resorting to simply taking what he wants but rather articulating the circumstances of his existence as homeless, marks the moment at which he begins to be the victim not the aggressor. For from here, we move into the third act with its *possibility* of redemption.

Both *Naked* and *Shoot the Moon* employ the common narrative convention of telling their stories as enacted on the women in the main characters' lives—wives, daughters, girlfriends, lovers. Within this structure, Sandy and Sophie are the "expendable" characters, eliminating themselves from the narrative. Sandy does this by telling George: "You're my friend, George. I like you. I love you. And if you don't come through, I'll find somebody else," therefore eliminating the moral and narrative dilemma of dual commitments and emotional entanglements for George. As a character, Sophie, the more sympathetic (because more developed) of the two, parallels the story functions Sandy and Sherry have in *Shoot the Moon*. Sophie also proves both sexually and narratively expendable, the former in how she seemingly functions as everyone's sexual victim. She removes herself narratively when, believing Johnny and Louise will reunite, she packs her suitcase and, distraught, abandons the flat—and the story.

Depicting the repercussions of George's and Johnny's behavior (to themselves and others) in the first acts, and laying out the specifics of the problem during the second acts—Johnny's social circumstances; George's uncontrolled anger and unacknowledged feelings—enables the third acts, with their possibilities of redemption, to occur.

Shortly after their separation and near the beginning of act 2, George returns to the family home, in the company of a police officer at the suggestion of his lawyer, to collect his books. As the ex-couple pack books and talk, George says to Faith, "We need to be grown up about this." The statement, referring to being accepting of their separation and his new live-in relationship, seems to annoy Faith.

Much later, when George brings Sherry home after she has run away and the two have made peace, he steps into a party-in-progress celebrating the completion of the tennis court. George makes polite conversation with Frank, complimenting the court, and Frank, acting as host of the household, offers George a drink. Next, Faith invites George and Sandy to come over sometime and play tennis with her and Frank, saying, "We have to be grown up about it. Don't you want that?" Echoing George's earlier words to her, Faith suggests that the two couples socialize with each other as an acceptance of the fact that the original husband and wife are now in other relationships.

But instead of returning quietly to his new home, George gets into his car and uses it as a battering ram to destroy the tennis court, smashing into various structures, including guests' cars, until the newly constructed tennis area is in shambles. This is certainly an effort on George's part to reclaim *his* home, *his* life—taking them back from Frank, returning them to what they had been before Faith's independence and his daughters' distance. Although George's violence is alarming, the narrative also seems to suggest that being "grown up" is not the answer. In denying his feelings of frustration, hurt, and jealousy, he has been dishonest—to himself and to his wife and daughters. Admitting his feelings and acting in concert with them enable him to "properly" take up his role as husband and father.

In response to George's destruction of the tennis courts, Frank grabs George and beats him, brutally and repeatedly, long after George is on the ground and unable to protect himself. In narrative terms, Frank has the right to be angry at what George has done to the tennis court, to his hard work. The problem is Frank's beating of George is so harsh and so prolonged that the punishment exceeds the crime; George hurt *property* but he did not hurt any *person*. Further, Frank goes after George for the wrong reasons, appearing to seek revenge for the destruction of his work, not to protect Faith and the family. If George has erred once again, we are meant to understand that at least he has done so out of love, out of an attempt to reclaim his family. In contrast is Frank's motive, which is just to get even. In the end, Frank—like Jeremy—turns out to be as angry and even more violent than George, for less admirable reasons.

During the beating, Faith and the girls, seeking to protect George, shout at Frank to stop. When he eventually does, the daughters, including Sherry, rush over to embrace their battered and immobile father. For her part, Faith refuses to respond to Frank and so he leaves. Instead, she walks over to where George lies on the ground and looks down at him with sympathy. George extends his hand toward her, in a gesture that asks her to place her own hand in his. The scene and film conclude here on a freeze frame of George's arm extended toward her. Faith does not respond in kind to George's gesture, but neither does she close down (as she did with Frank), leaving available the possibility that the two might yet reconcile. More to the point, the final image of a beaten George, embraced by his daughters and in supplication to Faith, signals forgiveness of him. This is not a vindication of what he has done but a sign that they (and we?) understand what he has gone through. The beating serves to bring George to his knees, to rid him of his arrogance. He is chastened and punished, the twin steps necessary for his potential rehabilitation.

By the time Johnny follows the person affixing posters (Darren Tunstall), we understand that his incessant, annoying chatter aimed at the taciturn poster man is Johnny's means of warding off his sense of isolation—talk to fill the night void. He rambles on frenetically, making jokes but little sense, till suddenly the posterer hits and kicks Johnny, then drives off, leaving him on the ground. Johnny gets up and makes his way down the street, into an alley, where he is suddenly surrounded and beaten terribly by a group of young men, motivated simply by the chance meeting. This act of violence seems both excessive and purposeless, even in a film punctuated by staccato outbursts of arbitrary violence. From this point on, Johnny is rendered not the perpetrator but the victim of violence and social circumstances.

Somehow Johnny manages to stagger back to Louise and Sophie's flat to fall on their doorstep, a battered, bleeding mess. His appearance evokes immediate concern and sympathy from Louise and Sophie. Tears in their eyes, they attempt to help him as best they can. Now they must deal with the evil Jeremy and the wounded Johnny, under their roof at the same time.

At the commotion, Jeremy, who had been asleep, gets up to taunt Johnny and the women. Johnny, huddled on the floor nearly unconscious and incoherent, is powerless to protect himself or the women. Indeed, he must rely on them to protect him (it is Louise who eventually manages to get Jeremy out). Johnny's powerlessness is made evident in the image of his broken and bleeding body on the ground, towered over by the threatening Jeremy, who is clad only in underwear, as he has been throughout his stay in the flat, a brazen emphasis of his comfort in, his ownership of, the situation: proprietor over both the flat and its occupants.

Johnny's brutal and emasculating beating is intended, like George's, to narratively settle the score for the injustices he has previously committed. Getting mercilessly pummeled brings Johnny to his knees, to the same position as the women in the narrative, no longer the threat but the victim. And in case we miss this point, when Sophie asks Johnny where he has been, he replies, "Down the via dolorosa." As Vincent Canby notes, "Johnny's being sarcastic, but the movie isn't" ("Cruising Nighttown" C3).

It is Johnny's severe beating that prompts Louise to relent, to take the risk of opening herself up to Johnny once again. It is Johnny's beating that prompts her to suggest they reunite and leave for Manchester together and that persuades her to ask for, and receive, a "cuddle" from him. She has let down her guard, built up from experience, doing the two things she had earlier refused to consider: trusting Johnny and returning to Manchester.

As she weighs her options and subsequently begins to count on Johnny to go through with their plans, Louise and we the audience are torn between her best interests (not Johnny) and the realization of her and our feelings for him: wishing they would reunite, fearing Johnny's ability to go through with it; hoping he will agree and so provide a "happy" ending, wanting him to say no for her greater good.

In this narrative universe fear wins out over hope. Johnny takes the money and abandons Louise, staying true to the character he is and the world in which he exists. At great length, *Naked* holds on to and concludes with the final image of a hobbling Johnny, the literal representation of the walking wounded, as he struggles to escape.

Naked is a fierce and risky film, especially in the characters and social conditions it portrays, but in narrative terms, like *Shoot the Moon*, it can be read as a plea for forgiveness by the men who have erred from the women they have hurt and demeaned. Such a conclusion would depend on how one reads Johnny's final act and the film's final image. Are we meant to read Johnny to be like Jeremy, so that Louise and Sophie are better off without him? Or do we feel sympathy for him as he limps off to the bleak circumstances of his life, unable to receive the affection Louise extends? To what degree are we relieved at his departure because the women have escaped his clutches? To what degree are we saddened by the desperation of his departure and his diminished existence? The latter, sympathy for Johnny, appears to be the stronger of the two interpretations, or at least an equally plausible reading.[7] In Linda Seger's terms he fails to receive love either as a healing force or as a reward.

Neither *Naked* or *Shoot the Moon* offers a definitive redemption for its central character. In the case of *Shoot the Moon* only the possibility of redemption is held out, along with George's extended hand. Redemption in the narrative terms of *Shoot the Moon* and *Naked* is posited as forgiveness. But forgiveness can be reached not only by the repentant acts of characters but also by a deeper *understanding* of them on the part of other characters and the audience. Both narratives do resolve with a deeper understanding of the male characters' conditions of existence, an understanding that accumulates through weightiness of details, resulting at some point in a shift in the balance of sentiment in favor of the characters, from blame and anger to forgiveness. Striking narrative equivalences exist between *Naked* and *Shoot the Moon* in the trajectories of the two main characters' stories and along a continuum of redemption based on whether, and to what degree, we can sympathize and forgive, although George's flaws in *Shoot the Moon* are presented as personal, psychological weaknesses in keeping with an individualist world view, while the fault in *Naked* lies less in Johnny than in the surrounding social environment.

This is not to collapse *Naked* and *Shoot the Moon* as somehow both "mainstream" or "independent." Their differences remain vivid. But it is to attempt to conceive of their distinctions and equivalences in narrative terms, in addition to form (alternative or Hollywood), setting ("mean streets" of London or suburbs of San Francisco), subject matter (urban underclass or middle class), and so on. That is, what might we mean narratively by *independent* or *alternative*?

Mike Leigh was right, in response to criticisms of *Naked* as misogynist, to argue that portraying a misogynist character does not necessarily then make the film misogynist (Howe, "It's the Movie" G1), just as, for instance, depicting a rape is not in itself sexually exploitative. Indeed, it is a meaningless argument considered separately from the processes of narrative signification. But similarly, the selection of subject matter (depicting an underclass rather than the middle class) or the selection of an anti-hero as central character does not then necessarily make that film alternative from a narratological perspective. For instance, there appears to be a tendency in Leigh's films for male characters to control the narrative—for men to incite and drive it forward, while the women are more likely to be affected by it. In *Secrets and Lies*, Maurice's (Timothy Spall) character has a disproportionate presence for a narrative that, at its core, explores various aspects of motherhood (Cynthia, Monica) and daughterhood (Hortense, Roxanne). Maurice is the "good soul" stuck, as he puts it, in the middle between the three women he loves—his sister, wife, and niece, all of whom happen to be excessively emotional. He is also the person who organizes the family reunion, guides everyone through the ensuing confrontation, pronounces on its meanings, and engineers the ultimate resolution.

Career Girls depicts two fascinating women characters but lacks apparent narrative purpose, prompting reviewers to refer to it as a "slight" or "minor" film (Rea, August 13, 1997: D4). Again, it is a less-central character, Ricky (Mark Benton), who is responsible for the film's ultimate events. Annie (Lynda Steadman) and Hannah (Katrin Cartlidge), the two college roommates reuniting for a weekend six years after graduation, are depicted as unhappy and unfulfilled. They seem to believe that all roads to their longed-for "true happiness" lies through men but, alas, Hannah is "too strong" for a relationship and Annie "too weak," as they acknowledge during a dinner conversation not long before the end of the film. Neither the narrative nor the characters themselves ever seem to imagine any other potential sources of happiness or success: not in the ways they have changed over the past six years, not in their careers (despite the film's title), and not in their friendship with each other.

Narrative Determinism

The narrative system of three-act structure and the ideological construct of redemption and forgiveness frequently operate in concert. The familiarity and prevalence of this narrative schema, embraced by Hollywood, make adherence to its conventions difficult to resist, whether consciously or otherwise. Initiated by establishing the flaws or dilemma for a character and then delineating what the causes of those flaws are, it proves conceptually difficult, as a third stage within this paradigm, *not* to focus on whether the characters realize or fail to realize their flaws, are redeemed or fail to be redeemed. The cultural omnipresence of this system that links rather than separates *Naked* narratologically to *Shoot the Moon* can be found in other seemingly unlikely independent films.

In *Trainspotting* (1996), for instance, this system surfaces as a "third-act problem." For most of its time, the narrative is unique: the story of a quintet of friends, rather than a single character, connected by class, friendship, and heroin. Their mode of existence centered around heroin use is explored not in order to condemn it but to show, along with its dangers, the pleasures it provides both as a drug and as an antidote to the miseries and meaninglessness of the larger, "legitimate" society which surrounds them.

The drug use is not depicted as attractive; there are too many disgusting and miserable consequences (the filthy toilet, withdrawal, an infant's death, imprisonment, and so on). But it is made comprehensible, especially in light of the futile social options available. One of the pivotal factors making the group's way of life sympathetic is the camaraderie between its members. They form their own subculture, connected by common interests, companionship, and loyalty.

Then, as we approach the end of the film, the narrative veers, becoming increasingly focused on a plot-event—a drug deal—and on a single figure, Renton (Ewan McGregor), as a potentially redeemable main character. Although Renton has been the voice-over narrator throughout the film, from here the story becomes increasingly his alone.

How Renton's potential redemption is achieved is significant: he must cheat and betray his friends by stealing, entirely for himself, the money they have made together from the drug deal. In the context of the narrative, his is an act of escape, of survival, a redemptive feat in which Renton opts for "going straight and choosing life."

There is no doubt that this resolution is intended to be ironic. Renton's choice for "life" is described as, "the job, the family, the fucking big television, the washing machine," and an endless litany of consumer goods and societal obligations. Simultaneously, however, as a smiling Renton steps into the hope-filled light of day, with passport and money in hand, the conclusion plays as straight-forwardly redemptive, as Renton's chance for a "future."

But treated in other ways narratively, Renton's betrayal of his friends could have played as an act lower and more debased than anything any member of the group has ever done for drugs. For Renton's betrayal to be potentially redemptive it must first be made acceptable, both morally and emotionally, to the audience, and in order for that to occur, the betrayal must be narratively justified. This is undertaken through multiple strategies.

First, the story becomes increasingly Renton's against his friends, rather than the group united against the larger social order, as it began. Instead of the film's earlier depiction of familiarity and camaraderie, it changes to show the intrusiveness and filthy habits of Renton's friends as they descend on his London flat. The antagonism among the friends, as though now enemies, becomes increasingly the narrative focus.

Second, the narrative demeans and vilifies the friends in comparison with Renton. The most notable instance of this is Begbie's (Robert Carlyle) extremely brutal, senseless beating of a man in a pub, in the process of which he also stabs Spud (Ewen Bremner) and threatens Renton. This is another instance of making an anti-hero (or morally questionable lead) forgivable by making another character's behavior (Jeremy's, Frank's) significantly worse. The other character in *Trainspotting* who undergoes a negative transformation is Sick Boy (Jonny Lee Miller), who is eliminated as a friend and transformed into a worthy object of betrayal because of his new career prostituting schoolgirls and pushing drugs and because he admits that, given the opportunity, he would steal the money from Renton and the others.

The exception to this negative character revision is Spud. He remains a sympathetic character who is loyal in his friendship with Renton, even to the extent of not betraying him to Begbie and Sick Boy when he sees Renton leaving with the money (which includes his own). So the third narrative tactic, employed in Spud's case, is for Renton to leave Spud's share of the money behind for him, as if to reassure us that he, Renton, is at heart a good guy, still worthy of our identification and deserving of any chances for redemption that come his way. And although Renton's intention is clear at the moment he leaves the money for Spud, the film makes it emphatic with a shot of Spud opening the locker and finding the money Renton has left him; indeed, this is the final shot of the film.

The narrative works to justify Renton's betrayals in order to make his potential redemption viable. This strikingly independent narrative reverts to the influences of normative realist cinema in its hopeful, "uplifting" outcome. Such linkages between the thematics of redemption and three-act structure serve to emphasize that the meanings created by narrative as cultural referent, as structure, and as form or style (in Bordwell's terms), that is, through representational and cultural/historical discourses, are inextricably interwoven.

Towards Independent Narrativity

There is, of course, no single kind of independent narrative; quite the contrary, a potentially infinite number are imaginable. But independent narratives are intended to be, in some measure, a departure from mainstream narrativity or normative realist film. This statement is made with the additional understanding that every text is capable of conveying a multiple number of narratives or potential narrative meanings, subject to various interpretations and changing historical and cultural circumstances. To analyze a narrative, then, is to pick one or more of these narrative trajectories, without exhausting the text's narrative meanings or excluding the possibility of other readings.

For instance, a comparative analysis of *Naked* and *Shoot the Moon* along an axis of gender relations and masculine behavior finds striking equivalences between the two films. Yet, while the material texts, the representational discourses, obviously remain the same, an examination based on the cultural discourse of class might well cause us to stress the strong dissimilarities between the two texts. George and Faith's large, idyllically rural home, as well as the privileged existence contained within, goes virtually unsignaled in *Shoot the Moon*, a matter of indifference or invisibility. This contrasts harshly with the reduced circumstances, squalor, or homelessness of the lives depicted in *Naked*. The latter film is staunchly and self-consciously set in the world of an urban underclass.

Shoot the Moon draws stereotypical class distinctions, principally through the character of Frank, who is used to defend George narratively (by beating him up). Frank is a building contractor who displays less-sophisticated, less-educated behavior than the middle to upper-middle-class Dunlaps. When Faith explains that she wants a gazebo behind the tennis court, Frank does not know what she is referring to.

> Faith: I was thinking about having a little gazebo. You know, like you see at Wimbledon.
> Frank: A what?....
> Faith: We'd have this tennis summer house, like the Japanese, where the children can have ice tea and chicken sandwiches.
> Frank: Japanese?

Later, during an awkward, preintimate encounter between the two, Faith makes nervous jokes that Frank does not understand. And against the narrative device of *Naked*'s homelessness, which motivates Johnny's movements and actions, there is the emblem of the tennis court itself, which Faith contracts Frank to build and which motivates her and George's actions. The court costs $12,000 and although Faith does not have the money at the moment, due to her separation, she is confident she will have it eventually.

Frank's depiction as less sophisticated and less educated pays off narratively when he becomes little more than a working class "thug," resorting to brute force in his savage beating of George. By doing so he also neatly excises himself from the story as unworthy of Faith's affections. In class contrast, Johnny's final beating in *Naked* engenders sympathy, stripping him of any feigned power he believes he has or pretends to have in the world, portraying him as the opposite of Jeremy, whose class and financial dealings bring him real power within the terms of that film. Jeremy leaves the flat intact, no mark on him, dressed again in his upscale suit and driving his expensive car. Jeremy remains unharmed, unchastened, and unpunished by the experiences depicted.

Within a matrix of gender relations and the representation of masculinity, Johnny and George are linked by their humbling beatings, Jeremy and Frank by their brutality. But within a narrative configuration based on the cultural framework of class, Johnny is more fittingly linked with Frank, and Jeremy with George. Further, while Johnny and George are linked or made parallel by their gender roles and serve similar narrative functions within that concept, they represent entirely opposing positions or narrative outcomes when class is the determining framework of analysis. In the latter instance, Johnny is shown to be socially powerless while Frank is "genuinely" brutal; Jeremy remains the figure of evil but George is deserving of forgiveness and Faith—love as a healing force and a reward. When contextualized by class, the two narratives signify differently; they no longer share striking similarities. This indicates that a narrative's meanings are shifting and relational, dependent on the framing historical and cultural discourses (class, gender, family, heterosexuality, and so on) through which a text is produced and interpreted.

Literary theorists have been more successful than those working in film in addressing the totalizing reductionism of narratology based on a singular structure or few structures. Under the influence of poststructuralism and cultural studies, literary narratology is working to add sociocultural, historical, and ideological or hegemonic processes in the creation of a *cultural semiotics*. For instance, in *Hermeneutic Desire and Critical Rewriting*, Marcel Cornis-Pope writes: "Recent narratology has advanced from questions of formal poetics and an immanent analysis of narrative articulations, to an evaluation of the sociocultural investments that inform the production and reception of narratives" (12).

Such a cultural semiotics considers rhetorical (formal, aesthetic), narrative, and cultural/historical processes together—in their simultaneity and interplay. It attempts to account for both rhetorical and referential aspects of narrativity. A narratology of cultural semiotics is concerned not only with representational aspects and processes (generic, structural, stylistic, syntactic) but equally with reading "as a process informed by cultural interests, interpretive conventions and changing historical conditions" (Cornis-Pope 70–71).

Out of similar concerns, film theorists such as Robert Stam have argued the usefulness of the work of the literary theorist, Mikhail Bakhtin, especially his concept of heteroglossia. Stam describes heteroglossia as "a notion of competing languages and discourses applying equally to 'text' and 'context.' The role of the artistic text, within a Bakhtinian perspective, is not to represent real life 'existents' but to stage the conflicts, the coincidences and competitions of languages and discourses, inherent in heteroglossia" ("From Realism" 197)

This concept, then, attempts to account for simultaneously competing and complementary discourses connected to a given text (for instance, gender against class paradigms in *Naked*), as well as tries to encompass the simultaneity of both representational (rhetorical, formal) and sociocultural discourses, whether competing or complementary.

An approach that emphasizes the multiplicity and diversity of discourses in operation within any cultural product at any historical moment attempts to mediate the dichotomous oppositions of form and content or aesthetics and ideology. Independent film strives to construct itself as a hybrid, borrowing from and owing allegiance to both Hollywood and avant-garde practices. A potentially rich means of conceptualizing independent film, then, is as an undertaking that modulates the oppositional framings of prevailing and alternative narrative practices. The means of tracking such modulation is through an understanding of narrativity as a complex, multiply layered, and pluralistic discourse. Through the interactions of representational with cultural/historical discourses—and, as the next chapter explores, with interpretive discourses—a narrative is at one and the same time the material text, the artifact, and the imaginary construct, the fabula.

The next chapter considers two models of independent narrative. One, *Orlando*, develops a more consistently alternative narrative form; the other, *The Piano*, pursues the more hybrid course between alternative and normative realist narrative practices. Both of these are compared to the narrativity of three-act structure in order to analyze what each narrative discourse offers and what its restrictions are.

Chapter 5 also brings to bear the additional strata of interpretive discourses and what their impact might be in the production of artifactual and cultural meanings. Through an analysis of reviews, the chapter traces some of the different ways that a film might be read, the products of the situated viewing positions of those doing the receiving. The point is to outline the significant stakes being contested in multiple, competing meanings, and to ascertain the social and political effects that are the outcomes of those interpretive acts.

CHAPTER FIVE

Psychic Cleavage: Reading the Art Against the Politics in Independent Film

Has Ada ever spoken to you?...I heard her voice. Here in my head.... She said, I'm afraid of my will, of what it might do. It's so strange and strong.
—Stewart to Baines, *The Piano*

Yet this Red Riding Hood falls head over heels in love with the wolf, who turns out to be not a sheep in wolf's clothing, but a recklessly romantic Prince with dirty fingernails.
—Vincent Canby

The Piano seduces and excites audiences with its uncritical portrayal of sexism and misogyny.
—bell hooks

The voice Stewart (Sam Neill) hears in his head is Ada's (Holly Hunter) "mind's voice" which the audience hears twice: in voice-over narration at the opening and closing of *The Piano*. The otherwise mute Ada describes her mind's voice to nine-year-old Flora (Anna Paquin) while attempting to explain the disappearance of the child's father. The scene is subtitled for the audience as mother communicates with daughter in sign language. Ada tells Flora that she did not need to speak with him (he remains unnamed) as she could, instead, lay her thoughts in his mind, "like they were a sheet." They were never married, however, because he got frightened and stopped listening.

The "fairy tale" ("Forceful Lessons" 18) Vincent Canby describes is a film "so good, so tough, so moving and, especially, so original" ("Early Favorite" C13)—similar high praise repeated by many other reviewers of *The Piano*.

hooks's indictment of the film as sexist and misogynist appears in an article in which she contrasts widespread criticism of gangsta rap to praise for *The Piano* (26–29). hooks argues that young, African American men are blamed as individuals for sexist, misogynist, and violent lyrics although no attempt is made to identify and critique the cultural context in which gangsta rap exists. It is that surrounding cultural context, the "larger structures of domination" (27), that socializes individual behavior and, indeed, is necessary for the continuation of those dominant systems. "It is much easier to attack gangsta rap than to confront the culture that produces that need" (29). The cultural context must change in order for, in the instance of gangsta rap, young black men to be socialized differently. At the same time, hooks contends that the similar omission of a cultural and historical context in *The Piano* results in a sexist portrayal of women that reinforces patriarchy and, in its depiction of the Maori, racism. "Violence against land, natives, and women in this film…is portrayed uncritically, as though it is natural, the inevitable climax of conflicting passions" (28). However, in stark contrast to gangsta rap, *The Piano* is applauded for doing what it does because it falls within the boundaries of high culture.

These three epigraphs mark helpful parameters for an examination of the reception of the 1993 film, written and directed by Jane Campion, and distributed by Miramax. While whole-heartedly agreeing with hooks's assessment of the widespread omission of social, political, economic, and psychic aspects in the analyses of cultural products dealing with gender, race, and many other issues, I would argue that her example of *The Piano* is a poor choice precisely because it is one of the rare filmic instances in which female sexuality and identity are expressed in cultural and ideological terms. Her indictment of *The Piano* as misogynist may reside more squarely with the film's critical reception than in her having exhausted potential readings of the narrative text itself. It is necessary to layer into the processes of meaning production the effects of interpretive, reception, or audience discourses. In the instance of this analysis, the primary interpretations assessed are those of reviewers of *The Piano*, a second tier of interpretation that comes after industry personnel and before a wider market of the film's targeted viewers. The issue at hand is how reviewers' readings influence the stabilization of a text's meanings.

It is difficult to determine the extent to which newspaper and magazine reviews affect public interpretations of films. While they may serve as indicators of how films can, and perhaps are, being read, they clearly do not speak for all viewers. However, their public role may help forge culturally negotiated interpretations of any given text; they may participate in the consolidation process of what come to be widely accepted readings. Certainly the movie industry perceives the influence of reviewers to be important, indicated, for instance, in the widespread incorporation of quotes from critical reviews in the body of a film's own promotional material. The use of quotations is meant to appeal to the "objectivity" and "expertise" signified by critical practice.

Speaking of the intraindustry influence of film reviewers, Martin Scorsese notes, "I kind of depend on the critics. They make it possible for certain people at certain studios at a given time to give me money for the next picture. That's the key thing" (qtd. in Hirschberg, "Two Directors" 94)

The influence of reviewers may be even greater for the independent industry, which considers positive reviews an important measure of a film's likely success in its decision to distribute a work, and one of the most effective means of promoting it subsequently. With some high-profile exceptions such as Miramax, which utilizes large advertising and promotional budgets, independent distributors rely heavily on positive national and local reviews. Conversely, the effect of negative reviews can be fatal to a film's outcome. For instance, a Zeitgeist distributed film, *Vermont Is for Lovers* (1993), never played in New York, the most important independent market in the United States as well as the homebase for the distribution company, because of a negative review by Vincent Canby in the *New York Times* after the film was screened at a festival in the city. According to Zeitgeist cofounder Emily Russo, "That made it impossible to open here effectively" (qtd. in Glucksman, "More Things Change" 28). Similarly, one can remember John Pierson's explanation, cited in chapter 3, of the significant extra work put into the New York release of *Slacker* (1991) in order to overcome a poor review in the *New York Times* (also by Canby). And although independent filmmakers may dread the possibility of negative reviews killing any chances for their film, they are simultaneously dependent on earning some critical attention before they can even hope to receive distribution because of the importance placed on positive reviews in distributors' assessments. The screening of a number of nondistributed films at the Lincoln Center, sponsored by the Independent Feature Project, is perceived as a positive move because it "will assure filmmakers a *New York Times* review, which may help garner national distribution" (Garrett, "New Venues" 16). A similar argument suggests that the "real award" in being chosen for the New York Film Festival is the "virtual guarantee" of a *New York Times* review (Basoli, "2000" 30).

However much mainstream reviewers influence positive or negative audience responses to a film or help shape specific readings of a film's narrative, their critical practice can stand as emblematic of common, dominant reading practices. That is to say, critical activity can indicate something about the contemporary processes and politics of hermeneutics. As Meaghan Morris argues:

> In the heterogeneity of a postindustrial culture, reviewers of film are not arbiters of taste, or judges, or even representative consumers, but mercenaries in the stabilizing force of the Thought Police. We do not decree what should be thought about any par-

ticular *film*; but we do help to patrol the limits of what is safely *or* adventurously thinkable as *cinema* at any given time. (111)

The permissible boundaries of film reviewing—what can be said about films and how—can tell us something of the way cinema may be culturally constructed at any historical moment. At the same time, widely accepted versions of a film's meanings are not the only way a work may be interpreted; reviewers' reception of a text should not be elided with the text itself, omitting alternative or multiple readings as, I believe, bell hooks does. By offering an alternate interpretation of *The Piano* from my own situated viewing position (as a feminist and a proponent of identity politics), I argue that instead of *The Piano* being excused in ways that gangsta rap is not, largely through its classification as high art, the film's reception actually mirrors the same cultural omissions hooks identifies. By praising it as high art, reviewers refuse to recognize the cultural and historical dynamics represented in the film. In other words, condemnation of gangsta rap without contextualization and high-art praise for *The Piano* may have parallel detrimental effects in marginalizing alternative cultural positions and function in similar ways in the continuation of prevailing ideological discourses and power structures.

Selling a Love Story

hooks's contention that *The Piano's* designation as an art film shields it from ideological scrutiny derives, in part, from reviewers' responses to the film. Her article quotes Roger Ebert: "One of the most enchanting, startlingly original, erotic love stories ever filmed!" (27). Ebert's sentiments, and some of his choice of words, are repeated from review to review: erotic, passionate or sensual, and most frequently of all, romantic.[1] These defining frames of reference are then recycled as the film's own claims through its print ads. Miramax, the U.S. distributor, selected an image of a smiling Holly Hunter, her eyes shut, as Harvey Keitel, standing behind her, kisses her cheek. The ads follow the standard practice of accompanying the image with reviewers' quotes. Varying with each specific market, a local film critic is cited, along with additional nonregional citations. For instance, one version of the ad in the *Los Angeles Times* reads, in bold print: "'A wildly beautiful love story!', Peter Travers, *Rolling Stone*; 'Breathtaking…exhilarating…a triumph!', Vincent Canby, *New York Times*; 'Passionate and romantic!', Kenneth Turan, *Los Angeles Times*". A comparable version in the *New York Times* includes: "'Exhilarating!', Vincent Canby, *New York Times*; 'A Masterpiece! A tidal wave of sensuality!', Jami

Bernard, *New York Daily News*; 'A riveting, erotic film!', David Ansen, *Newsweek*". In the *Philadelphia Inquirer*, Carrie Rickey's "A recklessly romantic, sensual and passionate film!" is accompanied by the same Roger Ebert quote cited in hooks' article.

Much less frequently cited in reviews are the disturbing aspects of the film's love story, and only rarely are links made between *The Piano*'s elements of violence or degradation and its eroticism, a link made explicitly and repeatedly within the text itself. George Baines's (Harvey Keitel) arrangement with Ada to barter the return of her piano for sexual favors, one black key at a time, is prostitution. Although no money changes hands in this business transaction, Baines has identified something equivalently crucial to Ada's survival. Ada's recognition of the transaction's nature is implicit in her lack of sexual response to Baines, remaining motionless when he touches her, until after the deal is canceled. Stewart, Ada's husband, nearly rapes her twice, the second time while she is still unconscious after he has chopped off her finger with an axe. This mutilation is Stewart's response to Ada's affair with Baines, accompanied by threats to repeat the action in the future if she continues to see him.[2] Stewart has the apparent legal right, as Ada's husband, to enact this punishment; no criminal repercussions occur. He also has the apparent right to physically barricade Ada in the house as a means of preventing her from seeing Baines—nailing shut the windows and doors from the outside.

Ada has no say in her piano being left on the beach, no say in its sale to Baines or in the requirement that she give him piano lessons. Her very presence in nineteenth-century New Zealand is the result of economic and legal constraints imposed on her as a woman, her father having arranged for her marriage to this unknown man. The implication exists that her father chose such a remote marriage because she had "erred" in the past (her illegitimate daughter), her previous sexual transgression making her unsuitable for a less distant, more desirable arrangement.

All the acts of violence or constraint imposed on Ada are tied to sexuality in some way, whether through the "transgression" of her previous sexual experience, Baines's desire for her, or Stewart's possessive rage in response to her affair. If there are no repercussions for Stewart, there certainly are for Ada; she suffers the consequences of other people's desires enacted on her. In addition, she is consistently punished for her own existence as both a woman and a sexual being, seemingly impossibly contradictory categories. This can be seen no more clearly than in the central metaphor of the film—her piano.

That the piano represents Ada's sexuality is made clear from the deep pleasure that transports her when she plays, ecstatically transforming her face and loosening her normally rigid body. It is also made evident in the ferocious desire with which she fights for the instrument she must have. It is the depth of her desire and the transformation it creates that Baines recognizes when he leads mother and daughter back to the abandoned piano, watching carefully as Ada plays her music while Flora plays on the beach.

Simultaneously, however, the piano also represents the repression of Ada's sexuality and the sublimation of her sexual desires into her music. Images of the repression of women's sexuality recur in the film, from the layers of hoops, skirts and underclothing that render Ada's body hidden and inaccessible to the dark and airless house into which she is barricaded to prevent her from seeing Baines. The contrast between Ada and Baines during his piano lessons is striking. He is able to display his desires, along with his body, for instance suddenly appearing naked, while she must conceal her desire and simultaneously police or withstand his. He has the ability to speak his desire, to ask for what he wants in progressive steps, from touching her arm to lying naked beside her, while her sexuality is silenced. The numerous instances of playfulness and physical affection between Ada and Flora indicate Ada's ability to be tender. Hers is not an individual failing of coldness, but the collision of her sexuality with external forms of repression.

The sublimation of Ada's sexuality into her music, the piano embodying her body, occurs because Ada, better than anyone, understands that—within the context in which she lives—sexual desire, both her own and others', is a dangerous force that will bring her punishment. Indeed, the unleashing of her sexual desires leads directly to her permanent physical mutilation by Stewart.

But unlike the classic cinematic depiction of women's sexuality as transgression meriting only punishment, Ada's sexuality is a force of power and ecstasy: the erotic, passionate, and sensual that critics describe. The fault lies, precisely, in the cultural context surrounding Ada. In this narrative perspective it is Stewart who errs for his desire to own her as he desires to own land; for his complete inability to understand that which he wishes to possess, whether Ada or the Maori's sacred burial ground. It is Baines who comes to realize he has erred in attempting to have her by buying her: "The arrangement is making you a whore and me wretched. I want you to care for me but you can't." From this narrative perspective it is Ada who does not err: she has kept her capacity to feel what she feels despite the pervasive tactics of oppression that surround her; she has nurtured the strong and delightful girl who is her "illegitimate" daughter.

In its complexity, the representation of women's sexuality in *The Piano* is unusual. The intensity of Ada's desires are inseparable from the threat of violence to body and soul. It is the film's encompassing portrait of the power of desire coupled with the potential for punishment that makes its representation of women's sexuality so compelling and, arguably, recognizable to many women's lived experiences.

While the piano symbolizes Ada's sexuality, its passion and repression, it has also become her voice. Ada has been mute from the age of six, we learn during her opening voice-over, the same age, "five or six," Stewart later tells Baines she began playing the piano.[3] We also learn from Ada's narration that her silence does not originate from a disability or illness but is the result of her own volition.

Ada's muteness recalls the feminist narrative thematic of silence in films such as Marleen Gorris's *A Question of Silence* (1981) in which three women, strangers to each other, beat and murder a man in a dress shop one day, a man they do not know. The women refuse to speak in their own defense. They resist all demands to explain their motivations because under the dominion of a patriarchal societal structure they cannot do so in any way that would make sense in terms of legal, psychiatric, and other discourses. Prevailing concepts of sanity, reason, and so on, would only serve to indict them in a world in which women have no language or voice of their own, and so, the women opt for the resistance of silence.

Ada's muteness has similar qualities of passive resistance. In the cinematic depiction of a world in which the individual cannot single-handedly overcome oppressive social structures, all that is left to Ada is a retreat into the resistance of silence. In Ada's case, because of the force of her will, her withdrawal is not the silence of timidity or defeat. Ada's muteness and her will are inseparable. Describing her decision to stop speaking through sheer force of will in the opening narration, Ada explains, "My father says it is a dark talent and the day I take it into my head to stop breathing will be my last." And during the film's closing voice-over, after her near drowning, she continues, "My will has chosen life. Still, it has had me spooked and many others besides." In classic realist or normative realist traditions, Ada's willfulness would be cause for narrative punishment. Here it is her will that enables her to survive (her drowning, her marriage), and it is her will that renders her silence a resistance. Together, Ada's sexuality, in its expression and repression; her silence; and her will—"so strange and strong" as her mind's voice tells Stewart—all comprise Ada's character and the force of her circumstances.

If, as I am arguing, the links between desire and violence, oppression and resistance, are so prevalent in *The Piano* how, then, does one account for reviewers omitting them? Indeed, praising *The Piano* as a sensual, sexually charged love story without specifying its disturbing elements of violence, degradation, intimidation, legally and economically mandated dependency, and so on, leaves that reading's viewers with an alarmingly perverse "romance" in which Ada is swept off her feet by a man who attempts to buy her body and affections (in an arrangement not dissimilar to the marriage deal cut between her father and Stewart) and that Ada apparently likes. Or at any rate, if she initially balks, her resistance is broken down by this "recklessly romantic Prince with dirty fingernails." In this reading, taken up by a wide spectrum of popular reviewers, as well as in the distributor's promotional campaign, the film becomes a traditional love story between three individuals: Ada the woman, Baines the good lover, Stewart the bad lover, thus reverting to hegemonic cultural notions of romance and an equally familiar cinematic exemplification of the romance genre. To see *The Piano* as simply "enchanting" or "charming" is to negate the context of power structures, the cultural/historical discourses, in which the individual characters are embedded. Without reference to acts depicted in the film such as rape, prostitution, and spousal abuse, reviewers fail to link sexuality and the treatment of women with patriarchal discourses, and therefore have to—or choose to—opt instead for the ever-reliable "wrong man" theory in which Baines supplants the hopeless Stewart and a gender equilibrium is successfully reimposed.

While Ada and Baines are romantically united in the film and this is indeed an erotic love story, the significance of their relationship makes little sense—except in the deeply disturbing terms of violence and possession as pleasure, the misogyny that hooks identifies—in the absence of reference to surrounding, depicted hegemonic relations. The omission of the dark elements of the film in many reviews was noted by some reviewers. In *Ms. Magazine*, Kathi Maio, while calling the film brilliant, noted that *The Piano* was winning most praise from male critics who were labeling it as "feminist." Maio writes that, in contrast, a number of women commentators were disturbed by the "grand passion" between Ada and Baines because it is based on a "sexual shakedown," Baines's extortionist arrangement of bargaining piano keys for physical intimacies with Ada (84). Ultimately, Maio argues that the film is a feminist story because of Ada's direct negotiations with Baines, unlike the marriage deal between two men; because Baines is capable of questioning his position in relation to Ada and comes to realize that "love cannot be coerced"; because Ada chooses who she will love. "In similar stories, only madness or death offers comfort to the woeful, willful heroine. But Ada refuses to become the mad woman in the attic or the tragic loser washed out to sea." In this argument, the film is successful despite the foundation of the central coupling in a sexual shakedown. In contrast, it is possible to argue that the film is compelling because of the source of the romantic relationship; its origination in a sexual-financial transaction, made possible by an imbalance of power, links the individual stories to larger cultural discourses.

Living in Culture

Although both men are colonizers, what separates Baines from Stewart is his potential to recognize that which eludes Stewart: the distinctions between possession and passion, ownership and love. What links Baines to Stewart, and to every other character in the film, is that he is not immune to nor can he live outside the bounds of ideology, that he, like all the characters, are historically and culturally constructed beings. Baines eventually cancels the deal and returns the piano, having come to realize what he wants from Ada is that which he cannot coerce—the reciprocity of her feelings. However, in the process his greater economic and social power is made clear because he has the means to obtain the piano from Stewart while Ada does not and because he can, and does, force lessons from her.

Ada's initial attitude toward Baines, informed by class, is further indication of every character's lack of immunity from hegemonic discourses. When Stewart first tells Ada about the lessons she must give, her response is, "He's an oaf. He can't read. He's ignorant." Ada initially disdains Baines for his illiteracy, personal hygiene, and living conditions in contrast to Stewart's more acceptable "landed gentry" surroundings and comportment: Stewart's combing his hair, for instance, before greeting Ada contrasts with the close-ups of Baines's dirty fingernails.

Unlike mainstream cinema's narrative of individualism in which single entities fight the system and prevail over hegemonic structures, no character in *The Piano* lives beyond the jurisdiction of ideological forces. Indeed, no world beyond hegemonic cultural/historical discourses and forces exists in the diegesis of the film. Nowhere can this be seen more clearly than with Flora, a character who sympathetically engages us and whose youthfulness might suggest a measure of innocence. Yet despite Flora's powerful will, which mirrors Ada's own, despite her strong imagination, which fabricates the colorful tales she tells, despite her adamant assertions to the contrary, Flora too falls prey to gender-divided power relations. Early on, as mother and daughter are alone and stranded on the beach, awaiting Stewart's arrival, Flora vows, "I'm not going to call him Papa. I'm not going to call him anything. I'm not even going to look at him." But by the time Stewart barricades Ada in the house (immediately following his first attempted rape of her in the woods, interrupted only by Flora's arrival), Flora has relented and blames her mother for the imprisonment, "You shouldn't have gone up there [to Baines], should you. I don't like it, nor does Papa."

It is Flora who betrays her mother by becoming, after all, the good daughter. As Carolyn Steedman notes, "[t]he essence of being a good child is taking on the perspective of those who are more powerful than you" (*Landscape* 44). Ada tells Flora to take a piano key in which she has burnt the words, "Dear George you have my heart Ada McGrath," to Baines, saying it belongs to him. Instead, Flora responds to the rule of the father, taking the key to Stewart and explaining, "Mother wanted me to give this to Mr. Baines. I thought maybe it wasn't the proper thing to do." The receipt of the engraved piano key results in the already frenzied Stewart chopping off Ada's finger with an axe and sending that to Baines instead—carried by a hysterical Flora, a cruel reward for the child's dutifulness to him.

Although every character is informed by and shares complicity in hegemonic social relations, and although those power relations prevail throughout the diegesis, for reviewers, particularly male reviewers, it may be more comfortable to see the film as a "grand passion" in Maio's words, the more familiar struggle between hero and miscreant, right and wrong man, than as an indictment of gendered power relations. It may be more palatable to believe that some individuals, like Baines (and perhaps themselves), comprehend and act on what wrong men, like Stewart, fail to get. This could account for the film's widespread interpretation as a high-art romance, leaving the text's references to and resonances of gendered power structures obscured or obliterated. While such a reading may represent the desired interpretation for many reviewers, it is also necessary to account for the aspects of this particular narrative that allow such a reading to become the reviewer-preferred one. As David Morley points out, "It is central to the argument that all meanings do not exist 'equally' in the message: it has been structured in dominance, although its meaning can never be totally fixed or 'closed'" (qtd. in Masterman 218–219).

While there has been much debate about the extent to which meanings are structured within the text ("structured in dominance"), instead of being the result of interpretive acts, following Morley's argument, the encoding process manages, guides, or enables potential readings to some significant degree. In the case of *The Piano* this occurs in complex ways, particularly in the overlap and competition among differing aesthetic and narrative representational discourses.

Combining Storytelling Modes

A striking aspect of *The Piano* is its strategy of combining prevailing and alternative modes of storytelling. In the accessibility of its storyline, a largely nonfragmented diegetic space predicated on psychological identification with central characters, and with the decision to cast recognizable Hollywood actors, *The Piano* reflects normative realist cinematic practices. In its visual appearance—both mise-en-scène and camera work—and in certain other narrative choices (for instance, the thematic motif of silence coinciding with a central concern of the feminist avant-garde), the film is an extension of alternative traditions. This strategy of combination creates a hybrid narrative form that is one of the hallmarks of independent film and that serves to open up certain narrative possibilities.

In its accessibility, and thus its potential for more widespread popularity, *The Piano* sidesteps some of the difficulties of a more "purely" but still successful art-house film like Sally Potter's *Orlando* (1993, released by Sony Classics), which received reviews praising its visual splendor but questioning the "slightness" of its content (Feay 18).[4] This perceived slightness, however, can be attributed as easily to *Orlando*'s unfamiliar narrative strategies than to any lesser ambitions on the film's part.

However, as an embodiment of alternative practice, *The Piano* avoids some of what have been argued are the possibly inherent pitfalls of normative realist cinema. For instance, experimental formal elements assist in keeping the audience aligned with Ada's story, so that they understand events from her perspective. Indeed, this occurs to a remarkable degree for a film in which the main character is mute. Camera, score, and mise-en-scène (e.g., its palette) supplant the convention of narrative "intermediaries," that is, characters who explain the purported central characters' circumstances (as we will see with *The Accused*)—disability or victimization apparently precluding them from doing so on their own behalf. In the process, the intermediaries arguably take over the narrative because it is they who undertake the dramatic journey, coming to see the world or themselves differently through contact with the "other."[5] Although Baines returns the piano to Ada, his behavior does not take over to the extent that the central narrative concern becomes the story of his redemption through her love[6] or of his struggle to avenge her mistreatment, as is too often the case in depictions of heterosexual romance. Rather than a struggle between the right and wrong men attempting to "protect" or possess her, the story remains Ada's: she escapes from Stewart through the strength of her mind's voice; she saves herself from drowning—neither are Baines's doing.

Further, and crucially, alternative narrative strategies help keep the story embedded in the discourses of distorted power relations instead of having the story revert to the individual who fights—and triumphs over—the system. This is evidenced in our ability to perceive Stewart's actions to be as pitiable as they are loathsome, he too being a product of the belief systems and hegemonic discourses that engulf him. Another, more common narrative course would be to depict Stewart as the singularly obsessive and often inexplicably motivated villain relied on by some Hollywood narratives, whose villainy can only be accounted for, seemingly, by individual choices. But as discussed above, no one in this film exists beyond or outside of patriarchal ideological structures, just as in *Orlando* no diegetic world is posited outside of categorization by gender. Filmmakers like Potter or Campion choose alternative narrative modes precisely because it frees them from the confines of normative realism's equation of cultural categories and sociopolitical problems with individualism and free will, and in turn, with the narrative representational codes of three-act structure.

Three-Act Structure

Examinations of *Orlando* and *The Accused* (1988), directed by Jonathan Kaplan and released by Paramount, can help provide insight into *The Piano*'s hybrid processes of signification. The subject matter of all three films has to do with gendered discourses of power. In content or political concerns the three films can be regarded as taking comparable positions in the representation of gender relations. At the same time, however, the films exist on a continuum of narrative practice from *The Accused*, most closely the product of Hollywood's search for mass audiences and humanistic messages (normative realism), to *Orlando* which refuses a coherent diegetic space and classical modes of character identification (linking it to avant-grade practices). The following analyses pinpoint some of the ways the narrative choices made by each film affect the cultural discourses mobilized. How do the specific narrative discourses employed enable and promote or conversely obscure and limit the representation of the politics of gendered power relations?

The Accused is a film that attempts to tackle difficult issues around rape, and in some aspects it succeeds. It also sparked public discussion on the subject of rape beyond the bounds of the text (Corliss, "Bad Women" 127). The film, based on a highly publicized actual event, tells the story of Sarah Tobias (Jodie Foster) who is gang-raped in a bar while a number of spectators cheer and goad the three rapists on. Kathryn Murphy (Kelly McGillis) is Sarah's court-appointed attorney who pursues a plea bargain in the case against the rapists but comes to realize she was wrong to have done so and subsequently brings the cheering onlookers to trial.

The Accused purposefully takes on issues concerning the legal system's (mis)treatment of rape victims. This is evident in the film's title with its subtext of ambiguity. Who is the accused in this instance? The men who raped and those who goaded the rapists on? Or Sarah, whose alcohol consumption, previous drug-related arrest, and sexual life, render her a bad witness and this a poor case? We see this thematic concern in the early scenes, which focus on the legal business of collecting evidence. Sarah is photographed, probed and questioned—no one is intentionally cruel, but the process itself is dehumanizing. The film critiques what occurs to the individual in the process of trying to make a case.

This critique is largely formulated through the issue of class and the relationship between Sarah and Kathryn. Distinctions between Sarah as working class and Kathryn as middle class are drawn in numerous ways, including dress, behavior, language, education, living conditions (trailer or modern apartment), and professions (waitress or lawyer). Sarah accuses Kathryn of wanting to plea bargain because Kathryn perceives her as a "low-class bimbo," verified by Kathryn who argues vociferously to her boss not to go to trial because she has "no case," largely as a result of who Sarah is.

Distinctions between the two main characters, once established, are used to argue out the value of different discourses, different kinds of experience. On Kathryn's side, it is a legal discourse; on Sarah's part, a personal discourse; for instance, in the competing claims of the needs of the individual who has been raped versus the requirements of legal process and evidence. A number of ways are depicted in which Sarah is shown to suffer repercussions from the rape (cutting off her long hair, a symbol of women's sexuality; her isolation and lack of support; the self-destructive accident in which she twice rams into the truck of one of the taunting men).

The narrative ostensibly positions Kathryn as wrong on both the class and experiential levels. It is Kathryn who realizes that she has made a mistake in plea bargaining, motivated by her own and others' perceptions of Sarah's character, and that she has erred for having made the decision without consulting her client, thus robbing Sarah of her voice. When Sarah is in the hospital after the car accident, she tells Kathryn, "He figures I'm a piece of shit. Everybody figures I'm a piece of shit. Why not? You told them that. I never got to tell nobody nothing. You did all my talking for me." In an interview, Jodie Foster elaborated on this aspect of Sarah's character: "All that matters to Sarah is that she tell her story.... If she tells her story, then it happened, and that means she's human"(qtd. in Taitz 15). It is this realization that prompts Kathryn so adamantly to take on the criminal solicitation case, too late to try the rapists but able yet to prosecute those who goaded. And in addition, it represents a last chance to give Sarah a voice, by providing her an opportunity to testify, as she so deeply desires, about her experiences from her own perspective.

In other words, it is Kathryn who learns from Sarah; it is Kathryn who changes. At the level of the cultural discourses set in motion by plot and character, the film validates Sarah's discourses, both class and experiential, or at least argues they should be valued equally with Kathryn's.

However, at the level of cultural discourses invoked by setting and genre—as a courtroom drama—the legal discourse increasingly takes over screen time, story focus, and Sarah's discourse of personal experience. In the last weighty portion of the film, Kathryn's language, not Sarah's, dominates the story and establishes the frame of reference by which we judge dramatic events. In the film's increasing narrative shift to courtroom drama, to weight placed on the outcome of the verdict and legal satisfaction, the moral and dramatic victories occur in Kathryn's terms. Sarah's experience is increasingly engulfed by the trial itself, by the outcome of the legal not the personal process. At the end of the film we are left with a sense that the repercussions of the rape itself have been overcome, that with the legal victory Sarah's psychological and emotional difficulties are also resolved. Certainly they are absent from the final moments of the film, in the beaming and legally victorious Sarah in the courtroom and on the courthouse steps.

The narrative of *The Accused* does contradictory things simultaneously on the levels of plot and character versus genre and in the cultural discourses that are summoned by these competing narrative elements. In story terms of plot and character, Sarah's class and experiential distinctions are validated. In terms of legal discourse, in the increasing shift to courtroom drama, Kathryn's class and experiential distinctions take precedence. In this sense, Sarah loses control of the story. The authority of experience gives way to the greater authority of the law; the personal shifts to the judicial; the dramatic outcome is dependent on the ability to argue and prove a case rather than on dealing with rape on a psychological level. The ability to argue and prove the case *becomes* the way of dealing with the rape.

Further, Sarah loses control of the story in the visual or formal representation of the rape itself. As Carol Clover points out (83), it is the testimony of the initially reluctant witness Ken Joyce (Bernie Coulson) that permits the visual presentation of the rape. Although Sarah too testifies, it is Ken's version, his words and his point of view that controls the camera. This is when we, the audience, *see* the rape, when it is made filmically "real" for us. Even the prosecution, in its summation, makes it clear that it and Sarah would have lost the case were it not for Ken's testimony. So, he also makes the rape "real" for the jury. In controlling the camera in the representation of the rape, Ken—not Sarah—validates the reality of the rape. While the film's story line pays lip service to Sarah's opportunity to speak for herself, its formal or aesthetic discourses, once again, reduce her to voicelessness. In this instance, the representational discourses of plot and character operate in opposition to aesthetic discourses.

If viewers are not familiar with the highly publicized case upon which the film is based, the text makes clear, at the beginning and throughout, that at the core of this story is a brutal gang-rape in a bar at which onlookers watched and cheered instead of intervening. Indeed, the opening scene of the film portrays Sarah running out of the bar immediately after having been raped. This initial sequence alerts the audience to the existence of a visual record of the events of that night. We are positioned, at this stage, on the exterior watching Sarah leaving from the door of the bar into the street. We have yet to be shown the interior, the visual record of what transpired on the other side of that door.

We are given signs to expect the enactment of the rape although it does not actually occur until late in the film. Its presentation is postponed, prolonged, deferred. And when it does arrive, it is played out in vivid, lengthy visual and audio detail. But the question is why? What is its dramatic necessity at this point, or at all? We have long believed Sarah's version of events, long sympathetically identified with her character. Emotional affiliation rests with Sarah and against the men on trial whom we want to see convicted (the text's equation to the reinstatement of justice)—all without having seen the gang-rape.

In the three-act structure of normative realist cinema, the third act encompasses the climax and resolution of the film. The climax is the dramatic high point, the moment of culminating action, conflict, excitement. The representation of the rape is promised, but withheld. In doing so, the narrative and sexual climaxes of *The Accused* coincide, heightening the impact of both.

We are left with the often-debated quandary, so frequently attributed to normative realist practices, of whether plot and character maintain a dominant authority, allowing the film to examine a genuinely important social issue. Or conversely, the extent to which other aspects of representational discourse (for instance, in the sequencing, duration, and mise-en-scène of the rape) subsume the social to a pretext that is portrayed merely to allow the representation of a pleasurable act of sexual violence. In other words, is the depiction of the rape—and of Sarah's entire story—exploitative, or is it disturbingly graphic but ultimately necessary? At issue is how certain story and aesthetic elements work together (or fail to) so that particular ideological constructs remain narratively dominant, and so, as referent to an outside reality, a social world beyond the film is sanctioned as is and, perhaps, further solidified.

As has often been noted, the narrative techniques and modes of representation of normative realism, with their emphasis on plot and character, are deeply embedded in the ideology of humanism. Originating with the Enlightenment, humanism is described by Jürgen Habermas as "the belief, inspired by modern science, in the infinite progress of knowledge and in the infinite advance toward social and moral betterment" (4). Humanism valorizes the human subject as the center of knowledge and action. It posits a notion of self or subjectivity derived from and commanded by the individual. The pervasively replicated humanist myth of individuals fighting and triumphing over the system mistakenly construes individuals and the cultural/historical discourses which construct them as separable. Whether the narrative structures of normative realism are ineffectual in their ability to interconnect social beings with power structures, or whether normative ideologies are rendered more effective by their seeming invisibility, the narrative practices of normative realism, as *The Accused* indicates, fail to make surrounding hegemonic forces apparent, much less the central subject of the film.

Alternative Narrative

If we turn to *Orlando* we can see how, in contrast, this film's adoption of alternative narrative techniques works to maintain the power of hegemonic discursive formations, not the individual, at center stage. *Orlando* follows the never-aging title character over four hundred years, initially as a young man, one day awakening to find herself transformed into a woman. One of the principal themes explored is gender distinctions as culturally, not biologically, determined. As such, the text explores gender as a fundamental organizing principle of experience. The film elaborates its ideas on gender through two approaches: in the first instance, as culturally imposed, and in the second instance, varying across time. On the one hand, there are the differences in treatment toward Orlando when she is a woman and when she is a man, such as the loss of her land, her more restrictive and cumbersome dress, and so on. On the other hand, there are depictions of gender traits as part of historical fashion, not inherent aspects of personality. This latter is bookended by the opening and closing voice-overs. In 1600, "There can be no doubt about his sex, despite the feminine appearance that every man of the time aspires to." And in the present day, "She—for there can be no doubt about her sex…with the slightly androgynous appearance that many females of the time aspire to." In order to convey this dual concept of gender as culturally imposed as well as varying across time, elements of mise-en-scène serve multiple purposes. Wardrobe, for instance, becomes more restrictive and cumbersome once Orlando is transformed into a woman. However, dress had also been excessively resplendent in her days as a man, prompting awareness of contrasts with modern concepts of masculinity and femininity.

Although the film tackles issues surrounding gender, an initially curious aspect is the casual, almost cursory, manner in which the moment of biological transformation is portrayed. Orlando, played by Tilda Swinton, simply wakes up one day to find she is now a woman. The character does not seem particularly disturbed by this, emphasized by her words, "Same person. No difference at all, just a different sex." There is no build-up of tension or suspense, no striking camera work, little that calls attention to the transformation. This can be contrasted to the moment of revelation in *The Crying Game* (1992) in which the entire first half of the film builds to the dramatic impact of both the main character Fergus's shock and the audience's shock. In *The Crying Game* the moment is heightened by distinct use of camera: a tilt down that settles on the body part, the male genitalia, previously concealed from us. In contrast, Orlando stands reflected in a mirror in wide shot, a full frontal view including her face, simply visualizing what, in a sense, we have known all along.

We have known it all along because of performance and visual presentation, again in contrast to *The Crying Game*. In the latter film much care is taken to conceal Dil's (Jaye Davidson) biological identity—indeed, much of the film's success hinges on this. In *Orlando*, we are aware that Swinton is a woman playing a man in the first portion of the film. Little attempt is made to alter her voice or mannerisms; neither Swinton's appearance nor her behavior are strikingly different after the transformation. However, because one of the subjects of the film is gender, and in particular its effects on women, Orlando's identity as female is given precedence, both as an actor and as a character.

If Orlando's change of biological sex is minimized formally, in terms of camera, mise-en-scène, and performance, the intent is to emphasize the extent to which gender is not embedded in the body or in the person but imposed on that body and person by outside social forces. Therefore Orlando, the physical being and character, stays relatively consistent while it is the world beyond her—its demands, expectations, and perceptions—that alter as a result of biological difference.

And indeed, land is bestowed on Orlando when she is a man but legally taken away from her when a woman. Same land, same person. Yet everything is different. In order to achieve this, the film takes its focus away from character and forces our attention to the surface. Instead of character development, we find an emphasis on the visual. The locus of audience interaction with text is pushed from identification with the psychic and emotional state of the character to appearance, manner, costuming, and so on. *Orlando* relies on the representational effects of spectacle, posing, and performance, rather than on character development, naturalistic acting, or psychological identification.

Here we can see how alternative modes of representation can be used to circumvent some of the deficiencies of hegemonic cinema's normative realism. It is *Orlando*'s careful undermining of the prominence of plot, diegetic space, and character identification that shifts the focus from Orlando the individual to surrounding, larger cultural and ideological discourses.

Although events occur in the film (the change of sex, relationships, etc.) they do not transpire in a cause-and-effect manner in which each event, hinged to the last, moves the dramatic action forward. Instead, the visuals are the structuring principle. We journey through the story by means of an accumulation of visual impressions or tableaus encompassing different eras and under the subjects Death, Love, Poetry, Politics, Society, Sex, and Birth. While these represent a reverse causality of life, from death to birth, they do so in a metaphorical rather than in a literal or plot sense. Diegetic fidelity is disrupted by the central character's recurring gazes and addresses directly to camera; disjunctions in narrative continuity are created by, for instance, entering a maze in one century, leaving it in another.

Characters are not drawn in terms of the complex, psychological portraits of normative realism. Orlando is not a character with well-defined personality traits. We know her largely as conforming to broad categories of man and woman across time. The tools to identify with her character are withheld because in this narrative view the individual does not have ultimate effect either on the world-at-large or over her own life. In this depiction, the surrounding culture constructs the individual. And so, there is a quality of acceptance on Orlando's part when she is faced with losing her house and land. She reads the legal document delivered to her, does not like it, but signs it anyway. In another film, one could easily imagine this as the central series of events, the dramatic struggle, in which the character takes on the legal establishment, fights for her rights, and wins or loses—in another film such as *The Accused*.

Moving away from the principal representational codes and conventions of normative realism permits a film like *Orlando* to break from a reinstatement of prevailing cultural/historical discourses and, instead, shift toward a critique of their replication. However, it should be noted, as Judith Mayne observes, "if, consequently, there is no such thing as an inherently radical technique, then there is no such thing as an inherently conservative one" (172). Attributes of mise-en-scène, for instance, in and of themselves do not bear the capacity to critique; instead, they are given significance in the context of their use and in contradistinction to existing conventions of a dominant cinema. The meanings of formal techniques are dependent, in other words, on the narrative operations of their positioning, functions, and uses.

Orlando and *The Piano* both serve as models for independent narrativity, the former by developing avant-garde attributes into a more narrative form; the latter by taking a more hybrid approach between alternative and normative realist discourses. In terms of alternative sensibilities, Ada's muteness serves as one way to deemphasize normative modes of identification with character. The audience has limited access to Ada's thoughts directly, certainly those that normally would occur through dialogue are not available, nor is there an intermediary character who interprets her. We search for clues to her emotional and psychic state elsewhere—in her relation to her music, in the film's strikingly moody camera work, in elements of mise-en-scène such as wardrobe. Indeed, costuming is as vital and vocal an element of storytelling in *The Piano* as it is in *Orlando*, in for instance, the use of hooped dresses and petticoats that encumber Ada as she tramps through the mud, that conceal her body and repress her sexuality, and that engulf her beneath the sea as she almost drowns.

In general, as reviewer Carrie Rickey writes of *The Piano*, "the exposition is principally visual" ("Mute Woman" W3). There is a kind of looseness in the film's cause-and-effect structure, for instance, in the sequencing of scenes. Framing and composition are used as frequently as event to elaborate story progression, such as in the repeated, striking two-shots of mother and daughter side-by-side, looking eerily similar in their poses, hats, and expressions, reminding us of the construction and transmission of cultural structures from generation to generation. Pictorial displays drive the story, from the high wide shot of the piano abandoned on the beach, denoting Ada's loss, to the image that begins on Ada's hand behind her back, travels up to her braided hair, and from there moves to the startlingly similar undergrowth of the New Zealand bush. In finding visual links between human appearance and place, we recognize the tangled circumstances in which Ada is caught. And, as in *Orlando*, rhythm and movement are established through the reliance on appearance and gaze of the main character in close-up. Although the diegesis is never ruptured, as in *Orlando*'s direct addresses to the camera, the piercing quality of Ada's returned look is constantly reiterated.

Ada's formidable will, taking the form of passive resistance, compares to *Orlando*'s acquiescence instead of action in response to the loss of her land. One cannot fight while barricaded in the master's house; no ability to speak exists when the only language available is the master's. Such elements, in keeping with avant-garde traditions, help the films maintain centrally in our field of attention both the individuals affected and the cultural and historical discourses from which they emerge and by which they are bound.

Simultaneously, *The Piano* weaves its narrative out of plot, character development, naturalistic acting, a coherent diegesis, and other normative realist representational codes. Such a merging of elements from two legacies, so often seen as oppositional, provides the audience with familiar pleasures of the text *and* keeps cultural formations and power relations foregrounded. In contrast to, among others, the feminist avant-garde of the 1970s and early 1980s, more recent film theory and independent practice have come to recognize elements of normative realist narrativity as significant, useful, and, indeed, pleasurable. By being inclusive of the pleasures of familiar modes of storytelling, a film such as *The Piano* increases its potential of receiving more extensive distribution and promotion. In gaining wide-reaching distribution, the possibility for greater audience address is created, a difficulty never satisfactorily resolved by the political avant-garde, and a significant consideration for socially or politically motivated filmmakers.

Reading Independent Narratives

I have argued that one of the achievements of *The Piano* is its merging of mainstream with avant-garde aesthetic and narrative legacies. In doing so, while also maintaining a popular audience address, discourses of individualism are prevented from subsuming those of gendered power relations. However, the problem remains precisely the strong tendency on the part of many reviewers to read the film as a story of individualism: a right versus wrong man romance, and thus obliterating the cultural/historical discourses enacted in the text. The foundation for this reading rests in the attributes of normative realism, which, as *The Accused* shows us, return too easily, some would argue inexorably, to the cult of individualism and free will. Simultaneously and seemingly contradictorily, the emphasis on nonnormative representational codes—the look of the camera and mise-en-scène standing in for more familiar forms of character identification—allow this film to be more easily interpreted as an "art" film.

At any given moment, *The Piano* stakes out the territory of one tradition, alternative or normative realist, but then must depart from these assumptions and codes in order to claim the ground of a differing narrative heritage. This creates gaps in its potential meanings or readings. In its hybrid strategy of combination, applicable to other independent films, the process of narrative signification is opened to slippage. A striking instance of this can be seen in the final portion of *The Piano* comprising, in a sense, three closing sequences: Ada's near-drowning and last minute, self-willed resurrection from "the cold grave, under the deep deep sea";[7] the epilogue describing Ada's, Flora's, and Baines's new life as a family in Nelson; and the final shot of the film, a long take showing Ada caught beneath the sea, not escaping, not setting her foot free from the rope that ties her to her sunken piano, instead, motionless too long to survive as the camera slowly pulls farther and farther back.

My reading of this latter, closing shot of the film is as metaphor, that although Ada survives we are left with a visualization of the deadly serious stakes at risk for her, for women, in that she almost drowned, that her will almost succumbed. Its purpose is to remind us that the cultural imperatives of power relations do take prisoners, despite Ada's own narrow escape. This could be considered an accurate, or certainly reasonable, way to interpret an experimental visual. In contrast, it has been suggested to me that the entire epilogue of Ada and Baines in their new life together is a "flash forward" that takes place in Ada's imagination in the moments just before her drowning (as is the case, for instance, at the conclusion of Lynne Ramsey's *Ratcatcher,* 2000). This reading, too, is dependent on the final long take of Ada motionless beneath the sea, a shot held too long to allow hope that she survives. But in this instance, in order to understand the epilogue as a flash forward occurring only in Ada's imagination, the closing image in which Ada fails to resurface is read as realism, as a literal rather than a metaphorical visual record. This reading, also, is a reasonable assumption in the context of mainstream cinema's realist practices. Both interpretations—metaphor or flash forward—are textually plausible readings.[8]

All readings remain potentially ambiguous, as David Morley points out; they are nonfixed or open within a certain range. That is, not all meanings are possible, but no single reading exhausts all potential meanings either. However, *The Piano*'s strategy of hybridity further erodes the codes, assumptions, and boundaries of particular representational traditions as determinants of meaning. Whether one understands the final portion of the film as shaped by the symbolic of an alternative filmic tradition or by the specificity of normative realism is not simply a question of preference but a fundamental distinction in the processes of narrativity between normative realist and alternative cinema.

If a viewer accepts the final image literally, the film's closure plumbs the depths of bleakness. For Ada, as for other women within this ideological fold (that is, all women in this diegetic perspective), no way out exists. Despite Ada's will, she has no effective resistance to the configurations and restraints of existing power relations except through death. However, a reading of the close that foregrounds the final shot as metaphorical, and therefore the flash forward-epilogue sequence as literal, veers dangerously close to Hollywood's happy endings predicated on myths of individualism. Despite the clink, clink, clink of Ada's newly crafted metal finger on the piano keys as she plays—the haunting audio reminder of the costs to body and spirit—the individual can triumph over injustice, and in her new life with Baines, Ada can reach a gender equilibrium within the construct of the family romance.

One may conjecture that Campion's discomfort with the limitations of either formula for closure prompted the multiple resolution in a kind of hedging of bets against the bleakness of one and the suddenly too well-lit, easy resolution of the other.[9] More critical to the discussion here, however, is the way the film's closure(s) indicates how a viewer might maneuver through differing processes of representational practices and the varying cultural discourses invoked by each, opting for a certain interpretation over another at any given moment.

Interweaving experimental aesthetic and narrative elements with those of normative realist cinema is precisely what makes interpretations of *The Piano* so given to slippage and, further, what makes the film exemplary of certain tendencies in contemporary independent film. Exemplary because of its hybridity, for instance, as in independent film's efforts to mediate binary oppositions such as form/content, art/politics, and Hollywood/avant-garde. Without the incorporation of nonnormative elements, *The Piano*'s narrative could not veer so adeptly from the individual's struggles to a critique of the historical structures that surround and construct us. It is not restricted to certain readings in the same ways as is the narrative of *The Accused*. Yet, it is this same incorporation of alternative practices and codes in *The Piano* that makes it possible to *refuse* the broadening of the scope of discussion from the individual to larger social forces.[10] Certain re/viewers opt instead to obliterate the cultural "big picture," obscuring it behind the film's experimental aspects: its visual uniqueness and departure from traditional narrative modes. Concealing it, in other words, under the rubric of art. That which leads Roger Ebert to describe *The Piano* as "startlingly original," Vincent Canby to call it "so original," and Jami Bernard to hail it as "A masterpiece!" also permits Canby to continue as follows. "This is filmmaking of such original effect that to ask Ms. Campion about her experiences as a woman director seems beside the point. She is a woman, a fact that shapes her own experiences; but it doesn't have anything to do with her artistic powers" (Canby, "Campion" 17).

Contrary to hooks's contention that *The Piano* is granted a dispensation because of its label as high art, crucial portions of the film's potential meanings are erased through its classification as such. Art films are designated as a separate category in which viewers (as well as, in many instances, their makers) are not held to account in similar ways as they are for social issue films. It is almost inconceivable, for instance, for a reviewer to omit the repercussions of rape or Sarah's silencing in *The Accused* and dwell on the work instead as a female buddy film. Yet *The Piano* was widely discussed in the popular press as an erotic romance without its many instances of violence and degradation meriting so much as mention. In this conceptualization, formal elements such as the look of the film can be enjoyed for their artistic qualities without having to link them back to the narrative's processes of meaning production. One can "appreciate" Ada's and Baines's travails without questioning one's own place in the depicted structures of power relations. Canby is able to state that Campion's existence as a woman has nothing to do with her artistic powers because he, along with the majority of mainstream reviewers, relies on humanist notions of art. Here, humanist modernism constructs the works it claims for its own as *above and beyond* social categories or cultural constructs such as gender, in favor of universal truth claims. And in doing so, it continues the submergence of voices such as Ada's.

Following hooks's line of argument, if gangsta rap is condemned by condemnation, *The Piano*, then, is condemned by high (art) praise. hooks interprets the film as the majority of reviewers do and on the basis of that same reading she criticizes, as misogynist, the film they praise. And within the perimeters of the reviewer-preferred reading, hooks's argument makes sense. However, too much is at stake in the act and politics of interpretation to surrender to others' readings so easily or to give away, without resistance, the possibility of alternate interpretations, as hooks does in this instance.

Speaking of the work of researchers, and I think by implication this argument can be extended to all readers, Ien Ang argues that the purpose of research is not "the search for (objective, scientific) knowledge," but the construction of interpretations, of certain ways of understanding the world, always historically located, subjective, and relative" ("Wanted" 105). Ang continues by saying that what is at stake here is, precisely, "a politics of interpretation" (105). In shifting conceptual frames from objective knowledge to constructed knowledge, certain questions are immediately problematized: Whose construction(s) prevail and why? Which, or whose, interpretations are admissible for consideration, discussion, and negotiation? In this formula, interpretation becomes a discursive construction of knowledge.

The point in this analysis of *The Piano* is not to suggest that independent film as a category of cinematic signification is unable to traverse the legacies of both mainstream and avant-garde, failing to surmount the density of one or the danger of prepackaged ideology in the other. Quite the contrary, the notion of hybridity as a property of independent film is one of independent cinema's defining and most promising traits. It is to suggest, however, that interpretation is both an act of representation and a political act: an act of representation in the sense of a determining moment in the production of an artifact's meanings, and political in the specifics of and struggle for control over those meanings. Films made by women or expressing women's experiences are insufficient without the corollary recognition, in the realm of reception, of what they seek to do and how they strive to do it. The struggle to represent unheard voices and marginalized lives cannot occur solely at the level of production or be placed only on the shoulders of filmmakers; they must exist equally in the critical activities of reviewers and viewers.

The issue is not only that acts of interpretation help construct their own object, "producing" the text in the process of decoding it, as noted by literary theorist Marcel Cornis-Pope (4). Specific readings can also be imposed at the expense of other interpretations that are thus dislodged. This matches the concept of the function of reviewers, described by Meaghan Morris, as paradigm guardians, determining what is safely or adventurously thought about film at any moment. Its opposite in Morris's terms, is the act of "political reviewing," and I would add political viewing, which "is a matter of changing what can be *said* about film" (121). Or as Edward Said notes, in his consideration of the debates around canonical texts and cultural literacy, too much emphasis has been placed on what should be read, rather than on how it should be read (328).

A film's meanings are solidified, among other sites, through the discussion surrounding its reception, for instance, in the press, in popular opinion such as word-of-mouth, and in other forms of negotiated opinion. Along with representational, institutional, and cultural/historical discourses, interpretation should be a recognized site of struggle with equivalent discursive implications in the maintenance or modification of existing power structures. The act of interpretation should not be surrendered without resistance; the existence of alternative readings should not, as in the case of *The Piano*, be dislodged so easily.

I return to *The Piano* for a final time, in order to look at its text-within-a-text performance of the Bluebeard "fairy tale" and to the Westerners who bring such dramatic enactments to their colonial outposts. Both populations of viewers, colonizing and indigenous, perform interpretations of the play within the film. The stage is set with the blood-soaked heads of Bluebeard's ex-wives poking through holes in the curtain, as Bluebeard, in shadow play, is about to behead another wife. Shouting, "Coward!" some of the Maori men storm the stage. The Europeans' response is condescending tolerance of Maori "naiveté" for their inability to distinguish reality from representation. But of course, and not without irony, the Maori are prescient. For the performance in which Bluebeard is to behead his wife but is halted by Maori intervention foreshadows Stewart taking an axe to Ada's finger. Further, it is the Maori who are depicted as understanding that representation and reality are inseparably integrated. The play within the film stands in for its external frame—the film itself. Bluebeard's assumption of ownership over his wives is mirrored in Stewart's, Ada's father's, and Baines's sense of prerogative over Ada. Both populations, European and Maori, carry out an act of interpretation of the same performance, and in the end, it is the Westerners who are shown to be naive for their conviction that one can neatly distinguish fact from fiction, reality from representation, and objective knowledge from discursive construct. It is the Westerners who, in error, see narrative representation as harmless entertainment, just as reviewers of the external frame, the film *The Piano*, see it as a harmless romance.

CHAPTER SIX

Independent Auteurism: From Modern Existentialism to Postmodernism as Nostalgia

Tarantino is Scorsese with quote marks around him.

—Paul Schrader

"Words are like onions," she said. "The more skins you peel off, the more meanings you encounter."

—Fatima Mernissi (61)

This final chapter considers an important emergent cultural/historical (economic, social, political) phenomenon, postmodernity, and explores how it is reflected in, partially formulated by, struggled over, or even solidified by way of independent film as a system of representation. Discussion centers around Quentin Tarantino's films because they have been so widely recognized and labeled as *postmodern*. What elements or features make them so? How much and in what ways are they a departure from earlier modernist versions or "visions" of the social and psychic order? I argue that ultimately Tarantino's films represent only a very limited view or version of postmodernism. Such representations do not limit the potential of postmodernism per se. However, they do carry the risk of narrowing how we might think of postmodernism, and therefore how we come to identify and construct it. The danger is that alternate versions or more encompassing possibilities of what postmodernism could be are dislodged or ruled out before they can even be envisioned.

Of the films examined in any detail in this study, *Pulp Fiction* (1994), distributed by Miramax, fits least well into operative notions of independent film, yet it is also perhaps the single film (and Quentin Tarantino the single filmmaker) that has come to most exemplify independent film of the 1990s. *Pulp Fiction* cost $8.5 million to make and featured an enviable list of known actors and stars (John Travolta, Samuel L. Jackson, Uma Thurman, Bruce

Willis, Harvey Keitel, Tim Roth) who vied to be in the film despite the relatively low pay. The film was distributed by Miramax but, in addition, it was also entirely financed by them—after being optioned to and turned down by TriStar, a major studio. The financing and distribution package meant the production did not have to go through the usual trials of patchwork funding, to be picked up for distribution (if fortunate) only on completion. And by this point, Tarantino was hardly a newcomer or unknown. *Pulp Fiction* was his second writing-directing effort (after *Reservoir Dogs*, 1992) and his fourth produced feature screenplay (*True Romance*, 1993; *Natural Born Killers*, 1994; both for Warner Brothers), all of which had brought him widespread attention.

It can be argued, however, that *Pulp Fiction* departs from a normative Hollywood paradigm in significant ways. The film was celebrated for its postmodern qualities, one of which was, as noted in the introduction to the published screenplay, that it "brilliantly finessed the divide between art-house cachet and commercial viability" (Dargis, "Foreword" n.p.). But this continues to beg the question. Why can it be considered independent *because* it brings to bear commercial viability (which is what Hollywood films do)?[1] And how precisely does it manage to stay on the "art-house cachet" side of the independent line?

We can begin to explore these questions by comparing the respective receptions of *Pulp Fiction* and the studio-made *Natural Born Killers* in two differing national contexts, Britain and the United States, looking particularly at the issue of violence, which is raised explicitly by both texts.

Natural Born Killers and Violence

Natural Born Killers is the story of two young lovers, Mickey and Mallory (Woody Harrelson and Juliette Lewis), who go on a cross-country killing spree that ends with fifty-two people dead and the couple turned into celebrities by media attention. It was directed by Oliver Stone, based on a screenplay by Quentin Tarantino. That Tarantino wrote the original screenplay was a widely reported fact, in part because of the writer's subsequent efforts to distance himself from the film. He declined a screenwriting credit (that went to David Veloz, Richard Rutowski, and Oliver Stone), settling instead for the separate and lesser credit, "Story by."

There is some evidence that Tarantino's objections were as much in response to *Natural Born Killers*'s being made at all as they were to any specific changes Stone made to the script or to the ultimate film he created. The rights to the *Natural Born Killers* screenplay had a complex, contested history well before they became Stone's, and Tarantino seems to have made several previous attempts to keep the script from going into production. At any rate, Tarantino was upset when word reached him that the script was being rewritten by Stone, although he had not yet read any of the specific changes (Hamsher 128). Further, at the time Tarantino distanced himself from the completed film, and until some time afterwards he had not actually seen it (Dawson 122).

Why Tarantino resisted *Natural Born Killers* being made is unclear. He himself has said he did not want to direct it.

> I wrote them all [*Reservoir Dogs, True Romance, Natural Born Killers*] to be my first film and then I *made* my first film, so I didn't want to do them anymore. The next film I directed, I wanted to be my *second* film and your second film is different from your first. And, more importantly, it's like the time had passed as far as what I wanted to do. It's like an old girlfriend, it has a shelf life. (brackets in original) (Dawson 103)

Further, there is a range of opinion on how greatly Tarantino's screenplay and the Veloz-Rutowski-Stone version vary, from "very different" (135) in the assessment of *Natural Born Killers*'s producer Jane Hamsher (135) to Gavin Smith's estimate in *Sight and Sound* that "roughly 80 per cent of his [Tarantino's] script survives intact" ("Stone" 9). But the point is that while the produced film is definitely the result of Stone's (and others') work, it also embodies to some extent Tarantino's conceptual, visual, and narrative concerns, and his name continues to be linked to it in the public's perception.

Smith also points out that when *Natural Born Killers* opened in the States in August 1994, "The anticipated firestorm of moral outrage in the U.S. media never materialized.... Though critics were divided between those who praised the film's audacity and those who dismissed it as irresponsible cynicism" (9). The film did in fact receive mixed reviews—rarely lukewarm, but rather conflicting, either praising or criticizing it. However, the contentiousness was largely not over the issue of the film's depiction of violence. Both positive and negative reviews (for instance, the *Philadelphia Inquirer* and the *New Yorker*, respectively) found the film's violence not excessively difficult to take, generally on the grounds that it was either purposefully satiric or simply cartoonish. Such critical acceptance of the violence seems to have prompted the *Los Angeles Times*, among other papers, to publish in its editorial pages negative views of the film based on its graphic use of violence, written by "ordinary" reader-citizens to counteract *Los Angeles Times*'s film critic Kenneth Turan's very positive and unoffended review (Softley F3; Myers F3; Turan, "Stone" B8).

For the most part, critical discussion was based not on *Natural Born Killers*'s use of violence but on whether the film worked as a narrative, on whether it was successful in satirizing a media-saturated society. J. Hoberman's internally contradictory review in the *Village Voice* is indicative; he argues that *Natural Born Killers* will "leave you impressed but unconvinced, torn between admiration and disgust, a desire to praise audacious filmmaking and the urge to laugh at rampaging idiocy" ("True Romance" 41).

In contrast, *Natural Born Killers*'s impending release in Britain sparked controversy precisely over the film's depictions of violence. Originally scheduled for November 1994, the film's theatrical release was postponed until February 1995, while the British Board of Film Classification considered whether it would even classify the film, a prerequisite for its being shown at all (ultimately it received an eighteen certificate—for viewers eighteen and older, similar to the Motion Picture Association of America's NC-17 rating). During its threat of censorship, the film was hotly and publicly debated for its depictions of violence, with many critics finding it distasteful.

Even reviewers in the United Kingdom who were against the film's being censored regarded it with wariness. For instance, Alexander Walker in the *Evening Standard* stated, "It is right, of course, that we approach such a film with caution, even suspicion," at the same time that he argued for its classification. Employing sarcasm, he wrote, "*Natural Born Killers* mirrors the toxic convulsions in America. We don't want that here, do we? Right: ban it" (45). He attributed the film's near censorship to a negative perception of American society and a British desire to resist its damaging influences.

Logically, the varying responses of the British and American press toward *Natural Born Killers* might be explained by differing national contexts and the respective place of violence, or relative lack of it, in each society. Reviewers in the United States, a more violent society, tend not to critique *Natural Born Killers*'s violence while reviewers in the United Kingdom do. However, this same pattern of response did not hold true for the reception of *Pulp Fiction*. While *Pulp Fiction* and *Reservoir Dogs* were much talked about in terms of their violence, they did not receive negative critical receptions in Britain similar to that of *Natural Born Killers*. The films were unequivocal critical successes in both national contexts, and the attitude toward their depictions of violence was considerably more lenient than was the case with *Natural Born Killers*.

Pulp Fiction and Violence

Reservoir Dogs opened in the United Kingdom in January 1993 and was still playing theatrically when *Pulp Fiction* had its British release in October 1994. *Reservoir Dogs*'s unusually lengthy theatrical run was because the film had become a cult favorite. In addition, its initial run was extended by the British

Board of Film Classification's refusal to classify it for video release. Release did not occur until June 1995, allowing theaters to continue offering the popular film.

That Tarantino was accepted in Britain can be seen in such events as his being asked to select nineteen of "his all-time favourite movies" for screening by the National Film Theatre in London during January 1995.[2] He is described in the NFT's program not in controversial terms but instead as "the most commercially successful, critically lauded and sought-after new young director in America" (4).

On *Pulp Fiction*'s depictions of violence, the reactions of most reviewers were quite unperturbed, in contrast to what they had been to *Natural Born Killers*. For instance, in the British edition of *Esquire*, in a review titled "Pulp Fiction Is Predictably Violent—and Predictably Wonderful," Greg Williams wrote, "Even his trademark explosive violence—which wrenches the guts and fills column inches in the outraged mid-market tabloids—is highly stylized, never gratuitous and balked at solely on the grounds of its realism" (32). Julie Burchill commented in the *London Sunday Times*:

> Tarantino is the ultimate straight-talker; his films are tight, elegant and sparse, completely character-driven, his justification of his films' violence the last word in unpretentiousness—"My films are violent because I've always thought that violence in films is cool"....While his [Stone's] excuses for the high body counts of his films are worthy of the lowest supermarket tabloid reporter: to *educate*, to tell us the *awful truth*. ("Blood" 7)

Burchill seems to have reversed conventional wisdom: tabloids presumably titillate while "proper" newspapers are supposed to inform. But her argument rests on the foundation that Tarantino's violence is justified and Stone's is not because Tarantino, unlike Stone, has no intended moral or message. Similarly, from the other side of the Atlantic, "Unlike Tarantino, Stone is obsessed with generating significance" (Hoberman, "True Romance" 41).

Debates about the place of violence in film are generally concerned with a few key problematics: whether the violence is "realistic" or not, for instance. The *Esquire* review attempts to have it both ways, calling *Pulp Fiction*'s violence both "highly stylized" and "realism." Another common, polarizing argument is whether the violence is gratuitous. *Esquire* is firm on this point, citing *Pulp Fiction*'s violence as "never gratuitous." Significantly, though, arguments for *Pulp Fiction*'s nongratuitous use of violence are built on its having, unlike *Natural Born Killers*, no moral, point, or lesson. This is the exact inverse of traditional arguments about filmic depictions of violence in which they are considered gratuitous precisely when they do not have a morally or narratively redemptive purpose. Indeed, those reviewers who find the film's brand of graphic violence unacceptable, condemn it using the very same arguments as those who acclaim it.

In one of the few entirely negative critiques of *Pulp Fiction*, Fintan O'Toole, writing in the *London Guardian*, calls Tarantino's style "sadism" and argues that his power:

> lies in the bold way he has dispensed with the excuses for violence on screen and gone straight for the thing itself. He does not go through the motions of constructing a pseudo-moral plot in which violence is enclosed within a struggle between good and evil. Nor does he try to use film violence as an image of a violent society in the hope of exposing the true nature of the world we live in. He just, in his own words, "does violence"....Unlike Scorsese's *Goodfellas*, *Pulp Fiction* does all it can to exclude a social context for the violence of its gangsters. (16–17)

O'Toole condemns the film on the same basis that others praise it. And this perspective is not limited to the popular press. Henry Giroux, for instance, writing in the *Harvard Educational Review*, calls "the new hyper-real avant-garde violent films," of which *Pulp Fiction* is a preeminent example, "an expression of the erosion of civil society" (306). He elaborates: "Tarantino's view of violence represents more than bad politics; it also breeds a dead-end cynicism. His films are filled with characters who have flimsy histories, are going nowhere, and live out their lives without any sense of morality or justice" (309).

Why, then, in many quarters is Stone's use of violence seen as more contemptible than Tarantino's?[3] Certainly, *Natural Born Killers* is as stylized and calls attention to itself as much as *Pulp Fiction* does: that is, it is clear that violence is the "subject" of Stone's film. The patchwork of film stocks and rapid cutting are meant to remind the viewer continually that the film is a media construction. The eroticization of violence (Mickey and Mallory, Scagnetti, the media) is supposed to compel and repulse us simultaneously. And *Natural Born Killers* is much more self-conscious in its use of violence than the majority of Hollywood action, horror, or crime films in which violence is prevalent and the avenging of violent deeds is made heroic. In most mainstream texts, violent acts are rendered "invisible" or their effects neutralized, whereas *Natural Born Killers*, in contrast, describes a world in which everything and everyone is brutal and brutalized. Given this, why is it more difficult to extend the kinds of defense granted *Pulp Fiction*, for instance, in this report of the reaction of a nineteen-year-old female fan from Manchester: "'The violence is realistic and gritty, it's done with a bit of panache. It has never been portrayed like this in films before'....Stallone and Arnie have killed dozens of people, she says, but nobody kicks up a fuss about their films" (Alderson 13). Indeed, the ordinariness and invisibility of the "body counts" in most action films (including those of *Pulp Fiction*'s Bruce Willis) are frequently used to praise *Pulp Fiction*'s violent depictions—precisely because they are made visible, meant to be registered and acknowledged.

Modernism and Morality

The difficulty for *Natural Born Killers*, condemned for its depictions of violence even while self-consciously attempting to call attention to violence, is that despite Stone's efforts to the contrary, the film retains the signifying practices of a humanist text, and its very attempts to denounce violence place it firmly within a modernist framework. It is one thing to make violence the subject of the film, as Tarantino does; but it is another thing to critique it, as Stone goes on to do. *Pulp Fiction* exists as an immersion in popular culture. *Natural Born Killers*'s modernist foundation lies in its attempts to critique. Stone's problem is that he has attempted to create a hybrid—a modernist morality tale and a story grounded in postmodern nonhumanism—and in the process he has achieved neither sufficiently.

In chapter 2, I briefly outlined the aesthetic realms of the modern and the postmodern, delineating aspects of their significance as systems of communication and expression. Here, I refer to these movements in their larger contexts, in which they represent "periodizing concepts" (Jameson 112–13), correlating aesthetic-expressive properties with social, economic, political, and ideological features. This is often rather awkwardly expressed by the use of the terms *modernism* or *postmodernism* to signify the traditionally more narrow sense of *culture*—the arts and other forms of knowledge exemplified by education, social etiquette, and class—while *modernity* and *postmodernity* represent the more inclusive, recent sense of *culture* as, in Raymond Williams's phrase, a whole way of life. So, for instance, "modernism [is part of] the culture of modernity" and "postmodernism is the culture of postmodernity" (Sarup, *Introductory Guide* 131).

In this more encompassing sense, modernity, the humanist project originating with the Enlightenment, is the belief in reason, progress, science, universal principles of justice and morality, and other "grand narratives" that structure or make sense of reality in such a way that the autonomous individual subject is at its center, functioning as the source of all agency. Postmodernity is the still-unfolding structuring of reality that locates "any universal or normative postulation of rational unanimity [as]...hostile to the challenges of otherness and difference" (Gandhi 27). In a postmodern configuration, the autonomous individual is replaced by a nonfixed, multiply identified subject who exists in a world of pluralism, heterogeneity, and cultural diversity instead of a world in which universally valid knowledge, principles, or master narratives are supposedly equally applicable to all human beings.

Modernism, the aesthetic movements beginning in the late nineteenth century and continuing to the 1960s, is part of modernity in the ways that it emphasizes "the aim of finding an inner truth beyond surface appearances" (Sarup, *Introductory Guide* 131) and in its belief, as with modernity, in "a unique self and private identity, a unique personality and individuality, which can be expected to generate its own unique vision of the world and to forge its own unique, unmistakable style" (Jameson 114). In modernism, the unique subject is represented by the artistic genius, the creator, the auteur.

Modernity's stress on the autonomous subject or self as the agent who can impose reason, order, and progress on existence is met and matched by modernism's stress on "unlimited self-realization, the demand for authentic self-experience and the subjectivism of a hyperstimulated sensitivity" (Sarup, *Introductory Guide* 144). Thus, the artist is able to see and feel things that the rest of us cannot.

Indeed, the two senses of culture—modernism and modernity—are inseparable because, while they may point to differing cultural structures, they are united by shared structuring principles. This is exemplified in Fintan O'Toole's scathing review of Tarantino's work, cited earlier, because "[u]nlike Scorsese's *Goodfellas*, *Pulp Fiction* does all it can to exclude a social context for the violence of its gangsters." Or as Leela Gandhi points out, "humanism has always functioned as an 'aesthetico-moral' ideology" (49), for instance, as with the narrative of redemption (see chap. 4). In arguing the failure of *Natural Born Killers*'s morally redemptive efforts in contrast to *Pulp Fiction*'s refreshing "unpretentiousness" in its lack of a message, reviewers are framing modern/postmodern arguments around changing concepts of the individual and the world that person occupies. In addition to formal and stylistic characteristics, it is its depiction of altered paradigms of self and society that renders *Pulp Fiction* a postmodern text.

From Existential to Ironic Heroes

A primary interest in postmodernism as representational practice is the degree to which it is able to depict multiply identified subjects in a multicultural and constantly shifting world. At stake are the ways in which postmodernism as representational and cultural production can promote or accommodate differences instead of being "hostile to the challenges of otherness and difference." Postmodernism provides a potential field for thinking through what it means to live in heterogeneity, while simultaneously keeping in play the diversity of multiple perspectives, values, lifestyles, and concerns, in contrast to contentions of modernism's narrativities of norms, absolutes, and universals.

The exception in *Pulp Fiction*'s refusal to tell a humanist-type morality tale may be the prominent story line of redemption concerning Jules (Samuel Jackson) who, by film's end, undergoes a conversion that causes him to retire as hitman. Moving from shouting biblical passages in which he doles out the vengeance of the Lord, Jules comes to realize that he is, instead, "the tyranny of evil men" and now wants to become a "shepherd." Within the context of the film it is difficult to know if Jules's redemption is meant to be taken seriously or, rather, greeted as another instance of high absurdity, similar to the other events we witness. Commentators who want to argue in favor of the film but are uneasy about its apparent amorality, tend to seize on Jules's redemption as an indicator of the film's essential moral purpose; for instance, "What lifts *Pulp Fiction* up from merry nihilism, in-jokes and postmodernist narrative strategies is the performance of Samuel L. Jackson, whose Scripture-spouting hitman, Jules, is the only human in *Pulp Fiction* who evinces any moral conscience.... Jackson's performance holds out the possibility of redemption, of human growth, and lends this frantically funny burlesque its few moments of human character" (Rickey, "Tarantino" W3). Other commentators, however, point to Jules's redemption as simply more of the morally arbitrary same: "He goes about his killing business with religious fervor, spouting Ezekiel at his terrified victims as if to justify his acts. And what changes his mind about his work? Not a crisis of conscience but a realisation of his own mortality. More self-preservation: the philosophical new Jules is as hard and cold as the old one" (Lipman 51).[4]

Paul Schrader, screenwriter of Martin Scorsese's *Taxi Driver* (1976) and *Raging Bull* (1980), as well as writer-director of such films as *American Gigolo* (1980), *Light Sleeper* (1991), and *Affliction* (1998), accounts for the modernist to postmodernist inversion of narrative morality, in which commentators defend *Pulp Fiction* because it has no overt moral intent, as a transition from existential heroes to ironic heroes.

> For all of this century, which is the history of movies, films have more or less worked on the existential hero because he [sic] was ideal for movies. He defined himself, he was self-starting, whether he was a hero or whether he was an anti-hero, whether he was the westerner or whether he was the rogue cop. What we have now is what strikes me as the ironic hero. And that is, everything in the ironic hero's life has quotations around it. He's quote unquote the protagonist who quote unquote loves someone or quote un-

quote kills someone. In the end it really doesn't make that much difference. Tarantino is Scorsese with quote marks around him.

Indeed, in commentary after commentary, Tarantino is continually compared to Scorsese; *Reservoir Dogs*, his debut, is seen as equivalent to *Mean Streets* (1973). And Tarantino himself cites *Taxi Driver* as one of his three favorite films (along with *Blow Out*, 1981; and *Rio Bravo*, 1958). Schrader continues, "What *Pulp Fiction* has done is move the serious movie protagonist into a territory that is very new and very uncertain.... And what I'm saying is that it's the first post-existential art movie." By existential hero, Schrader means the individual who operates within a rule- (or misrule-) governed universe—modernity—and who must make moral decisions based on that "reality." Scorsese's stories are emblematic of a world of good and evil, even, or especially, when his main characters are antiheroes.

For instance, Pam Cook describes Scorsese's *Cape Fear* (1991) as a "violent rape movie in which women apparently collude in their own punishment at the hands of a rapist. Yet, for the most part critics, even when shocked by the film's brutality, prefer to discuss it in formal and/or moral terms—as 'cinema' or as a treatise on good and evil" ("Cape Fear" 132). Cook's point is that the prism of modernist auteurism provides a protective point of view in which "cinema" and the "formal" equate with an art cinema and a director-as-auteur beyond reproach or accountability (not dissimilar to the way reviewers read *The Piano* as an art film, as I discussed in chap. 5). And further, that the "moral" of modernist auteurism refers only to universalizing themes such as the abstraction of good and evil, and not the particular, localized morality of specific power relations in specific circumstances.

Although it appears accurate to describe *Pulp Fiction*, in comparison to Scorsese's work, as a postmodern text, it is also important to recognize it as a very narrow conception of what postmodernism might be, just as Scorsese represents only a very narrow series of possibilities of a modernist worldview. This is evidenced in Schrader's assumption, above, borne out in textual practice, that only "he" might be the hero—the solitary, traditional (i.e. white, heterosexual) male.

It is also apparent in the dominance of the gangster and crime genres for both Hollywood auteurism (Scorsese, Coppola, De Palma) and for independent film. What has variously been called art shock, violent chic, and art house designer violence is the single most prevalent, one could well say overrepresented, genre in independent film, including: *Blood Simple* (1984), *Henry: Portrait of a Serial Killer* (1990), *La Femme Nikita* (1990), *Straight out of Brooklyn* (1991), *Love Crimes* (1991), *Bad Lieutenant* (1992), *One False Move* (1992),

Man Bites Dog (1992), *Laws of Gravity* (1992), *Gun Crazy* (1993), *Killing Zoe* (1994), *Red Rock West* (1994), *The Last Seduction* (1994), *Heavenly Creatures* (1994), *Things to Do in Denver When You're Dead* (1995), *Little Odessa* (1995), *Albino Alligator* (1996), *From Dusk to Dawn* (1996), *Kiss or Kill* (1996), *Copland* (1997), *Jackie Brown* (1997), *Rounders* (1998), *Suicide Kings* (1998), *The Opportunists* (2000), and *The Way of the Gun* (2000).[5] So while there is a modern/postmodern transition causing Tarantino and Scorsese to tell their stories differently—ironically instead of existentially as Shrader observes—they continue to tell much the same stories.

Postmodern Appropriations

Certainly one of the reasons Tarantino's work is viewed as postmodern is that it makes extensive appropriations of and references to pop culture. Indicative are the celebrated openings of *Pulp Fiction* and *Reservoir Dogs* with their consumer and popular citations: what a Big Mac is called in France; theorizing the meaning of the lyrics to Madonna's "Like a Virgin." Such appropriation largely has been praised for its humor and cleverness, "This is the kind of stuff most of us actually do spend much of our time talking about, and it puts us on a level of understanding with the characters....[I]t is to Tarantino's credit that he has managed to work modern, junk and retro culture into his script with such ease" (Lipman 51). Some appropriations, however, have caused controversy over whether they are homage or plagiarism.

The short, black wig worn by Uma Thurman as Mia Wallace in *Pulp Fiction* is seen as borrowed from Anna Karina, lead in a number of Jean-Luc Godard films, and so it is perceived as an homage to that director. The biblical passage, Ezekiel 25:17, so pivotal to Jules's character, was used earlier in a kung fu film and was spoken by a black character, which Tarantino freely admits: "The guy reading it was a black guy and he was reading it like...'the path of the righteous myannnnn,' and I looked it up in the Bible and it was so great" (B. Lowry 28).

Viewed as more disturbing are the similarities between *Reservoir Dogs* and *City on Fire*, a 1989 Hong Kong film directed by Ringo Lan. In *Quentin Tarantino: The Cinema of Cool*, a largely favorable view as the title suggests, author Jeff Dawson summarizes a segment of *City on Fire*:

> a gang of code-named robbers (Brother Jo, Brother Chow, Brother Fu and Brother Nam) leg it after a bungled diamond heist. The heist has been bungled because one of them, a psychopath, started shooting. The cops were lying in wait, tipped off by

Brother Chow, an undercover cop. In the getting away, Brother Chow is 'minded' by the older Brother Fu who sickens Chow by emptying a pair of barettas through the wind-screen of a police car. Chow shoots an innocent bystander and gets wounded himself. Fu carries him to the rendezvous, a disused warehouse. Fearing that they were set up, the boss (Big Song) is called. Big Song accuses Chow of being a cop and pulls his gun on him. Fu protests Chow's innocence and pulls his gun, too. A four-way stand-off ensues. (90)[6]

Tarantino's response is, again, strikingly upfront: "I love *City On Fire* and I have the poster for it framed in my house. It's a great movie. I steal from every movie. I steal from every single movie ever made. I love it.... Great artists *steal*, they don't do *hommages*" (Dawson 91).

On the one hand, the controversy over whether forms of appropriation are "homage" or "theft" can be understood as the reworking, in process, of modernist concepts of "originality," the enormous emphasis placed by modernism on the value of the new and unknown.[7] "The paradox is that Tarantino takes these stale ingredients and makes them fresh which, I suppose, is the paradox of postmodernism" (Rickey, "Tarantino" W3). And even more generously, "The miracle of Quentin Tarantino's *Pulp Fiction* is how, being composed of second-hand, debased parts, it succeeds in gleaming like something new.... When it works we call it postmodernism; when it doesn't, it's vampirism" (Ansen, "Redemption" 71).

On the other hand, significant issues are at stake over credit and credibility in the transition to a cultural production of appropriation. In Tarantino's favor, the editor of *UK Premiere*, Matt Mueller, argues:

> Nothing's really original in terms of what he's doing but it's *how* he does it, how he puts it together. The way he combines all these elements is what makes it so unique. It's like Elvis or Buddy Holly, when they created rock and roll. They took black music that had been around for years and years and made it accessible for a popular audience. He's doing for movies what they did for music. (qtd. in Dawson 89)

But this argument evades a crucial issue based on the "availability" of black music. As African American jazz saxophonist Archie Shepp put it, "You own the music and we make it" (qtd. in Kofsky 12). In some quarters, cultural production as appropriation is not so new.

Postmodern appropriation seems to work best when it is acknowledged or, better yet, hailed. The difficulties within a postmodern paradigm surrounding concepts of appropriation when unacknowledged become evident in Tarantino's dealings with friend and writing collaborator Roger Avary. The stories for *True Romance* and *Natural Born Killers* originated in a script by Avary, *The Open Road*. Tarantino rewrote the script, which became the foundation for both *True*

Romance and *Natural Born Killers* (the latter began as a story within a story in the *True Romance* frame, as a fictionalized version of the couple's exploits that the Clarence character writes during their cross-country run) (Dawson 124; Hamsher 26). As partners, they attempted to get *True Romance* produced, but after three years without success, Tarantino sold the script to director Tony Scott. Avary receives no credit despite initiating the story, collaborating on rewrites, or the fact that Scott hired him to rewrite *True Romance*'s ending (Dawson 107).

The development of *Pulp Fiction* becomes even more blurred. Credit for the film reads: "Written and Directed by Quentin Tarantino; Stories by Quentin Tarantino and Roger Avary." The original idea for *Pulp Fiction* as three distinct crime stories began as a collaboration between Tarantino and Avary. Tarantino came up with the stories for segment one, about Vincent and Jules, and segment three, concerning a bank heist gone wrong. The latter was subsequently rewritten as the separate, feature-length *Reservoir Dogs*. Avary contributed segment two, about a boxer who refuses to throw a fight. He also subsequently rewrote that into a feature-length screenplay titled *Pandemonium Reigns*.

In Avary's account:

> When Quentin had done *Reservoir Dogs*, he called me up and said, "Roger, they're offering me all these different projects, but the one thing I gotta do is *Pulp Fiction*." And I said, "Great, go to it." So we went back and we got *Pandemonium Reigns* and we squashed it back down and it became *The Gold Watch*. We took a scene that I had written for *True Romance* and that had been written out of the script (about someone's head being blown off inside a car) and things that Quentin had written for other movies and we just kind of rushed everything together. We got together in Amsterdam and mostly the middle story is mine. (qtd. in Dawson 144)

By which Avary means that he wrote the majority of *The Gold Watch*, concerning the boxer Butch (Bruce Willis) and Marsellus Wallace (Ving Rhames), as well as initially coming up with the idea.

According to Dawson, "Until Avary, too, received an Oscar for his troubles, there had been some doubt as to the extent of his contribution to the overall picture, with a swell of media opinion suggesting that Avary had almost been duped out of his share of the credit" (145). The decision to award screenwriting Oscars to both was made by the Academy of Motion Pictures Arts and Sciences, in Avary's case based on the "Stories by" credit.

Avary, because he needed the money, sold his rights in *Pulp Fiction* to Tarantino for Writers Guild minimum and the stories credit. Avary, in fact, responds with equanimity to these events: "Any decision that I made, I made under counsel, with attorneys and with agents. It was ultimately my decision and made of clear mind and body and I certainly, especially at this point, don't regret anything I've done. Even before I got the Oscar, I didn't regret what happened because the certain sacrifices that I made enabled me to get *Killing Zoe* made" (Dawson 145).

Tarantino's version, reported to the *Los Angeles Times*, is:

> Roger wrote a script that I wanted to use, so I bought it from him....Then I came up with all the other ideas and characters and so I adapted his screenplay the way you would adapt a book. But having said that, I don't want Roger getting credit for monologues. *I* write the monologues (qtd. in Dawson 146).

Tarantino seems to be referring specifically to the monologue delivered by Christopher Walken, which explains the history of the watch, passed down from soldier to soldier and father to son, and its importance to Butch. But here, in the case of his collaborating with Avary, Tarantino is much less inclined to embrace or even admit to "stealing" as an artistic practice, as he had with *City on Fire*, or to allowing his own work to be "appropriated."

Interestingly, the most contentious question of authorship between the two occurs over Tarantino's cameo role in *Sleep with Me* (1994) in which, during a party scene, he argues the homoerotic aspects of *Top Gun* (1986). "I came up with my own speech. It was a theory me and a friend worked out. *Top Gun* as a gay-theme movie," he explains in the *New York Times* (B. Lowry 27). And in *The Cinema of Cool* he explains, "Roger came up with the original theory about it and then the two of us proceeded to perfect it. Like a comedy team, kept expanding on it" (Dawson 202). The normally reticent Avary sharply disagrees: "That was a routine I came up with. I spent hours trying to convince everybody that it's true.... It annoyed me the way I found out about it more than anything. I was in a restaurant with Eric Stoltz [who is in both *Sleep with Me* and *Killing Zoe*] and I was telling him about it and he goes, 'Oh my God, Quentin just improvised that'" (Dawson 202).

Difficulties in distinguishing between kinds of borrowings mark a postmodern problematic. Part of the issue may not be the appropriation per se but its acknowledgment, for instance Tarantino's open claim of stealing from *City on Fire* or of getting the Ezekiel passage from a Kung Fu movie versus his denial of Avary's input. From Avary's point of view Tarantino is not always eager to hand out credit where credit is due (Dawson 202). The greater dilemma appears to arise with accountable rather than unaccountable appropriation, that is, situations in which accountability in the form of financial tangibles such as fees and shared writing credits are due. Both Tarantino's work and postmodernism raise issues of what is and what is not appropriate appropriation.

Postmodernism and Pop Culture

Other widely recognized postmodern attributes in Tarantino's work include fragmentation and pastiche. Much has been made of *Pulp Fiction*'s piecemeal structure, in which stories stop and restart and time is nonchronological, but this is hardly the first instance of nonlinear narrative, a mainstay of avant-garde modernist film throughout its existence. However, the specific quality of *Pulp Fiction*'s fragmentation may have frequently been overlooked because of Tarantino's own propensity to compare his films' structures to that of novels (B. Lowry 28; Dawson 68,141). But the way in which *Pulp Fiction*'s structure departs from the nonlinearity of art films, as Pat Dowell in *Cineaste* points out, "should be familiar":

> Every day Americans are quite at home with stories that come to a rest, divided into segments to be interrupted by other stories and then resume. The interruptions are called commercials and increasingly they are commercials for other stories both on television and in the movies. Channel surfing also segments the stories we watch. In *Pulp Fiction* Tarantino starts episodes and lets them come to what feel like commercial breaks. The setup scene of Honeybunny and Pumpkin in the coffee shop planning their robbery is exactly like the tease that opens most television shows before the first commercial; audiences don't expect it in a movie and so don't frame it as such, but, after surfing in and out of other episodes, Tarantino eventually returns to it. (4)[8]

Certainly, returning to the same show after a suspension in time (usually a week) is another attribute of televisual fragmentation. It is not simply that *Pulp Fiction* is nonlinear but also that its fragmentation mimics some of the narrative dynamics of television. Or as Carrie Rickey puts it, *Pulp Fiction*'s five stories "dovetail like the subplots on a *Seinfeld* episode" ("Tarantino" W3).

Tarantino's films are pastiche, for instance, in terms of their very conscious compilation of historical eras. Discussion of Madonna's lyrics establish *Reservoir Dogs* as set in the 1990s, but the music ("Stuck in the Middle with You") and other references evoke the 1970s, while the black suits and ties of the cast recall 1950s film noir and gangster films.[9] Equally, the feeling of "it looks like the 1950s, is set in the 1990s but acts like the 1970s" (Dawson 79) is repeated in *Pulp Fiction* with its present-time references to McDonald's, Flock of Seagulls, and so on, its casting of 1970s movie icon John Travolta as Vincent Vega, and then setting him in a 1950s retro diner staffed by Buddy Holly and Marilyn

Monroe look-alikes and Douglas Sirk–named menu items. Operating in a similar manner is Tarantino's awareness that Bruce Willis as Butch "has the look of a 50s actor," comparing him to Aldo Ray (Dargis, "Pulp Instincts" 10).

One of Tarantino's most heralded personal characteristics is his memory. Much has been written about his prodigious ability to retain cinematic details.[10] He seems to imbibe films and television, to recollect them whole. The press' most frequently reiterated Tarantino persona is "video store geek," due to his abilities of recollection and because he worked at a film aficionado's video rental store in Los Angeles before making films. It was at this store, Video Archives, where he met Avary, another young man who prided himself on his encyclopedic knowledge of film. "'When we first met we had a great competition,' Avary recalls. 'We hated each other. It was *Who knows more?* And he won. Quentin is a database'." And Tarantino takes care to set the record straight, "People think I learned about movies because I worked there. But I worked there because I knew about movies" (Hirschberg, "Tarantino" 120).

However, his memory extends beyond a capacity for filmic data. "'Quentin has a mind for dialogue,' says Avary. 'He can repeat a conversation you've had ten or fifteen years ago verbatim'" (Dawson 35). As with his *Top Gun* parody in *Sleep with Me*, a good deal of his dialogue originates as conversation, his own and others, which he retains and reformulates. Managing to draft *Reservoir Dogs* in three weeks, Tarantino explains, "I wrote it real quick, but that's slightly deceptive simply because I had done some homework on it before, but dialogue's real easy for me to write and since this movie is nearly *all* dialogue it's just getting guys talking to each other and then jotting it down" (46). Tarantino combines a strong ear for dialogue with a strong memory.

Pat Dowell writes that *Pulp Fiction* "reproduces the everyday experience of living in a fragmented society, in which each of us must stitch together a coherent narrative out of the bombardment of information and drama that is our daily passage in a market culture" (5). Another effect of postmodernism is that "the amount of information available to the subject and required of it exceeds its capacities" (Miller 45), potentially overwhelming the subject and leaving her or him without the means to make sense of the world. The significance of Tarantino's skills of retention is that they give him the ability to remember, select, and condense information in this era of ceaseless visual and aural input. His specific kind of appropriation and referentiality seeks to celebrate or at least to graciously live with the abundance or excess of information surrounding us all. As Amanda Lipman points out, even "if we are not supposed to empathise with the characters themselves, we cannot help recognising the junk culture world they inhabit" (51). The artifacts in this world may not be "junk" per se—the information age conveys a lot of useful, valuable material—but it has the feel of junk in that it is overwhelming, in that it is so difficult to know how to compartmentalize, interpret, or live with it. And this is something Tarantino's texts offer, to help make sense of it all. Rather than empathizing with single, conflicted characters as we do with an existentialist text, we connect with the surrounding context, the world Tarantino's characters inhabit. The transition in Tarantino's film is from an individuated, psychological imaginary to a *cultural imaginary*, based on commonality of mediated experience, that is, dependent on shared cultural habitation and memory.

A Postmodern Cultural Imaginary

How such a cultural imaginary functions in *Pulp Fiction* can be explored by looking at the presence of John Travolta, both in his casting and in the treatment of his persona within the film. Playing Vincent Vega caused the surprising revival of Travolta's career that had twenty years previously seemed unstoppable but that had languished in the previous decade as Travolta made such films as the *Look Who's Talking* series (1989, 1991, and 1992). As Martin Amis describes meeting Travolta: "For me, it was like stepping into a Warhol poster—a Mao, an Elvis. It was like bumping into Jim Morrison, or Jimi Hendrix. You feel that John Travolta is so iconic that he ought to be dead. And he isn't: not anymore" (Amis 17). Travolta's resurrection in *Pulp Fiction* captured an iconic place he holds in popular culture as well as seemed to retrieve something from the historical past. His presence appropriated double qualities of *place* in popular culture: elevation and time. For example, Bruce Willis, too, is an iconic cultural figure in his persona as action hero, but he's never "gone missing." He's been a consistent presence since the success of *Die Hard* in 1988. Travolta reached similar heights of popularity as Willis, or exceeded them, but his presence in *Pulp Fiction* also conveys the sense of history, of the popular past retrieved and saved. The casting choice of Travolta is, in itself, a recoupment for popular memory, an act of documenting popular history.

Tarantino was a fan of Travolta's from his 1970s films and especially from his performance in *Blow Out*, one of Tarantino's favorites. As Julie Burchill comments, "Tarantino's specialty is not in *discovering* great new actors, but in giving a second chance to disgraced or neglected ones" in the same way that "television commercials no longer commission new jingles, but instead use classic pop songs for that instant hit of nostalgia" (Burchill, "Shooting" 6). It is that "hit of nostalgia" to which Tarantino is so attuned. A collector of film and television series lunch boxes, figurines, and board games, during his "audition" encounter with Travolta, Tarantino had him play the games from both *Welcome*

Back, Kotter (the 1970s television series in which Travolta played Vinnie Barbarino) and *Grease* (1978) (Hirschberg, "Tarantino" 122; Biskind 97). Travolta won both rounds which Tarantino attempted to explain away: "I was thrown off my game on *Welcome Back, Kotter* because I normally play Barbarino" (qtd. in Biskind 97).

Many commentators focus on *Pulp Fiction*'s first segment, "Vincent Vega & Marsellus Wallace's Wife," which begins with Vincent and Jules's early morning hit and ends with Mia Wallace's near overdose, as the film's most successful. They often find Vincent's character to be the lead or link across the various stories (Lipman 51),[11] and dwell specifically on the dance sequence. For instance, Gavin Smith describes it as "Mia and Vincent pairing for a cool, beyond-chic twist on the restaurant's dance floor" ("Tarantino" 32), and *Mademoiselle*'s take is, "It's hard not to smile when Travolta—20 pounds overweight, stringy hair hanging down to his shoulders—gets up to do the twist with Thurman in a sweet lampoon of his Brooklyn dance-king moves" (Frankel 91). The effectiveness of Travolta in the film rests not simply on his having been cast but also on how his persona is treated. While Willis's presence in *Pulp Fiction* plays on the action figure, and Samuel Jackson as Jules is a play on the blaxploitation hero, neither character quite pinpoints the moment of play and persona as successfully as Travolta does when he dances.

It is a more effective send up precisely because he does and does not repeat his past persona. From Amis:

> The rebirth had to be a revamp, a kind of travesty. Accordingly, the physically graceful but emotionally gawky American calf—Tony/Danny/Bud—was obliged to reappear as a corrupt and jowelly ruin. This is why the dance scene with Uma Thurman is so central. It is a post-modern *coup de théâtre*. The audience colludes. Every movie goer knows what Travolta can do on a dance floor. Watching his drugged gyrations is like watching the aged Picasso drawing a stickman. (20)

While Amis ascribes a tone of regret to this scene because of the changes in Travolta, for those in the audience who grew up with Travolta and are of his generation it also offers a moment of hope. Despite the years and the paunch, it holds out the possibility that one can still remain in the game. In an interview with Travolta, Steven Rea calls the dance sequence "a sublime set-piece": "Slowly, the stoned, stony-faced Vincent gets into the groove, doing that grinding-out-the-cigarette move as Chuck Berry rocks the speakers" ("Look" F1). Travolta responds that the scene was an opportunity for him because he was able to do novelty dances and because he is fond of dancing in character. "I got to be in character…[and] do dances that Vincent and I would have grown up with, do it high—you know, within the character—and look the way I did with that gut and that whole thing." As for the audience, "they either see what I see, or they go on a memory trip of whatever they want to remember—*Grease, Saturday Night Fever, Urban Cowboy*. But everybody wins. It's so satisfying" (F4). It is the similarities *and* differences between the 1970s and 1990s Travolta personas, all in play at this moment on the dance floor that gives the sequence its effect and poignancy.

Further, it is not solely that Travolta dances but also how he dances. Burchill suggests, "The only possible improvement one could make to this section would be to have Thurman and Travolta dance, not to Chuck Berry, but to the Bee Gees, or even You're The One That I Want; though perhaps the fact that Tarantino resisted this is to his credit" ("Shooting" 7). Indeed, it is precisely the scene's minimalist quality that is so much a part of its effect. It is a moment, not of excess, but of discretion:

> You brace yourself for a big Travolta moment. Will he nip to the men's room and come back in a white suit and black shirt? Will he roll his hands and point at the glitter ball? No way; the two of them take to the floor and quietly twist, while the camera stands to one side, snatches a couple of closeups, then fades them out halfway through. It's a triumph of discretion, the only one in the movie. (Lane 97)

Indeed, the sequence is surprisingly understated, lasting a minute and forty-five seconds through the chorus and two verses of Chuck Berry's "You Never Can Tell" before fading out at the beginning of the refrain to the chorus. The camera work is equally circumspect, composed of only four shots: wide shot with the two twisting, which is held for a while, until Travolta does his up-on-his-toes move. Cut to a medium close shot, which starts on Travolta then pans to and holds on Thurman; the camera drifts back to Travolta as if it is going to settle on him then immediately pans back to Thurman and holds on her as she does the Swim. Cut to a close-up of Travolta doing the Batman then pan to Thurman doing the same, which then widens to a medium shot of Travolta twisting, tilts down to his feet, and keeps moving to Thurman's feet. Cut to a medium shot of Thurman, which dollies right to include Travolta, holds on the two for a moment, then drifts back to a solo shot of Thurman as the scene fades out from there.

Initially puzzling, the camera stays on Thurman for as long or even longer than on Travolta. And it is Thurman who gets the solo number when the two return to the Wallace residence. But the camera choices make sense if one recalls that Thurman, a 1990s star, appeals to the twenty-something audience of the film, while Travolta resonates for its forty-something viewers. The two dancing together is an intergenerational moment of viewing pleasure, a shared cultural meeting ground. For the forty-something viewers, the high point of "Vincent Vega & Marsellus Wallace's Wife" is Travolta's resurrection as he dances. For the twenty-something audience, the story's high point is Thurman's resurrection with a hypodermic needle to her heart.

Further, the restrained quality of the dance sequence, its "triumph of discretion," leaves us wanting more; we are not satisfied, certainly not satiated. It retains its moment or state of longing, the desire that is nostalgia. It is the desire to revisit a certain time or event that is so critical to the structure of feeling that is nostalgia, not the revisiting itself.

Although frequently described as such, Travolta's presence in the dance scene is not really a parody (while displaying it to excess would have made it so) but rather an immersion in a moment of popular memory. The affectionate mood of the scene, "its sweet lampoon," lacks the critical distance necessary for satire or parody; its "sweetness" conveys the engagement and the play involved in revisiting. The irony of the distant, circumspect camera is that it helps create the opposite effect—not the critical distance of satire and parody but the pleasures and immediacy of immersion.

It is appropriate that this older, now overweight 1970s icon dances to Chuck Berry in the 1950s aura of Jackrabbit Slim's with a 1990s movie star partner. The scene encapsulates, plays on, and immerses itself in popular memory. As a site and citation of cultural recollection it is not only deeply nostalgic but one could well add, about nostalgia. Because it is so deeply embedded in shared cultural memory, the discursive effect of *Pulp Fiction* is nostalgia, seemingly at odds with its striking contemporariness—but this is another paradox of certain manifestations of postmodernism. Although postmodernism is so "futuristic" in its outlook, there is a running thread that is deeply nostalgic.

History and Nostalgia

Jean Baudrillard describes a new postmodern uncertainty of meaning, free floating and indeterminate. "All the great humanist criteria of value, all the values of a civilisation of moral, aesthetic, and practical judgement, vanish in our system of images and signs" (qtd. in Pribram, *Seduction* 201–2). Despite his disclaimer that postmodernity is neither "optimistic nor pessimistic," Baudrillard paints a bleak and nostalgic picture of what remains for the "survivors" of modernity: "Suddenly there is a curve in the road, a turning point. Somewhere, the real scene has been lost, the scene where you had rules for the game and some solid stakes that everyone could rely on" (204). One wonders, here, who is meant by "everyone." Just how inclusive were those rules and "solid stakes that everyone could rely on"?

Similarly, Fredric Jameson describes postmodern culture as one that displays "an alarming and pathological symptom of a society that has become incapable of dealing with time and history" (117). Jameson argues that postmodernism is ahistorical because "it is incapable of achieving aesthetic representations of our own current experiences," remaining instead, "condemned to seek the historical past through our own pop images and stereotypes about that past, which itself remains forever out of reach" (117–18). The mediated, pastiche quality of the postmodern appears to delimit our ability to locate ourselves historically because, unlike modernity, originality and authenticity are no longer possible. Those modernist qualities are apparently a prerequisite for access to a "real," and so the historical. Instead, history is destined to be replaced in postmodernity by nostalgia as the future.

But it could be argued as easily, in opposition to Jameson's position, that the postmodern, by identifying work in terms of its diversity—calling attention to its time, place, and voices of origin—*historicizes*, precisely by removing cultural knowledges from the abstract realms of the universal, the absolute, and the eternal. As Leela Gandhi notes, a postcolonial-poststructuralist intervention focuses "on 'history' as the grand narrative through which Eurocentrism is 'totalised' as the proper account of all humanity" (171). Even if Jameson is right that one course of postmodernism is about nostalgia, which is the stream that perhaps most concerns him, Baudrillard, and Tarantino, and even if they themselves are nostalgic for a vanishing series of rules and solid stakes, it does not mean that their position represents all potential currents in postmodernity. A postmodern historicism might well be the representation of otherness and the accounting of difference, multiplicity, and diversity.

For if we accept that *Pulp Fiction* in its postmodern countenance is deeply nostalgic, we must also ask what it is nostalgic for. Here we return to its modernist, auteurist roots, to the similar ground covered by both Scorsese and Tarantino. This brings us, once again, to Paul Schrader's contention that "Tarantino is Scorsese with quote marks around him," and to a consideration of just how this is so.

Reservoir Dogs and Masculinity

As John Fried rightly observes in *Cineaste*, just because *Pulp Fiction* refuses to conform to the contours of humanist moralism with its sins and redemptions (as Stone attempts to do with *Natural Born Killers*), this does not automatically make the text apolitical. "In fact, it is precisely the film's play on classic *film noir*, blaxploitation, and kung fu films, among other action genres, that leads one directly to the core of its power politics: masculinity and the anxiety of the male hero" (6). Tarantino's texts dwell repeatedly on the codes of masculinity and the pleasures of male community, from the identical, trendy "uniform" of black suit, white shirt, and black tie signaling membership in a certain club, to the hip hit partnership of Vincent and Jules.

Reservoir Dogs abounds in references to masculinity: about being or failing to be a "real man." Lack of sufficient masculinity is often couched in terms of femininity, homosexuality, or infancy. For instance, just before undercover cop Mr. Orange (Tim Roth) goes to meet with the other gang members to plan the diamond robbery, he pauses to look at himself in the mirror, saying, to bolster his courage, "Don't pussy out on me now. They don't know. They don't know shit. You're not gonna get hurt. You're fucking Baretta. They believe every word cause you're supercool," in which the antithesis of masculinity is to be compared to female genitalia. As he gets into the waiting car we watch from the point of view of a tailing police vehicle and listen to the comments of its offscreen occupants:

> Cop V/O #1: There goes our boy.
> Cop V/O #2: I swear, the guy has to have rocks in his head the size of Gibraltar to work undercover.
> Cop V/O #1: Do you want one of these?
> Cop V/O #2: Yeah, give me the bear claw.

Their exchange serves to contradict the comment about undercover work, revealing Mr. Orange not to be crazy but the "real" cop. They might have the pastry but he's got the testosterone.

When, after the robbery gone bad, Mr. Blonde (Michael Madsen) arrives at the warehouse, the designated meeting place, he finds Mr. White (Harvey Keitel) and Mr. Pink (Steve Buscemi) shouting at each other, guns drawn. Mr. Blonde calls a halt to their fighting by rendering them children, "You kids shouldn't play so rough, somebody's gonna start crying."

At the core of *Reservoir Dogs* is a love story of sorts, between Mr. Orange and Mr. White, two mismatched guys from opposite sides of the tracks (one cop, one robber). The events of the film test their identities as professionals and as men. Indeed, the story is based on their identities as men coming into conflict with their self-constructions as professionals.

Although positioned on opposite sides of the law, the two adhere to strict and similar codes of behavior based on notions of what it means to be a professional. Mr. White, a seasoned pro, complains about Mr. Blonde who screws up the robbery when he begins shooting people, "What you're supposed to do is act like a fucking professional. A psychopath isn't a professional. I can't work with a psychopath. You don't know what those sick assholes are gonna do next." In Mr. White's world, as in that of the police, you shoot only in self-protection, to control the situation, and to accomplish the mission. Both sides are playing the same war game in a world populated by three categories of people: cops, robbers, and "real people" (civilians):

> Mr. Pink: I tagged a couple of cops. Did you kill anybody?
> Mr. White: A few cops.
> Mr. Pink: No real people?
> Mr. White: Just cops.

The two sides simply have a different version of who the bad guy is. For the cops it is the robbers; for the robbers it is the police informer in their midst.

Within these strictures of professionalism, a crucial value, because it is necessary to the success of the mission, is loyalty. We see this in Marvin (Kirk Baltz), the cop Mr. Blonde disfigures; despite being beaten and then tortured he does not reveal that Mr. Orange is the "rat" in their midst, the one who set them up for the bungled robbery and can now identify them. But within the code of masculinity, loyalty is elevated beyond a component of professionalism to a transcending virtue in its own right. It is loyalty that comes closest to love in this worldview.

Strictly speaking, Mr. Pink is the "winner" of the story's events—he survives with his life and escapes with the diamonds. But he is not the most honorable of the characters; indeed, of the group who makes it to the warehouse he may be the least admirable or honorable—he is motivated by professionalism, yes, but not by loyalty. As he says to Mr. White, when he learns that White has told the wounded Mr. Orange his first name, Larry, and where he's from, "You're acting like a first year fucking thief; I'm acting like a professional." And Mr. Pink is correct. In opening up to Mr. Orange, in telling him his name, and later by protecting him at all costs, Mr. White acts out of sentiment, not professionalism. But we are meant to relate to Mr. White's character, not Mr. Pink's, because it is White who takes the code of masculinity to its purest, highest levels, who lives for the ideals of the code itself and no longer simply for the material gains reaped by adherence to the code. This is a very romantic view of masculinity in its willingness to place loyalty above all else, above and beyond professionalism, above even personal survival. And so fittingly, other aspects of the relationship between Mr. Orange and Mr. White are embedded in the discourse of romanticism.

The most overtly homoerotic relationship in the film is between Nice Guy Eddie (Chris Penn) and Mr. Blonde, a relationship based on (ultimately self-destructive) loyalty. But the most tender, loving—and blindly loyal—relationship is that between Mr. Orange and Mr. White. Immediately following the opening credits there is an abrupt cut to Mr. Orange wounded and bleeding in the back seat of a car, in the aftermath of the robbery gone wrong. We hold on him as he grasps the hand of an off-camera person who attempts to talk him through his fear and pain. The camera pans right, across the clasped hands, to reveal Mr. White in the front seat, driving. This is the first view we have of Mr. White in the scene—as an extension of their entwined and clasped hands.

When they reach the warehouse, as Mr. White helps Mr. Orange inside he infantilizes him by cooing, "Who's a tough guy? Come on, who's a tough guy?" and "We made it. We fucking make it. Look where we are," using the words and intonations of baby talk. Once he is lying down, still bleeding profusely, Orange confesses to White that he is scared—outside the bounds of usual masculine admissibility—and asks White to hold him. White cradles him like a sick lover: Orange is in the protected, traditionally female, diminished position in the lower portion of the frame of coupled embraces. At one moment, White whispers in Orange's ear—we cannot hear what—and Orange laughs, the gestures of a shared lovers' secret. White tells him, "You go ahead and be scared. You've been brave enough for one day," suggesting that the reprieve from the strict boundaries of permissible masculine behavior helps unite the two.[12]

Their relationship culminates at the end of the film when Joe (Lawrence Tierney) draws a gun on Mr. Orange, believing him to be the police informer. White draws his gun on Joe: "Joe, you're making a terrible mistake. I'm not gonna let you make it." Nice Guy Eddie, Joe's son, aims his gun at Mr. White. White: "Joe, if you kill that man you die next. Repeat, if you kill that man you die next." And indeed, they all shoot each other.

White has erred in trusting Orange, in allowing his feelings to supersede his code of professionalism. Orange has transgressed the code of his profession, too: by watching without acting when White shoots and kills two policemen through the windshield of their car (and by continuing to care about White afterwards); in being shot by a woman whose car they hijack, and killing her in response, although she's a civilian, a "real person," who cannot be expected to know, be accountable to, or to live by their codes.

And now, at the end of the film, Orange commits the ultimate transgression. A badly wounded White crawls over to Orange and embraces him, cradling him lovingly and protectively, although he too is shot. Orange embraces him in return and then admits he is a cop. Until this moment he has never blown his cover: not as he watched while fellow officers were killed; not in order to save himself in the immediate aftermath of the bungled robbery. But here, when he is virtually free and clear, when the cops have arrived at the warehouse, signaling his rescue, he confesses to White. Not out of necessity, duress, or a sense of professionalism—quite the contrary. Out of an act of loyalty to White, honesty in exchange for the other's trust in him, he tells White, "I'm a cop, Larry. It's true, Larry, I'm a cop." His hand cradling one side of Orange's face, his gun aimed directly at the other side, White, crying and moaning, says "Sorry" as he shoots Orange and the cops shoot him. Both have sacrificed themselves out of loyalty to and love for the other.

The cumulative effect of the film's central relationship does not read as a comedy of errors or as a parody of this display of excessive masculinity. In its romanticism, there is something we are meant to view as supposedly tragically or ennoblingly heroic in this mutual self-sacrifice. This is the tale and the tone of two star-crossed lovers dying in each other's arms.

Pulp Fiction and Masculinity

Within a similar paradigm of masculinity, the segment in which Vincent escorts Mia Wallace for the evening in *Pulp Fiction* is actually an interaction between Vincent and Marsellus. This is made evident in the segment's title: "Vincent Vega & Marsellus Wallace's Wife" (not Vincent Vega & Mia Wallace). Here Mia is the extension of her husband, serving as the vehicle for interaction between the two men: the boss, the film's most powerful male; and the hero, the character for whom we feel (along with Jules) the greatest empathic connection. If we do not "identify" with Vincent in normative narrative terms, we at least journey through much of the story with him.

What *Pulp Fiction* introduces beyond *Reservoir Dogs* are the links between masculine identity and power. The subtextual tension, including sexual, surrounding Vincent's "date" with Mia is set up by the story of Marsellus's past behavior toward underlings who have shown excessive affection for his wife—purportedly having a man thrown out of a fourth floor window for giving Mia a foot massage.

Vincent works for Marsellus; Marsellus calls the shots. And Mia makes Marsellus's power clear, and by transference her own, over the twist contest, for instance, when Vincent initially resists participating: "I do believe Marsellus, my husband, your boss, told you to take me out and do whatever I wanted. Now, I want to dance. I want to win. I want that trophy." The code of professionalism and honor among men/gangsters prohibits Vincent from having sex with his boss's wife. But even more important, given Marsellus's reputation and power over Vincent, self-preservation mitigates against doing so. And so Vincent stands in the bathroom, arguing with himself not to sleep with Mrs. Wallace, just at the moment that she is in the living room overdosing on his heroin. But the imbalance of power is remedied, at least symbolically, when Vincent drives a hypodermic needle straight into Mia's heart, the adrenaline the cure for her overdose, and does so with enough force and aggression (and excitement for the audience) to get back at her for having power over him and for Marsellus having power over him, and so not being able to fuck her in the first place.

The links between practices of masculinity and power are made even more apparent in the film's next segment, "The Gold Watch." That the watch itself is a symbol of masculinity is made clear in the recounting of its history by Captain Koons (Christopher Walken) in which, as John Fried notes, we are told "how at the end of each war it passed from man to man, literally from ass to ass—and how it is now Butch's turn to guard the grail of masculinity" (Fried 6).

Although enemies (Marsellus is out to kill Butch) when the two are captured by a pair of "redneck" S/M homosexuals, Maynard and Zed (Duane Whitaker and Peter Greene), with intent to torture and sodomize, Butch turns back from his close escape in order to rescue Marsellus. He does so ostensibly out of honor and solidarity: the "honor of thieves" and the solidarity between two men who, like the cops and robbers in *Reservoir Dogs*, share similar codes of behavior within a common framework of existence. And Butch also turns back because the two men share the solidarity of heterosexuality.

The greatest threat to heterosexual masculinity is homosexuality, and it is this peril that the two must now jointly confront.[13] The incident causes them to bond as "men," certainly, but not as a result of their achievements; rather, through their humiliation (Marsellus) and near-humiliation (Butch).

However, this is also the moment when Butch can turn the tables of power and exact his retaliation on Marsellus. That is, he can exert the superiority of his own masculinity. Previously Marsellus had greater power over Butch (ordering him to throw a fight; having him hunted down when he disobeys). Now Butch gains the upper hand because it is Marsellus who has been sodomized and not Butch. It is Butch who knows about the disgrace that undermines Marsellus's masculinity, the masculinity that has served as the foundation of Marsellus's power and authority. And indeed, the two strike a bargain. In exchange for Butch's vow of silence, Marsellus allows him to escape with his life and with Marsellus's money.

Tarantino and Avary, among others, celebrate what Scorsese celebrates—the "legit" society of men whether on the right side of the law or not (usually not). As Amy Taubin argues about recent gay films, particularly the work of Gregg

Araki (*The Living End*, 1992) and Tom Kalin (*Swoon*, 1992), the new "queer cinema has much more in common with male violence films (with Quentin Tarantino's *Reservoir Dogs* or Nick Gomez's *Laws of Gravity*, for example) than it does with any feminist cinema. Like Tarantino and Gomez, Araki and Kalin are also the sons of Scorsese, whose films define and critique masculinity through violence but also make Robert De Niro a homoerotic object of desire" (Taubin, "Queer Male Cinema" 179).[14] Such "male violence films" share a continuous thread, a common emphasis not disrupted by generation.

And while it might be argued that Tarantino parodies the excesses of masculine behavior (everyone dying at the end of *Reservoir Dogs*; the high absurdity of Maynard and Zed; the Captain Koons-gold watch monologue), "there is more going on here than a simple play on the artifice of masculinity. With each pathological twist and turn of its plot, the film reveals its preoccupation with the necessity to protect the boundaries of masculinity" (Fried 7), just as Scorsese's films, in Taubin's words above, "define and critique" it. In both instances, masculinity is being updated, modernized (or postmodernized) for contemporary usage.

Tarantino is right in tacitly acknowledging that the codes of masculinity used in Scorsese's modernist or existential texts no longer encapsulate the contemporary moment as they once did, and so he updates them with, for instance, the quotidian, pop culture conversation of his gangsters. Or to be more accurate, the altered circumstances are that such existential heroes no longer exist as they were *believed to* in the modernist world and within the modernist text. However, Tarantino realizes they can still be *longed for* or *fantasized* within a postmodern practice of nostalgia as the future.

So *Pulp Fiction* both mourns the loss of and celebrates the modernist male, and in so doing, attempts to update him. "Although *Pulp Fiction* certainly revels in deconstructing codes of masculinity, a surfeit of macho images and rhetoric still permeate the film, gratifying spectators who long nostalgically for traditional heroes" (Fried 7). For "traditional" hero, read heterosexual, white male. The sweet sentiment of nostalgia shapes itself as a paean to the loss of the pleasures of male community: the good old days of wars, westerns, and gangsters—the guys.

The problem is that both these concepts of reality represented by Scorsese and Tarantino—modernist or postmodernist; existential or ironic—are circumscribed. They are composed of an overemphasis on a male code of ethics and on a certain type of masculinity as generalizable identity. Masculine identity (white, heterosexual) becomes universally applicable, conveyed by the power of art. The presence of the auteur as cultural visionary and spokesperson elevates a particular worldview to the heights of universal truth, which then becomes model and meaning for "everyone." In fact, however, it is only a narrow paradigm of reality—only one potential model out of a much larger spectrum of possibilities. But the rest of the spectrum is overlooked in that process of elevation to artistic genius in which the auteur becomes spokesperson for "his" entire era. What is constructed within a very specific framework is then too easily interpreted as the entirety.

While Tarantino's work does indeed pinpoint or mark an important cultural shift, the transition from modern to postmodern representation, it does so only within the narrow, exclusionary framework of masculinity and the valorization of auteurism. Within this frame, some worldviews, experiences, and personal truths count, to be elevated to the universal. Such a convergence of auteurism and the dominance of masculine identity are then mistaken for the defining truths of, in the instance of Tarantino, what postmodern culture is or might be.

This becomes clear in the issues surrounding race raised by Tarantino's work. For of course there is another dynamic at work in the power plays between Vincent and Marsellus and between Marsellus and Butch. In this world of masculine supremacy as it is fantasized, it is not surprising that the white man proves more powerful than the black man, in the face of the threat the black man poses, nor is it surprising who is "actually" sodomized.

Representing Race/A White Imaginary

As much as his depictions of violence, Tarantino's representations of race have provoked controversy. Praised in some quarters for his prominent African American characters—Jules in *Pulp Fiction*, Pam Grier as *Jackie Brown*—he is reviled elsewhere for his racist dialogue and use of racial epithets.

Tarantino's own position toward race seems, initially, both curious and contradictory. On the one hand, screenwriter L. M. Kit Carson's comment that *Reservoir Dogs* was a real "white guy movie" was apparently extended as a compliment, and was accepted as such (Hoberman, "True Romance" 61). In *Pulp Fiction*, in the segment "The Bonnie Situation" Tarantino, as the character Jimmy, gives himself some of the nastiest, racist language in the film. "Several writers (J. Hoberman first, I think) have noted already that Tarantino has given himself a role in which he gets to throw the word 'nigger' around, and, I might add, '*dead nigger*' at that. Strangely racist as that may seem, the personal appropriation for the director represents, I think, the wannabe posturing of a hip white guy" (Dowell 5).[15] There is, as Dowell points out, too much "wannabe" in Jimmy's character and Tarantino's persona to write either off as motivated by stock "white guy" racism. The character Jimmy is friends with Jules and in the briefest of shots it turns out that he is married to a black woman. This makes it more difficult to know, as a consequence, how to accept his language usage. Does his friendship and marriage make him black by extension and so use of the word *nigger* is somehow okay? Or are we meant to read the text in such a way that his close relationships with African Americans make him all right (that is, nonracist) *despite* his repeated use of the word? Equally puzzling is why Jules seems so fearful of Jimmy, the only character in the film who renders Jules nervous and whom he attempts to placate.

As for Tarantino, his work is too filled with the effects and details of black culture, too immersed in it, to allow one to write him off as simply prejudicially dismissive of this "other." Dowell suggests that "*Pulp Fiction* fancies itself postracist," that is, "beyond tacky social problems like racism" (5). But he may be closer to the mark in describing Tarantino's representations of race as "the wannabe posturing of a hip white guy," wanting to be black. Sharon Willis augments this view with the crucial point that the white male posturing in Tarantino's films is in imitation of widespread but narrowly circumscribed images and conceptions of black men. Tarantino's depictions reduce black masculinity to "a cultural icon for the dominant culture," in which minority representation exists for the benefit or use of principally white men and their self-images ("Fathers" 60).

Devon Jackson, writing in the *Village Voice*, describes himself as very similar to Tarantino (in race, age, background), except he is offended by the filmmaker's depictions of race, which he attributes entirely to a wannabe mentality: "In his world, blacks are the epitome of cool; as are their language and style; hence, 'nigga' is a cool word. Put all of the above into the character who is white and that white person becomes ultracool" (39). Jackson calls Tarantino's vision of race a "training manual on how to appropriate nigga culture—its imagination, style, and form" (39).

Tarantino's harshest critic on this issue is Spike Lee, who argues very similar points about Tarantino's representations of race. He complains about the excessive use of the word *nigger* in *Jackie Brown, Pulp Fiction,* and *Reservoir Dogs,* saying, "I want Quentin to know that all African-Americans do not think that word is trendy or slick." Lee adds, hitting on the wannabe accusation, "What does he want to be made—an honorary black man?" (qtd. in Gregorian 6). Apparently so, according to Tarantino's defense in response. "I think as a writer, I have the right to create my characters, and I should be hindered only by my talent. I have a talent for writing black characters, because they are me. And I know the truth of me" (qtd. in Lawson B11).

At stake, then, is not only the propriety of certain word usage, but Tarantino's claim that he has a talent for writing black characters because he is them. What is in contestation here is the *appropriation* of *identity*. It is not only the use of the word *nigger*, but how it is used and who gets to use it, especially in the instance of a white man "posturing" as black. This can be likened to gay and lesbian reappropriations of the word—and meanings—of *queer*. Who gets to use it, in what contexts, and with what significances? The issue becomes clearer when considering the different contexts of usage in various Tarantino films. Although used and disapproved of in *Reservoir Dogs*, the word *nigger* did not spark the same controversy as it did when it was used in *Pulp Fiction* and *Jackie Brown*. In *Reservoir Dogs* it can be read as spoken by a bunch of racist, sexist, homophobic white guys sitting around talking "in character." In *Pulp Fiction*, however, it is spoken across races by Jules to Vincent and by Jimmy to Jules, who accepts it without apparent reaction. Therefore, it appears to be giving tacit approval, on the part of blacks (represented by Jules), for white usage.

Appropriation or consumption of others' identities as postmodern practice is a legitimate threat. In this era of much ballyhooed "border crossings," it is critical to consider which borders are being traversed, who they belong to, who is crossing them, and on what bases. Fatima Mernissi's analogy in the epigraph of this chapter, which speaks of peeling an onion to get at multiple layers of truths, told to her by her grandmother, is a reminder that postmodernism did not invent multiplicity of meanings nor relational knowledge.

Mernissi grew up in a harem in Fez, Morocco, in the 1940s and 1950s. She describes a harem as a domestic unit of extended family which "carried on the tradition of women's seclusion.... What defines it as a harem is not polygamy, but the men's desire to seclude their wives, and their wish to maintain an extended household rather than break into nuclear units" (34–35). The front gate of the harem or household, guarded by a doorkeeper, is one of many *hudud* or Islamic sacred frontiers—boundaries, borders or limits, not to be crossed, in this instance, by women. *Hudud* might be geographically tangible as in the harem's front gate or an imaginary frontier "in the mind of the powerful" (3). But despite the restriction, "women dreamed of trespassing all the time. The world beyond the gate was their obsession" (1–2). For women to cross the frontier marked by the household gate was to "trespass," to step into a world in which they were not invited or permitted—the *Dreams of Trespass* of Mernissi's title— to move into forbidden spaces and places.

In the current postmodern play with the concept of border crossings, it is of course a myth to assume that open borders exist for the less powerful. Those who advocate the fluid crossing of borders of identity often fail to consider whether the frontiers they cite are reciprocal—equally open to both sides. While the less powerful seem to understand well that their movement into a colonizer's territory is viewed as trespassing, culturally endowed postmodern border crossers frequently forget that their own journeys into the identity formations of others may not be welcomed as the free and open transversal they posit it to be. These are not dreams but acts of trespass.

Mernissi's perspective mapped onto the territory that *Pulp Fiction* carves out for itself serves as a reminder that the usurpation or appropriation of other cultural positions even when, perhaps especially when, self-consciously apprehended as a compliment—wannabeism or homage—does not equate to the creation of a heterogeneous, pluralistic society. At the turn of the twenty-first century, fear of the loss of mastery over grand narratives such as masculinity is not, by far, the only possible conception of a postmodern world. For some, postmodernism may mark a nostalgia for a specific past; for others, however, history is only now being created in the contours of heterogeneous postmodern identities.

Postmodern narrativity—in the complex sense of representational and cultural/historical discourses invoked in combination—will continue to play a significant role in the makeup of independent film. What is left open to question, however, are the forms such a postmodern independent cinema might take. Will it remain largely an expression of the loss of and the longing for universal mastery (auteurist, masculine, white)? This may prove so if, as in *Pulp Fiction*'s case, a postmodern narrative trajectory is based on the appropriation of other cultures. Or rather, how well might postmodern narrativity express a plurally identified society—a world of difference and multiplicity? Such an alternative depends on the ability of independent film to participate in the construction of representational, institutional, interpretive, and cultural/historical discourses that enable multiple identities to simultaneously and inclusively coexist, that is, an independent cinema that puts into practice a more fully heterogeneous conceptualization of cultural production.

CONCLUSION

Having begun chapter 1 with a description of the influence of independent film on the Academy Awards throughout the 1990s, it seems fitting to conclude with the 2000 and 2001 Oscars, as both Hollywood and independent film move into the new century. In 2000, *American Beauty,* released by the newest studio, Dreamworks, won Best Picture, Best Actor, Best Director, Best Screenplay and Best Cinematography. In 2001, *Crouching Tiger, Hidden Dragon* received ten Oscar nominations including Best Picture, second in number only to Dreamworks/Universal's twelve nominations for *Gladiator*.[1] The subtitled film, whose original language is Mandarin and stars an all-Asian cast, was distributed in the United States by Sony Classics. Although I have discussed how Hollywood has affected independent film, I have said less about how independent film has affected Hollywood.

Critically lauded as well as award-winning, *American Beauty*, a tale of unrequited pedophilia, found approval in some independent quarters as well. For instance, the editors of *Filmmaker* describe the film as having, along with Hollywood stars, "indie subject matter (the dysfunctional suburban American family)," allowing it "to have its cake and eat it too" (Editors 20). And that the film is "all the more radical for its refusal to locate redemption within the familial and work-centered relationships so upheld by most mainstream entertainment" (16). Like *Happiness* (1998), *American Beauty*'s story of pedophilia also takes as its target of desire a friend of the leading character's child. With its voyeurism, adultery, homophobia masking homoeroticism, and so on, *American Beauty* provides *Happiness* with some credible competition. Yet *Happiness* was considered inappropriate for release by Universal and its then-subsidiary, October (see chap. 1). What then makes *American Beauty* not only acceptable for its studio, Dreamworks, but also applauded by the conservative Academy and widely patronized by the viewing public, as was demonstrated by its earning $130 million at the box office? In terms of the entire Academy slate for 2000, as John Gibson noted on MSNBC the day after the Oscar ceremony, the principal awards went to "a dysfunctional family, a crossdresser, and an abortionist" (the latter two being Hillary Swank, Best Actress for *Boys Don't Cry* and Michael Caine, Best Supporting Actor in *The Cider House Rules*).

Of course, there are differences between the films. Lester Burnham (Kevin Spacey) of *American Beauty* does not have sex with the object of his desire, while Bill Maplewood (Dylan Baker) in *Happiness* does (off-screen). But Lester's last-second circumspection is due to his discovery that Angela (Mena Suvari) is a virgin and not a "slut" as he had assumed and fantasized previously. Another difference between the two films is that *American Beauty*'s pedophile dies at the end of the film, the traditional "fitting" punishment and closure of normative realist cinema. Still, Bill Maplewood is caught and punished—not with death, but with jail. Despite Lester's nonconsummation of the sexual relationship and his ultimate punishment by death, *American Beauty*, with its recurring images of a naked Angela displayed on a bed or floating in a bath of red rose petals, remains visualized on the body of its young teenage character (her age is unspecified in the film). And like Bill Maplewood, Lester Burnham is not vilified; quite the contrary, he is "humanized" to a greater extent than the *Happiness* character, although the sympathetic treatment of Maplewood was the reason most commentators provided for Universal's censoring of the film.

It is reasonable to argue that one of the factors that has made *American Beauty* not only acceptable but appreciated is the increased presence, prominence, and cultural effects of independent film. Additionally, *American Beauty* is another indication of studio need to compete with the independent industry, either by buying up independent prestige units or by vying directly with individual films.

But as telling as "content" issues is the way in which the distribution and marketing of *American Beauty* was handled. For example, borrowing a page from the independent manual, Dreamworks opened the film in only five cities, "then slowly rolled [it] out across the country" (Chetwynd and Seiler E5), thus following the independent practice of a slow release strategy built on positive reviews and word-of-mouth. This approach is rare to Hollywood, where studios normally rely on a film's big opening weekend. Dreamworks also mirrored Miramax's previously successful Oscar strategy. Indeed, the two companies went head-to-head, waging multimillion-dollar Academy Award campaigns, Dreamworks for *American Beauty* and Miramax for *The Cider House Rules*. This "high-priced, high intensity" competition (Waxman G6) was a repeat of the previous year's struggle between Dreamworks's *Saving Private Ryan* and Miramax's *Shakespeare in Love*—except that Dreamworks lost that one.

In the week before the March 25, 2001, Oscar ceremony, *Crouching Tiger, Hidden Dragon* crossed $100 million in domestic box-office gross, marking a new record for a foreign-language film (Puig, "Tiger" D1). In a cover story the preceding month, *Inside*, a magazine devoted to business developments in the major media industries, describes *Crouching Tiger, Hidden Dragon* as "an almost perfect piece of new-paradigm cinema" because it is "cross-cultural, cross-generational, smart, kinetic, epic in scope but modestly budgeted." As such it is "the antithesis of a bloated formula film," Hollywood's standard old-paradigm offering (Cieply 48).

Similarly, *USA Today* attributes *Crouching Tiger, Hidden Dragon*'s financial success to its producers taking advantage of new circumstances arising from "the sweeping globalization of filmmaking" (Martin, "Tiger" D1). *Crouching Tiger, Hidden Dragon*'s budget of $15 million coupled with its appeal in foreign territories, particularly Asia, at a time when half of a film's grosses can come from international sales (see chap. 1), not only ensures the film's financial well-being but establishes it as a model in making films for a global audience (see also Basoli, "Ang Lee").

Yet this "new-paradigm" model displays a number of familiar, well-tested, and long-relied-upon traits of independent film. For instance, the film's distributor, Sony Classics, throughout its history and in its previous incarnations as Orion Classics and United Artists Classics, has always been indebted to world cinema for a sizeable portion of its releases (although it should be noted that *Crouching Tiger, Hidden Dragon* is an Asian and American coproduction). International films have long enriched concepts of independent film for American audiences and American filmmakers as well as being an important source for "product."

Crouching Tiger, Hidden Dragon's cross-cultural, cross-generational success has been attributed to its mixed-genre narrative approach, combining martial arts traditions with the conventions of romance. Sony Classics acknowledges that it purposefully marketed the film's martial arts aspects to the much-desired demographic of teenage boys (Puig, "Tiger" D1), while the film's prominent female leads and themes of romance appealed to other viewers. But again, the incorporation of multiple genres or a play on genre is a recurrent feature of independent narratives (*Poison, The Crying Game*), as is appealing to specifically targeted audience segments. Similarly, modest budgets and a reliance on character-driven rather than star-led storytelling are also long-established traditions in independent film.[2] It could well be argued that the significance of *Crouching Tiger, Hidden Dragon*'s success resides in its bringing independent sensibilities along with an international perspective to American audiences and to Hollywood's attention. *Inside*'s cautionary tale (to Hollywood) suggests that certain independent traits may well be better suited to a changing global cinematic landscape based on a complex understanding of multiple, disparate audiences.

As Hollywood continues to borrow from independent paradigms (*American Beauty*, the lessons of *Crouching Tiger, Hidden Dragon*), it is impossible to predict if independent film will be appropriated into insignificance or if it will continue to exist in something approaching its current configurations as a distinct, valuable cinematic entity. Ironically, it is precisely independent film's successes of the past two decades that make absorption or cooptation an imminent danger. Alternatively, independent film may well evolve into as yet unknown forms of representation and unforeseen avenues of production and dissemination. Two current developing technologies promise to have an indelible impact on independent film: digital video and the Internet.

The prospect of originating on digital video (DV) received a firm boost with the success of the highly respected Danish film, *The Celebration* (1998). Shot on digital video, it was then transferred to 35 mm film for release. Miguel Arteta cites *The Celebration* as his inspiration for shooting *Chuck & Buck* (2000) on DV (Bowen, "Arrested Development" 74) as does Gary Winick, the cofounder of InDigEnt (Independent Digital Entertainment), which is producing ten DV-originating films for $100,000 each, financed by the Independent Film Channel (Patterson 26). InDigEnt films include *Tape* (2001) and *Women in Film* (2001). Other DV-originated films that have been picked up for release include *Timecode* (2000), *Groove* (2000), *Signs & Wonders* (2001), *Center of the World* (2001), extensive portions of *The Blair Witch Project* (1999); and all Dogme '95 films: *The Idiots* (1999), *Mifune* (1999), *julien donkey-boy* (1999), and *Dancer in the Dark* (2000). *The Celebration* is a Dogme film as well; its director, Thomas Vinterberg, is also the author (with von Trier) of the Dogme manifesto.[3] Part of the attention generated by Dogme can be attributed to its insistence on originating features in DV and to curiosity about how they fare subsequently.

The primary motive for independents to shoot on DV is sharply reduced production costs. DV tape is far less expensive than film stock, and the very small, lightweight, and highly portable qualities of a DV camera eliminate the need for a camera department and require less (or in Dogme's case, no) lighting, which all translate into smaller crews. Although the cost of transferring to 35 mm remains considerable, that expense can be picked up by the distributor, shifting costs from producers to end users. Or at any rate, filmmakers can defer the expense of a transfer until they have the assurance of a distribution deal, negotiated on the basis of the video version.

But the reduced costs associated with DV also bring other, nonfinancial benefits. Independent film producers who have moved into or undertaken DV productions point out that lowered production costs effectively result in greater creative freedom and more control over stories for filmmakers (G. Holland 37).

Another advantage to DV production is that is allows attention to be focused on the film's performances, by reducing the technical and time requirements of film camera and lighting, for example. DV's inherent depth of field minimizes the need for actors to hit their marks to ensure a shot's focus, giving performers greater freedom of movement. And the relatively inexpensive camera and tape costs make it possible to work with two cameras simultaneously, increasing editing options and decreasing the need for short takes or retakes. All these attributes mean "the actors [don't] lose any momentum" (Arteta qtd. in Bowen, "Arrested Development" 76). Indeed, the reasoning behind Dogme's rules, including its use of DV, is to minimize the technical and formal requirements of production in favor of a film's performances and narrative.

Whether DV will substantially replace film stock ultimately depends on if its currently limited image quality can continue to improve without incurring significantly higher costs. Alberto Garcia, the postproduction supervisor on *Chuck & Buck*, reminds us that consumer DV cameras already outstrip the performance of professional nondigital video (Garcia 75), and high expectations are being placed on Sony's 24 frames-per-second high-definition camera (Südderman 59).

Taking a contrary view, James Schamus questions whether DV will prove to be a significant asset for independent filmmakers. He argues that although DV does democratize the production process by reducing its costs, the significant expenditure for independents at the turn of the twenty-first century is not production but marketing and promotion, which can be greater (and for independents frequently is) than the cost of making the film itself. The only way DV will have a measurably positive effect is if there are corollary "efficient and cost-effective ways" to reach an independent film's intended and potential audiences (qtd. in Pincus, "Manifest Destiny" 107–8).

For independents who believe in the possibilities made available by new technologies, their response to Schamus is the Internet. The Internet has the potential to influence independent film in two principal ways: first, as a promotional and marketing site; and second, as a distribution outlet where independent projects (no longer actually film) can be exhibited or streamed.

The financial success of *The Blair Witch Project*, in particular, has drawn attention to the Internet's potentially critical role as a marketing site for independents. The Web appears to have the capability to reach both a wide audience base (large numbers) and a specifically targeted or focused one (a certain demographic) for relatively low costs, certainly low in comparison to traditional marketing techniques. The key to *The Blair Witch Project* Web site's success seems to be based on what one of the film's producers, Greg Hale, calls "Story Augmentation"—using the site to function as an expansion of the narrative beyond the bounds of the film. Originally designed by Eduardo Sánchez, who codirected the film with Daniel Myrick, the site gave information on the fictional legend of the Blair witch, provided detailed backstories on its main characters including personal journals and family photo albums, and displayed what appeared to be crime scene photos, expert testimony, and news reports on the missing trio (Pincus, "Sticky Fingers" 55; Merritt 410). Adam Pincus calls this "narrative spillover" (56), the expansion of the story beyond the finiteness of the film's frame. Narrative spillover serves to enhance a site's "stickiness," which is measured in two ways. The first measure is the amount of time a visitor stays on the site (an average of eleven minutes in *The Blair Witch Project*'s case); and the second is the number of times a visitor returns to the site. Narrative spillover—what happened before and after the events in the film; other kinds of information to that depicted on screen; or alternate perspectives to those of the film's characters—enables producers to launch a Web site well before the film's release (or even before shooting is completed), helping to create a buzz for it. Stickiness also may enable a site to sustain or even promote interest well after a film's theatrical release, helping to increase its video and DVD sales, for instance.

Another successful independent film Web site is the one belonging to *Pi* (1998). Employing a different strategy, one better suited to this particular film, the site nevertheless also carefully targeted its potential audience. Designed by the film's principal lead, Sean Guillette, the site stressed interactivity, focusing on the concepts and ideas foregrounded in the film. This strategy resulted in ongoing and continually growing discussions between everyone from "math geeks" to "migraine sufferers" (Guillette qtd. in Pincus, "Sticky Fingers" 53).

That the Net's marketing potential is taken seriously by the entire film industry—and not just by independents—is indicated by the solicitous treatment accorded 28-year-old Texan Harry Knowles, founder of the Ain't It Cool News Web site where film reviews frequently appear. Universal's head of marketing, Marc Shmuger, describes Knowles as "a tastemaker with a great deal of influence," and Dreamworks provided Knowles and 200 of his friends with an exclusive advance screening of *Gladiator* (Puig, "Moviemakers" E2). But expectations notwithstanding, the Internet's marketing effectiveness and its costs remain unknown.

Although still in its infancy, the Internet may also serve as a distribution outlet for independent projects through the exhibition process of video streaming. Currently, Internet exhibition of projects either created for other venues (cinema, television) or specifically designed for the Web is restricted by the quality limitations of live-action streaming. But many believe it holds enormous potential for independents. Marco Masoni, for instance, argues that the Web will not "kill" video, film, or television but rather will transform their concepts, traditions, and skills, just as it will transform independents from filmmakers to mediamakers (48). Others suggest that the Web may prove particularly welcoming for experimental film- and videomakers and that it may well be better suited for shorts instead of features. Works created specifically for the Internet are appearing already. One example is Icuna (icuna.com), which has commissioned one-minute pieces from filmmakers like Percy Adlon, Alex Cox, and Jay Rosenblatt (Rich, "Times" 24).

All this makes it difficult to anticipate the paths independent film—or independent media—will take in the future. I hope, however, that I have convincingly outlined some of the significant ways independent film has become established, from 1980 to the present, as a recognizable system of cinematic representation.

Among the attributes marking independent film as a distinct cultural formation are an institutional/industrial infrastructure with its own mechanisms of distribution, marketing strategies, exhibition venues, and so on; its formulation as a hybrid between Hollywood and alternative discourses, borrowing from each, replicating neither but owing allegiance to both; the field's interventions in dichotomized concepts of cultural production and its attempts to mediate such oppositions as form and content, aesthetics and ideology, art and politics; its incorporation of emerging postmodern representational and cultural practices; and the efforts it makes to represent a heterogeneous, pluralistic, and multicultural society, carving out for itself a representational niche concerned with identity politics. Using its own series of aesthetics, narrativity, subject matter, political concerns, social agendas, target audiences or markets, institutional structures, and industrial practices, independent cinema has become a significant cultural site for filmmaking and for cultural politics, for practice and for theory.

Illustrations

Fig. 1: Using Danny Glover and humor to sell *To Sleep with Anger*. Courtesy of the Academy of Motion Picture Arts and Sciences.

Fig. 2: *Daughters of the Dust*'s kaleidoscope of women characters: from left, Eula Peazant (Alva Rogers), Yellow Mary (Barbara-O), and Nana Peazant (Cora Lee Day). © 1992 Kino International Corporation.

Fig. 3: Outspoken, confident Chantel (Ariyan Johnson) from *Just Another Girl on the I.R.T.* Photographic still provided courtesy of Miramax Films. All rights reserved.

Illustrations 211

Fig. 4: Johnny (David Thewlis) *Naked*'s dangerous lead character. *Naked* copyright 1993, Fine Line Features. All rights reserved. Photo by Simon Mein. Photo appears courtesy of New Line Productions, Inc.

Fig. 5: The central women characters in *Naked* attempt to console each other. Sophie (Katrin Cartlidge) on left, and Louise (Lesley Sharp). *Naked* copyright 1993, Fine Line Features. All rights reserved. Photo by Simon Mein. Photo appears courtesy of New Line Productions, Inc.

Illustrations 213

Fig. 6: The disintegrating marriage of George and Faith Dunlap (Albert Finney and Diane Keaton) in *Shoot the Moon*. Courtesy of the Academy of Motion Picture Arts and Sciences.

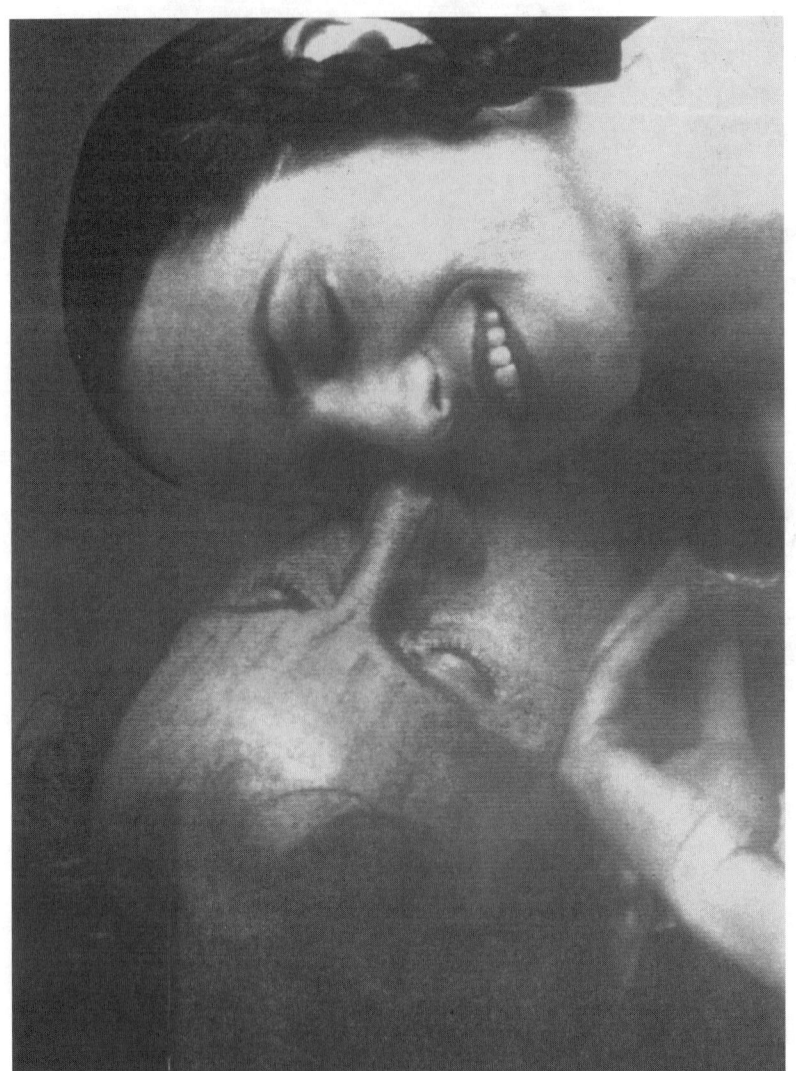

Fig. 7: *The Piano's* disturbing grand passion. George Baines (Harvey Keitel) and Ada McGrath (Holly Hunter). Photographic still provided courtesy of Miramax Films. All rights reserved. Photo by Grant Matthews and Polly Walker.

Illustrations

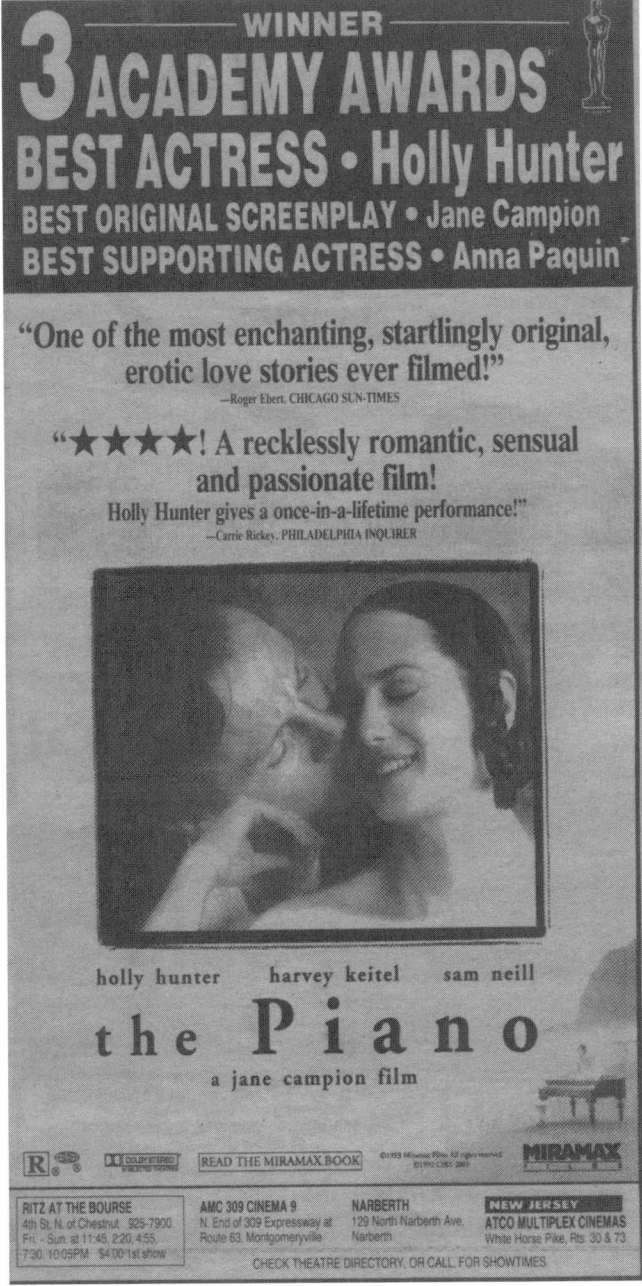

Fig. 8: The same image as used in the film's promotional materials. The ad (from the *Philadelphia Inquirer*) framed by reviewer quotations ensuring a love story.

Fig. 9: Mother and daughter's (Anna Paquin) matching appearance and strong gazes in *The Piano*. Photographic still provided courtesy of Miramax Films. All rights reserved. Photo by Grant Matthews and Polly Walker.

Fig. 10: Sarah Tobias (Jodie Foster) gets to tell her story in *The Accused*. Courtesy of the Academy of Motion Picture Arts and Sciences.

Fig. 11: But it is Ken Joyce's (Bernie Coulson) testimony that controls the representation of the rape. Joyce being questioned by Kathryn Murphy (Kelly McGillis). Courtesy of the Academy of Motion Picture Arts and Sciences.

Illustrations 219

Fig. 12: Mia Wallace (Uma Thurman) and Vincent Vega (John Travolta) do a dance turn in *Pulp Fiction*. Photographic still provided courtesy of Miramx Films. All rights reserved. Photo by Linda R. Chen.

Fig. 13: Brothers in arms: Mr. White (Harvey Keitel) and Mr. Orange (Tim Roth) from *Reservoir Dogs*. Photographic still provided courtesy of Miramx Films. All rights reserved. Photo by Linda R. Chen.

NOTES

Introduction

1. This is not to suggest that much Hollywood originated fare is "pure entertainment." Quite the contrary, "entertainment" is constructed by the same social, political, and ideological considerations and constraints as any other form of cultural production. It is only to point out that many Hollywood films are presented or marketed as entertainment in contrast to the intentional, self-conscious pursuit of "art" or "political content" by many independent producers and consumers.
2. "To boost *The Postman*'s Oscar prospects and broaden its audience, Miramax says, it has spent $2.5 million since January. In fact, *Newsweek* has learned, Miramax spent $6 million—and an additional $1 million targeting Academy voters, buying more ads in *Variety* than any other studio" (*Newsweek* 72). In addition to Best Picture, *Il Postino* was nominated for Best Director, Best Actor (Massimo Troisi), Best Screenplay, and Best Original Dramatic Score. It won for Best Original Dramatic Score.
3. Although attempting to be as inclusive as possible in the definition of independent film, I have excluded any studio-financed or distributed film from this study, with the exception of striking instances such as *Roger & Me* and *El Mariachi* (1993). Studio interest in such films reflects Hollywood's desire to capitalize on the independent successes of recent years.
4. For instance, a notable example of a significant independent producer is Christine Vachon who has served as producer or executive producer for such films as *Poison* (1991), *Swoon* (1992), *Go Fish* (1994), *Safe* (1995), *Kids* (1995), *Stonewall* (1996), *I Shot Andy Warhol* (1996), *Happiness* (1998), *Velvet Goldmine* (1998), and *Boys Don't Cry* (1999).
5. For example, John Pierson's *Spike, Mike, Slackers & Dykes: A Guided Tour Across a Decade of American Independent Cinema* and Emanuel Levy's *Cinema of Outsiders: The Rise of American Independent Film* limit their discussions to American-made films. International contexts are also an important source for the financing and distribution of American independent film,

Chapter One

1. *Filmmaker: The Magazine of Independent Film* is a quarterly published by the Independent Feature Project (New York) and the Independent Feature Project West (Los Angeles).
2. I discuss *Pulp Fiction's* storytelling structure and style in chapter 6. I cover categories of art cinema, including foreign films and historical epics, in chapter 2.
3. For instance, *USA Today* defines specialty films as those that open on five hundred or fewer screens (Chetwynd D3).
4. Written by Danish filmmakers Lars von Trier (*Breaking the Waves; The Idiots*, 1999) and Thomas Vinterberg (*The Celebration*, 1998), the ten rules (called "The Vow of Chastity") are intended to deemphasize the technical and aesthetic aspects of production as well as the director as auteur in order to focus instead on the characters/actors and settings. The rules are: location shooting only; no sound added apart from that made with image; hand-held camera; no lighting except that found at location; no optical work or filters; no superficial action; no temporal or geographical alienation (displacement); no genre movies; shot on DV with film transfer to 35 mm; director must not be credited.
5. For more on the great difficulties of financing, producing, and securing distribution for independent films, see Chuck Kleinhans, "Independent Features: Hopes and Dreams."
6. Although the Sundance Film Festival has come to dominate independent festivals in the publicity and distribution deals it is able to secure for independent films, it has also provoked the most discussion about whether it is even an "independent" festival any longer. This is because of its repeated screenings of higher-budget films with experienced directors, and star or known casts. For instance, Caryn James speaks of a "direct link between Hollywood and Park City" (where the festival is held) and notes, "Even the hardest-nosed business people, the distributors who come here prepared to buy movies, now astutely describe this festival in terms of pop-culture celebrity. Their tone is usually stunned, as if visualizing money flying out of their pockets" (James 1, 26). At 1999's Sundance, Robert Redford acknowledged that the event has become more a marketplace than a festival (Taubin, "Slippery Slopes" 148; Puig, "Sundance Market" D4).

Notes

7 For instance, Paul Schrader comments, "Ever since the liberation movements of blacks and women, of gays and grays, those segments of the population that were overlooked in movies are now addressed.... Parts of the audience that were overlooked are now being addressed to the extent that they have economic clout" (qtd. in Rickey, "Divide" 26).

8 See also, for instance, "High Risk Distribs" 7 and John Pierson, 19, 114.

9 Although the youth market in toto is important to Hollywood, the working assumption is that girls and young women will go to "guy" films but not vice versa, therefore the boys and young male market is more specifically targeted. The exception to this has been the so-called date movies, dramas or romantic comedies that appeal to young women but that have enough other elements (casting, action) to make them acceptable to men. This was one of the most widely held explanations for the astronomical success of *Titanic*.

10 It should also be noted that a widely regarded attribute of the new Hollywood was the rise, in the 1970s and 1980s, of American auteurs such as Francis Ford Coppola, Martin Scorsese, Robert Altman, and Brian DePalma. The work of these filmmakers also influenced and, arguably, paved the way for independent fare. The problem with the designation *the new Hollywood* is that it is too unified and singular a category to describe a wide array of differing, sometimes competing, contemporaneous attributes and events.

11 The figures vary depending on their source. Neal Gabler in the *New York Times* cites $57 million (78); David Lieberman provides two different figures, $59.7 and $61 million (B2). Jack Valenti, head of the Motion Picture Association of America (MPAA), supplies $60 million (T. Lowry B2). However, as all numbers are based on MPAA sources the discrepancies are due presumably to changing calculations predicated on date given. See also *Philadelphia Inquirer* March 6, 1997: C2.

12 See, for instance, Gabler 77; T. Lowry B2; Goodwin 2; Giannetti and Eyman 533, 537; Clark, "Profits" D1; Martin, "Studios Bank" D6.

13 Bart analyzed the blockbusters of the summer of 1998, all of which grossed over $100 million in domestic theatrical box office: *Armageddon, Saving Private Ryan, Godzilla, There's Something about Mary, Deep Impact, Mulan, Doctor Doolittle, Lethal Weapon 4, The Truman Show*. All the films made at least as much in foreign grosses as they did domestically, and in half the cases significantly more. For instance, *Godzilla* grossed $136 million domestically and $240 million in foreign theatrical markets, although it was widely perceived as a big disappointment for Sony (Ryan F1, F5).

14 All figures quoted are for domestic theatrical box-office grosses and do not include foreign theatrical, videocassette, or domestic and foreign television revenues. Sources for figures are *Filmmaker 3*: insert preceding 42; *Filmmaker 4*: 37; *Filmmaker 5*: 40; *Filmmaker 6*: 49 and insert preceding 49; and Levy 515-26.

15 See, for instance, Rickey, "Divide" 18+ and Gabler 76-78. Both bemoan the trend toward specific demographics, fearing it will splinter audiences and eliminate common ground (Rickey) or further exacerbate the divide between "entertainment" and "art" (Gabler).

16 As the selection panel was composed of industry insiders, it should be expected that panelists would be likely to nominate films with which they had been involved. Although many documentaries appeared on the list, for the purposes of the discussion at hand I have excluded them and, rather, focused on narrative films—the dominant fare at repertory houses.

17 John Waters has stated, "I've always said that what I do is make exploitation films for art theaters" (qtd. in Hoberman and Rosenbaum 152). Waters cites his three major influences as American underground film (the Kuchar Brothers, Andy Warhol, Kenneth Anger), exploitation and nudist camp movies, and European art films (Bowen, "Flash" 51).

18 Studio divestiture of theater ownership, while causing the B studios to decline, at the same time provided an opportunity for independent film. Beginning in the 1950s, exhibitors could program nonstudio fare, for instance, foreign films, enabling the influences of European cinema (e.g., Italian neorealism, Ingmar Bergman, the French New Wave) in the 1950s and 1960s in the United States.

19 Orion itself was formed by former United Artists executives in the wake of UA's absorption by MGM, creating MGM/UA in 1981.

20 Harvey Weinstein denies charges of Miramax inaccurately reporting their box-office take (Johnson and Harris S21). However, Miramax/Dimension was accused of doing the same thing with *Scream 2*, inflating the opening weekend box office by $6 million. Miramax subsequently acknowledged having done this, saying it had overestimated the number of screens at which the movie had played (Orwall B1; Klady 16).

21 Fox Searchlight's *The Full Monty*, for instance, had a general rather than an art-house release, reaching 783 theatres simultaneously at its peak (Rea, "On Movies," October 5, 1997: F9).

22 The fall 2000 series consisted of *Titanic Town, Human Resources, Barenaked in America, One, A Time for Drunken Horses*, and *Non-Stop*. (Hernandez

and Brooks; Parks G27; Shooting Gallery Web Site). The Shooting Gallery/Loews 2001 series included *Last Resort, When Brendan Met Trudy, Too Much Sleep, The Day I Became a Woman,* and *The Low Down.*

23 For instance, Marcus Hu cites Alive, Atlantic, Cineplex, Island, Vestron, Film Dallas, and Spectrafilm as going out of business in the late 1980s, in the wake of the short-lived boom of video dollars, followed in the early 1990s by Avenue, Cinecom, and Circle (34).

24 At the time of his comments, Sayles' ten films and their distributors were: *The Return of the Secaucus Seven* (1980), Libra/Specialty; *Baby It's You* (1983), Paramount; *Lianna* (1983), United Artists Classics; *The Brother from Another Planet* (1984), Cinecom; *Matewan* (1987), Cinecom; *Eight Men Out* (1988), Orion; *City of Hope* (1991), Goldwyn; *Passion Fish* (1992), Miramax; *The Secret of Roan Inish* (1994), First Look; *Lone Star* (1996), Sony Classics. He has since released two more films, *Men with Guns* (1998), Sony Classics; and *Limbo* (1999), Screen Gems. *Baby It's You* was produced and released by a studio, Paramount. Of the remaining nine films, Libra, United Artists Classics, Cinecom, Orion, and Goldwyn are no longer in business, accounting for six of the nine films (Cinecom distributed two).

25 Although this study focuses on the distribution activities of companies, most of the mini-majors produce films as well. The substantial marketing costs include newspaper and TV advertising, print costs for wider releases beyond the arthouse circuit, and expensive Academy Award campaigns. On the last, see Rawsthorn, "Independent Films" (6).

26 Universal's studio head Ron Meyer is reported to have said "he would do everything in his power to keep the studio from releasing the film" (Puig, "Happiness" D1). For additional reports on the October/Universal jettisoning of *Happiness*, see Pener 12 and Ansen, "Comedy" 87.

27 James Schamus of Good Machine points out that in order to get out of its contractual obligation to distribute the film without putting it in the hands of one of its competitors, Universal paid for Good Machine's marketing of *Happiness*, putting the studio in the ironic position of simultaneously suppressing and promoting the film ("Pursuit of Happiness 34+).

28 Stephen Holden wrote, "Though not graphic, the scenes centering on this deeply troubled character are all the more disturbing because he is almost sympathetic and because the boys he molests are his 11-year-old son's classmates" (41).

29 *The Full Monty* received four Academy Award nominations: the prestigious Best Picture, Best Director, Best Original Screenplay, and Best Original

Score (Musical or Comedy). It won for Best Original Score. *Life Is Beautiful* received seven nominations including Best Picture, and it won for three: Best Actor, Best Foreign Film, and Best Dramatic Score. *Crouching Tiger, Hidden Dragon* obtained ten nominations and collected four awards. For more on *Crouching Tiger, Hidden Dragon*, see Conclusion.

Chapter Two

1   This argument is not intended to dismiss formulations of realism as an important part of alternative production. For independent cinema, filmmakers such as Mike Leigh and Ken Loach for instance, represent significant practitioners.
2   It should also be noted that while Cartwright and Fonoroff argue here for an entirely nonnarrative tradition, alternative cinema has created almost every imaginable hybrid as well, for instance experimental documentaries such as the work of Marlon Riggs (*Tongues Untied*, 1989; *Affirmations*, 1990), and a large and varied range of experimental narratives. Jane Campion's *Passionless Moments*, 1983, serves as only a single instance.
3   A blended personal and political approach has also been an important strategy for certain independent documentaries such as *Silverlake Life: The View from Here* (1993).
4   See, for instance, "It isn't fashionable to talk about the alarming low number of American women directing independent features.... independent film is no more hospitable to female directors than Hollywood is" (Dargis, "Even" 13).
5   Collage, for example, is also a characteristic of modernism. Certain traits may not represent complete breaks from past modernist usage but instead signify developments or evolutions of stylistic features with variations in intent and result. In terms of collage or referentiality, for instance, modernist efforts are more likely to draw from other art or classical sources; the postmodern from the popular.

Chapter Three

1   For instance, *School Daze* (1988), *Do the Right Thing* (1989), *Jungle Fever* (1991), *Malcolm X* (1992), *Get on the Bus* (1996), *He Got Game* (1998), *The Original Kings of Comedy* (2000), and *Bamboozled* (2000).
2   For a more detailed discussion of this point, and the implications for an independent women's cinema, see Pribram, "Institutional Power" 3–5.

Notes

3   Comparable but equally rare attempts to reach young women in the independent area include *Girls Town* (1996) and *Manny and Lo* (1996). Justin Wyatt points out that another factor in both Hollywood's and independent film's emphasis on young audiences is that this market is easier than the adult market to target efficiently, particularly through television (178–179).

4   Michael Barker, copresident and founding partner, Sony Pictures Classics, Cold Spring Film Workshop, Cold Spring on-the-Hudson, New York, July 11 and 12, 1992.

5   Other sources on the film's distribution history include Godfrey17; Pribram, "Institutional Power" 3–5; Rhines 2.

6   Dash found it fittingly ironic that foreign-film distributor Kino was to release *Daughters of the Dust*. It underlined reluctant reception to the work as though it were "a foreign film. An American-made foreign film" (qtd. in Mills, "Dash" C1, C3).

7   For more on the interconnectedness between distributor confidence, size of advertising budget, and public awareness of a film, see Wyatt (189).

8   Producer's representative is a position found particularly in independent film, not within a Hollywood paradigm. In the latter, a film's distribution rights are tied up with its financing-producing while in the independent arena financing and distribution are often distinct stages. A producer's rep views available films, decides which are significant and marketable, has them play the "right" festival circuit to create a buzz or at least to achieve enough positive response to ensure their marketability, and then shepherds and negotiates the deal with the distributor for a percentage of the advance. Pierson no longer acts as a producer's rep; he is currently the host of *Split Screen* on the Independent Film Channel.

9   Pierson did business with Goldwyn (his comments were written before the company went out of business), for instance, they distributed *Go Fish* (1994), a film he handled. An example of standard industry perspective on casting known actors comes from Rick Sands, Chairman of Worldwide Distribution at Miramax: "If you ultimately want to sell the movie, you're much better off with any sort of name talent than without it" (qtd in Martin, "Name Game" 47).

10 A more recent Hollywood trend for black films is romantic comedies or dramas, for instance, *Waiting to Exhale* (1995), *Booty Call* (1997), *Love Jones* (1997), *The Wood* (1999), and *The Best Man* (1999).

11 In addition to *To Sleep with Anger*, Goldwyn's catalog includes *Hollywood Shuffle* (1987), *Straight out of Brooklyn* (1991), *Mississippi Masala* (1992), *Livin' Large* (1992), *Fear of a Black Hat* (1994), and *You So Crazy* (1994).

12   In the independent arena, a film's actual production costs are of concern to the film's producers but are not taken into account in the distributor's calculations, unless they have financed or cofinanced it themselves. *To Sleep with Anger* cost $1.2 million to make; *Daughters of the Dust*'s budget was $1.25 million (*Filmmaker 3:* insert preceding 42).

13   This figure comes from Susan Jacobs of New York's Film Forum (qtd. in Godfrey 17). Jacobs also commented that she did not hear complaints about the film's difficulty or comprehensibility from black women as she did from "the white crowd."

14   On the film's popularity with black women and sold-out performances see also Rule C15; Mills, "Dash" C1, C3.

15   Similarly, it is reported that *The Full Monty* "just barely squeezed into" the 1997 Sundance Festival after "a last-minute plea from Fox Searchlight president Lindsay Law" (Kilday 56).

I was present at a week-long course on independent film led by John Pierson at the Maine Photographic Workshop in the summer of 1990. During that week, Pierson screened two films for workshop participants: *Slacker* and *All The Vermeers in New York*. Pierson told us he was trying to decide which of the two to represent next. After the screening, one member of the workshop, a college-aged man, responded extremely enthusiastically to *Slacker*, stating repeatedly, "I went to school with people just like that!" while the "older" members of the workshop (those in our thirties) were not as intrigued. Nor did we respond with comparable enthusiasm to the screening of *All the Vermeers in New York*, which it appeared had been targeted to our demographic. I've since wondered if the outcome might have been different had the older test viewers been as gripped by *All the Vermeers* as our younger colleague had been by *Slacker*. Michael Barker of Orion Classics, which distributed *Slacker*, was also present at the workshop.

16   Another reviewer noted: "I realize this is supposed to represent the 'new black aesthetic' but it sure looks like *Vogue*, Fellini, even Spielberg to me" (Brown, "How" 52). See also B. Ruby Rich's incisive critique of critical reception to the film's aesthetics, "In the Eyes of the Beholder" (60+). It should also be noted that reviews of *Daughters of the Dust* grew more positive with the film's success and evident audience popularity; presumably black women's responses suggested to reviewers that the film merited a second or closer examination.

17   See chapter 5 in this volume for criticisms of *Orlando* (1993), which are similar to those aimed at *Daughters of the Dust* because of *Orlando*'s supposed emphasis on superficiality and devotion to appearance.

18 Nana Peazant is played by Cora Lee Day, Yellow Mary Peazant by Barbara-O, Eula Peazant by Alva Rogers, Haagar Peazant by Kaycee Moore, and Viola Peazant by Cheryl Lynn Bruce.
19 Two different versions of the Ibo captives' story are told within the film, one by Eula, the other by Bilal Muhammed (Umar Abdurrahamn).
20 "The History of the World is but the Biography of Great Men" (qtd. in Gay 158).
21 An example of interaction cited in Carter's article occurs with the film *Eraser* (1996) when star Vanessa Williams is comforted by federal agents after narrowly escaping her pursuers. A federal agent assures her, "Don't worry, you'll be fine." Williams answers, "No, I'm not going to be fine," to which a man in the audience responds, "Vanessa, you'll always be fine!"
22 From its start of production, *Daughters of the Dust* was guaranteed television broadcast on PBS because the film had been largely funded by American Playhouse.
23 While Pierson has represented more films about young men grappling with identity than any other genre or kind, it should be noted he has also represented such diverse films as *Parting Glances* (1986), *She's Gotta Have It* (1986), *Working Girls* (1987), *Roger and Me* (1987), and *Go Fish* (1994). He also helped obtain production funds for *The Blair Witch Project* (1999).
24 See David J. Fox and Nina J. Easton, who explain that one of the reasons films such as *New Jack City* and *Boyz N the Hood* make money is that they "draw teenagers who will stand in long lines and see a movie more than once" (F1). That Miramax's releasing strategy may have been a miscalculation of *Just Another Girl on the I.R.T.*'s likeliest audiences is indicated by the film's box-office take of $479,000 (*Filmmaker 3:* insert preceding p. 42). In addition, Miramax's wide-release strategy entailed higher film print and promotional costs.
25 Even advocate Pierson says, "The movie tends to split into two halves" and the story is "not entirely coherent" (100).
26 This is not to say that there is an equally viable political position for every category of identity. As Madan Sarup notes, identities can be "reactionary" as well as "progressive" (*Identity* 184). The tendency for cultural theorists has been to focus on categories of identity viewed as progressive (people of color, women, gays and lesbians, working classes), while ignoring categories that summon political opposition (whites, upper classes, religion, nationalism, regionalism).

Chapter Four

1. Edward Branigan argues that it is necessary to distinguish *narrative* and *nonnarrative* from *fiction* and *nonfiction*. Accordingly, he identifies four categories of narrative: narrative fiction, such as the novel; narrative nonfiction, such as history; nonnarrative fiction, for instance, many kinds of poetry; and nonnarrative nonfiction, such as the essay (Branigan 1).
2. For instance, John Pierson views Sayles as more occupied with literary concerns than with visual style, and as such considers him not much of a "catalyst" or "creative spark" for young filmmakers (18–19).
3. That there are "virtually no theoretical studies of the representational dimension of film narrative" seems a rather questionable statement given the amount of work in representation and ideology within film studies. Perhaps Bordwell refers to a lack of a systematized theoretical framework.
4. de Lauretis's work, for instance chapter 5 of *Alice Doesn't*, "Desire in Narrative," serves as an example of the work on narrative as representation that Bordwell overlooks.
5. *Discourse* in this usage seems comparable to Bordwell's application of *narration*. For a more detailed explanation of the differences between *fabula/syuzhet* and *histoire/discours*, see Burgoyne 107.
6. This is not to say there is no difference between consensual and nonconsensual sex; obviously there is. Rather, it is to point out that the narrative squeezes the viewer into a position of judgment based on "It's not as bad as—."
7. For instance: "But the film also suggests that there is something humanly valuable that could have been salvaged in Johnny; and Leigh, without sentimentalizing him, leaves the audience at the end with a profound feeling of loss" (Quart 45).

Chapter Five

1. *Erotic:* Hinson, "Piano" D6; Buck 127; Canby, "Forceful Lessons" 18 and "Early Favorite" C15; Travers 76; and Rickey, "Hunter" E1. *Passionate* or *sensual:* Hinson, "Piano" D6; Turan, "Piano" F16; Canby, "Forceful Lessons 18; Travers 76; and Bernard 6C. *Romantic:* Cantwell 51; Rickey, "Mute Woman" W3; Hinson, "Piano" D6; Turan, "Piano" F1; Buck 127; Canby, "Forceful Lessons" 13 and "Campion" 17; and Corliss, "Wuthering Eighty-Eights" 80.

Notes

2   Handing Ada's severed finger to Flora, Stewart instructs her, "You give this to Baines. Tell him if he ever tries to see her again, I'll take off another and another and another."

3   That Ada's muteness is countered by her music further links the piano to the expression/repression of her sexuality and emotions: "One is tempted to speculate that the different kinds of drama have their corresponding sense deprivations: for tragedy, blindness, since tragedy is about insight and illumination; for comedy, deafness, since comedy is concerned with problems in communication, misunderstandings and their consequences; and for melodrama, muteness, since melodrama is about expression" (Peter Brooks qtd. in Modleski 538).

4   In describing *Orlando* as an "epistemological costume drama," Georgia Brown wrote "Potter's movie... seems light, also didactic, fare with striking tableaus" (Brown, "My Brilliant Careers" 51). *Orlando* did well at the box office, especially by art film standards, in both Britain and the United States. However, a distinction can be seen in how the two films, both foreign films for American audiences, fared at the 1994 Academy Awards. *The Piano* received eight nominations: Best Picture, Best Actress, Best Supporting Actress, Best Director, Best Original Screenplay, Best Cinematography, Best Costume Design, and Best Editing. It won three Oscars: Best Screenplay (Jane Campion), Best Actress (Holly Hunter), and Best Supporting Actress (Anna Paquin). *Orlando* received a single nomination, for Best Costume Design.

5   Examples of intermediaries might include Anne Sullivan (Anne Bancroft) for Helen Keller (Patty Duke) in *The Miracle Worker* (1962), the Liam Neeson and Natasha Richardson characters in *Nell* (1994), Tom Cruise's Charlie Babbitt, for brother Raymond (Dustin Hoffman) in *Rainman* (1988), Joe Miller (Denzel Washington) as legal and narrative representative for Andy Beckett (Tom Hanks) in *Philadelphia* (1993), as well as Kelly McGillis's character in *The Accused*.

6   Some reviewers did choose to see it this way. For instance, the "sensual awakening" in the headline of Jami Bernard's review in the *New York Daily News* ("*The Piano* Fine-Tunes a Sensual Awakening") is Baines's, not Ada's (6C).

7   From the Thomas Hood (1799–1845) poem used in the final voice-over to close the film.

8   Voice-over accompanying the final shot can also be interpreted in keeping with either visual version: "At night I think of my piano in its ocean grave.

And sometimes of myself floating above it. Down there everything is so still and silent that it lulls me to sleep. It is a weird lullaby, and so it is. It is mine. 'There is a silence where hath been no sound. / There is a silence where no sound may be. / In the cold grave, under the deep deep sea.'"

9 Another imaginable resolution would be if Ada were to leave only with her daughter. But Campion has staked out for herself the terrain of heterosexual relationships—the belief that men and women can live together, including as lovers and partners, despite the cultural obstacles—and so resolves the film within those confines.

10 But what characters' problems might be is deemed, in a number of instances, to remain a "mystery," while often simultaneously falling back on individual failings as explanation. For instance, "Yet on some deeper level they remain mysterious, as if Campion had insisted that the characters remain half-hidden in shadow.... She [Ada] suffers, but the source of her pain is mysterious and undiagnosed. Judging from Campion's previous films, her primary affliction is femininity itself.... [H]er women are haunted creatures at the mercy of their emotions" (Hinson, "Piano" D6).

Chapter Six

1 Gavin Smith in *Film Comment* argues that *Reservoir Dogs* will "prove pivotal in the history of the American independent film, for legitimizing its relationship to Hollywood genre" ("Tarantino" 32).

2 The films were (in screening order): *Ride in the Whirlwind* (1965), *Assault on Precinct 13* (1976), *One-Eyed Jacks* (1961), *Casualties of War* (1989), *Le Doulos* (1962), *Magnificent Obsession* (1954), *His Girl Friday* (1940), *Bande à part* (1964), *Taxi Driver* (1976), *Blow Out* (1981), *Rio Bravo* (1958), *Pulp Fiction* (1994), *Reservoir Dogs* (1992), *Abbott and Costello Meet Frankenstein* (1948), *Winchester 73* (1950), *The Good, the Bad and the Ugly* (1966), *The Thing* (1982), *A Bout de souffle* (1960), and Jim McBride's remake, *Breathless* (1983). Presumably the NFT had Tarantino select a program of his favorites because it was not possible to do a retrospective of the director's work.

3 Stone's version of the instructions he gave for the rewriting of the script is as follows: "I want to expand the script for more of a social political commentary about the 90s, more about Mickey and Mallory [versus Wayne Gayle] and more about violence and aggression and the implications of violence in this century" (Dawson 132).

4 See also Pat Dowell in *Cineaste,* who makes no distinction between Jules's conversion and other events in the film. "*Pulp Fiction*'s various protagonists

succeed and fail on a relatively random basis that has little to do with their actions. Most of what they do doesn't make a difference in their destinies (since life is like a box of chocolates). A pothole or a trip to the bathroom at the wrong moment means life or death (more than once for Vincent Vega), or a kid's bad aim with a handgun becomes a miracle for Jules" (5).

5. Richard Corliss in *Time* ("Adding" 95) argues that filmmakers like Tarantino, Tom Kalin, Stacy Cochran, Abel Ferrara, and Hal Hartley "follow the lead of Joel and Ethan Coen's *Blood Simple* (1984), which targeted as its audience the cinema intelligentsia bored with both the languid pace of European festival films and the exhausted formulas of Hollywood. These movie-goers wanted a little kick with their chic. To their rescue ride the art-house outlaws."

6. On the similarities between *Reservoir Dogs* and *City on Fire* see also Dowell (4-5).

7. Appropriation is also an attribute of modernism, for instance, in the work of T. S. Eliot or Cubist paintings, as noted in chapter 2.

8. *Pulp Fiction*'s narrative fragmentation in the Vincent story line could also, arguably, be viewed as a "cheat." Tarantino takes the narrative risk of killing off one of his main characters, yet provides the audience with the impression that he is alive and well, at film's end, as he leaves the diner with Jules.

9. That the wardrobe had more to do with evoking a 1950s filmic ambiance than with invoking realism is expressed by *Reservoir Dogs*'s crime consultant and cast member, Eddie Bunker, regarding the identifiability of the gang: "I mean it was absurd. There were these guys going to pull this big robbery and they're sitting in a coffee shop all dressed alike" (Dawson 79).

10. For instance, in *Vanity Fair* Lynn Hirschberg declared that Tarantino arguably knows more "about movies than any other person on the planet" ("Tarantino" 96).

11. It should be noted most mainstream press commentators are white; it is very possible black reviewers would lean more heavily toward Jules/Samuel Jackson as the lead or connecting character. The issue is further obscured by the fact that Miramax, in a bid not to have the actors cancel each other out, promoted Travolta for the Best Actor category of the Academy Awards, but Jackson as Best Supporting Actor (Dowell 5). Each received nominations as designated; neither ultimately won. Again, racial stereotypes (who is the lead and who the "sidekick" in white-black partnerings) may well have factored into the way the actors were split into respective categories.

12. Although she also analyzes Tarantino's films as treatises on masculinity, Sharon Willis argues that the relationship between Mr. White and Mr. Or-

ange, and between Tarantino's male characters in general, is that of surrogate father and son ("Fathers" 47).
13. Saying the pawn shop scene "reeks of homophobia," Devon Jackson writes of the connection between heterosexual masculinity and the fear of homosexuality: "These two faggots are deviants of the worst kind: queers who pass themselves off as he-men" (40).
14. The similarities across generations are evident in, for instance, J. Hoberman's description of Scorsese's innovativeness, which is specifically compared to Tarantino's: "*Mean Streets* synthesized American exploitation flicks and European art movies—creating a jagged, rock-scored, in-your-face, wildly gestural mode, characterized by conversational gambits seemingly inspired by Abbott and Costello, and a frenzied, if not tormented, maleness" ("Back" 31).
15. Another example of wannabe posturing might be director Warren Beatty's *Bulworth* (1998).

Conclusion

1. *Crouching Tiger, Hidden Dragon* won 4 Oscars for Best Foreign Language Film, Best Art Direction, Best Cinematography, and Best Dramatic Score. In something of a controversy, none of the film's actors were nominated (Barker A2).
2. A number of *Crouching Tiger, Hidden Dragon*'s actors are stars to Asian audiences or to martial arts fans. The point here is that from the specific perspective of a general American audience who went to see the film in large numbers, the film was a character piece, not a star vehicle.
3. For the Dogme movement, see chapter 1 and n. 4.

FILMOGRAPHY

1980–2001
Based on Independent Films, Filmmakers, and Distributors Cited in the Text

By Title

The Accompanist, Claude Miller, 1993, Sony Classics.
The Addiction, Abel Ferrara, 1995, October.
The Adjuster, Atom Egoyan, 1992, Orion Classics.
Adrenaline Drive, Shinabu Yaguchi, 2000, Shooting Gallery.
An Affair of Love, Frédéric Fonteyne, 2000, Fine Line.
After Dark, My Sweet, James Foley, 1990, Avenue.
Afterglow, Alan Rudolph, 1997, Sony Classics.
Aimée and Jaguar, Max Färberböck, 2000, Zeitgeist.
Albino Alligator, Kevin Spacey, 1996, Miramax.
Alice and Martin, André Téchiné, 2000, USA Films.
All about My Mother, Pedro Almodóvar, 1999, Sony Classics.
All Over Me, Alex Sichel, 1997, Fine Line.
All the Vermeers in New York, Jon Jost, 1992, Strand.
Amateur, Hal Hartley, 1994, Sony Classics.
Amélie, Jean-Pierre Jeunet, 2001, Miramax.
American Desi, Piyush Dinker Pandya, 2001, Eros International.
American Dream, Barbara Kopple, 1992, Miramax.
American Movie, Chris Smith and Sarah Price, 1999, Sony Classics.
American Psycho, Mary Harron, 2000, Lions Gate.
Amongst Friends, Rob Weiss, 1993, Fine Line.
Amores Perros, Alejandro González Iñárrito, 2000, Lions Gate.
Angelo, My Love, Robert Duvall, 1983, Cinecom.
Angels and Insects, Philip Haas, 1996, Goldwyn.
Antonia and Jane, Beeban Kidron, 1991, Miramax.
Antonia's Line, Marleen Gorris, 1996, First Look.
Apartment Zero, Martin Donovan, 1989, Skouras.
The Atomic Cafe, Kevin Rafferty, Jayne Loader and Pierce Rafferty, 1982, Libra.

Autumn Tale, Eric Rohmer, 1999, October.

Babette's Feast, Gabriel Axel, 1987, Orion Classics.
Bad Lieutenant, Abel Ferrara, 1992, Aries.
The Ballad of Gregorio Cortez, Robert Young, 1983, Embassy.
The Ballad of Little Jo, Maggie Greenwald, 1994, Fine Line.
Barcelona, Whit Stillman, 1994, Fine Line.
Barenaked in America, Jason Priestley, 2000, Shooting Gallery.
Bar Girls, Marita Giovanni, 1994, Orion Classics.
The Basketball Diaries, Scott Kalvert, 1995, Fine Line.
Basquiat, Julian Schnabel, 1996, Miramax.
The Beans of Egypt, Maine, Jennifer Warren, 1994, IRS.
Beautiful Creatures, Bill Eagles, 2001, Universal Focus.
Beautiful Thing, Hettie MacDonald, 1997, Sony Classics.
Beau Travail, Claire Denis, 2000, New Yorker.
Bedrooms and Hallways, Rose Troche, 1998, First Run.
Before Night Falls, Julian Schnabel, 2001, Fine Line.
Begotten, E. Elias Merhige, 1991, World Artists.
Beijing Bicycle, Wang Xiaoshuai, 2001, Sony Classics.
Belizaire the Cajun, Glenn Pitre, 1986, Skouras.
Better Housekeeping, Frank Novak, 2001, Universal Focus.
Better Living through Circuitry, Jon Reiss, 2000, Seventh Art.
Better than Sex, Jonathan Teplitzky, 2000, Goldwyn Films.
Betty Blue, Jean-Jacques Beineix, 1986, Alive.
Beyond Silence, Caroline Link, 1996, Miramax.
Bhaji on the Beach, Gurinder Chadha, 1994, First Look.
The Big Dis, Gordon Erikson, 1990, First Run.
Big Night, Stanley Tucci and Campbell Scott, 1996, Goldwyn.
The Big One, Michael Moore, 1998, Miramax.
Billy Elliot, Stephen Daldry, 2000, Universal Focus.
Billy's Hollywood Screen Kiss, Tommy O'Haver, 1998, Trimark.
Black and White, James Toback, 1999, Screen Gems.
The Blair Witch Project, Daniel Myrick and Eduardo Sánchez, 1999, Artisan.
Blair Witch 2: Book of Shadows, Joe Berlinger, 2000, Artisan.
Blair Witch 3, Daniel Myrick and Eduardo Sánchez, 2001, Artisan.
Blood Simple, Joel Coen, 1984, Circle.
The Bloody Child, Nina Menkes, 1996, World Artists.
Born in Flames, Lizzie Borden, 1983, First Run.
Box of Moonlight, Tom DiCillo, 1997, Trimark.
Boyfriends and Girlfriends, Eric Rohmer, 1987, Orion Classics.

Boys Don't Cry, Kimberly Peirce, 1999, Fox Searchlight.
Bread and Roses, Ken Loach, 2000, Lions Gate.
Breaking the Waves, Lars von Trier, 1996, October.
A Brief History of Time, Errol Morris, 1992, Triton.
Broken Mirrors, Marleen Gorris, 1984, no distributor.
Brother, Takeshi Kitano, 2001, Sony Classics.
The Brother from Another Planet, John Sayles, 1984, Cinecom.
Brother of Sleep, Joseph Vilsmaier, 1995, Sony Classics.
Brother's Keeper, Joe Berlinger, 1992, self-distributed.
The Brothers McMullen, Edward Burns, 1995, Fox Searchlight.
Buena Vista Social Club, Wim Wenders, 1999, Artisan.
Buffalo 66, Vincent Gallo, 1998, Lions Gate.
Burnt by the Sun, Nikita Mikhalkov, 1994, Sony Classics.
But I'm a Cheerleader, Jamie Babbit, 2000, Lions Gate.
Butterfly, Jose Luis Cuerda, 2000, Miramax.
Bye Bye Brazil, Carlos Diegues, 1980, Unifilms.

Café au Lait, Mathieu Kassovitz, 1993, New Yorker.
Camille Claudel, Bruno Nuytten, 1988, Orion Classics.
Career Girls, Mike Leigh, 1997, October.
Carla's Song, Ken Loach, 1996, Shadow.
The Castle, Rob Sitch, 1999, Miramax.
The Caveman's Valentine, Kasi Lemmons 2001, Universal Focus.
Cecil B. Demented, John Waters, 2000, Artisan.
The Celebration, Thomas Vinterberg, 1998, October.
The Celluloid Closet, Rob Epstein and Jeffrey Friedman, 1996, Sony Classics.
The Center of the World, Wayne Wang, 2000, Artisan.
Central Station, Walter Salles, 1998, Sony Classics.
Chameleon Street, Wendell B. Harris Jr., 1991, Northern Arts.
Chan Is Missing, Wayne Wang, 1982, New Yorker.
Character, Mike van Diem, 1997, Sony Classics.
Chasing Amy, Kevin Smith, 1997, Miramax.
Children of Heaven, Majid Majidi, 1999, Miramax.
Chocolat, Claire Denis, 1989, Orion Classics.
Chocolat, Lasse Hallström, 2000, Miramax.
Choose Me, Alan Rudolph, 1984, Island.
Chuck & Buck, Miguel Arteta, 2000, Artisan.
Chungking Express, Wong Kar-wai, 1995, Miramax/Rolling Thunder.
Chunhyang, Im Kwon Taek, 2001, Lot 47.
Chutney Popcorn, Nisha Ganatra, 1999, First Look.

Cinema Paradiso, Giuseppe Tornatore, 1990, Miramax.
City of Hope, John Sayles, 1991, Goldwyn.
The City of Lost Children, Marc Caro and Jean-Pierre Jeunet, 1995, Sony Classics.
La Ciudad, David Riker, 1999, Zeitgeist.
Claire of the Moon, Nicole Conn, 1992, Strand.
Clean, Shaven, Lodge Kerrigan, 1995, Strand.
Clerks, Kevin Smith, 1994, Miramax.
The Clockwatchers, Jill Sprecher, 1998, Artistic License.
Close to Eden, Nikita Mikhalkov, 1992, Miramax.
Un Coeur en Hiver, Claude Sautet, 1993, October.
The Color of Paradise, Majid Majidi, 2000, Sony Classics.
The Colors Trilogy: Blue, Krzysztof Kieslowski, 1993, Miramax.
The Colors Trilogy: Red, Krzysztof Kieslowski, 1994, Miramax.
The Colors Trilogy: White, Krzysztof Kieslowski, 1994, Miramax.
Combination Platter, Tony Chan, 1993, Arrow.
Come Back to the 5 & Dime Jimmy Dean, Jimmy Dean, Robert Altman, 1982, Cinecom.
Committed, Lisa Kreuger, 2000, Miramax.
The Cook, the Thief, His Wife and Her Lover, Peter Greenaway, 1990, Miramax.
Cookie's Fortune, Robert Altman, 1999, October.
Copland, James Mangold, 1997, Miramax.
Criminal Lovers, François Ozon, 2000, Strand.
Cronos, Guillermo Del Torro, 1993, October.
Crossover Dreams, Leon Ichaso, 1985, Miramax.
Crouching Tiger, Hidden Dragon, Ang Lee, 2000, Sony Classics.
Croupier, Mike Hodges, 2000, Shooting Gallery.
Crush, Alison Maclean, 1993, Strand.
The Crying Game, Neil Jordan, 1992, Miramax.
The Cup, Khyentse Norbu, 1999, Fine Line.

Dancer in the Dark, Lars von Trier, 2000, Fine Line.
Dancing at Lughnasa, Pat O'Connor, 1998, Sony Classics.
Danzón, Maria Novaro, 1991, Sony Classics.
Daughters of the Dust, Julie Dash, 1992, Kino.
The Day I Became a Woman, Marziyeh Meshkini, 2001, Shooting Gallery.
The Daytrippers, Greg Mattola, 1997, CFP.
Dead Man, Jim Jarmusch, 1996, Miramax.
Dear Diary, Nanni Moretti, 1994, Fine Line.
The Deep End, Scott McGhee and David Siegel, 2001, Fox Searchlight.

Filmography

Delicatessen, Marc Caro and Jean-Pierre Jeunet, 1991, Miramax.
Denise Calls Up, Hal Salwen, 1996, Sony Classics.
Desert Blue, Morgan J. Freeman, 1998, Goldwyn Films.
Desert Hearts, Donna Deitch, 1986, Goldwyn.
Different for Girls, Richard Spence, 1997, First Look.
Dim Sum: A Little Bit of Heart, Wayne Wang, 1985, Orion Classics.
The Dinner Game, Francis Veber, 1998, Lions Gate.
Distant Voices, Still Lives, Terence Davies, 1989, Avenue.
Diva, Jean-Jacques Beineix, 1981, United Artists Classics.
Dogma, Kevin Smith, 1999, Lions Gate.
The Doom Generation, Gregg Araki, 1995, Trimark.
Double Happiness, Mina Shum, 1994, Fine Line.
The Double Life of Veronique, Krzysztof Kieslowski, 1991, Miramax.
Down by Law, Jim Jarmusch, 1986, Island.
Down in the Delta, Maya Angelou, 1998, Miramax.
The Dreamlife of Angels, Erick Zonca, 1998, Sony Classics.
Drowning by Numbers, Peter Greenaway, 1987, Miramax.
Drugstore Cowboy, Gus Van Sant, 1989, Avenue.

East Is East, Damien O'Donnell, 2000, Miramax.
East Palace, West Palace, Zhang Yuan, 1997, Strand.
East-West, Régis Warnier, 1999, Sony Classics.
Eat Drink Man Woman, Ang Lee, 1994, Goldwyn.
Eating Raoul, Paul Bartel, 1982, Quartet.
Edith and Marcel, Claude Lelouch, 1983, Miramax.
Edward II, Derek Jarman, 1992, Fine Line.
8 ½ Women, Peter Greenaway, 2000, Lions Gate.
The Emperor and the Assassin, Chen Kaige, 1999, Sony Classics.
Enchanted April, Mike Newell, 1992, Miramax.
The English Patient, Anthony Minghella, 1996, Miramax.
Enormous Changes at the Last Minute, Mirra Bank and Ellen Hovde, 1985, First Run.
Entre Nous, Diane Kurys, 1983, United Artists Classics.
Equinox, Alan Rudolph, 1992, IRS.
Erendira, Ruy Guerra, 1983, Miramax.
Eternity and a Day, Theo Angelopoulos, 1998, Phaedra.
Eureka, Shinji Aoyama, 2001, Shooting Gallery.
Europa, Europa, Agnieszka Holland, 1991, Orion Classics.
Everybody's Fine, Giuseppe Tornatore, 1990, Miramax.
Everything Relative, Sharon Pollack, 1996, Tara.

Eve's Bayou, Kasi Lemmons, 1997, Lions Gate.
Exotica, Atom Egoyan, 1994, Miramax.
The Eyes of Tammy Faye, Fenton Bailey and Randy Barbato, 2000, Lions Gate.

Faithless, Liv Ullmann, 2001, Goldwyn Films.
Fallen Angels, Wong Kar-wai, 1995, Kino.
Faraway, So Close!, Wim Wenders, 1993, Sony Classics.
Farewell My Concubine, Chen Kaige, 1993, Miramax.
Far from Poland, Jill Godmilow, 1984, Film Forum.
Fast, Cheap, and Out of Control, Errol Morris, 1997, Sony Classics.
Fear, Anxiety and Depression, Todd Solondz, 1989, Goldwyn.
Fear of a Black Hat, Rusty Cundieff, 1994, Goldwyn.
Felicia's Journey, Atom Egoyan, 1999, Artisan.
Female Perversions, Susan Streitfeld, 1996, October.
La Femme Nikita, Luc Besson, 1990, Goldwyn.
First Love, Last Rites, Jesse Peretz, 1998, Strand.
The Five Senses, Jeremy Podeswa, 2000, Fine Line.
Flirt, Hal Hartley, 1995, CFP.
Flirting, John Duigan, 1990, Goldwyn.
The Flower of My Secret, Pedro Almodóvar, 1996, Sony Classics.
Following, Christopher Nolan, 1998, Zeitgeist.
Forbidden Love: The Unashamed Stories of Lesbian Lives, Aerlyn Weissman and Lynne Fernie, 1992, Women Make Movies.
Four Rooms, Allison Anders, Alexandre Rockwell, Robert Rodriguez, Quentin Tarantino, 1996, Miramax.
Frame Up, Jon Jost, 1993, World Artists.
Freeze Die Come to Life, Vitali Kanevski, 1990, International Film Exchange.
Fresh, Boaz Yakin, 1994, Miramax.
A Friend of the Deceased, Vyacheslav Krishtofovich, 1998, Sony Classics.
From Dusk to Dawn, Robert Rodriguez, 1996, Miramax.
From the Journals of Jean Seberg, Marc Rappaport, 1995, Planet Pictures.
The Full Monty, Peter Cattaneo, 1996, Fox Searchlight.
The Funeral, Abel Ferrara, 1996, October.
The Funeral, Juzo Itami, 1984, Republic.

Gal Young 'Un, Victor Nunez, 1979, First Run.
The Garden, Derek Jarman, 1990, International Film Circuit.
Gas Food Lodging, Allison Anders, 1992, Cineville.
Genealogies of a Crime, Raoul Ruiz, 1997, Strand.
The General, John Boorman, 1998, Sony Classics.
Genghis Blues, Roko Belic, 1999, Roxie.
George Washington, David Gordon Green, 2000, Cowboy.

Ghost Dog: The Way of the Samurai, Jim Jarmusch, 2000, Artisan.
Girlfight, Karyn Kusama, 2000, Screen Gems.
Girl on the Bridge, Patrice Leconte, 1999, Paramount Classics.
Girl 6, Spike Lee, 1996, Fox Searchlight.
Girls Town, Jim McKay, 1996, October.
The Glass Shield, Charles Burnett, 1994, Miramax.
Gods and Monsters, Bill Condon, 1998, Lions Gate.
Go Fish, Rose Troche, 1994, Goldwyn.
Gohatto, Nagisa Oshima, 1999, New Yorker.
The Golden Bowl, James Ivory, 2001, Lions Gate.
Golden Eighties, Chantal Akerman, 1982, World Artists.
The Governess, Sandra Goldbacher, 1998, Sony Classics.
Goya in Bordeaux, Carlos Saura, 2000, Sony Classics.
Gregory's Girl, Bill Forsyth, 1982, Goldwyn.
Groove, Greg Harrison, 2000, Sony Classics.
Guantanamera, Tomás Gutiérrez Alea and Juan Carlos Tabio, 1997, CFP.
Guinevere, Audrey Wells, 1999, Miramax.
Gummo, Harmony Korine, 1997, Fine Line.
Gun Crazy, Tamra Davis, 1993, First Look.

Haiku Tunnel, Jacob Kornbluth and Josh Kornbluth, 2001, Sony Classics.
The Handmaid's Tale, Volker Schlöndorf, 1990, Cinecom.
The Hanging Garden, Thom Fitzgerald, 1997, Goldwyn Films.
Happiness, Todd Solondz, 1998, Good Machine.
Happy, Texas, Mark Illsley, 1999, Miramax.
Harry Is Here to Help, Dominik Moll, 2001, Miramax.
Hav Plenty, Christopher Cherot, 1997, Miramax.
Hearts of Darkness, Fax Bahr and George Hickenlooper, 1991, Triton.
Heavenly Creatures, Peter Jackson, 1994, Miramax.
Heavy, James Mangold, 1996, CFP.
Hedwig and the Angry Inch, John Cameron Mitchell, 2001, Fine Line.
Henry: Portrait of a Serial Killer, John McNaughton, 1990, Greycat.
Henry V, Kenneth Branagh, 1989, Goldwyn.
Henry Fool, Hal Hartley, 1998, Sony Classics.
High Art, Lisa Cholodenko, 1998, October.
High Heels, Pedro Almodóvar, 1991, Miramax.
High Hopes, Mike Leigh, 1989, Skouras.
The Hit, Stephen Frears, 1984, Island.
Hollywood Shuffle, Robert Townsend, 1987, Goldwyn.
Hoop Dreams, Steve James, 1994, Fine Line.
The Hours and the Times, Christopher Münch, 1991, Strand.

Household Saints, Nancy Savoca, 1993, Fine Line.
The House of Yes, Mark S. Waters, 1997, Miramax.
Howard's End, James Ivory, 1992, Sony Classics.
How to Be a Woman and Not Die in the Attempt, Ana Belén, 1999, First Look.
Humanité, Bruno Dumont, 2000, WinStar.
Human Resources, Laurent Cantet, 2000, Shooting Gallery.
Human Traffic, Justin Kerrigan, 2000, Miramax.

The Icicle Thief, Maurizio Nichetti, 1989, Aries.
The Idiots, Lars von Trier, 1999, USA Films.
Illtown, Nick Gomez, 1998, Shooting Gallery.
Incident at Oglala, Michael Apted, 1991, Miramax.
The Incredibly True Adventure of Two Girls in Love, Maria Maggenti, 1995, Fine Line.
Inside Monkey Zetterland, Jefery Levy, 1992, IRS.
In the Bedroom, Todd Field, 2001, Miramax.
In the Company of Men, Neil LaBute, 1997, Sony Classics.
In the Mood for Love, Wong Kar-wai, 2000, USA Films.
In the Soup, Alexandre Rockwell, 1992, Triton.
Irma Vep, Olivier Assayas, 1996, Zeitgeist.
I Shot Andy Warhol, Mary Harron, 1996, Goldwyn.
I Stand Alone, Gaspar Noé, 1998, Strand.
I've Heard the Mermaids Singing, Patricia Rozema, 1987, Miramax.

Jackie Brown, Quentin Tarantino, 1997, Miramax.
Jean de Florette, Claude Berri, 1986, Orion Classics.
Jeffrey, Christopher Ashley, 1995, Orion Classics.
Jerry and Tom, Saul Rubinek, 1998, Miramax.
Jesus' Son, Alison Maclean, 2000, Lions Gate.
Johnny Suede, Tom DiCillo, 1991, Miramax.
Journey of Hope, Xavier Koller, 1990, Miramax.
Judy Berlin, Eric Mendelsohn, 2000, Shooting Gallery.
Julie Johnson, Bob Gosse, 2001, Universal Focus.
julien donkey-boy, Harmony Korine, 1999, Fine Line.
Jump, Justin McCarthy, 1999, Arrow.
Just Another Girl on the I.R.T., Leslie Harris, 1993, Miramax.

Kama Sutra: A Tale of Love, Mira Nair, 1997, Trimark.
Kansas City, Robert Altman, 1996, Fine Line.
Kicked in the Head, Matthew Harrison, 1997, October.
Kicking & Screaming, Noah Baumbach, 1995, Trimark.

Filmography

Kids, Larry Clark, 1995, Shining Excalibur.
Kikujiro, Takeshi Kitano, 1999, Sony Classics.
Killing Zoe, Roger Avary, 1994, October.
Kill-Off, Maggie Greenwald, 1989, Films Around the World.
Kiss of the Spider Woman, Hector Babenco, 1985, Island.
Kiss or Kill, Bill Bennett, 1996, October.
Kolya, Jan Sverák, 1996, Miramax.
Koyaanisqatsi, Godfrey Reggio, 1983, Island.
The Krays, Peter Medak, 1990, Miramax.

Ladybird, Ladybird, Ken Loach, 1994, Goldwyn.
The Last Days, James Moll, 1998, October.
The Last Days of Chez Nous, Gillian Armstrong, 1993, Fine Line.
The Last Good Time, Bob Balaban, 1994, Goldwyn.
The Last Metro, François Truffaut, 1980, United Artists Classics.
Last Night at the Alamo, Eagle Pennell, 1984, Cinecom.
The Last of England, Derek Jarman, 1988, International Film Circuit.
Last Resort, Pawel Pawlikowski, 2001, Shooting Gallery.
The Last Seduction, John Dahl, 1994, October.
The Last Time I Committed Suicide, Stephan Kay, 1997, Roxie.
Late August, Early September, Olivier Assayas, 1999, Zeitgeist.
Late Bloomers, Julia Dyer, 1996, Strand.
Latin Boys Go to Hell, Ela Troyano, 1997, Strand.
Lawn Dogs, John Duigan, 1997, Strand.
Laws of Gravity, Nick Gomez, 1992, RKO.
Leningrad Cowboys, Aki Kaurismäki, 1989, Orion Classics.
Letter to Brezhnev, Chris Bernard, 1984, Circle.
Let's Talk about Sex, Troy Beyer, 1998, Fine Line.
Lianna, John Sayles, 1983, United Artists Classics.
L.I.E., Michael Cuesta, 2001, Lot 47.
The Life and Times of Rosie the Riveter, Connie Field, 1980, First Run.
Life Is Beautiful, Roberto Benigni, 1998, Miramax.
Life Is Sweet, Mike Leigh, 1991, October.
Like Water for Chocolate, Alfonso Arau, 1993, Miramax.
Limbo, John Sayles, 1999, Screen Gems.
The Limey, Steven Soderbergh, 1999, Artisan.
Liquid Sky, Slava Tsukerman, 1983, Cinevista.
Little Odessa, James Gray, 1995, Fine Line.
Little Vera, Vasili Pichul, 1988, Miramax.

Little Voice, Mark Herman, 1998, Miramax.
The Living End, Gregg Araki, 1992, October.
Living in Oblivion, Tom DiCillo, 1995, Sony Classics.
Living on Tokyo Time, Steven Okasaki, 1987, Skouras.
Livin' Large, Michael Schultz, 1992, Goldwyn.
Lock, Stock and Two Smoking Barrels, Guy Ritchie, 1999, Gramercy.
The Lonely Passion of Judith Hearne, Jack Clayton, 1987, Island.
Lone Star, John Sayles, 1996, Sony Classics.
Longtime Companion, Norman Rene, 1990, Goldwyn.
Lost Highway, David Lynch, 1997, October.
Love & Death on Long Island, Richard Kwietniowski, 1997, Lions Gate.
Love & Sex, Valerie Breiman, 2000, Lions Gate.
Love Crimes, Lizzie Borden, 1991, Miramax.
Love Is the Devil, John Maybury, 1998, Strand.
Lovers, Vicente Aranda, 1991, Aries.
Lovers of the Arctic Circle, Julio Medem, 1999, Fine Line.
Loving Jezebel, Kwyn Bader, 2000, Universal Focus.
The Low Down, Jamie Thraves, 2001, Shooting Gallery.
The Luzhin Defense, Marleen Gorris, 2000, Sony Classics.

Maborosi, Hirokazu Kore-eda, 1996, Milestone.
Macho Dancer, Lino Brocka, 1988, Strand.
Madame Bovary, Claude Chabrol, 1991, Goldwyn.
The Madness of King George, Nicholas Hytner, 1994, Goldwyn.
Magdalena Viraga, Nina Menkes, 1986, World Artists.
Mala Noche, Gus Van Sant, 1986, Frameline.
Malèna, Giuseppe Tornatore, 2000, Miramax.
Man Bites Dog, Remy Belvaux, André Bonzel and Benoit Poelvoorde, 1992, Roxie.
Man Facing Southeast, Eliseo Subiela, 1987, Film Dallas.
Manny and Lo, Lisa Krueger, 1996, Sony Classics.
Man of the Year, Dirk Shafter, 1996, Seventh Art.
Manon of the Spring, Claude Berri, 1986, Orion Classics.
The Man Who Cried, Sally Potter, 2000, Universal Focus.
Map of the Human Heart, Vincent Ward, 1993, Miramax.
El Mariachi, Robert Rodriguez, 1993, Columbia.
Marianne and Juliane, Margarethe von Trotta, 1981, New Yorker.
Matador, Pedro Almodóvar, 1986, World Artists.
Matewan, John Sayles, 1987, Cinecom.
Ma Vie en Rose, Alain Berliner, 1997, Sony Classics.

Me Myself I, Philippa Karmel, 1999, Sony Classics.
Mediterraneo, Gabriele Salvatores, 1991, Miramax.
Memento, Christopher Nolan, 2001, Newmarket Capital Group.
Memory of Appearances, Raoul Ruiz, 1986, International Film Circuit.
Men with Guns, John Sayles, 1998, Sony Classics.
Metropolitan, Whit Stillman, 1990, New Line.
Me You Them, Andrucha Waddington, 2001, Sony Classics.
Mifune, Soren Kragh-Jacobsen, 1999, Sony Classics.
The Million Dollar Hotel, Wim Wenders, 2000, Lions Gate.
Mindwalk, Bernt Capra, 1991, Triton.
Mississippi Masala, Mira Nair, 1992, Goldwyn.
Mi Vida Loca, Allison Anders, 1994, Sony Classics.
The Moderns, Alan Rudolph, 1988, Alive.
Mona Lisa, Neil Jordan, 1986, Island.
The Monster, Roberto Benigni, 1994, CFP.
Mrs. Brown, John Madden, 1997, Miramax.
Mrs. Dalloway, Marleen Gorris, 1998, First Look.
Mrs. Parker and the Vicious Circle, Alan Rudolph, 1994, Fine Line.
Much Ado about Nothing, Kenneth Branagh, 1993, Goldwyn.
MURDER and Murder, Yvonne Rainer, 1996, Zeitgeist.
Muriel's Wedding, P.J. Hogan, 1995, Miramax.
The Music of Chance, Philip Haas, 1993, IRS.
My Beautiful Laundrette, Stephen Frears, 1986, Orion Classics.
My Brilliant Career, Gillian Armstrong, 1980, Analysis.
My Dinner with Andre, Louis Malle, 1981, New Yorker.
My First Mister, Christine Lahti, 2001, Paramount Classics.
My Left Foot, Jim Sheridan, 1989, Miramax.
My Life's in Turnaround, Don Ward and Eric Schaeffer, 1994, Arrow.
My Name Is Joe, Ken Loach, 1999, Artisan.
My New Gun, Stacy Cochran, 1992, IRS.
My Own Private Idaho, Gus Van Sant, 1991, Fine Line.
My Son the Fanatic, Udayan Prasad, 1998, Miramax.
Mystery Train, Jim Jarmusch, 1989, Orion Classics.
Mystic Pizza, Donald Petrie, 1988, Goldwyn.
My Twentieth Century, Ildiko Enyedi, 1990, Aries.

Naked, Mike Leigh, 1993, Fine Line.
The Nasty Girl, Michael Verhoeven, 1990, Miramax.
Nelly and Monsieur Arnaud, Claude Sautet, 1996, New Yorker.
Nenette and Boni, Claire Denis, 1997, Strand.

Next Stop, Wonderland, Brad Anderson, 1998, Miramax.
Night and Day, Chantal Akerman, 1992, International Film Circuit.
Night on Earth, Jim Jarmusch, 1991, Fine Line.
Nil by Mouth, Gary Oldman, 1998, Sony Classics.
Nobody's Fool, Evelyn Purcell, 1986, Island.
Non-Stop, Sabu, 2000, Shooting Gallery.
El Norte, Gregory Nava, 1983, Cinecom.
Northern Lights, John Hanson and Rob Nilsson, 1979, First Run.
Notes from Underground, Gary Walkow, 1995, Northern Arts.
Not One Less, Zhang Yimou, 1999, Sony Classics.
Nowhere, Gregg Araki, 1997, Fine Line.

The Object of Beauty, Michael Lindsay-Hogg, 1991, Avenue.
Once Were Warriors, Lee Tamahori, 1994, Fine Line.
One, Tony Barbieri, 2000, Shooting Gallery.
One False Move, Carl Franklin, 1992, IRS.
On the Ropes, Nanette Burstein and Brett Morgan, 2000, WinStar.
On the Run, Bruno de Almeida, 1998, Phaedra.
On Top of the Whale, Raoul Ruiz, 1982, International Film Circuit.
Open Your Eyes, Alejandro Amenábar, 1997, Artisan.
The Opportunists, Myles Connell, 2000, First Look.
The Opposite of Sex, Don Roos, 1998, Sony Classics.
Orlando, Sally Potter, 1993, Sony Classics.
Orphans, Peter Mullan, 2000, Shooting Gallery.
Oscar and Lucinda, Gillian Armstrong, 1997, Fox Searchlight.
Our Lady of the Assassins, Barbet Schroeder, 2001, Paramount Classics.

Paris Is Burning, Jennie Livingstone, 1991, Miramax.
Parting Glances, Bill Sherwood, 1986, Cinecom.
Party Girl, Daisy von Scherler Mayer, 1995, First Look.
Passion Fish, John Sayles, 1992, Miramax.
Passion of Mind, Alain Berliner, 2000, Paramount Classics.
Patti Rocks, David Burton Morris, 1988, Film Dallas.
Pecker, John Waters, 1998, Fine Line.
Pelle the Conqueror, Bille August, 1989, Miramax.
Permanent Vacation, David Veloz, 1998, Artisan.
Persuasion, Roger Michell, 1995, Sony Classics.
Pi, Darren Aronofsky, 1998, Artisan.
The Piano, Jane Campion, 1993, Miramax.

Picture Bride, Kayo Hatta, 1995, Miramax.
The Pillow Book, Peter Greenaway, 1996, CFP.
The Player, Robert Altman, 1992, Fine Line.
Poison, Todd Haynes, 1991, Zeitgeist.
Pollock, Ed Harris, 2000, Sony Classics.
Ponette, Jacques Doillon, 1996, Arrow.
Il Postino, Michael Radford, 1995, Miramax.
The Price of Milk, Harry Sinclair, 2000, Lot 47.
Prick up Your Ears, Stephen Frears, 1987, Goldwyn.
Priest, Antonia Bird, 1995, Miramax.
The Princess and the Warrior, Tom Tykwer, 2001, Sony Classics.
Privilege, Yvonne Rainer, 1991, Zeitgeist.
The Promise, Margarethe von Trotta, 1994, Fine Line.
Prospero's Books, Peter Greenaway, 1991, Miramax.
Pulp Fiction, Quentin Tarantino, 1994, Miramax.
Pushing Hands, Ang Lee, 1992, Good Machine.

The Quarry, Marion Hänsel, 1998, First Run.
Queen Margot, Patrice Chéreau, 1994, Miramax.
Queen of Diamonds, Nina Menkes, 1991, World Artists.
A Question of Silence, Marleen Gorris, 1981, Quartet/Sigma.

Raining Stones, Ken Loach, 1994, Northern Arts.
Raise the Red Lantern, Zhang Yimou, 1991, Orion Classics.
Ran, Akira Kurosawa, 1984, Orion Classics.
The Rat, Steve Barron, 2001, Universal Focus.
Ratcatcher, Lynne Ramsay, 2000, First Look.
Red Firecracker, Green Firecracker, Ping He, 1994, October.
Red Rock West, John Dahl, 1994, Roxie.
The Red Violin, François Girard, 1998, Lions Gate.
Remembering the Cosmos, Junichi Suzuki, 1999, Phaedra.
Requiem for a Dream, Darren Aronofsky, 2000, Artisan.
Reservoir Dogs, Quentin Tarantino, 1992, Miramax.
Restless, Jule Gilfillan, 1998, Arrow.
The Return of the Secaucus Seven, John Sayles, 1980, Libra/Specialty.
Rhapsody in August, Akira Kurosawa, 1991, Orion Classics.
Rhythm Thief, Matthew Harrison, 1994, Strand.
River of Grass, Kelly Reichardt, 1995, Strand.
River's Edge, Tim Hunter, 1987, Island.
The Road Home, Zhang Yimou, 1999, Sony Classics.

Rock Hudson's Home Movies, Mark Rappaport, 1992, Planet Pictures.
Roger & Me, Michael Moore, 1989, Warner Bros.
Roja, Mani Rathnam, 1992, Phaedra.
Romance, Catherine Breillat, 1999, Trimark.
A Room with a View, James Ivory, 1986, Cinecom.
Roosters, Robert Young, 1993, IRS.
Rosa Luxembourg, Margarethe von Trotta, 1986, New Yorker.
Rosetta, Jean-Pierre Dardenne and Luc Dardenne, 1999, USA Films.
Rounders, John Dahl, 1998, Miramax.
Ruby in Paradise, Victor Nunez, 1993, October.
Run Lola Run, Tom Tykwer, 1999, Sony Classics.

Safe, Todd Haynes, 1995, Sony Classics.
The Safety of Objects, Rose Troche, 2001, Renaissance.
Salaam Bombay!, Mira Nair, 1988, Cinecom.
Sammy & Rosie Get Laid, Stephen Frears, 1987, Cinecom.
Sankofa, Haille Gerima, 1994, Mypheduh.
Sans Soleil, Chris Marker, 1982, New Yorker.
Saving Grace, Nigel Cole, 2000, Fine Line.
The Scent of Green Papaya, Tran Anh Hung, 1993, First Look.
Schizopolis, Steven Soderbergh, 1996, Northern Arts.
The Secret of Roan Inish, John Sayles, 1994, First Look.
Secrets & Lies, Mike Leigh, 1996, October.
Series 7, Daniel Minahan, 2001, USA Films.
Set Me Free, Léa Pool, 2000, Artistic License.
sex, lies & videotape, Steven Soderbergh, 1989, Miramax.
Shadow Magic, Ann Hu, 2000, Sony Classics.
Shadow of the Vampire, E. Elias Merhige, 2000, Lions Gate.
Shakespeare in Love, John Madden, 1998, Miramax.
Shallow Grave, Danny Boyle, 1995, Gramercy.
Shall We Dance?, Masayuki Suo, 1997, Miramax.
Shanghai Triad, Zhang Yimou, 1995, Sony Classics.
Sherman's March, Ross McElwee, 1986, First Run.
She's Gotta Have It, Spike Lee, 1986, Island.
Shine, Scott Hicks, 1996, Fine Line.
Shower, Zhang Yuan, 1999, Sony Classics.
Sid and Nancy, Alex Cox, 1986, Goldwyn.
Sidewalks of New York, Edward Burns, 2000, Paramount Classics.
Sidewalk Stories, Charles Lane, 1989, Island.
Signs & Wonders, Jonathan Nossiter, 2001, Strand.

Filmography

Silverlake Life: The View from Here, Tom Joslin and Peter Friedman, 1993, Zeitgeist.
Simple Men, Hal Hartley, 1992, Fine Line.
Slacker, Richard Linklater, 1991, Orion Classics.
Slam, Marc Levin, 1998, Trimark.
Sleepwalk, Sara Driver, 1987, First Run.
Sling Blade, Billy Bob Thornton, 1996, Miramax.
Slums of Beverly Hills, Tamara Jenkins, 1998, Fox Searchlight.
Smithereens, Susan Seidelman, 1982, New Line.
Smoke Signals, Chris Eyre, 1996, Miramax.
Smooth Talk, Joyce Chopra, 1986, Spectra Films.
The Snapper, Stephen Frears, 1994, Miramax.
A Soldier's Daughter Never Cries, James Ivory, 1998, October.
Songcatcher, Maggie Greenwald, 1999, Trimark.
Southern Comfort, Kate Davis, 2001, HBO Theatrical.
Southpaw, Liam McGrath, 2000, Shooting Gallery.
Spanking the Monkey, David O. Russell, 1994, Fine Line.
Spetters, Paul Verhoeven, 1980, Goldwyn.
Star Maps, Miguel Arteta, 1997, Fox Searchlight.
Starstruck, Gillian Armstrong, 1982, Cinecom.
Steal This Movie!, Robert Greenwald, 2000, Lions Gate.
Stonewall, Nigel Finch, 1996, Strand.
The Story of Qui Ju, Zhang Yimou, 1992, Sony Classics.
Straight out of Brooklyn, Matty Rich, 1991, Goldwyn.
Strangers in Good Company, Cynthia Scott, 1992, First Run.
Stranger than Paradise, Jim Jarmusch, 1985, Goldwyn.
Strawberry and Chocolate, Tomás Gutiérrez Alea and Juan Carlos Tabio, 1994, Miramax.
Strawberry Fields, Rea Tajiri, 1999, Phaedra.
SubUrbia, Richard Linklater, 1996, Sony Classics.
Subway, Luc Besson, 1985, Island.
Such a Long Journey, Sturla Gunnarsson, 2000, Shooting Gallery.
Sugar Town, Allison Anders and Kurt Voss, 1999, October.
Suicide Kings, Peter O'Fallon, 1998, Artisan.
Sunday, Jonathan Nossiter, 1997, CFP.
Sunshine, István Szabó, 1999, Paramount Classics.
Superstar: The Life and Times of Andy Warhol, Chuck Workman, 1991, Aries.
Sure Fire, Jon Jost, 1993, World Artists.
Surname Viet Given Name Nam, Trinh T. Minh-Ha, 1989, Women Make Movies.

Suzhou River, Lou Ye, 2000, Strand.
The Sweet Hereafter, Atom Egoyan, 1997, Fine Line.
Sweetie, Jane Campion, 1990, Avenue.
Swoon, Tom Kalin, 1992, Fine Line.

A Tale of Summer, Eric Rohmer, 1997, Artificial Eye.
Tampopo, Juzo Itami, 1987, Republic.
Tango, Carlos Saura, 1998, Sony Classics.
The Tao of Steve, Jenniphr Goodman, 2000, Sony Classics.
Tape, Richard Linklater, 2001, Lions Gate.
A Taxing Woman, Juzo Itami, 1988, New Yorker.
The Tempest, Derek Jarman, 1980, World Northal.
Thank You and Good Night, Jan Oxenberg, 1991, Aries.
The Thief, Pavel Chukhraj, 1998, Stratosphere.
The Thin Blue Line, Errol Morris, 1988, Miramax.
Things to Do in Denver When You're Dead, Gary Felder, 1995, Miramax.
The Third Miracle, Agnieszka Holland, 2000, Sony Classics.
30 Days, Aaron Harnick, 2000, Arrow.
32 Short Films about Glenn Gould, François Girard, 1993, Goldwyn.
Three Lives and Only One Death, Raoul Ruiz, 1996, New Yorker.
Three Seasons, Tony Bui, 1999, October.
Tie Me Up! Tie Me Down! Pedro Almodóvar, 1990, Miramax.
Timecode, Mike Figgis, 2000, Screen Gems.
A Time for Drunken Horses, Bahman Ghobadi, 2000, Shooting Gallery.
Time Regained, Raoul Ruiz, 2000, Kino.
A Time to Live, Hou Hsiao-hsien, 1985, International Film Circuit.
The Times of Harvey Milk, Robert Epstein, 1984, Cinecom.
Titanic Town, Roger Michell, 2000, Shooting Gallery.
Together Alone, P.J. Castellaneta, 1992, Frameline.
To Live, Zhang Yimou, 1994, Goldwyn.
Tom and Viv, Brian Gilbert, 1994, Miramax.
Too Much Sleep, David Maquiling, 2001, Shooting Gallery.
Topsy-Turvy, Mike Leigh, 1999, October.
To Sleep with Anger, Charles Burnett, 1990, Goldwyn.
Totally Fu**ed Up, Gregg Araki, 1994, Strand.
Toto le Héros, Jaco Van Dormael, 1992, Triton.
A Touch of Evil, Tony Au, 1995, October.
Tous les Matins du Monde, Alain Corneau, 1992, October.
Toute une Nuit, Chantal Akerman, 1982, World Artists.
Track 29, Nicholas Roeg, 1988, Island.

Filmography

Trainspotting, Danny Boyle, 1996, Miramax.
Trees Lounge, Steve Buscemi, 1996, Live.
Trick, Jim Fall, 1999, Fine Line.
The Trip to Bountiful, Peter Masterson, 1985, Island.
Trixie, Alan Rudolph, 2000, Sony Classics.
Trouble in Mind, Alan Rudolph, 1986, Alive.
Troublesome Creek: A Midwestern, Steven Ascher and Jeanne Jordan, 1995, Artistic License.
Trust, Hal Hartley, 1990, Fine Line.
Tumbleweeds, Gavin O'Connor, 1999, Fine Line.
The 24 Hour Woman, Nancy Savoca, 1999, Artisan.
Twin Falls Idaho, Michael Polish, 1999, Sony Classics.
Two Family House, Raymond De Felitta, 2000, Lions Gate.

The Unbelievable Truth, Hal Hartley, 1990, Miramax.
Under the Olive Trees, Abbas Kiarostami, 1994, Miramax.
Up at the Villa, Philip Haas, 2000, USA Films.
Urbania, Jon Shear, 2000, Lions Gate.
The Usual Suspects, Bryan Singer, 1995, Gramercy.

The Van, Stephen Frears, 1996, Fox Searchlight.
The Vanishing, George Sluizer, 1988, Tara.
Variety, Bette Gordon, 1985, Horizon.
Velvet Goldmine, Todd Haynes, 1998, Miramax.
Venus Beauty Institute, Tonie Marshall, 1999, Lot 47.
Vermont Is for Lovers, John O'Brien, 1993, Zeitgeist.
Vertical Ray of the Sun, Anh Hung Tran, 2000, Sony Classics.
Vincent, Paul Cox, 1987, Roxie.
The Virgin Suicides, Sofia Coppola, 1999, Paramount Classics.
Vive l'Amour, Tsai Ming-liang, 1994, Strand.
Voyage to the Beginning of the World, Manoel de Oliveira, 1997, Strand.

Waiting for Guffman, Christopher Guest, 1997, Sony Classics.
Waiting for the Moon, Jill Godmilow, 1987, Skouras.
Waking Ned Devine, Kirk Jones, 1998, Fox Searchlight.
Walking and Talking, Nicole Holofcener, 1996, Miramax.
The War Room, D. A. Pennebaker and Chris Hegedus, 1993, October.
The War Zone, Tim Roth, 1999, Lot 47.
The Waterdance, Michael Steinberg and Neal Jimenez, 1992, Goldwyn.
Water Drops on Burning Rocks, François Ozon, 2000, Zeitgeist.

The Watermelon Woman, Cheryl Dunye, 1996, First Run.
The Way of the Gun, Christopher McQuarrie, 2000, Artisan.
The Wedding Banquet, Ang Lee, 1993, Goldwyn.
Welcome to the Dollhouse, Todd Solondz, 1996, Sony Classics.
West Beirut, Ziad Doueiri, 1999, Cowboy.
What Happened Was…, Tom Noonan, 1994, Goldwyn.
When Brendan Met Trudy, Kieron J. Walsh, 2001, Shooting Gallery.
When the Cat's Away, Cèdric Klapisch, 1997, Sony Classics.
When We Were Kings, Leon Gast, 1997, Gramercy.
The Whole Wide World, Dan Ireland, 1996, Sony Classics.
The Widow of Saint-Pierre, Patrice Leconte, 2001, Lions Gate.
Wild Reeds, André Téchiné, 1994, Strand.
Wilde, Brian Gilbert, 1997, Sony Classics.
The Wind Will Carry Us, Abbas Kiarostami, 2000, New Yorker.
Wings of Desire, Wim Wenders, 1988, Orion Classics.
The Wings of the Dove, Iain Softley, 1997, Miramax.
Winter Sleepers, Tom Tykwer, 2000, WinStar.
Without Air, Neil Abramson, 1995, Phaedra.
Wittgenstein, Derek Jarman, 1993, Zeitgeist.
The Wizard of Loneliness, Jenny Bowen, 1988, Skouras.
Woman on Top, Fina Torres, 2000, Fox Searchlight.
Women, Luis Galvão Teles, 1997, WinStar.
Women in Film, Bruce Wagner, 2001, Lions Gate.
Women on the Verge of a Nervous Breakdown, Pedro Almodóvar, 1988, Orion Classics.
Working Girls, Lizzie Borden, 1987, Miramax.

Xiu Xiu: The Sent-Down Girl, Joan Chen, 1998, Stratosphere.

Yi Yi, Edward Yang, 2001, WinStar.
You Can Count on Me, Kenneth Lonergan, 2000, Paramount Classics.
The Young Poisoner's Handbook, Benjamin Ross, 1996, CFP.
Young Soul Rebels, Isaac Julien, 1991, Miramax.
You So Crazy, Thomas Schlamme, 1994, Goldwyn.

Zebrahead, Anthony Drazan, 1992, Triumph.
Zentropa, Lars von Trier, 1991, Miramax.

Filmography

By Distributors

Alive
Betty Blue, Jean-Jacques Beineix, 1986.
The Moderns, Alan Rudolph, 1988.
Trouble in Mind, Alan Rudolph, 1986.

Analysis
My Brilliant Career, Gillian Armstrong, 1980.

Aries
Bad Lieutenant, Abel Ferrara, 1992.
The Icicle Thief, Maurizio Nichetti, 1989.
Lovers, Vicente Aranda, 1991.
My Twentieth Century, Ildiko Enyedi, 1990.
Superstar: The Life and Times of Andy Warhol, Chuck Workman, 1991.
Thank You and Good Night, Jan Oxenberg, 1991.

Arrow
Combination Platter, Tony Chan, 1993.
Jump, Justin McCarthy, 1999.
My Life's in Turnaround, Don Ward and Eric Schaeffer, 1994.
Ponette, Jacques Doillon, 1996.
Restless, Jule Gilfillan, 1998.
30 Days, Aaron Harnick, 2000.

Artifical Eye
A Tale of Summer, Eric Rohmer, 1997.

Artisan
The Blair Witch Project, Daniel Myrick and Eduardo Sánchez, 1999.
Blair Witch 2: Book of Shadows, Joe Berlinger, 2000.
Blair Witch 3, Daniel Myrick and Eduardo Sánchez, 2001.
Buena Vista Social Club, Wim Wenders, 1999.
Cecil B. Demented, John Waters, 2000.
The Center of the World, Wayne Wang, 2000.
Chuck & Buck, Miguel Arteta, 2000.
Felicia's Journey, Atom Egoyan, 1999.
Ghost Dog: The Way of the Samurai, Jim Jarmusch, 2000.
The Limey, Steven Soderbergh, 1999.
My Name Is Joe, Ken Loach, 1999.

Open Your Eyes, Alejandro Amenábar, 1997.
Permanent Vacation, David Veloz, 1998.
Pi, Darren Aronofsky, 1998.
Requiem for a Dream, Darren Aronofsky, 2000.
Suicide Kings, Peter O'Fallon, 1998.
The 24 Hour Woman, Nancy Savoca, 1999.
The Way of the Gun, Christopher McQuarrie, 2000.

Artistic License
The Clockwatchers, Jill Sprecher, 1998.
Set Me Free, Léa Pool, 2000.
Troublesome Creek: A Midwestern, Steven Ascher and Jeanne Jordan, 1995.

Avenue
After Dark, My Sweet, James Foley, 1990.
Distant Voices, Still Lives, Terence Davies, 1989.
Drugstore Cowboy, Gus Van Sant, 1989.
The Object of Beauty, Michael Lindsay-Hogg, 1991.
Sweetie, Jane Campion, 1990.

CFP
The Daytrippers, Greg Mattola, 1997.
Flirt, Hal Hartley, 1995.
Guantanamera, Tomás Gutiérrez Alea and Juan Carlos Tabio, 1997.
Heavy, James Mangold, 1996.
The Monster, Roberto Benigni, 1994.
The Pillow Book, Peter Greenaway, 1996.
Sunday, Jonathan Nossiter, 1997.
The Young Poisoner's Handbook, Benjamin Ross, 1996.

Cinecom
Angelo, My Love, Robert Duvall, 1983.
The Brother from Another Planet, John Sayles, 1984.
Come Back to the 5 & Dime Jimmy Dean, Jimmy Dean, Robert Altman, 1982.
The Handmaid's Tale, Volker Schlöndorf, 1990.
Last Night at the Alamo, Eagle Pennell, 1984.
Matewan, John Sayles, 1987.
El Norte, Gregory Nava, 1983.
Parting Glances, Bill Sherwood, 1986.
A Room with a View, James Ivory, 1986.

Salaam Bombay!, Mira Nair, 1988.
Sammy & Rosie Get Laid, Stephen Frears, 1987.
Starstruck, Gillian Armstrong, 1982.
The Times of Harvey Milk, Robert Epstein, 1984.

Cineville
Gas Food Lodging, Allison Anders, 1992.

Cinevista
Liquid Sky, Slava Tsukerman, 1983.

Circle
Blood Simple, Joel Coen, 1984.
Letter to Brezhnev, Chris Bernard, 1984.

Columbia
El Mariachi, Robert Rodriguez, 1993.

Cowboy
George Washington, David Gordon Green, 2000.
West Beirut, Ziad Doueiri, 1999.

Embassy
The Ballad of Gregorio Cortez, Robert Young, 1983.

Eros International
American Desi, Piyush Dinker Pandya, 2001.

Film Dallas
Man Facing Southeast, Eliseo Subiela, 1987.
Patti Rocks, David Burton Morris, 1988.

Film Forum
Far from Poland, Jill Godmilow, 1984.

Films Around the World
Kill-Off, Maggie Greenwald, 1989.

Fine Line
An Affair of Love, Frédéric Fonteyne, 2000.

All Over Me, Alex Sichel, 1997.
Amongst Friends, Rob Weiss, 1993.
The Ballad of Little Jo, Maggie Greenwald, 1994.
Barcelona, Whit Stillman, 1994.
The Basketball Diaries, Scott Kalvert, 1995.
Before Night Falls, Julian Schnabel, 2001.
The Cup, Khyentse Norbu, 1999.
Dancer in the Dark, Lars von Trier, 2000.
Dear Diary, Nanni Moretti, 1994.
Double Happiness, Mina Shum, 1994.
Edward II, Derek Jarman, 1992.
The Five Senses, Jeremy Podeswa, 2000.
Gummo, Harmony Korine, 1997.
Hedwig and the Angry Inch, John Cameron Mitchell, 2001.
Hoop Dreams, Steve James, 1994.
Household Saints, Nancy Savoca, 1993.
The Incredibly True Adventure of Two Girls in Love, Maria Maggenti, 1995.
julien donkey-boy, Harmony Korine, 1999.
Kansas City, Robert Altman, 1996.
The Last Days of Chez Nous, Gillian Armstrong, 1993.
Let's Talk about Sex, Troy Beyer, 1998.
Little Odessa, James Gray, 1995.
Lovers of the Arctic Circle, Julio Medem, 1999.
Mrs. Parker and the Vicious Circle, Alan Rudolph, 1994.
My Own Private Idaho, Gus Van Sant, 1991.
Naked, Mike Leigh, 1993.
Night On Earth, Jim Jarmusch, 1991.
Nowhere, Gregg Araki, 1997.
Once Were Warriors, Lee Tamahori, 1994.
Pecker, John Waters, 1998.
The Player, Robert Altman, 1992.
The Promise, Margarethe von Trotta, 1994.
Saving Grace, Nigel Cole, 2000.
Shine, Scott Hicks, 1996.
Simple Men, Hal Hartley, 1992.
Spanking the Monkey, David O. Russell, 1994.
The Sweet Hereafter, Atom Egoyan, 1997.
Swoon, Tom Kalin, 1992.
Trick, Jim Fall, 1999.
Trust, Hal Hartley, 1990.

Tumbleweeds, Gavin O'Connor, 1999.

First Look
Antonia's Line, Marleen Gorris, 1996.
Bhaji on the Beach, Gurinder Chadha, 1994.
Chutney Popcorn, Nisha Ganatra, 1999.
Different for Girls, Richard Spence, 1997.
Gun Crazy, Tamra Davis, 1993.
How to Be a Woman and Not Die in the Attempt, Ana Belén, 1999.
Mrs. Dalloway, Marleen Gorris, 1998.
The Opportunists, Myles Connell, 2000.
Party Girl, Daisy von Scherler Mayer, 1995.
Ratcatcher, Lynne Ramsay, 2000.
The Scent of Green Papaya, Tran Anh Hung, 1993.
The Secret of Roan Inish, John Sayles, 1994.

First Run
Bedrooms and Hallways, Rose Troche, 1998.
The Big Dis, Gordon Erikson, 1990.
Born in Flames, Lizzie Borden, 1983.
Enormous Changes at the Last Minute, Mirra Bank and Ellen Hovde, 1985.
Gal Young 'Un, Victor Nunez, 1979.
The Life and Times of Rosie the Riveter, Connie Field, 1980.
Northern Lights, John Hanson and Rob Nilsson, 1979.
The Quarry, Marion Hänsel, 1998.
Sherman's March, Ross McElwee, 1986.
Sleepwalk, Sara Driver, 1987.
Strangers in Good Company, Cynthia Scott, 1992.
The Watermelon Woman, Cheryl Dunye, 1996.

Fox Searchlight
Boys Don't Cry, Kimberly Peirce, 1999.
The Brothers McMullen, Edward Burns, 1995.
The Deep End, Scott McGhee and David Siegel, 2001.
The Full Monty, Peter Cattaneo, 1996.
Girl 6, Spike Lee, 1996.
Oscar and Lucinda, Gillian Armstrong, 1997.
Slums of Beverly Hills, Tamara Jenkins, 1998.
Star Maps, Miguel Arteta, 1997.
The Van, Stephen Frears, 1996.

Waking Ned Devine, Kirk Jones, 1998.
Woman on Top, Fina Torres, 2000.

Frameline
Mala Noche, Gus Van Sant, 1986.
Together Alone, P.J. Castellaneta, 1992.

Goldwyn
Angels and Insects, Philip Haas, 1996.
Big Night, Stanley Tucci and Campbell Scott, 1996.
City of Hope, John Sayles, 1991.
Desert Hearts, Donna Deitch, 1986.
Eat Drink Man Woman, Ang Lee, 1994.
Fear, Anxiety and Depression, Todd Solondz, 1989.
Fear of a Black Hat, Rusty Cundieff, 1994.
La Femme Nikita, Luc Besson, 1990.
Flirting, John Duigan, 1990.
Go Fish, Rose Troche, 1994.
Gregory's Girl, Bill Forsyth, 1982.
Henry V, Kenneth Branagh, 1989.
Hollywood Shuffle, Robert Townsend, 1987.
I Shot Andy Warhol, Mary Harron, 1996.
Ladybird, Ladybird, Ken Loach, 1994.
The Last Good Time, Bob Balaban, 1994.
Livin' Large, Michael Schultz, 1992.
Longtime Companion, Norman Rene, 1990.
Madame Bovary, Claude Chabrol, 1991.
The Madness of King George, Nicholas Hytner, 1994.
Mississippi Masala, Mira Nair, 1992.
Much Ado about Nothing, Kenneth Branagh, 1993.
Mystic Pizza, Donald Petrie, 1988.
Prick up Your Ears, Stephen Frears, 1987.
Sid and Nancy, Alex Cox, 1986.
Spetters, Paul Verhoeven, 1980.
Straight out of Brooklyn, Matty Rich, 1991.
Stranger than Paradise, Jim Jarmusch, 1985.
32 Short Films about Glenn Gould, François Girard, 1993.
To Live, Zhang Yimou, 1994.
To Sleep with Anger, Charles Burnett, 1990.
The Waterdance, Michael Steinberg and Neal Jimenez, 1992.

The Wedding Banquet, Ang Lee, 1993.
What Happened Was…, Tom Noonan, 1994.
You So Crazy, Thomas Schlamme, 1994.

Goldwyn Films
Better than Sex, Jonathan Teplitzky, 2000.
Desert Blue, Morgan J. Freeman, 1998.
Faithless, Liv Ullmann, 2001.
The Hanging Garden, Thom Fitzgerald, 1997.

Good Machine
Happiness, Todd Solondz, 1998.
Pushing Hands, Ang Lee, 1992.

Gramercy
Lock, Stock and Two Smoking Barrels, Guy Ritchie, 1999.
Shallow Grave, Danny Boyle, 1995.
The Usual Suspects, Bryan Singer, 1995.
When We Were Kings, Leon Gast, 1997.

Greycat
Henry: Portrait of a Serial Killer, John McNaughton, 1990.

HBO Theatrical
Southern Comfort, Kate Davis, 2001.

Horizon
Variety, Bette Gordon, 1985.

International Film Circuit
The Garden, Derek Jarman, 1990.
The Last of England, Derek Jarman, 1988.
Memory of Appearances, Raoul Ruiz, 1986.
Night and Day, Chantal Akerman, 1992.
On Top of the Whale, Raoul Ruiz, 1982.
A Time to Live, Hou Hsiao-hsien, 1985.

International Film Exchange
Freeze Die Come to Life, Vitali Kanevski, 1990.

IRS
The Beans of Egypt, Maine, Jennifer Warren, 1994.
Equinox, Alan Rudolph, 1992.
Inside Monkey Zetterland, Jefery Levy, 1992.
The Music of Chance, Philip Haas, 1993.
My New Gun, Stacy Cochran, 1992.
One False Move, Carl Franklin, 1992.
Roosters, Robert Young, 1993.

Island
Choose Me, Alan Rudolph, 1984.
Down by Law, Jim Jarmusch, 1986.
The Hit, Stephen Frears, 1984.
Kiss of the Spider Woman, Hector Babenco, 1985.
Koyaanisqatsi, Godfrey Reggio, 1983.
The Lonely Passion of Judith Hearne, Jack Clayton, 1987.
Mona Lisa, Neil Jordan, 1986.
Nobody's Fool, Evelyn Purcell, 1986.
River's Edge, Tim Hunter, 1987.
She's Gotta Have It, Spike Lee, 1986.
Sidewalk Stories, Charles Lane, 1989.
Subway, Luc Besson, 1985.
Track 29, Nicholas Roeg, 1988.
The Trip to Bountiful, Peter Masterson, 1985.

Kino
Daughters of the Dust, Julie Dash, 1992.
Fallen Angels, Wong Kar-wai, 1995.
Time Regained, Raoul Ruiz, 2000.

Libra
The Atomic Cafe, Kevin Rafferty, Jayne Loader and Pierce Rafferty, 1982.

Libra/Specialty
The Return of the Secaucus Seven, John Sayles, 1980.

Lions Gate
Amores Perros, Alejandro González Iñárrito, 2000.
Bread and Roses, Ken Loach, 2000.
Buffalo 66, Vincent Gallo, 1998.
But I'm a Cheerleader, Jamie Babbit, 2000.
The Dinner Game, Francis Veber, 1998.

Filmography

Dogma, Kevin Smith, 1999.
8 ½ Women, Peter Greenaway, 2000.
Eve's Bayou, Kasi Lemmons, 1997.
The Eyes of Tammy Faye, Fenton Bailey and Randy Barbato, 2000.
Gods and Monsters, Bill Condon, 1998.
The Golden Bowl, James Ivory, 2001.
Jesus' Son, Alison Maclean, 2000.
Love & Death on Long Island, Richard Kwietniowski, 1997.
Love & Sex, Valerie Breiman, 2000.
The Million Dollar Hotel, Wim Wenders, 2000.
The Red Violin, François Girard, 1998.
Shadow of the Vampire, E. Elias Merhige, 2000.
Steal This Movie!, Robert Greenwald, 2000.
Tape, Richard Linklater, 2001.
Two Family House, Raymond De Felitta, 2000.
Urbania, Jon Shear, 2000.
The Widow of Saint-Pierre, Patrice Leconte, 2001.
Women in Film, Bruce Wagner, 2001.

Live
Trees Lounge, Steve Buscemi, 1996.

Lot 47
Chunhyang, Im Kwon Taek, 2001.
L.I.E., Michael Cuesta, 2001.
The Price of Milk, Harry Sinclair, 2000.
Venus Beauty Institute, Tonie Marshall, 1999.
The War Zone, Tim Roth, 1999.

Milestone
Maborosi, Hirokazu Kore-eda, 1996.

Miramax
Albino Alligator, Kevin Spacey, 1996.
Amélie, Jean-Pierre Jeunet, 2001, Miramax.
American Dream, Barbara Kopple, 1992.
Antonia and Jane, Beeban Kidron, 1991.
Basquiat, Julian Schnabel, 1996.
Beyond Silence, Caroline Link, 1996.
The Big One, Michael Moore, 1998.
Butterfly, Jose Luis Cuerda, 2000.
The Castle, Rob Sitch, 1999.

Chasing Amy, Kevin Smith, 1997.
Children of Heaven, Majid Majidi, 1999.
Chocolat, Lasse Hallström, 2000.
Cinema Paradiso, Giuseppe Tornatore, 1990.
Clerks, Kevin Smith, 1994.
Close to Eden, Nikita Mikhalkov, 1992.
The Colors Trilogy: Blue, Krzysztof Kieslowski, 1993.
The Colors Trilogy: Red, Krzysztof Kieslowski, 1994.
The Colors Trilogy: White, Krzysztof Kieslowski, 1994.
Committed, Lisa Kreuger, 2000.
The Cook, the Thief, His Wife and Her Lover, Peter Greenaway, 1990.
Copland, James Mangold, 1997.
Crossover Dreams, Leon Ichaso, 1985.
The Crying Game, Neil Jordan, 1992.
Dead Man, Jim Jarmusch, 1996.
Delicatessen, Marc Caro and Jean-Pierre Jeunet, 1991.
The Double Life of Veronique, Krzysztof Kieslowski, 1991.
Down in the Delta, Maya Angelou, 1998.
Drowning by Numbers, Peter Greenaway, 1987.
East Is East, Damien O'Donnell, 2000.
Edith and Marcel, Claude Lelouch, 1983.
Enchanted April, Mike Newell, 1992.
The English Patient, Anthony Minghella, 1996.
Erendira, Ruy Guerra, 1983.
Everybody's Fine, Giuseppe Tornatore, 1990.
Exotica, Atom Egoyan, 1994.
Farewell My Concubine, Chen Kaige, 1993.
Four Rooms, Allison Anders, Alexandre Rockwell, Robert Rodriguez, Quentin Tarantino, 1996.
Fresh, Boaz Yakin, 1994.
From Dusk to Dawn, Robert Rodriguez, 1996.
The Glass Shield, Charles Burnett, 1994.
Guinevere, Audrey Wells, 1999.
Happy, Texas, Mark Illsley, 1999.
Harry Is Here to Help, Dominik Moll, 2001.
Hav Plenty, Christopher Cherot, 1997.
Heavenly Creatures, Peter Jackson, 1994.
High Heels, Pedro Almodóvar, 1991.
The House of Yes, Mark S. Waters, 1997.
Human Traffic, Justin Kerrigan, 2000.

Incident at Oglala, Michael Apted, 1991.
In the Bedroom, Todd Field, 2001.
I've Heard the Mermaids Singing, Patricia Rozema, 1987.
Jackie Brown, Quentin Tarantino, 1997.
Jerry and Tom, Saul Rubinek, 1998.
Johnny Suede, Tom DiCillo, 1991.
Journey of Hope, Xavier Koller, 1990.
Just Another Girl on the I.R.T., Leslie Harris, 1993.
Kolya, Jan Sverák, 1996.
The Krays, Peter Medak, 1990.
Life Is Beautiful, Roberto Benigni, 1998.
Like Water for Chocolate, Alfonso Arau, 1993.
Little Vera, Vasili Pichul, 1988.
Little Voice, Mark Herman, 1998.
Love Crimes, Lizzie Borden, 1991.
Malèna, Giuseppe Tornatore, 2000.
Map of the Human Heart, Vincent Ward, 1993.
Mediterraneo, Gabriele Salvatores, 1991.
Mrs. Brown, John Madden, 1997.
Muriel's Wedding, P.J. Hogan, 1995.
My Left Foot, Jim Sheridan, 1989.
My Son the Fanatic, Udayan Prasad, 1998.
The Nasty Girl, Michael Verhoeven, 1990.
Next Stop, Wonderland, Brad Anderson, 1998.
Paris Is Burning, Jennie Livingstone, 1991.
Passion Fish, John Sayles, 1992.
Pelle the Conqueror, Bille August, 1989.
The Piano, Jane Campion, 1993.
Picture Bride, Kayo Hatta, 1995.
Il Postino, Michael Radford, 1995.
Priest, Antonia Bird, 1995.
Prospero's Books, Peter Greenaway, 1991.
Pulp Fiction, Quentin Tarantino, 1994.
Queen Margot, Patrice Chéreau, 1994.
Reservoir Dogs, Quentin Tarantino, 1992.
Rounders, John Dahl, 1998.
sex, lies & videotape, Steven Soderbergh, 1989.
Shakespeare in Love, John Madden, 1998.
Shall We Dance?, Masayuki Suo, 1997.
Sling Blade, Billy Bob Thornton, 1996.
Smoke Signals, Chris Eyre, 1996.

The Snapper, Stephen Frears, 1994.
Strawberry and Chocolate, Tomás Gutiérrez Alea and Juan Carlos Tabio, 1994.
The Thin Blue Line, Errol Morris, 1988.
Things to Do in Denver When You're Dead, Gary Felder, 1995.
Tie Me Up! Tie Me Down! Pedro Almodóvar, 1990.
Tom and Viv, Brian Gilbert, 1994.
Trainspotting, Danny Boyle, 1996.
The Unbelievable Truth, Hal Hartley, 1990.
Under the Olive Trees, Abbas Kiarostami, 1994.
Velvet Goldmine, Todd Haynes, 1998.
Walking and Talking, Nicole Holofcener, 1996.
The Wings of the Dove, Iain Softley, 1997.
Working Girls, Lizzie Borden, 1987.
Young Soul Rebels, Isaac Julien, 1991.
Zentropa, Lars von Trier, 1991.

Miramax/Rolling Thunder
Chungking Express, Wong Kar-wai, 1995.

Mypheduh
Sankofa, Haille Gerima, 1994.

Newmarket Capital Group
Memento, Christopher Nolan, 2001.

New Line
Metropolitan, Whit Stillman, 1990.
Smithereens, Susan Seidelman, 1982.

New Yorker
Beau Travail, Claire Denis, 2000.
Café au Lait, Mathieu Kassovitz, 1993, New Yorker
Chan Is Missing, Wayne Wang, 1982.
Gohatto, Nagisa Oshima, 1999.
Marianne and Juliane, Margarethe von Trotta, 1981.
My Dinner with Andre, Louis Malle, 1981.
Nelly and Monsieur Arnaud, Claude Sautet, 1996.
Rosa Luxembourg, Margarethe von Trotta, 1986.
Sans Soleil, Chris Marker, 1982.
A Taxing Woman, Juzo Itami, 1988.

Three Lives and Only One Death, Raoul Ruiz, 1996.
The Wind Will Carry Us, Abbas Kiarostami, 2000.

Northern Arts
Chameleon Street, Wendell B. Harris Jr., 1991.
Notes from Underground, Gary Walkow, 1995.
Raining Stones, Ken Loach, 1994.
Schizopolis, Steven Soderbergh, 1996.

October
The Addiction, Abel Ferrara, 1995.
Autumn Tale, Eric Rohmer, 1999.
Breaking the Waves, Lars von Trier, 1996.
Career Girls, Mike Leigh, 1997.
The Celebration, Thomas Vinterberg, 1998.
Un Coeur en Hiver, Claude Sautet, 1993.
Cookie's Fortune, Robert Altman, 1999.
Cronos, Guillermo Del Torro, 1993.
Female Perversions, Susan Streitfeld, 1996.
The Funeral, Abel Ferrara, 1996.
Girls Town, Jim McKay, 1996.
High Art, Lisa Cholodenko, 1998.
Kicked in the Head, Matthew Harrison, 1997.
Killing Zoe, Roger Avary, 1994.
Kiss or Kill, Bill Bennett, 1996.
The Last Days, James Moll, 1998.
The Last Seduction, John Dahl, 1994.
Life Is Sweet, Mike Leigh, 1991.
The Living End, Gregg Araki, 1992.
Lost Highway, David Lynch, 1997.
Red Firecracker, Green Firecracker, Ping He, 1994.
Ruby in Paradise, Victor Nunez, 1993.
Secrets & Lies, Mike Leigh, 1996.
A Soldier's Daughter Never Cries, James Ivory, 1998.
Sugar Town, Allison Anders and Kurt Voss, 1999.
Three Seasons, Tony Bui, 1999.
Topsy-Turvy, Mike Leigh, 1999.
A Touch of Evil, Tony Au, 1995.
Tous les Matins du Monde, Alain Corneau, 1992.
The War Room, D. A. Pennebaker and Chris Hegedus, 1993.

Orion Classics
The Adjuster, Atom Egoyan, 1992.
Babette's Feast, Gabriel Axel, 1987.
Bar Girls, Marita Giovanni, 1994.
Boyfriends and Girlfriends, Eric Rohmer, 1987.
Camille Claudel, Bruno Nuytten, 1988.
Chocolat, Claire Denis, 1989.
Dim Sum: A Little Bit of Heart, Wayne Wang, 1985.
Europa, Europa, Agnieszka Holland, 1991.
Jean de Florette, Claude Berri, 1986.
Jeffrey, Christopher Ashley, 1995.
Leningrad Cowboys, Aki Kaurismäki, 1989.
Manon of the Spring, Claude Berri, 1986.
My Beautiful Laundrette, Stephen Frears, 1986.
Mystery Train, Jim Jarmusch, 1989.
Raise the Red Lantern, Zhang Yimou, 1991.
Ran, Akira Kurosawa, 1984.
Rhapsody in August, Akira Kurosawa, 1991.
Slacker, Richard Linklater, 1991.
Wings of Desire, Wim Wenders, 1988.
Women on the Verge of a Nervous Breakdown, Pedro Almodóvar, 1988.

Paramount Classics
Girl on the Bridge, Patrice Leconte, 1999.
My First Mister, Christine Lahti, 2001.
Our Lady of the Assassins, Barbet Schroeder, 2001.
Passion of Mind, Alain Berliner, 2000.
Sidewalks of New York, Edward Burns, 2000.
Sunshine, István Szabó, 1999.
The Virgin Suicides, Sofia Coppola, 1999.
You Can Count on Me, Kenneth Lonergan, 2000.

Phaedra
Eternity and a Day, Theo Angelopoulos, 1998.
On the Run, Bruno de Almeida, 1998.
Remembering the Cosmos, Junichi Suzuki, 1999.
Roja, Mani Rathnam, 1992.
Strawberry Fields, Rea Tajiri, 1999.
Without Air, Neil Abramson, 1995.

Planet Pictures
From the Journals of Jean Seberg, Marc Rappaport, 1995.
Rock Hudson's Home Movies, Mark Rappaport, 1992.

Quartet
Eating Raoul, Paul Bartel, 1982.

Quartet/Sigma
A Question of Silence, Marleen Gorris, 1981.

Renaissance
The Safety of Objects, Rose Troche, 2001.

Republic
The Funeral, Juzo Itami, 1984.
Tampopo, Juzo Itami, 1987.

RKO
Laws of Gravity, Nick Gomez, 1992.

Roxie
Genghis Blues, Roko Belic, 1999.
The Last Time I Committed Suicide, Stephan Kay, 1997.
Man Bites Dog, Remy Belvaux, André Bonzel and Benoit Poelvoorde, 1992.
Red Rock West, John Dahl, 1994.
Vincent, Paul Cox, 1987.

Screen Gems
Black and White, James Toback, 1999.
Girlfight, Karyn Kusama, 2000.
Limbo, John Sayles, 1999.
Timecode, Mike Figgis, 2000.

Seventh Art
Better Living through Circuitry, Jon Reiss, 2000.
Man of the Year, Dirk Shafter, 1996.

Shadow
Carla's Song, Ken Loach, 1996.

Shining Excalibur
Kids, Larry Clark, 1995.

Shooting Gallery
Adrenaline Drive, Shinabu Yaguchi, 2000.
Barenaked in America, Jason Priestley, 2000.
Croupier, Mike Hodges, 2000.
The Day I Became a Woman, Marziyeh Meshkini, 2001.
Eureka, Shinji Aoyama, 2001.
Human Resources, Laurent Cantet, 2000.
Illtown, Nick Gomez, 1998.
Judy Berlin, Eric Mendelsohn, 2000.
Last Resort, Pawel Pawlikowski, 2001.
The Low Down, Jamie Thraves, 2001.
Non-Stop, Sabu, 2000.
One, Tony Barbieri, 2000.
Orphans, Peter Mullan, 2000.
Southpaw, Liam McGrath, 2000.
Such a Long Journey, Sturla Gunnarsson, 2000.
A Time for Drunken Horses, Bahman Ghobadi, 2000.
Titanic Town, Roger Michell, 2000.
Too Much Sleep, David Maquiling, 2001.
When Brendan Met Trudy, Kieron J. Walsh, 2001.

Skouras
Apartment Zero, Martin Donovan, 1989.
Belizaire the Cajun, Glenn Pitre, 1986.
High Hopes, Mike Leigh, 1989.
Living on Tokyo Time, Steven Okasaki, 1987.
Waiting for the Moon, Jill Godmilow, 1987.
The Wizard of Loneliness, Jenny Bowen, 1988.

Sony Classics
The Accompanist, Claude Miller, 1993.
Afterglow, Alan Rudolph, 1997.
All about My Mother, Pedro Almodóvar, 1999.
Amateur, Hal Hartley, 1994.
American Movie, Chris Smith and Sarah Price, 1999.
Beautiful Thing, Hettie MacDonald, 1997.
Beijing Bicycle, Wang Xiaoshuai, 2001.

Brother, Takeshi Kitano, 2001.
Brother of Sleep, Joseph Vilsmaier, 1995.
Burnt by the Sun, Nikita Mikhalkov, 1994.
The Celluloid Closet, Rob Epstein and Jeffrey Friedman, 1996.
Central Station, Walter Salles, 1998.
Character, Mike van Diem, 1997.
The City of Lost Children, Marc Caro and Jean-Pierre Jeunet, 1995.
The Color of Paradise, Majid Majidi, 2000.
Crouching Tiger, Hidden Dragon, Ang Lee, 2000.
Dancing at Lughnasa, Pat O'Connor, 1998.
Danzón, Maria Novaro, 1991.
Denise Calls Up, Hal Salwen, 1996.
The Dreamlife of Angels, Erick Zonca, 1998.
East-West, Régis Warnier, 1999.
The Emperor and the Assassin, Chen Kaige, 1999.
Faraway, So Close!, Wim Wenders, 1993.
Fast, Cheap, and Out of Control, Errol Morris, 1997.
The Flower of My Secret, Pedro Almodóvar, 1996.
A Friend of the Deceased, Vyacheslav Krishtofovich, 1998.
The General, John Boorman, 1998.
The Governess, Sandra Goldbacher, 1998.
Goya in Bordeaux, Carlos Saura, 2000.
Groove, Greg Harrison, 2000.
Haiku Tunnel, Jacob Kornbluth and Josh Kornbluth, 2001.
Henry Fool, Hal Hartley, 1998.
Howard's End, James Ivory, 1992.
In the Company of Men, Neil LaBute, 1997.
Kikujiro, Takeshi Kitano, 1999.
Living in Oblivion, Tom DiCillo, 1995.
Lone Star, John Sayles, 1996.
The Luzhin Defense, Marleen Gorris, 2000.
Manny and Lo, Lisa Krueger, 1996.
Ma Vie en Rose, Alain Berliner, 1997.
Me Myself I, Philippa Karmel, 1999.
Men with Guns, John Sayles, 1998.
Me You Them, Andrucha Waddington, 2001.
Mifune, Soren Kragh-Jacobsen, 1999.
Mi Vida Loca, Allison Anders, 1994.
Nil by Mouth, Gary Oldman, 1998.
Not One Less, Zhang Yimou, 1999.
The Opposite of Sex, Don Roos, 1998.

Orlando, Sally Potter, 1993.
Persuasion, Roger Michell, 1995.
Pollock, Ed Harris, 2000.
The Princess and the Warrior, Tom Tykwer, 2001.
The Road Home, Zhang Yimou, 1999.
Run Lola Run, Tom Tykwer, 1999.
Safe, Todd Haynes, 1995.
Shadow Magic, Ann Hu, 2000.
Shanghai Triad, Zhang Yimou, 1995.
Shower, Zhang Yuan, 1999.
The Story of Qui Ju, Zhang Yimou, 1992.
SubUrbia, Richard Linklater, 1996.
Tango, Carlos Saura, 1998.
The Tao of Steve, Jenniphr Goodman, 2000.
The Third Miracle, Agnieszka Holland, 2000.
Trixie, Alan Rudolph, 2000.
Twin Falls Idaho, Michael Polish, 1999.
Vertical Ray of the Sun, Anh Hung Tran, 2000.
Waiting for Guffman, Christopher Guest, 1997.
Welcome to the Dollhouse, Todd Solondz, 1996.
When the Cat's Away, Cèdric Klapisch, 1997.
The Whole Wide World, Dan Ireland, 1996.
Wilde, Brian Gilbert, 1997.

Spectra Films
Smooth Talk, Joyce Chopra, 1986.

Strand
All the Vermeers in New York, Jon Jost, 1992.
Claire of the Moon, Nicole Conn, 1992.
Clean, Shaven, Lodge Kerrigan, 1995.
Criminal Lovers, François Ozon, 2000.
Crush, Alison Maclean, 1993.
East Palace, West Palace, Zhang Yuan, 1997.
First Love, Last Rites, Jesse Peretz, 1998.
Genealogies of a Crime, Raoul Ruiz, 1997.
The Hours and the Times, Christopher Münch, 1991.
I Stand Alone, Gaspar Noé, 1998.
Late Bloomers, Julia Dyer, 1996.
Latin Boys Go to Hell, Ela Troyano, 1997.
Lawn Dogs, John Duigan, 1997.

Love Is the Devil, John Maybury, 1998.
Macho Dancer, Lino Brocka, 1988.
Nenette and Boni, Claire Denis, 1997.
Rhythm Thief, Matthew Harrison, 1994.
River of Grass, Kelly Reichardt, 1995.
Signs & Wonders, Jonathan Nossiter, 2001.
Stonewall, Nigel Finch, 1996.
Suzhou River, Lou Ye, 2000.
Totally Fu**ed Up, Gregg Araki, 1994.
Vive l'Amour, Tsai Ming-liang, 1994.
Voyage to the Beginning of the World, Manoel de Oliveira, 1997.
Wild Reeds, André Téchiné, 1994.

Stratosphere
The Thief, Pavel Chukhraj, 1998.
Xiu Xiu: The Sent-Down Girl, Joan Chen, 1998.

Tara
Everything Relative, Sharon Pollack, 1996.
The Vanishing, George Sluizer, 1988.

Trimark
Billy's Hollywood Screen Kiss, Tommy O'Haver, 1998.
Box of Moonlight, Tom DiCillo, 1997.
The Doom Generation, Gregg Araki, 1995.
Kama Sutra: A Tale of Love, Mira Nair, 1997.
Kicking & Screaming, Noah Baumbach, 1995.
Romance, Catherine Breillat, 1999.
Slam, Marc Levin, 1998.
Songcatcher, Maggie Greenwald, 1999.

Triton
A Brief History of Time, Errol Morris, 1992.
Hearts of Darkness, Fax Bahr and George Hickenlooper, 1991.
In the Soup, Alexandre Rockwell, 1992.
Mindwalk, Bernt Capra, 1991.
Toto le Héros, Jaco Van Dormael, 1992.

Triumph
Zebrahead, Anthony Drazan, 1992.

Unifilms
Bye Bye Brazil, Carlos Diegues, 1980.

United Artists Classics
Diva, Jean-Jacques Beineix, 1981.
Entre Nous, Diane Kurys, 1983.
The Last Metro, François Truffaut, 1980.
Lianna, John Sayles, 1983.

Universal Focus
Beautiful Creatures, Bill Eagles, 2001.
Better Housekeeping, Frank Novak, 2001.
Billy Elliot, Stephen Daldry, 2000.
The Caveman's Valentine, Kasi Lemmons, 2001.
Julie Johnson, Bob Gosse, 2001.
Loving Jezebel, Kwyn Bader, 2000.
The Man Who Cried, Sally Potter, 2000.
The Rat, Steve Barron, 2001.

USA Films
Alice and Martin, André Téchiné, 2000.
The Idiots, Lars von Trier, 1999.
In the Mood for Love, Wong Kar-wai, 2000.
Rosetta, Jean-Pierre Dardenne and Luc Dardenne, 1999.
Series 7, Daniel Minahan, 2001.
Up at the Villa, Philip Haas, 2000.

Warner Brothers
Roger & Me, Michael Moore, 1989.

WinStar
Humanité, Bruno Dumont, 2000.
On the Ropes, Nanette Burstein and Brett Morgan, 2000.
Winter Sleepers, Tom Tykwer, 2000.
Women, Luis Galvão Teles, 1997.
Yi Yi, Edward Yang, 2001.

Women Make Movies
Forbidden Love: The Unashamed Stories of Lesbian Lives, Aerlyn Weissman and Lynne Fernie, 1992.

Surname Viet Given Name Nam, Trinh T. Minh-Ha, 1989.

World Artists
Begotten, E. Elias Merhige, 1991.
The Bloody Child, Nina Menkes, 1996.
Frame Up, Jon Jost, 1993.
Golden Eighties, Chantal Akerman, 1982.
Magdalena Viraga, Nina Menkes, 1986.
Matador, Pedro Almodóvar, 1986.
Queen of Diamonds, Nina Menkes, 1991.
Sure Fire, Jon Jost, 1993.
Toute une Nuit, Chantal Akerman, 1982.

World Northal
The Tempest, Derek Jarman, 1980.

Zeitgeist
Aimée and Jaguar, Max Färberböck, 2000.
La Ciudad, David Riker, 1999.
Following, Christopher Nolan, 1998.
Irma Vep, Olivier Assayas, 1996.
Late August, Early September, Olivier Assayas, 1999.
MURDER and Murder, Yvonne Rainer, 1996.
Poison, Todd Haynes, 1991.
Privilege, Yvonne Rainer, 1991.
Silverlake Life: The View from Here, Tom Joslin and Peter Friedman, 1993.
Vermont Is for Lovers, John O'Brien, 1993.
Water Drops on Burning Rocks, François Ozon, 2000.
Wittgenstein, Derek Jarman, 1993.

No Distributor
Broken Mirrors, Marleen Gorris, 1984.

Self-Distributed
Brother's Keeper, Joe Berlinger, 1992.

WORKS CITED

Alderson, Kate. "After Quentin, the Rest Is Pulp." *London Times,* January 30, 1995.
Amedeo, Michael. "Panel: No Formula for Success on Indie Films." *Hollywood Reporter,* April 17, 1996.
Amis, Martin. "Look Who's Smirking." *London Sunday Times,* February 26, 1995.
Anderson, John. *Sundancing: Hanging out and Listening in at America's Most Important Film Festival.* New York: Spike, 2000.
Ang, Ien. "Ethnography and Radical Contextualism in Audience Studies." *The Audience and Its Landscape.* Ed. James Hay, Lawrence Grossberg, and Ellen Wartella. Boulder: Westview, 1996.
———. "Wanted: Audiences. On the Politics of Empirical Audience Studies." *Remote Control: Television, Audience, and Cultural Power.* Ed. Ellen Seiter, Hans Borchers, Gabriele Kreutzner, and Eva-Maria Warth. London: Routledge, 1989.
Ansen, David. "A Comedy of Cruelty." *Newsweek,* October 12, 1998.
———. "The Redemption of Pulp." *Newsweek,* October 10, 1994.
Bambara, Toni Cade. Preface. *Daughters of the Dust: The Making of an African-American Women's Film.* New York: New Press, 1992.
———. "Reading the Signs, Empowering the Eye: *Daughters of the Dust* and the Black Independent Cinema Movement." *Black American Cinema.* Ed. Manthia Diawara. New York: Routledge, 1993.
Barker, Olivia. "The Asianization of America." *USA Today,* March 22, 2001.
Basoli, A.G. "Ang Lee: The Irony and the Ecstasy." *MovieMaker* 8 (winter 2001).
———. "The 2000 New York Film Festival." *MovieMaker* 8 (winter 2001).
Bernard, Jami. "*The Piano* Fine-Tunes a Sensual Awakening." *New York Daily News,* rep. in *Centre Daily Times,* January 7, 1994.
Bey, Isisara. "A Seat on the Aisle." *American Visions* 8 (June 1993).
Biskind, Peter. "An Auteur Is Born." *Premiere* (November 1994).
Bobo, Jacqueline. *Black Women as Cultural Readers.* New York: Columbia

University Press, 1995.

Bordwell, David. *Narration in the Fiction Film*. Madison: University of Wisconsin Press, 1985.

Bordwell, David, and Kristin Thompson. *Film Art: An Introduction*. 5th ed. New York: McGraw-Hill, 1997.

Bowen, Peter. "Arrested Development." *Filmmaker* 8 (spring 2000).

———. "Flash in the Pan." *Filmmaker* 7 (fall 1998).

Box Office Guru. <boxofficeguru.com>

Boyd, Valerie. "*Daughters of the Dust.*" *American Visions* 6 (1991).

Branigan, Edward. *Narrative Comprehension and Film*. New York: Routledge, 1992.

Brown, Georgia. "How We Grew." *Village Voice*, January 21, 1992.

———. "My Brilliant Careers." *Village Voice*, June 15, 1993.

———. "Swept Away." *Village Voice*, June 4, 1996.

Brunt, Rosalind. "The Politics of Identity." *New Times: The Changing Face of Politics in the1990s*. Ed. Stuart Hall and Martin Jacques. London: Verso, 1990.

Buck, Joan Juliet. "Strange Melodies." *Vogue* (December 1993).

Burchill, Julie. "Blood out of Stone." *London Sunday Times*, February 26, 1995.

———. "Shooting for the Hip." *London Sunday Times*, October 23, 1995.

Bürger, Peter. "The Negation of the Autonomy of Art by the Avant-Garde." *Postmodernism: A Reader*. Ed. Thomas Docherty. New York: Columbia University Press, 1993.

Bürger, Peter. *Theory of the Avant-Garde*. Minneapolis: University of Minnesota Press, 1984.

Burgoyne, Robert. "Film-narratology." Stam, Burgoyne, and Flitterman-Lewis.

Canby, Vincent. "Brains, a Gift of Gab and Headed for Trouble." *New York Times*, March 19, 1993.

———. "Cruising Nighttown in Quest of the Ultimate Light." *New York Times*, October 15, 1993.

———. "Early Cannes Favorite: A Post-Freudian Romance." *New York Times*, May 18, 1993.

———. "Forceful Lessons of Love and Cinematic Language." *New York Times*, October 16, 1993.

———. "Jane Campion Stirs Romance with Mystery." *New York Times*, May 30, 1993.

Cantwell, Mary. "Jane Campion's Lunatic Women." *New York Times Magazine*, September 19, 1993.

Carter, Kevin L. "Blacks' Reaction to Films Add Theater to the Theater." *Philadelphia Inquirer*, July 14, 1996.

Cartwright, Lisa, and Nina Fonoroff. "Narrative Is *Narrative*: So What Is New?" *Multiple Voices in Feminist Film Criticism*. Ed. Diane Carson, Linda Dittmar, and Janice Welsch. Minneapolis: University of Minnesota Press, 1994.
Chetwynd, Josh. "Film Glut Freezes out Independents." *USA Today*, December 28, 1998.
Chetwynd, Josh, and Andy Seiler. "Inside Movies." *USA Today*, September 15, 2000.
Cieply, Michael. "Who Will Save Hollywood?" *Inside*, February 6, 2001.
Citron, Michelle. "Women's Film Production: Going Mainstream." *Female Spectators: Looking at Film and Television*. Ed. E. Deidre Pribram. London: Verso, 1988.
Clark, Mike. "Profits Can Really Soar Overseas." *USA Today*, December 31, 1997.
———. "Smaller Films Were the Bigger Stars of the Year." *USA Today*, December 27, 1996.
Clover, Carol. "High and Low: The Transformation of the Rape-revenge Movie." Cook and Dodd.
Cook, Pam. "*Cape Fear* and Femininity as Destructive Power." Cook and Dodd.
———, ed. *The Cinema Book*. London: BFI, 1987.
———. "The Point of Expression in Avant-Garde Film." *Catalogue: British Film Institute Productions*. Ed. Elizabeth Cowie. London: BFI, 1978.
Cook, Pam, and Philip Dodd, eds. *Women and Film: A Sight and Sound Reader*. London: Scarlet, 1994.
Corliss, Richard. "Adding Kick to the Chic." *Time*, November 16, 1992.
———. "'Bad' Women and Brutal Men: A Hit Movie Reopens the Debate on Rape in the '80s." *Time*, November 21, 1988.
———. "Independents' Day." *Time*, February 24, 1997.
———. "Wuthering Eighty-Eights." *Time*, November 22, 1993.
Cornis-Pope, Marcel. *Hermeneutic Desire and Critical Rewriting: Narrative Interpretation in the Wake of Poststructuralism*. New York: St. Martin's, 1992.
Coste, Didier. *Narrative as Communication*. Minneapolis: University of Minnesota Press, 1989.
Cox, Dan. "Fine Line Challenges Miramax for Indie Champ Title." *Variety*, October 14-20, 1996.
Crane, Diane. *The Transformation of the Avant-Garde: The New York Art World, 1940–1985*. Chicago: University of Chicago Press, 1987.
Danto, Arthur C. *After the End of Art: Contemporary Art and the Pale of History*.

Princeton: Princeton University Press, 1997.

Dargis, Manohla. "Even in Independent Film, a Suit Is a Suit Is a Suit." *New York Times,* January 31, 1999.

———. Foreword. *Pulp Fiction: A Quentin Tarantino Screenplay.* New York: Hyperion, 1994.

———. "Pulp Instincts." *Sight and Sound* 4 (May 1994).

———. "The Vision Thing." *Filmmaker* 3 (spring 1995).

Dash, Julie. *Daughters of the Dust: The Making of an African-American Women's Film,* New York: New Press, 1992.

"Daughters of the Dust." *Variety,* February 11, 1991.

Davis, Zeinabu Irene. "An Interview with Julie Dash." *Wide Angle* 13 (July–October 1991).

Dawes, Amy. "'No-Budget' Filmmakers Tell Secrets of Their Quiet Success." *Variety,* January 28, 1991.

Dawson, Jeff. *Quentin Tarantino: The Cinema of Cool.* New York: Applause, 1995.

de Lauretis, Teresa. *Alice Doesn't: Feminism, Semiotics, Cinema.* Bloomington: Indiana University Press, 1984.

"Dialogue between bell hooks and Julie Dash." *Daughters of the Dust: The Making of an African-American Woman's Film.* New York: New Press, 1992.

DiCillo, Tom. *Box of Moonlight & Notes from Overboard: A Film-Maker's Diary.* London: Faber and Faber, 1997.

Dowell, Pat. "Pulp Friction: Two Shots at Quentin Tarantino's *Pulp Fiction.*" *Cineaste* 21 (July 1995).

Eagleton, Terry. *The Ideology of the Aesthetic.* Oxford: Blackwell, 1990.

Eco, Umberto. *Serendipities: Language and Lunacy.* Trans. William Weaver. New York: Columbia University Press, 1998.

The Editors. "Festivals." *Filmmaker* 8 (fall 1999).

Elsen, Jon. "Goldwyn Sues MGM over Name." *New York Post Online, Business News,* October 31, 1997.

"Faithful." *Filmmaker* 8 (fall 1999).

Feay, Suzi. "Woolf Whistles." *Time Out,* March 10-17, 1993.

Ferncase, Richard. *Outsider Features: American Independent Films of the 1980s.* Westport: Greenwood, 1996.

Filmmaker 3 (winter 1995).

Filmmaker 4 (winter 1996).

Filmmaker 5 (fall 1996).

Filmmaker 6 (winter 1998).

Foster, Hal, ed. *The Anti-Aesthetic: Essays on Postmodern Culture.* Port Townsend: Bay, 1983.

Frankel, Martha. "*Pulp Fiction.*" *Mademoiselle* (October 1994).
Fried, John. "Pulp Friction: Two Shots at Quentin Tarantino's *Pulp Fiction.*" *Cineaste* 21 (July 1995).
Frow, John. *Cultural Studies and Cultural Value*. Oxford: Clarendon, 1995.
Gabler, Neal. "The End of the Middle." *New York Times Magazine,* November 16, 1997.
Gandhi, Leela. *Postcolonial Theory: A Critical Introduction*. New York: Columbia University Press, 1998.
Garcia, Alberto. "Master of His Digital Domain." *Filmmaker* 8 (spring 2000).
Garner, Jack. "*Daughters* Is Pretty, and Pretty Hard to Follow." *Gannett News Service*, May 13, 1992. < Lexis-Nexis >.
Garrett, Steven. "Beach Blanket Bingo." *Filmmaker* 7 (spring 1999).
———. "New Venues." *Filmmaker* 8 (winter 2000).
Gay, Peter. *The Naked Heart*. Vol. 4 of *The Bourgeois Experience: Victoria to Freud*. New York: Norton, 1995.
Geffner, David. "Cars, Soap, and Celluloid: Marketing Independent Film in a Studio Film Age." *Filmmaker* 7 (summer 1999).
———. "Is Sundance Reaching 'Critical Mass'?" *MovieMaker* 8 (winter 2001).
Germain, David. "With *Blair Witch* as Role Model, Sundance Films Head for Theaters." Associated Press in *The Columbia, SC State,* April 28, 2000.
Giannetti, Louis, and Scott Eyman. *Flashback: A Brief History of Film*. 3rd ed. Englewood Cliffs: Prentice-Hall, 1996.
Gibson, John. "Feedback." *MSNBC*. Broadcast March 27, 2000.
Gilroy, Paul. *The Black Atlantic: Modernity and Double Consciousness*. Cambridge: Harvard University Press, 1993.
Giroux, Henry A. "*Pulp Fiction* and the Culture of Violence." *Harvard Educational Review* 65 (summer 1995).
Glaister, Dan. "Sale Threat to British Film Industry." *London Guardian,* May 22, 1998.
Gledhill, Christine. Cook, *Cinema Book*.
Glucksman, Mary. "The More Things Change." *Filmmaker* 3 (winter 1995).
———. "Pushing Films." *Filmmaker* 3 (spring 1995).
———. "The State of Things." *Filmmaker* 3 (fall 1994).
Godfrey, Rebecca. "Straight Outta Sea Island." *Off-Hollywood Report* 7 (spring 1992).
Godzich, Wlad. Foreword. Coste.
Gomery, Douglas. *The Hollywood Studio System*. New York: St. Martin's, 1986.
Goodwin, Christopher. "It's the Pictures That Got Small." *London Sunday Times,* May 17, 1998.

Gregorian, Dareh. "Spike Warns Tarantino to Watch His Language." *New York Post*, December 18, 1997.
Gritten, David. "For Director Mike Leigh, Life's Not Always Sweet." *Los Angeles Times*, December 23, 1993.
Grossberg, Larry. "Postmodernity and Affect: All Dressed up with No Place to Go." *Communications* 10 (1988).
Grove, Martin. "Showbiz Today." *CNN*. Broadcast October 24, 1994.
Grover, Ronald. "All That Glitters Is Not Goldwyn." *Business Week*, July 24, 1995.
Gubernick, Lisa. "We Don't Want to Be Walt Disney." *Forbes*, October 16, 1989.
Habermas, Jürgen. "Modernity—An Incomplete Project." Foster.
Hall, Stuart. "What Is This 'Black' in Black Popular Culture?" *Black Popular Culture: A Project by Michelle Wallace*. Ed. Gina Dent. Seattle: Bay, 1992.
Hall, Stuart, and Paddy Whannel. *The Popular Arts*. London: Hutchinson Educational, 1964.
Hamsher, Jane. *Killer Instinct*. New York: Broadway, 1997.
Haraway, Donna. *Simians, Cyborgs, and Women: The Reinvention of Nature*. London: Free Association, 1991.
Harris, Dana. "Outside Investors Become Siders." *Daily Variety*, November 27, 2000.
———. "Suburbia's Mean Streets Enter *Girls Town*." *The Independent Film and Video Monthly* (April 1996).
Harvey, Sylvia. *Independent Cinema?* Stafford: West Midlands Arts, 1978.
———. *May '68 and Film Culture*. London: BFI, 1980.
Hekman, Susan J. *Moral Voices, Moral Selves: Carol Gilligan and Feminist Moral Theory*. University Park: Pennsylvania State University Press, 1995.
Hernandez, Eugene. "Dispatch from IndieWood—Miramax Drops Kevin Smith's *Dogma*." *IndieWIRE*, April 9, 1999. <indiewire.com>.
Hernandez, Eugene, and Brian Brooks. "Shooting Gallery Series Take 2." *IndieWIRE*, August 11, 2000. <indiewire.com>.
Hernandez, Eugene, and Mark Rabinowitz. "Bingham Ray on the Record, Part I." *IndieWIRE*, December 17, 1999. <indiewire.com>.
———. "Bingham Ray on the Record, Part 1A." *IndieWIRE*, December 17, 1999. <indiewire.com>.
"High Risk Distribs." *Off-Hollywood Report* 6 (winter 1990–91).
Hinson, Hal. "*I.R.T.*: Express Lane to the Inner City." *Washington Post*, April 2, 1993.
———. "*The Piano*: Symphony of a Troubled Heart." *Washington Post*, November 19, 1993.

Hirschberg, Lynn. "Tarantino Bravo." *Vanity Fair* (July 1994).
———. "Two Directors." *New York Times Magazine,* November 16, 1997.
Hoban, Phoebe. "A Building *Dust* Storm." *New York Magazine,* March 30, 1992.
Hoberman, J. "Back on the Wild Side." *Premiere* (August 1992).
———. "True Romance." *Village Voice,* August 30, 1994.
Hoberman, J., and Jonathan Rosenbaum. *Midnight Movies.* New York: Harper, 1983.
Holden, Stephen. "Shouts of Rage at the Way We Are." *New York Times,* September 13, 1998.
Holland, Gill. "Filmmaking Year Zero." *Filmmaker* 8 (winter 2000).
Holland, Patricia. *The Television Handbook.* London: Routledge, 1997.
hooks, bell. "Sexism and Misogyny: Who Takes the Rap?" *Z Magazine* 7 (February 1994).
Hope, Ted. "Indie Film Is Dead…Long Live Indie Film." *Filmmaker* 4 (fall 1995).
Horn, John. "Sundance Festival Buries Indie Films in Money." Associated Press in *Philadelphia Inquirer,* February 1, 1998.
Howe, Desson. "It's the Movie of the Decade. No No, It's Just a Decadent Movie." *Washington Post,* January 30, 1994.
———. "*Naked*: Baring the Soul." *Washington Post,* January 28, 1994.
Hu, Marcus. "Guerrilla Releasing: A Guide to No-Budget Film Distribution." *Filmmaker* 1 (summer 1993).
Hudson, Dawn. "Letters." *Filmmaker* 3 (summer 1995).
IMDb. Internet Movie Database. <Imdb.com>.
"In-House Boutiques." *Off-Hollywood Report* 5 (winter 1990–91).
"Introduction." "The Two Hollywoods." Special issue of *New York Times Magazine,* November 16, 1997.
Jackson, Devon. "Quentin Tarantino's Negro Problem—and Hollywood's." *Village Voice,* March 28, 1995.
Jacobson, Harlan. "Women Floor the Audiences." *USA Today,* January 31, 2000.
Jacobson, Sarah. "Being and Nothingness." *Filmmaker* 6 (summer 1998).
Jakobson, Roman. "On Realism in Art." *Readings in Russian Poetics: Formalist and Structuralist Views.* Ed. Ladislav Matejka and Krystyna Pomorska. Cambridge: MIT Press, 1971.
James, Caryn. "Hollywood Breathes in the Spirit of Sundance." *New York Times,* February 2, 1997.
Jameson, Fredric. "Postmodernism and Consumer Society." Foster.

Jarman, Derek. "The Last Reel." Diary excerpts. *London Guardian Weekend Magazine.* June 17, 2000.

Johnson, Ross, and Dana Harris. "How Healthy Is *The Patient?*" *Hollywood Reporter,* September 16, 1997. New York special issue.

Johnston, Sheila. "Film Narrative and the Structuralist Controversy." Cook, *Cinema Book.*

Jones, Jacquie. "*Daughters of the Dust.*" *Cineaste* 19 (1992).

Jost, Jon. *Off-Hollywood Report* 7 (spring 1992).

Kael, Pauline. *New Yorker,* January 18, 1982.

Kempley, Rita. "*Naked*: London Britches Falling Down." *Washington Post,* January 28, 1994.

Kilday, Gregg. "Independent Thinking." *Entertainment Weekly,* September 19, 1997.

Kim, Walter. "Robert Redford Has This Problem." *New York Times Magazine,* November 16, 1997.

King, Thomas R., and Richard Turner. "Disney Agrees to Buy the Distributor of *Crying Game* at Possibly $60 Million." *Wall Street Journal,* May 3, 1993.

Klady, Leonard. "Miramax Mixup over *Scream.*" *Variety,* December 22, 1997–January 4, 1998.

Kleinhans, Chuck. "Independent Features: Hopes and Dreams." *The New American Cinema.* Ed. Jon Lewis. Durham: Duke University Press, 1998.

Knowles-Borishade, Adetokunbo F. "Paradigm for Classical African Orature." *Black Studies Journal* 21 (June 1991).

Kofsky, Frank. *Black Nationalism and the Revolution in Music.* New York: Pathfinder, 1970.

Kozloff, Sarah. "Narrative Theory and Television." *Channels of Discourse, Reassembled: Television and Contemporary Criticism.* Ed. Robert C. Allen. 2nd ed. Chapel Hill: University of North Carolina Press, 1992.

Kuhn, Annette. "History of Narrative Codes." Cook, *Cinema Book.*

Lane, Anthony. "Degrees of Cool." *New Yorker,* October 10, 1994.

Lawson, Terry. "Tarantino Still Sure of Himself." *Knight-Ridder Newspapers,* rep. in *Wilkes-Barre Times Leader,* December 26, 1997.

Lechner, Jack. "Once Is Not Enough." *Filmmaker* 9 (fall 2000).

Levy, Emanuel. *Cinema of Outsiders: The Rise of American Independent Film.* New York: New York University Press, 1999.

Lewis, Michael. "The Capitalist: The Money Pit." *New York Times Magazine,* November 16, 1997.

Lieberman, David. "Movie-Industry Costs Give Hollywood a Wake-Up Call." *USA Today,* March 6, 1997.

Lipman, Amanda. "*Pulp Fiction.*" *Sight and Sound* 4 (November 1994).

Lipsky, Jeff. "Wielding Influence: Jeff Lipsky on Distributing Cassevetes." *Filmmaker* 5 (fall 1996).
Los Angeles Times, November 26, 1993.
Lowery, Mark, and Nadirah Z. Sabir. "The Making of Holly-Hood." *Black Enterprise* (December 1994).
Lowry, Beverly. "Criminals Rendered in 3 Parts, Poetically." *New York Times,* September 11, 1994.
Lowry, Tom. "Hollywood Banks on Blockbusters." *USA Today,* December 26, 1996.
Lucey, Paul. *Story Sense: Writing Story and Script for Feature Films and Television.* New York: McGraw-Hill, 1996.
Macauley, Scott. "Take My Film…Please!" *Filmmaker* 3 (fall 1994).
———. "True Romance." *Filmmaker* 3 (summer 1995).
Macdonald, Mariane. "Profile." *London Independent,* May 22, 1996.
Magiera, Marcy. "Gramercy's Goal Is a Challenge for DDB." *Advertising Age,* February 1, 1993.
Maio, Kathi. "The Key to *The Piano.*" *Ms. Magazine,* (March-April 1994).
Martin, Reed. "The Name Game." *Filmmaker* 9 (winter 2001).
———. "Studios Bank on Burgeoning Overseas Box Office." *USA Today,* December 13, 2000.
———. "*Tiger* Tale Catches Global Star-Making Trend." *USA Today,* December 13, 2000.
Maslin, Janet. "Meeting Halfway." *New York Times Magazine,* November 16, 1997.
Masoni, Marco. "Nothing but Net." *Filmmaker* 8 (winter 2000).
Masterman, Len. *Teaching the Media.* London: Routledge, 1994.
Mayne, Judith. "Paradoxes of Spectatorship." *Viewing Positions: Ways of Seeing Film.* Ed. Linda Williams. New Brunswick: Rutgers University Press, 1995.
McCarthy, T. "Falls Short of Target." *Variety,* January 20, 1982.
McCarthy, Todd, and Charles Flynn, eds. *King of the Bs: Working within the Hollywood System.* New York: Dutton, 1975.
McKay, Jim. "Girls, Girls, Girls—Part II." *IndieWIRE,* August 22, 1996. <indiewire.com>.
McNary, Dave. "Universal Applies Focus to Its Specialty Pic Unit." *Daily Variety,* June 29, 2000.
Mercer, Kobena. *Welcome to the Jungle: New Positions in Black Cultural Studies.* London: Routledge, 1994.
Mernissi, Fatima. *Dreams of Trespass: Tales of a Harem Girlhood.* Reading: Addison-Wesley, 1994.
Merritt, Greg. *Celluloid Mavericks: The History of American Independent Film.*

New York: Thunder's Mouth, 2000.

Metz, Christian. *The Imaginary Signifier: Psychoanalysis and the Cinema.* Trans. C. Britton, A. Williams, B. Brewster, and A. Guzzetti. Bloomington: Indiana University Press, 1982.

Miller, Toby. *The Well-Tempered Self: Citizenship, Culture, and the Postmodern Subject.* Baltimore: Johns Hopkins University Press, 1993.

Mills, David. "A Dash of Difference." *Washington Post,* February 28, 1992.

———. "Out of Obscurity." *Washington Post,* October 28, 1990.

Modleski, Tania. "Time and Desire in the Woman's Film." *Film Theory and Criticism.* Ed. Gerald Mast, Marshall Cohen, and Leo Braudy. Oxford: Oxford University Press, 1992.

Moran, Jim, and Holly Willis. "The War of Independents." *Filmmaker* 6 (winter 1998).

Morris, Meaghan. *The Pirate's Fiancée: Feminism, Reading, Postmodernism.* London: Verso, 1988.

Myers, Jennifer. "Young Viewers May Not Perceive the Satire." *Los Angeles Times,* September 12, 1994.

Natale, Richard. "Indie Films No Longer Penny-Ante Affair." *Los Angeles Times,* April 14, 1995. Calendar.

Newsweek, March 25, 1996.

New York Times, December 10, 1993.

NFT. "Quentin Tarantino's Choice." Program of National Film Theatre/British Film Institute, January 1995.

Nicholson, David. "Reaching for Realism in Black Filmmaking." *Washington Post,* October 28, 1990.

"1997's Most Influential People: Harvey Weinstein, Movie Mogul." *Time,* April 21, 1997.

Orenstein, Peggy. "The Movies Discover the Teen-Age Girl." *New York Times,* August 11, 1996.

Orwall, Bruce. "Miramax Admits It Overstated *Scream 2* Ticket Sales." *Wall Street Journal,* December 22, 1997.

O'Toole, Fintan. "Bloody Minded." *London Guardian,* February 3, 1995.

Owens, Craig. "The Discourse of Others: Feminists and Postmodernism." Foster.

Parks, Louis B. "The Indies Are 'In.'" *Houston Chronicle,* February 24, 2000.

Patterson, Tristan. "What I Really Want to Do...." *Filmmaker* 8 (summer 2000).

Pener, Degen. "*Happiness* Is...." *Entertainment Weekly,* July 17, 1998.

Philadelphia Inquirer, July 21, 1991.

Philadelphia Inquirer, March 25, 1994.

Works Cited

Philadelphia Inquirer, March 6, 1997.
Pierson, John. *Spike, Mike, Slackers & Dykes: A Guided Tour across a Decade of American Independent Cinema.* New York: Hyperion, 1995.
Pincus, Adam. "Manifest Destiny." *Filmmaker* 8 (fall 1999).
———. "Sticky Fingers." *Filmmaker* 8 (spring 2000).
Pomorska, Krystyna. "Russian Formalism in Retrospect." *Readings in Russian Poetics: Formalist and Structuralist Views.* Ed. Pomorska and Ladislav Matejka. Cambridge: MIT Press, 1971.
Pribram, E. Deidre. "Institutional Power and Independent Film Funding." *Afterimage* 21 (summer 1993).
———. "Seduction, Control, and the Search for Authenticity: Madonna's *Truth or Dare.*" *The Madonna Connection: Representational Politics, Subcultural Identities, and Cultural Theory.* Ed. Cathy Schwichtenberg. Boulder: Westview, 1993.
Puig, Claudia. "*Happiness* Has a Dark Side." *USA Today,* October 21, 1998.
———. "Little Girl Power in Hollywood." *USA Today,* July 29, 1998.
———. "Moviemakers Abuzz about Power of the Net." *USA Today,* July 21, 2000.
———. "Sundance: A Film Market, Certainly, but Still Surprising." *USA Today,* January 26, 1999.
———. "Sundance's Shifting Beat." *USA Today,* January 21, 1999.
———. "*Tiger* Cuts through Foreign-Film Reluctance." *USA Today,* March 22, 2001.
Quart, Leonard. *Film Quarterly* 47 (spring 1994).
Rabinowitz, Mark. "Sony Launches New Division for Mid-Level Pics." *IndieWIRE,* December 7, 1998. <indiewire.com>.
Rainer, Peter. "*Just Another Girl on the I.R.T.* Moving in the Right Direction." *Los Angeles Times,* April 2, 1993.
Ratner, Megan. "Borderlines." *Filmmaker* 4 (summer 1996).
Rawsthorn, Alice. "Independent Films Are Becoming an Important Source of Profit for Major Studios." *Financial Times,* January 23, 1996.
———. "Movie Makers Vie for the Sundance Kid's Acclaim." *Financial Times,* January 23, 1996.
Rea, Steven. *Philadelphia Inquirer,* August 13, 1997.
———. "Driving Through Trouble." *Philadelphia Inquirer,* March 16, 1997.
———. "Look Who's Stalking." *Philadelphia Inquirer,* October 12, 1994.
———. "Movie Madness." *Philadelphia Inquirer,* September 8, 1996.
———. "On Movies." *Philadelphia Inquirer,* May 11, 1997.
———. "On Movies." *Philadelphia Inquirer,* October 5, 1997.
———. "On Movies." *Philadelphia Inquirer,* March 22, 1998.

Rhines, Jesse Algeron. "Distributing Difference." *Afterimage* 21 (summer 1993).
Rich, B. Ruby. "In the Eyes of the Beholder." *Village Voice,* January 28, 1992.
———. "Times When Less Is More Profound." *New York Times,* August 6, 2000.
Rickey, Carrie. "Divide and Conquer: Selling the Movies." *Philadelphia Inquirer Magazine,* November 19, 1995.
———. "Holly Hunter: Without Words." *Philadelphia Inquirer,* November 14, 1993.
———. "A Mute Woman Struggles for Voice in *The Piano*." *Philadelphia Inquirer,* November 19, 1993.
———. "Tarantino Mashes Mirth, Mayhem into a Postmodern Pulp." *Philadelphia Inquirer,* October 14, 1994.
Rohter, Larry. "An All-Black Film (Except the Audience)." *New York Times,* November 20, 1990.
Rosen, David, with Peter Hamilton. *Off-Hollywood: The Making and Marketing of American Specialty Films*. A Study of American Independent Feature Films Commissioned by the Sundance Institute and the Independent Feature Project, 1987.
Rule, Sheila. "Director Defies Odds with First Feature, *Daughters of the Dust*." *New York Times,* February 12, 1992.
Ryan, Desmond. "Multinationals Are Changing the Movies and Film Fans Are Not Going to Be Pleased." *Philadelphia Inquirer,* March 28, 1999.
Said, Edward W. *Culture and Imperialism*. New York: Random, 1993.
Sarris, Andrew. "Whatever Happened to Forever?" *Village Voice,* January 20-26, 1982.
Sarup, Madan. *Identity, Culture and the Postmodern World*. Edinburgh: Edinburgh University Press, 1998.
———. *An Introductory Guide to Post-Structuralism and Postmodernism*. London: Harvester Wheatsheaf, 1993.
Schamus, James. "American Independents Depending on Europe." *Off-Hollywood Report* 6 (winter 1992).
———. "Don't Worry, Be Happy." *Filmmaker* 4 (fall 1995).
———. "The Pursuit of *Happiness*: Making an Art of Marketing an Explosive Film." *The Nation,* April 5, 1999.
Schatz, Thomas. "The New Hollywood." *Film Theory Goes to the Movies*. Ed. Jim Collins, Hillary Radner, and Ava Preacher Collins. New York: Routledge, 1993.
Schickel, Richard. "Love, Rage and the Quotidian." *Time,* February 1, 1982.
Schiff, Steven. *Lolita: The Book of the Film*. New York: Applause, 1998.
Schrader, Paul. *Moving Pictures*. BBC2. Broadcast March 12, 1995.

Works Cited

Schulte-Sasse, Jochen. "Foreword: Theory of Modernism versus Theory of the Avant-Garde." Bürger.
"Seagram Buys Polygram from Philips for $10.6 bn." *London Independent,* May 22, 1998.
Seger, Linda. *Making a Good Script Great.* 2nd ed. Hollywood: Samuel French, 1994.
Shohat, Ella, and Robert Stam. *Unthinking Eurocentrism: Multiculturalism and the Media.* New York: Routledge, 1994.
Shooting Gallery Web Site. <movies.yahoo.com/sgfilmseries>.
Smith, Gavin. "Oliver Stone: Why Do I Have to Provoke?" *Sight and Sound* (December 1994).
———. "Quentin Tarantino." *Film Comment* 30 (July 1994).
Softley, Jeff. "Stone's Method Only Shatters His Message." *Los Angeles Times,* September 12, 1994.
Stam, Robert. "From Realism to Intertextuality." Stam, Burgoyne, and Flitterman-Lewis.
———. "The Origins of Semiotics." Stam, Burgoyne, and Flitterman-Lewis.
Stam, Robert, Robert Burgoyne, and Sandy Flitterman-Lewis, eds. *New Vocabularies in Film Semiotics: Structuralism, Post-Structuralism, and Beyond.* New York: Routledge, 1992.
Stark, Jim. "Garage Movies: Part I." *Off-Hollywood Report* 5 (July-August 1990).
Steedman, Carolyn. "Culture, Cultural Studies, and the Historians." *Cultural Studies.* Ed. Lawrence Grossberg, Cary Nelson, and Paula Treichler. New York: Routledge, 1992.
———. *Landscape for a Good Woman: A Story of Two Lives.* London: Virago, 1986.
Steinmetz, Johanna. "One Man's Families." *Chicago Times,* December 8, 1991.
Sterngold, James. "For Artistic Freedom, It's Not the Worst of Times." *New York Times,* September 20, 1998.
Sterritt, David. "How 'Festival Overload Syndrome' Affects Critics." *Chronicle of Higher Education,* August 4, 2000.
Südderman, Martin. "The First 24P Hi-Definition Indie." *Filmmaker* 9 (winter 2001).
Sullivan, Monica. *VideoHound's Independent Film Guide.* Farmington Hill: Visible Ink, 1999.
Taitz, Sonia. "Jodie Foster: Tough Hero." *New York Times,* October 16, 1988.
Tasker, Yvonne. "Approaches to the New Hollywood." *Cultural Studies and Communications.* Ed. James Curran, David Morley, and Valerie Walkerdine. London: Arnold, 1996.
Taubin, Amy. "Queer Male Cinema and Feminism." Cook and Dodd.

———. "Slippery Slopes." *Village Voice,* February 16, 1999.
"The Two Hollywoods." *New York Times Magazine,* November 16, 1997.
Thompson, Kristen, and David Bordwell. *Film History: An Introduction.* New York: McGraw-Hill, 1994.
Thomson, Patricia. "The Screenplay's the Thing." *The Independent* (December 1988).
"To Sleep with Anger." *Variety,* January 31, 1990.
Travers, Peter. "Sex and *The Piano.*" *Rolling Stone,* December 9, 1993.
Tudor, Andrew. "Genre." *Film Genre Reader.* Ed. Barry Keith Grant. Austin: University of Texas Press, 1986.
Turan, Kenneth. "Mike Leigh's Raw, *Naked* Truth." *Los Angeles Times,* December 16, 1993.
———. "*The Piano* Plays an Intoxicating Tune." *Los Angeles Times,* November 19, 1993.
———. "Stone Removes the Gloves in *Killers.*" *Los Angeles Times,* August 26, 1994.
Turner, Graeme. *British Cultural Studies: An Introduction.* 2nd ed. London: Routledge, 1996.
"USA Snapshots." *USA Today,* 5 November 1998.
Walker, Alexander. "Banning the Bloodshed Denies Our Freedom." *London Evening Standard,* November 3, 1994.
Wallace, Michelle. *Invisibility Blues: From Pop to Theory.* London: Verso, 1994.
Waxman, Sharon. "Going for the Gold in More Ways than One." *Washington Post,* March 26, 2000.
Wechsler, Pat. "The Focused Filmmaker." *Washington Post,* April 2, 1993.
Weeks, Janet. "*Scream* Movies Cultivate Special Audience: Girls." *New York Times,* December 12, 1997.
Weiskind, Ron. "Independents' Day." *Pittsburgh Post-Gazette,* December 8, 1996.
Williams, Greg. "*Pulp Fiction* Is Predictably Violent—and Predictably Wonderful." *Esquire* [British edition] (November 1994).
Williams, Jeannie. "Weinsteins Picture Philanthropic Future." *USA Today,* September 18, 1997.
Williams, Raymond. *Keywords: A Vocabulary of Culture and Society.* 2nd ed. Oxford: Oxford University Press, 1983.
Willis, Sharon. *High Contrast: Race and Gender in Contemporary Hollywood Film.* Durham: Duke University Press, 1997.
———. "The Fathers Watch the Boys' Room." *Camera Obscura* 32 (September 1993-January 1994).
Winters, Laura. "Making a Cellblock an Unlikely Garden of Free Expression."

New York Times, October 4, 1998.
Wolff, Janet. *Aesthetics and the Sociology of Art.* 2nd ed. Ann Arbor: University of Michigan Press, 1993.
Wolff, Janet, and John Seed, eds. *The Culture of Capital: Art, Power and the Nineteenth-Century Middle Class.* Manchester: Manchester University Press, 1988.
Wollen, Peter. "Mexico/Women/Art." Wollen, *Readings and Writings.*
———. "'Ontology' and 'Materialism' in Film." Wollen, *Readings and Writings.*
———. *Readings and Writings: Semiotic Counter-Strategies.* London: Verso, 1982.
———. "Semiotic Counter-Strategies: Retrospect 1982." Wollen, *Readings and Writings.*
———. "The Two Avant-Gardes." Wollen, *Readings and Writings.*
Wyatt, Justin. *High Concept: Movies and Marketing in Hollywood.* Austin: University of Texas Press, 1994.
Zeig, Sande. "Queens of England." *Filmmaker* 1 (summer 1993).

TITLE INDEX

A

Accused, The, xx, 152–156, 158, 231n.5
Adjuster, The, 58
Adrenaline Drive, 33, 61, 64
Affair of Love, An, 22, 61
Aimée and Jaguar, 63
Albino Alligator, 177
All about My Mother, 65
All the Vermeers in New York, 31–32, 88, 228n.15
Amateur, 13, 58
Amélie, 63
American Desi, 72
American Dream, xviii, 73
American Psycho, 28
Amongst Friends, 104
Amores Perros, 65
Angels and Insects, 59
Antonia and Jane, 72
Antonia's Line, 65, 72
Apartment Zero, 35
Atomic Cafe, The, xviii
Autumn Tale, 58

B

Babette's Feast, xiv, 22, 66
Bad Lieutenant, xv, 176
Ballad of Little Jo, The, 72
Barcelona, 58
Basquiat, 59
Beautiful Thing, 72
Beau Travail, 63
Before Night Falls, 22, 59
Beijing Bicycle, 23, 62
Belizaire the Cajun, 35
Better Housekeeping, 26
Better than Sex, 35
Betty Blue, 63

Beyond Silence, 63
Bhaji on the Beach, 68, 72
Big Dis, The, 29
Big One, The, 73
Billy Elliot, 26
Billy's Hollywood Screen Kiss, 72
Black and White, 26
Blair Witch Project, The, 18, 27, 30, 39, 75, 202, 203–204, 229n.23
Blair Witch 2: Book of Shadows, 27
Blair Witch 3, 27
Blood Simple, xi, xv, 19, 35, 176, 233n.5
Bloody Child, The, 54
Born in Flames, 29, 55, 72
Box of Moonlight, 18, 31
Boyfriends and Girlfriends, 58
Boys Don't Cry, ix, 25, 32, 72, 200
Bread and Roses, 72
Breaking the Waves, 4, 28, 62
Brief History of Time, A, 30
Broken Mirrors, 65
Brother, 66
Brother from Another Planet, The, 28, 225n.24
Brother of Sleep, 63
Brother's Keeper, xviii
Brothers McMullen, The, 12, 25, 31, 32, 39
Buena Vista Social Club, xviii
Buffalo 66, 28, 41
Burnt by the Sun, 65
But I'm a Cheerleader, 72
Bye Bye Brazil, 62

C

Camille Claudel, 59
Career Girls, 72, 115, 135
Carla's Song, 72
Castle, The, 24

Caveman's Valentine, The, 26, 84
Celebration, The, 28, 55, 62, 202
Celluloid Closet, The, xviii, 73
Center of the World, The, 27, 37, 202
Central Station, 23, 62
Chan Is Missing, 15, 19, 68, 72, 82
Character, 66
Chasing Amy, 104
Children of Heaven, 64
Chocolat, 63
Chuck & Buck, 27, 202, 203
Chungking Express, 63
Chunhyang, 35, 65
Chutney Popcorn, 73
Cinema Paradiso, xiv, 64
City of Hope, 51, 225n.24
Ciudad, La, 72
Claire of the Moon, 31, 72
Clean, Shaven, 32
Clerks, ix, 6, 13, 17, 55, 104
Close to Eden, 66
Coeur en Hiver, Un, 28, 63
Colors Trilogy: Blue, White and Red, The, 58
Combination Platter, 29
Come Back to the 5 & Dime Jimmy Dean, Jimmy Dean, 34
Cook, the Thief, His Wife and Her Lover, The, 37, 58
Cookie's Fortune, 28
Copland, 177
Criminal Lovers, 63
Cronos, 65
Crossover Dreams, 72
Crouching Tiger, Hidden Dragon, xi, xix, 12, 23, 25, 26, 39, 61, 66, 199, 200–202, 234nn.1, 2
Croupier, 33
Crush, 32
Crying Game, The, xi, 4, 18, 23, 36, 69, 157, 201
Cup, The, 22, 66

D

Dancer in the Dark, 62, 202
Dancing at Lughnasa, 25
Danzón, 65

Daughters of the Dust, xiv, xix, 18, 19, 43, 55, 72, 83, 105, 106, 109, 110, 227n.6, 228nn.12, 16, 17, 229n.22
  appearance in, 92–94
  and audiences, 103–104, 107–108
  distribution, 86-88, 91–92
  history in, 95–100
  narrative, 100–103
Day I Became a Woman, The, 64
Daytrippers, The, 28
Dear Diary, 22, 64
Deep End, The, 25
Delicatessen, 63
Desert Blue, 35
Desert Hearts, xiv, 28, 35, 72, 82
Dim Sum: A Little Bit of Heart, 72
Dinner Game, The, 28
Distant Voices, Still Lives, 58
Diva, 22, 61, 63
Dogma, 28, 37
Double Happiness, 72
Double Life of Veronique, The, 66
Down by Law, 13, 58, 60
Down in the Delta, 84
Dreamlife of Angels, The, 63
Drowning by Numbers, 58
Drugstore Cowboy, xi, 35

E

East is East, 72
East Palace, West Palace, 62
East-West, 66
Eat Drink Man Woman, 66
Eating Raoul, 34
Edith and Marcel, 63
Edward II, 58
8 1/2 Women, 28, 58
Emperor and the Assassin, The, 23, 62
Enchanted April, 59
English Patient, The, 3, 4, 5, 11, 18, 23, 26, 59
Enormous Changes at the Last Minute, 29
Entre Nous, 22, 61, 63
Erendira, 61, 65
Eternity and a Day, 66
Eureka, 64

Title Index

Europa, Europa, 22, 66
Eve's Bayou, 28, 72, 83
Exotica, 58

F

Fallen Angels, 61, 63
Faithless, 35
Faraway, So Close!, 63
Farewell My Concubine, 62
Fast, Cheap & Out of Control, xviii
Felicia's Journey, 58
Female Perversions, 58
Femme Nikita, La, 176
Flirt, 13, 28
Flower of My Secret, The, 65
Forbidden Love: The Unashamed Stories of Lesbian Lives, 73
Freeze Die Come to Life, 65
Fresh, 83
Friend of the Deceased, A, 66
From Dusk to Dawn, 177
Full Monty, The, xi, 25, 32, 39, 73, 224n.21, 225–226n.29, 228n.15
Funeral, The (Ferrara), xv
Funeral, The (Itami), 61, 64

G

Gal Young 'Un, 29
Gas Food Lodging, 72, 115
Genealogies of a Crime, 58
General, The, xv
Genghis Blues, 73
Ghost Dog: The Way of the Samurai, 27
Girl 6, 25
Girlfight, 26, 72
Girl on the Bridge, 25
Girls Town, 28, 69, 72, 227n.3
Glass Shield, The, 72, 83
Gods and Monsters, 28, 59
Go Fish, xv, 17, 28, 55, 68, 72, 227n.9, 229n.23
Gohatto, 65
Golden Bowl, The, 59
Golden Eighties, 61
Governess, The, 23
Goya in Bordeaux, 66
Gregory's Girl, 28
Groove, 202

Guantanamera, 62
Gummo, 22, 58
Gun Crazy, 177

H

Handmaid's Tale, The, 34
Hanging Garden, The, 35
Happiness, xi, 12, 17, 38–39, 55, 58, 199–200, 225nn.26, 27
Hav Plenty, 18, 83
Hearts of Darkness, 30
Heavenly Creatures, 177
Heavy, 28, 76
Henry Fool, 58
Henry: Portrait of a Serial Killer, xv, 32, 176
Henry V, 59
High Art, 18, 28, 72
High Heels, 66
High Hopes, 72, 115
Hollywood Shuffle, 83
Hoop Dreams, xi, xviii, 73
Hours and the Times, The, 54, 72
Howard's End, xiv, 23, 36, 59
How to Be a Woman and Not Die in the Attempt, 66
Humanité, 29
Human Traffic, 73

I

Icicle Thief, The, 58
Idiots, The, 29, 62, 202
Incident at Oglala, 73
Incredibly True Adventure of Two Girls in Love, The, 17–18, 22, 69–70, 72, 114
In the Company of Men, 23
In the Mood for Love, 64
In the Soup, 30
Irma Vep, 63
I Shot Andy Warhol, 18, 28, 59, 75–76
I Stand Alone, 63
I've Heard the Mermaids Singing, 58

J

Jackie Brown, 177, 194, 195
Jean de Florette, 63
Jerry and Tom, 24
Journey of Hope, 66
Judy Berlin, 33

Julie Johnson, 26
julien donkey-boy, 58, 202
Jump, 29
Just Another Girl on the I.R.T., xix, 83, 87, 104–106, 108, 109, 110, 229n.24

K

Kama Sutra: A Tale of Love, 64
Kids, 37
Kikujiro, 23, 65
Killing Zoe, xv, 177, 180
Kiss or Kill, 177
Kolya, 62
Krays, The, xv

L

Ladybird, Ladybird, 28, 55, 72
Last Metro, The, 22, 61, 63
Last of England, The, 54, 58
Last Seduction, The, xv, 28, 177
Late August, Early September, 63
Late Bloomers, 72
Latin Boys Go to Hell, 32, 72
Laws of Gravity, 104, 177, 193
Leningrad Cowboys, 62
Lesson in History, A, 98–100
L.I.E., 35
Lianna, 225n.24
Life and Times of Rosie the Riveter, The, 29
Life Is Beautiful, xiv, xix, 4, 18, 23, 32, 39, 61, 64, 225–226n.29
Life is Sweet, 28, 72, 115
Like Water for Chocolate, xi, 65
Limbo, 26, 225n.24
Limey, The, xv
Little Odessa, 177
Little Vera, 65
Living End, The, xiv, 19, 28, 55, 72, 193
Living in Oblivion, 18, 23, 30–31
Living on Tokyo Time, 35
Lone Star, 23, 51, 225n.24
Longtime Companion, 72
Lost Highway, xv
Love & Sex, 28
Love Crimes, 176
Love Is the Devil, 32, 59
Lovers, 66

M

Maborosi, 65
Macho Dancer, 73
Madame Bovary, 59
Madness of King George, The, 59
Mala Noche, 32, 72
Malèna, 64
Man Bites Dog, 32, 61, 177
Manon of the Spring, 63
Man Facing Southeast, 55, 61
Manny and Lo, 227n.3
Man Who Cried, The, 26
Mariachi, El, 221n.3
Marianne and Juliane, 63
Matewan, 34, 51, 225n.24
Ma Vie en Rose, 23, 61, 72
Mediterraneo, 64
Memento, 58
Men with Guns, 51, 225n.24
Metropolitan, 34, 58
Me You Them, 62
Mifune, 62, 202
Mindwalk, 30
Mississippi Masala, 28, 72
Mi Vida Loca, xiv, 23, 69, 72
Moderns, The, 35, 59
Monster, The, 28
Mrs. Brown, 59
Mrs. Dalloway, 59
Mrs. Parker and the Vicious Circle, 59
Much Ado about Nothing, 28, 59
MURDER and Murder, 72
My Beautiful Laundrette, xi, 22, 59, 73
My Brilliant Career, 72
My Dinner with Andre, 58
My First Mister, 26
My Left Foot, 23, 59
My Life's in Turnaround, 29
My Name is Joe, 27, 55, 72
My New Gun, 72
My Own Private Idaho, 21, 61, 72
My Son the Fanatic, 59, 72
Mystery Train, 13, 22, 58, 60
My Twentieth Century, 64

N

Naked, xx, 22, 72, 115–116, 125–135, 136,

Title Index

138–139, 140
Nasty Girl, The, 55, 63
Natural Born Killers, xx, 168–170, 171–173, 174, 178–179, 187
Nenette and Boni, 32, 63
Next Stop, Wonderland, 24
Night and Day, 61
Night on Earth, 13, 21
Non-Stop, 61, 65
Norte, El, 28, 34
Northern Lights, 29
Not One Less, 62

O

One False Move, xv, 83, 176
On the Ropes, xviii, 29, 73
On the Run, 65
On Top of the Whale, 58
Open Your Eyes, 66
Opportunists, The, 177
Opposite of Sex, The, 25
Orlando, xi, xx, 23, 43, 54, 72, 140, 151, 152, 156–159, 228n.17, 231n.4
Orphans, 33
Oscar and Lucinda, 59
Our Lady of the Assassins, 26

P

Paris Is Burning, xi, xviii, 73
Parting Glances, 72, 82, 229n.23
Passion Fish, 225n.24
Passion of Mind, 25
Pecker, 22
Pelle the Conqueror, 67
Permanent Vacation, 27
Persuasion, 59
Pi, 27, 204
Piano, The, xx, 4, 23, 72, 140, 141–142, 164–165, 176, 231n.4,
  alternative narrative, 150–152, 158–163
  reviews, 142–145, 230n.1
  "romance," 144–145, 147–150
  sexuality, 145–147
  violence in, 145, 147–148
Picture Bride, 72
Pillow Book, The, 58
Player, The, xvi, 21
Poison, xiv, 10, 12, 43, 55, 58, 72, 201
Pollock, 25, 59
Ponette, 29
Postino, Il, xi, xvi, 4, 17, 18, 64, 221n.2
Price of Milk, The, 35
Prick up Your Ears, 28, 59
Priest, 37
Princess and the Warrior, The, 63
Privilege, 54, 72
Promise, The, 63
Prospero's Books, 58
Pulp Fiction, xv, xx, 4, 5, 10, 18, 23, 24, 39, 75, 167–168, 233n.8
  appropriations in, 177–181, 196–197
  masculinity in, 191–194
  "morality" in, 173–176
  and nostalgia, 187
  and pop culture, 181–186
  race in, 194–197
  violence in, 170–173
Pushing Hands, 66

Q

Quarry, The, 29
Queen Margo, 59
Question of Silence, A, 65, 72, 147

R

Raining Stones, 72
Raise the Red Lantern, 62
Ran, 58, 61, 65
Ratcatcher, 73, 161
Red Firecracker, Green Firecracker, 67
Red Rock West, 177
Red Violin, The, xiv, 59
Remembering the Cosmos, 65
Requiem for a Dream, 27
Reservoir Dogs, xi, xv, xx, 13, 17, 19, 75, 168, 169, 170–171, 176, 177, 179, 182, 187–191, 192, 193, 194–196, 233n.9
Restless, 29
Return of the Secaucus Seven, The, 15, 19, 35, 51, 225n.24
Rhapsody in August, 58, 65
River of Grass, 58
Road Home, The, 62
Roger & Me, xvi, xviii, 221n.3, 229n.23
Roja, 64
Room with a View, A, 28, 34, 59

Rosa Luxembourg, 63
Rosetta, 29, 62
Rounders, 177
Ruby in Paradise, 28
Run Lola Run, xv, 23, 58

S

Safe, 18, 23
Salaam Bombay!, 28, 64
Sammy & Rosie Get Laid, 28, 59, 72
Sankofa, 72
Sans Soleil, 63
Saving Grace, 22
Scent of Green Papaya, The, 66
Schizopolis, 58
Secret of Roan Inish, The, 225n.24
Secrets & Lies, xi, 3, 28, 72, 115, 135
Series 7, 29
sex, lies & videotape, 23, 36, 61
Shadow Magic, 67
Shadow of the Vampire, 28
Shakespeare in Love, 4, 11, 18, 23, 26, 39, 59, 200
Shallow Grave, 22
Shanghai Triad, 61, 62
Sherman's March, 29
She's Gotta Have It, xi, 6, 15, 18, 19, 72, 82, 83, 229n.23
Shine, xiv, 3, 4, 5, 22, 39, 59
Shoot the Moon, xx, 116, 124–135, 136, 138–139
Shower, 67
Sid and Nancy, 28, 59
Sidewalks of New York, 25
Sidewalk Stories, 72, 83
Signs and Wonders, 32, 202
Silverlake Life: The View from Here, 73, 226n.3
Simple Men, 13, 58
Slacker, xiv, 18, 68, 92, 104, 143, 228n.15
Slam, 69, 72, 84
Sleepwalk, 29
Sling Blade, 4, 5
Slums of Beverly Hills, 25
Smithereens, 15, 21
Smoke Signals, 72
Smooth Talk, 59

Snapper, The, 73
Southern Comfort, 73
Southpaw, 33
Spetters, 62
Star Maps, 25
Steal This Movie!, 28
Stonewall, 72
Story of Qui Ju, The, 62
Straight Out of Brooklyn, xi, 17, 28, 55, 72, 83, 176
Strangers in Good Company, 29
Stranger than Paradise, xi, 15, 19, 28, 35, 54, 58, 60
Strawberry and Chocolate, 62
Strawberry Fields, 72
Subway, 63
Such a Long Journey, 33, 72
Suicide Kings, xv, 177
Sunday, 28
Sunshine, 25, 64
Surname Viet Given Name Nam, 54
Suzhou River, 62
Sweet Hereafter, The, 22, 58
Sweetie, 55
Swoon, 18, 21, 72, 193

T

Tale of Summer, A, 58
Tampopo, 65
Tango, 66
Tao of Steve, The, 23
Tape, 202
Taxing Woman, A, 65
Thank You and Good Night, xviii
Thief, The, 65
Thin Blue Line, The, xi, xviii, 73
Things to Do in Denver When You're Dead, 177
30 Days, 29
32 Short Films about Glenn Gould, 28
Three Lives and Only One Death, 58
Three Seasons, xiv, 28, 72
Tie Me Up! Tie Me Down!, 37, 66
Timecode, 26, 202
Times of Harvey Milk, The, xviii, 28
Time to Live, A, 66
Together Alone, 32

Title Index

To Live, 28, 62
Tom and Viv, 59
Topsy Turvy, 59, 115
To Sleep with Anger, xix, 18, 28, 83, 87, 88, 89, 90–91, 92, 107, 108, 109, 110, 228n.12
Totally Fu**ed Up, 32
Toto le Héros, 30, 67
Touch of Evil, A, 64
Tous les Matins du Monde, 28
Toute une Nuit, 62
Trainspotting, xi, xx, 73, 76, 93, 136–137
Trick, 72
Trust, 19, 21, 58
Tumbleweeds, 22, 72
24 Hour Woman, The, 72

U

Unbelievable Truth, The, 58
Under the Olive Trees, 64
Up at the Villa, 59
Urbania, 28
Usual Suspects, The, 22

V

Van, The, 25, 73
Vanishing, The, 32, 67
Velvet Goldmine, 10, 11, 18
Venus Beauty Institute, 35
Vermont Is for Lovers, 143
Vertical Ray of the Sun, 67
Vincent, 32
Virgin Suicides, The, 25
Vive l'Amour, 66
Voyage to the Beginning of the World, 65

W

Waiting for the Moon, 35, 58
Waking Ned Devine, 25
Walking and Talking, 12
War Room, The, xviii, 28
War Zone, The, 35
Water Drops on Burning Rocks, 63
Watermelon Woman, The, 29, 73
Way of the Gun, The, xv, 177
Wedding Banquet, The, xv, 12, 73
Welcome to the Dollhouse, 23, 76
West Beirut, 67

What Happened Was…, 13
When the Cat's Away, 63
Wilde, 59
Wild Reeds, 63
Wind Will Carry Us, The, 64
Wings of Desire, The, 22, 58
Wings of the Dove, The, 59
Winter Sleepers, 29, 63
Wittgenstein, 13, 54, 58
Wizard of Loneliness, The, 35
Woman on Top, 25
Women, 65
Women in Film, 202
Women on the Verge of a Nervous Breakdown, xiv, 22, 54, 66
Working Girls, xiv, 72, 82, 115, 229n.23

X-Y-Z

Xiu Xiu: The Sent-Down Girl, 62
Yi Yi, 29, 62
You Can Count on Me, 25
Young Poisoner's Handbook, The, 28
Young Soul Rebels, 55, 73
You So Crazy, 37
Zentropa, 58

INDEX

A

Academy Awards, xvi, 3–5, 31, 39, 179, 199–200, 221n.2, 231n.4, 233n.11
actors, in independent film, 7, 25, 90, 157, 167–168, 182, 183–186, 234nn.1,2
Adams, Marlin, 91
aesthetic avant-garde, xix, 45–48, 50, 51, 54, 68, 71, 160
African American cinema, 72, 73, 83–84, 85–86. See also *Daughters of the Dust, Just Another Girl on the I.R.T., To Sleep with Anger*
African Americans
    audiences, 81, 86, 87, 88, 89–91, 92, 100, 101–102, 104, 105, 107–108, 229n.24
    marketing to, 89, 90, 91–92, 105
    history, 94–100, 100–101, 102
Alive Pictures, 7, 35, 225n.23
alternative film, xix, 9, 41, 42, 43–44, 50, 52, 69, 77, 87, 114, 160, 226n.2
alternative narrative, 9, 47–48, 50–52, 60, 70, 72, 99, 114, 115, 134, 137–140, 150–152
    in *Daughters of the Dust*, 96, 100–101, 105
    in *Orlando*, 156–160
    in *The Piano*, 150–152, 158–160, 161, 162
Ang, Ien, 163
Anger, Kenneth, 67
Antonioni, Michelangelo, 55, 56, 60
appropriation of identity, 194–197
appropriation, postmodern, 74, 177–181
Aries Film Releasing, 7, 32
Arrow Entertainment, 6, 29,
art films/cinema, xiv, 55–58, 70, 71, 84, 108, 144, 162–163, 176
auteurism, xx, 57, 60, 68, 76, 176, 187, 193–194, 223n.10
    categories of, 58–60
    international, xiv, 8–9, 55, 60–61, 61t–67t
Artisan Entertainment, 6, 18, 25, 26, 27, 30, 34, 37
Atlantic Releasing, 225n.23
audience, interpretive, and reception discourses, xii, xiii, xvii–xviii, xxi, 77, 86, 87, 103, 106–107, 108, 110, 123, 140, 142, 144, 163–164, 205
audiences, 8, 14, 85–86, 87, 89–90, 92, 105, 106, 107–108, 163–164, 201, 203, 205, 229n.24
    specialized, 18, 27, 82, 84–85, 88, 89, 92, 100, 104, 204
auteurism, xx, 57, 60, 68, 76, 176, 187, 193–194, 223n.10
avant-garde
    aesthetic, xix, 45–48, 50, 51, 54, 68, 71, 160
    political, xix, xxi, 45, 48–52, 53, 71–72, 160
avant-garde film, xiv, 9, 11, 41, 43, 57, 70–71, 114
    influence on independent film, xiii, xiv, xx, 9, 12–13, 52–55, 77, 114, 152, 159, 163
Avary, Roger, 178, 179–180, 182, 192
Avenue Pictures, 7, 32, 35, 225n.23

B

B films/studios, xvi, 19, 20, 21, 36
Bakhtin, Mikhail, 186–187
Bambara, Toni Cade, 86, 93, 100, 102
Barenholtz, Ben, 34–35
Barker, Michael, 22–23, 34, 227n.4, 228n.15

Baudrillard, Jean, 186–187
Bergman, Ingmar, xiv, 55, 56, 60
Bernard, Tom, 22–23, 34, 40
Bertolucci, Bernardo, xiv
blaxploitation, 19, 85, 184, 188
blockbusters, 16–17, 223n.13
Bloom, Marcie, 23
Bobo, Jacqueline, 86, 94–95
Bordwell, David, 55, 117–118, 119, 121, 122, 230nn.3,4,5
Boyd, Valerie, 95
Brakhage Stan, 67, 68
branding, 26–27
Branigan, Edward, 119–120, 230n.1
Brecht, Bertolt, 49, 51
Brunt, Rosalind, 82
Buñuel, Luis, 56, 60
Bürger, Peter, 48–49
Burgoyne, Robert, 120, 121
Burnett, Charles, 83, 88, 89

C

Cahiers du Cinéma, 50
Campion, Jane, 142, 152, 161, 162, 226n.2, 232nn.9,10
Canby, Vincent, 106, 141, 143, 162–163
Carter, Kevin, 101, 102
Cartwright, Lisa, 47, 51, 53–54, 67, 70, 226n.2
Cassavetes, John, 19, 35, 60
CFP (Cinepix Film Properties), 6, 28
Chabrol, Claude, 57, 60
Cherot, Christopher, 18
Chubb, Caldecott, 89
Cinecom International, 7, 27, 28, 34, 225nn.23,24
cinematic codes, 49
Cineplex, 225, n.23
Cinéthique, 46
Circle Releasing, 7, 35, 225n.23
Citron, Michelle, 53, 54, 68
class in films, 72–73, 130, 133, 134, 136, 138–139, 149, 153
Clover, Carol, 154
Cook, Pam, 176
Corman, Roger, 20–21
Cornis-Pope, Marcel, 139, 164

Coste, Didier, 119, 123
Cowboy Pictures, 29
Crane, Diane, 71
crime and gangster independent films, xv, 176–177, 192–193, 233n.5. See also *Pulp Fiction, Reservoir Dogs, Natural Born Killers*
Cubism, 45–46
cult films, 19, 20, 21
cultural/historical discourses, xii, xiii, xv, xvii, xx, xxi, 71–72, 77, 78, 83, 87, 93–94, 100, 106–107, 110, 111, 115, 116, 117, 119, 121, 122, 123, 124, 125, 137, 139, 140, 148, 149, 153–154, 156, 158, 167, 197, 205
cultural product/commodity, xviii, 3, 11, 14, 27, 44

D

Dana, Jonathon, 30
Danto, Arthur, 74–75
Dargis, Manohla, 11, 168
Dash, Julie, 81, 83, 86, 87–88, 91, 92, 93–94, 99, 100, 102, 103–104, 107, 108, 227n.6
de Lauretis, Theresa, 118, 123, 230n.4
de Sica, Vittorio, 56, 60
Deren, Maya, 67
Deutchman, Ira, 21, 22, 25, 34
DiCillo, Tom, 30–31
Dinerstein, David, 25
discursive formation/field, xi, xii–xiii, xix, xxii, 3, 11, 77, 205
distributors, independent, xviii, xix, 6–7, 14, 21–33, 53, 82–83, 84, 85–86, 87–92, 103–104, 107, 110, 143, 202, 204–205, 253–273
  influential personnel, 21–25, 27–30, 31–32, 33–35
  micro, 7, 29–30, 31–33
  mini-major, 6–7, 10, 28, 31, 36, 87
documentary films, xviii, 3, 73, 226n.3
Dogme '95, 11, 52, 202, 203, 222n.4
Dowell, Pat, 181, 182, 194–195, 232n.4
DV (digital video) production, 202–203

E

Eagleton, Terry, 45, 46, 50

Index

Eco, Umberto, 73
Eisenstein, Sergei, 49
"entertainment," xv, 75, 165, 221n.1
experimental film, xiii, xix, 19, 20, 41–42, 43–44, 47–48, 53, 58
exploitation films, 19, 20–21

F

Fagan, Steve, 29
Fassbinder, R.W., 50
Fellini, Federico, 55, 60
feminist avant-garde, xx, xxi, 47, 53, 54, 68, 147, 159
Film Dallas, 225n.23
Filmmaker, 5, 13, 18–19, 31, 41, 199, 222n.1
Fine Line Features, xvi, 3, 4, 6, 7, 21–22, 25, 26, 32, 34, 37, 115, 125
First Look Pictures, 6, 29, 225n.24
First Run Features, 6, 29
Fonoroff, Nina, 47, 51, 53–54, 67, 70, 226n.2
foreign-language independent films, xviii–xix, 8–9, 60–61, 61t-67t, 200–201
Foucault, Michel, 113
Fox Searchlight Pictures, 24–25, 31, 34, 39, 228n.15
Frameline, 29
French New Wave, 56–57, 60
Fried, John, 187–188, 193

G

Gandhi, Leela, 173–174, 187
gay and lesbian films, 69–70, 72, 73, 82, 84, 86, 192–193
gender and independent film, xx, xxi, 72, 73, 82, 84, 115, 116, 125, 127–128, 129, 130, 131, 134–135, 138, 139, 141–142, 145, 146, 147–148, 149–150, 152–153, 156–157, 160, 161, 162, 163, 188, 227n.3
genres in independent film, xv, 69, 75, 90–91, 148, 176, 188, 201, 232n.1
Gigliotti, Donna, 22–23
Gilmore, Geoffrey, 26
Gilroy, Paul, 81–82, 100, 108, 109
Gledhill, Christine, xi
Godard, Jean-Luc, 49, 57, 60, 74, 177

Goldman, Bo, 124
Goldwyn Company, xix, 6, 12, 28, 32, 37, 89–91, 107, 225n.24, 227nn.9,11
Goldwyn Films, 35
Good Machine, 12, 13, 38, 225n.27
Gramercy Pictures, 3, 22, 29
Grossberg, Larry, 14–15

H

Habermas, Jürgen, 155
Hall, Stuart, 56, 95, 107
Haraway, Donna, 113
Harris, Leslie, 83, 104, 106
Harvey, Sylvia, 45, 46–47, 48, 71
Hawks, Howard, 56
Hekman, Susan, 113
history, representation of, 59, 83, 93–100, 183, 187, 197
Hitchcock, Alfred, 56
Hoberman, J., 21, 194
Holland, Patricia, 116
Hollywood, influence of
 representational, xiii–xiv, xx, 5, 10, 12–13, 40, 41, 42, 116, 150–152
 economic, xiv, 5, 10, 12–13, 23–24, 25–26, 29, 36–37, 39–40
 studio ownership, 6–7, 23–24, 29, 36–40, 225nn.26,27
Hollywood appropriations of independent film, 3–4, 11, 36, 199–200, 202, 221n.3
homophobia in *Pulp Fiction*, 188, 192, 234n.12
hooks, bell, 93–94, 141–142, 162–163
Hope, Ted, 13–14, 105
Hu, Marcus, 31–32
Hudlin, Warrington, 101, 102

I

identity cinema, xix, 69–73, 82–87, 107, 108, 109
identity politics, xiv–xv, xix, xxi, xxii, 9, 14, 52, 81–83, 85–87, 102–103, 105–107, 108–110, 229n.26
independent, history of term, xv–xvi
independent film
 actors, 7, 25, 90, 157, 167–168, 182, 183–186, 234nn.1,2

aesthetics, xiv–xv, xx, 9, 13, 52, 54–55, 58, 69, 70, 71, 77, 93–94, 114, 115, 151, 155, 157, 158, 159, 162
and alternative film, xix, 9, 41, 42, 43–44, 50, 52, 69, 77, 87, 114, 160
art cinema, influence of, xiv, 8–9, 57–59, 84, 108, 144, 162–163
audiences, 8, 14, 85–86, 87, 89–90, 92, 105, 106, 107–108, 163–164, 201, 203, 205, 229n.24
    specialized, 18, 27, 82, 84–85, 88, 89, 92, 100, 104, 204
and avant-garde film, xiii, xiv, xx, 12–13, 43, 50, 52–55, 71–72, 77, 152, 159, 163
box-office earnings, 17–18, 23, 24, 27, 31, 32, 33, 36, 88, 91, 224n.14
budgets/financing, 5–6, 15–16, 26, 201, 202, 228n.12
and cultural politics, xiv, xxiii, 9, 14, 52–53, 69–73, 76, 82–87, 163–164, 196–197. See also identity politics, multiculturalism
as cultural product/commodity, xviii, 3, 11, 14, 27
defining, xi, xiii, xv, xvi–xvii, 3–15, 77
directors, xvi–xvii, 7–8, 41, 58–59, 60–61, 61t–67t, 69–70, 72, 75–76, 193, 202, 204, 226n.4
as discursive formation, xi, xii–xiii, xix, xxii, 3, 11, 77, 205
distribution, xviii, xix, 6–7, 14, 21–35, 53, 82–83, 84, 85–86, 87–92, 103–104, 107, 110, 143, 202, 204–205, 253–273
distribution rights, cost of, 24, 27, 29, 30, 91
DV (digital video) production, 202–203
and experimental film, xiii, 41–42, 43–44, 58
foreign-language, xviii–xix, 8–9, 60–61, 61t–67t, 200–201
gender in, xx, xxi, 72, 73, 82, 84, 115, 116, 125, 127–128, 129, 130, 131, 134–135, 138, 139, 141–142, 145, 146, 147–148, 149–150, 152–153, 156–157, 160, 161, 162, 163, 188, 227n.3
genre, xv, 69, 75, 90–91, 148, 176, 188, 201, 232n.1
history of, 4, 15–21
and identity politics, xiv–xv, xix, xxi, xxii, 9, 14, 52, 81–83, 85–87, 102–103, 105–107, 108–110, 229n.26
international, xviii-xix, 8–9, 60–61, 61t–67t, 200–201
Internet, impact of, 27, 30, 203–205
marketing and promotion, 8, 14, 18, 23, 24, 25, 27, 30, 31, 32, 33, 88–90, 91–92, 105, 106–107, 143, 144, 200, 203–204, 221n.2, 225n.25
narrative, xx, 9, 72, 75, 76, 96, 100–101, 105, 114, 114–115, 116, 134, 135–136, 137–140, 150–152, 156–160, 161, 162, 165, 175, 181, 197
race and ethnicity in, 72, 73, 81–84, 85–86, 89–92, 105–106, 141–142, 164, 194–196, 197, 233n.11. See also *Daughters of the Dust, Just Another Girl on the I.R.T., A Lesson in History, To Sleep with Anger*
release pattern, 8, 23, 30, 88, 200, 222n.3, 224n.21
reviewers and reviewing, 3, 5, 17, 36, 37, 38, 88, 89–90, 92, 93, 96, 99, 106, 108, 141, 142–144, 144–145, 147–148, 150, 162–163, 165, 171–172, 174, 175, 178, 195, 228n.16, 231nn.6,10
sexual identity in, 69–70, 72, 73, 82, 84, 86, 190–191, 192–193
as specialty film, xvi, 8, 89–90, 107–108, 222n.3. See also audiences, specialized
studio ownership, 6–7, 23–24, 29, 36–40, 225nn.26,27
violence in, xx, 75, 125, 129, 130, 132–133, 146, 148, 170, 171–173, 176–177, 193, 233n.5
Independent Feature Project, xvi, 4, 143
institutional and material discourses, xii, xiii, xvii, xix, xxi, 11–12, 77, 78, 82–83, 86, 87, 110, 205. See also distribution, marketing and promotion
international cinema, as independent films, xviii–xix, 8–9, 60–61, 61t–67t, 200–201

Index

Internet
  as distribution outlet, 203, 204–205
  for promotion and marketing, 27, 30, 203–204
interpretive, audience, and reception discourses, xii, xiii, xvii-xviii, xxi, 77, 86, 87, 103, 106–107, 108, 110, 123, 140, 142, 163–164, 205
IRS Releasing, 7
Island Pictures, 7, 32, 225n.23

J

Jackson, Samuel, 175, 184, 233n.11
Jakobson, Roman, 42, 120
Jameson, Fredric, 173, 174, 187
Jarman, Derek, 13
Johnson, Sheila, 121, 122
Jones, Jacquie, 95
Jost, Jon, 31- 32, 88

K

Kaplan, Jonathan, 152
Kino International, 29, 88, 91, 92, 227n.6
KJM3 Entertainment Group, 91–92
Knowles-Borishade, Adetokunbo, 100–101
Kozloff, Sarah, 118
Kuhn, Annette, 55–56
Kureishi, Hanif, 59
Kurosawa, Akira, 56, 60

L

Law, Lindsay, 25
Lee, Spike, 8, 83, 195
Leigh, Mike, xx, 28, 115, 125, 134, 135, 226n.1
lesbian films, 69–70, 72, 73, 82, 84
Levy, Emanuel, 57, 221n.5
Libra Films, 35, 225n.24
Lions Gate, 6, 25, 28, 37
Lipsky, Jeff, 28, 35
Lot 47 Films, 6, 29, 35
Lucey, Paul, 117

M

Mauceri, Marc, 29
Macauley, Scott, 13, 69–70
Maggenti, Maria, 69–70, 71, 114, 115
Malin, Amir, 27, 28, 34

marketing and promotion, 8, 14, 23, 24, 27, 30, 31, 33, 88, 89–90, 91–92, 106–107, 143
  niche or target marketing, 18, 19, 25, 32, 89–90, 105, 144, 200, 203–204, 221n.2, 225n.25
masculinity, 116, 125, 138, 139, 234n.14
  in *Pulp Fiction*, 191–194, 195
  in *Reservoir Dogs*, 188–191
Masterman, Len, 56
material and institutional discourses, xii, xiii, xvii, xix, xxi, 11–12, 77, 78, 82–83, 86, 87, 110, 205. See also distribution, marketing and promotion
Mayne, Judith, 158
meaning production, xii, xiii, xx, 9, 77, 108, 110, 120, 121, 122, 162, 163, 164
Menken, Marie, 68
Mercer, Kobena, 86, 105, 109
Mernissi, Fatima, 167, 196–197
Metz, Christian, 121–122
micro distributors, 7, 29–30, 31–33
mini-major distributors, 6–7, 28, 31, 36, 87
Miramax Films, xvi, 3, 4, 5, 6, 7, 10, 11, 17, 18, 23–25, 26, 32, 36–37, 39, 104, 142, 143, 167, 168, 200, 221n.2, 224n.20, 225n.24, 229n.24, 233n.11
modernism, xx, 45, 48–49, 73, 75, 76, 173, 174, 175–176, 177, 178, 187, 193, 194
modernity, 14, 98, 173–174
Moran, Jim, 41, 43, 54, 84
Morley, David, 150, 161
Morris, Meaghan, 143–144, 164
Morrison, Toni, 81, 102, 103, 104
MPAA (Motion Picture Association of America) ratings, 37
multiculturalism, xxi–xxii, 82, 103, 108, 109–110, 174, 205
multiple readings, xviii, xx, 77, 106, 107, 108, 109, 110, 111, 138, 139, 144, 161, 164

N

narrative, 53–54, 154, 155
  avant-garde/experimental film, 11, 47–48, 50–52, 70
  independent film, xx, 9, 72, 75, 76, 105, 114–115, 116, 135–136, 175, 181, 197

narrative, alternative, 9, 60, 72, 99, 100, 134, 137–140
 in *Daughters of the Dust*, 96, 100–101, 105
 in *Orlando*, 156–160
 in *The Piano*, 150–152, 158–160, 161, 162, 165
narrative theory/narratology, xx, 113–115, 116–124, 125, 139–140, 230nn.1,3,4
New Yorker Films, 6, 29, 35
nonnarrative avant-garde/experimental film, 11, 47, 68, 70
Northern Arts Entertainment, 6, 29
normative realism, xx, 42, 50, 114, 115, 116, 124, 137, 147, 150, 151, 152, 155, 156, 158, 159–160, 161, 162

O

October Films, 3, 4, 6, 7, 24, 25, 26, 27, 28–29, 34, 35, 36, 37, 38, 199
Ordesky, Mark, 22
Orion Classics, 6, 22–23, 32, 34, 92, 201, 228n.15

P

Paramount Classics, 25
Parker, Alan, 124
pedophilia
 in *American Beauty*, 199, 200
 in *Happiness*, 38–39, 199, 200
personal cinema, xix, 67–69
Peters, Maybelle, 98, 99, 100
Phaedra Cinema, 29
Pierson, John, 5, 23, 34, 90, 92, 103–104, 143, 221n.5, 227nn.8,9, 228n.15, 229nn.23,25
political avant-garde, xix, xxi, 45, 48–52, 53, 71–72, 160
Pomorska, Krystyna, 118
postmodernism/postmodernity, xx, 14, 52–53, 73–76, 167, 173–176, 177, 186–187, 193, 194
 appropriation, 74, 177–181, 194–197
 heterogeneity, 14–15, 53, 73, 75, 175, 187, 197
 and nostalgia, 183, 186, 187, 193, 197
 stylistic traits, 14, 73–74, 181–183
Potter, Sally, 43, 47, 151, 152

producer's representative, 90, 227n.8
promotion and marketing, 8, 14, 18, 19, 23, 24, 25, 27, 30, 31, 32, 33, 88–90, 91–92, 105, 106–107, 143, 144, 200, 203–204, 221n.2, 225n.25
Propp, Vladimir, 117, 121

R

race and ethnicity in independent films, 72, 73, 81–84, 85–86, 89–92, 105–106, 141–142, 164, 194–196, 197, 233n.11. See also *Daughters of the Dust, Just Another Girl on the I.R.T., A Lesson in History, To Sleep with Anger*
Ray, Bingham, 24, 25, 27, 28, 35
realism, 42, 45, 52, 226n.1
reception, audience, and interpretive discourses, xii, xiii, xvii–xviii, xxi, 77, 86, 87, 103, 106–107, 108, 110, 123, 140, 142, 144, 163–164, 205
redemption, 117, 135–136, 151, 171–172, 174, 175, 187
 in *Naked* and *Shoot the Moon*, 116, 128, 131, 132, 134
 in *Trainspotting*, 136–137
Redford, Robert, 13
Renoir, Jean, 56
repertory films, 18–19, 21
representational discourses, xii, xiii, xvii, xx, xxi, 11, 43–44, 77, 78, 82, 83, 87, 100, 105, 108, 110–111, 114, 116, 121, 122, 123, 124, 137, 140, 150, 152, 154, 155, 158, 197, 205
Resnais, Alain, 55, 57, 60
reviewers and reviewing, 3, 5, 17, 36, 37, 38, 88, 89–90, 92, 93, 96, 99, 106, 108, 141, 142–144, 144–145, 147–148, 150, 162–163, 165, 171–172, 174, 175, 178, 195, 228n.16, 231nn.6,10
Rosenbaum, Jonathan, 21
Rosenblatt, Jay, 5, 205
Rossellini, Roberto, 60
Rothman, Tom, 28, 34, 89–90, 107
Roxie Releasing, 6, 29
Russo, Emily, 143

S

Said, Edward, 164

Index

Sarup, Madan, 173–174, 229n.26
Savoy Pictures, 7
Sayles, John, 8, 33–34, 51, 114, 115, 225n.24, 230n.2
Seventh Art Releasing, 29
Schamus, James, 12, 13, 14, 30, 84, 203
Schmidt, John, 28
Schrader, Paul, xx, 167, 175–176, 177, 187, 223n.7
Schulte-Sasse, Jochen, 48
Scorsese, Martin, xx, 57, 143, 174, 175, 176, 177, 187, 192–193, 234n.14
Screen Gems, 25, 26, 225n.24
Seger, Linda, 117, 134
Shining Excalibur, 37
Shohat, Ella, 97
Shooting Gallery, 32–33, 224–225n.22
sixteen millimeter technology, 18, 67
Skouras Pictures, 35
Smith, Gavin, 169, 232n.1
Sony Pictures Classics, 6, 7, 22, 23, 25, 26, 30–31, 34, 36, 151, 199, 201, 225n.24
specialty film divisions, 21, 22, 24–25, 25–26, 36
Spectrafilm, 7, 225n.23
Stam, Robert, 97, 120, 139–140
Stark, Jim, 13
Steedman, Carolyn, 113, 149–150
Stone, Oliver, 168–169, 171, 172, 173, 232n.3
Strand Releasing 6, 29, 31–32
studio ownership, effects of, 6–7, 23–24, 29, 36–40, 225nn.26,27
Sundance Film Festival, 4, 13, 24, 26, 27, 88, 92, 104, 222n.6, 228n.15
surrealist films, 46, 67
structuralist films, 46, 47, 68

T

Tarantino, Quentin, xx, 57, 61, 167, 168–169, 171, 172, 173, 174, 176, 178–184, 187, 188, 193–196, 234n.14
Taubin, Amy, 192–193
three-act structure, 116–117, 124, 125, 135, 137, 152, 155
Thurman, Uma, 185–186
Todorov, Tzvetan, 117

Townsend, Robert, 85
Travolta, John, 183–186, 233n.11
Triton Pictures, 7, 30
Truffaut, François, xiv, 57, 60
Tudor, Andrew, 55
Turner, Graeme, 42

U

United Artists Classics, 22, 34, 201, 225n.24
Universal Focus, 25, 26
Urman, Mark, 33, 39
USA Films, 6, 22, 29, 35

V

Varda, Agnès, 60
Variety
    on *Daughters of the Dust*, 88, 93, 96
    on *To Sleep with Anger*, 88
violence
    in independent films, xx, 75, 176–177, 193, 233n.5
    in *Naked* and *Shoot the Moon*, 125, 128, 129, 130, 131–132, 132–133
    in *Natural Born Killers*, 168, 169–170, 171, 172, 176
    in *The Piano*, 145, 146, 147, 148
    in *Pulp Fiction*, 168, 171–173
    in *Reservoir Dogs*, 170
Visconti, Luchino, 60
Vitale, Ruth, 22, 25

W

Wallace, Michelle, 97, 98
Weinstein, Bob, 23, 24, 37
Weinstein, Harvey, 23, 36, 37
Whannel, Paddy, 56
Williams, Raymond, 97–98, 173
Willis, Holly, 41, 43, 54, 84
Willis, Sharon, 107, 195, 233n.12
WinStar Cinema, 29
Wishman, Seymour, 29
Wollen, Peter, 45–46, 49, 51–52, 70, 82
women's films, 68, 72, 73, 82, 115, 163, 226n.4

Y-Z

young audiences, 84–85, 201, 223n.9, 227n.3
Zeitgeist Films, 6, 10, 29, 143

The History & Art of Cinema

Frank Beaver, *General Editor*

Framing Film is committed to serious, high-quality film studies on topics of national and international interest. The series is open to a full range of scholarly methodologies and analytical approaches in the examination of cinema art and history, including topics on film theory, film and society, gender and race, politics. Cutting-edge studies and diverse points of view are particularly encouraged.

For additional information about the series or for the submission of manuscripts, please contact:

> Peter Lang Publishing, Inc.
> Acquisitions Department
> 275 Seventh Avenue, 28th floor
> New York, NY 10001

To order other books in this series, please contact our Customer Service Department at:

> (800) 770-LANG (within the U.S.)
> (212) 647-7706 (outside the U.S.)
> (212) 647-7707 FAX

Or browse online by series at:

> WWW.PETERLANGUSA.COM